Gendered Crossings

Diálogos Series

KRIS LANE, SERIES EDITOR

Understanding Latin America demands dialogue, deep exploration, and frank discussion of key topics. Founded by Lyman L. Johnson in 1992 and edited since 2013 by Kris Lane, the Diálogos Series focuses on innovative scholarship in Latin American history and related fields. The series, the most successful of its type, includes specialist works accessible to a wide readership and a variety of thematic titles, all ideally suited for classroom adoption by university and college teachers.

Also available in the Diálogos Series:

From Shipmates to Soldiers: Emerging Black Identities in the Río de la Plata by Alex Borucki

Women Drug Traffickers: Mules, Bosses, and Organized Crime by Elaine Carey

Searching for Madre Matiana: Prophecy and Popular Culture in Modern Mexico by Edward Wright-Rios

Africans into Creoles: Slavery, Ethnicity, and Identity in Colonial Costa Rica by Russell Lohse

Native Brazil: Beyond the Convert and the Cannibal, 1500–1900 edited by Hal Langfur

Emotions and Daily Life in Colonial Mexico edited by Javier Villa-Flores and Sonya Lipsett-Rivera

The Course of Andean History by Peter V. N. Henderson

Masculinity and Sexuality in Modern Mexico edited by Anne Rubenstein and Víctor M. Macías-González

A History of Mining in Latin America: From the Colonial Era to the Present by Kendall Brown

Modernizing Minds in El Salvador: Education Reform and the Cold War, 1960–1980 by Héctor Lindo-Fuentes and Erik Ching

For additional titles in the Diálogos Series, please visit unmpress.com.

Gendered Crossings

WOMEN AND MIGRATION IN THE SPANISH EMPIRE

Allyson M. Poska

University of New Mexico Press • Albuquerque

Published 2016
Printed in the United States of America
21 20 19 18 17 16 1 2 3 4 5 6

LIBRARY OF CONGRESS CATALOGING-IN-PUBLICATION DATA

Poska, Allyson M.
Gendered crossings : women and migration in the Spanish Empire /
Allyson M. Poska.
pages cm. — (Diálogos Series)
Includes bibliographical references and index.
ISBN 978-0-8263-5642-0 (cloth : alk. paper) — ISBN 978-0-8263-5643-7 (pbk. : alk. paper) —
ISBN 978-0-8263-5644-4 (electronic) 1. Women immigrants—
Latin America—Social conditions. 2. Women immigrants—Latin America—Economic
conditions. 3. Women immigrants—Cultural assimilation—
Latin America. 4. Latin America—Emigration and immigration. 5. Latin America—Emigration
and immigration—Social aspects. 6. Europe, Southern—
Emigration and immigration—Economic aspects. I. Title.
JV6347.P67 2016
304.8082'09171246—dc23
2015016156

Paperback edition cover illustration: Spanish frigate like those that carried the colonists
from La Coruña to Montevideo. Reproduced with permission
from the Mariner's Museum. Newport News, Virginia.
Designed by Catherine Leonardo
Composed in Minion Pro 10.25/13.5
Display type is Minion Pro

Contents

Illustrations

MAPS

FIGURES

TABLES

Acknowledgments

THE BEST AND MOST ENJOYABLE INTELLECTUAL ENDEAVORS ARE THE product of collaboration, and many scholars generously shared their time and knowledge with me as I worked on this project. Liz Lehfeldt, Carla Rahn Phillips, Sarah Chambers, Susan Socolow, Allison Games, Fabrício Prado, Alex Borucki, Nancy Shoemaker, Betsy Lewis, Jeffrey Erbig, Porter Blakemore, Ed Pompeian, Álvaro Caso Bello, and Jeff McClurken were willing to read drafts and/or answer questions about a dizzying array of topics from ships and whales to slaves and forts. Silvana Buscaglia kindly provided maps of the excavations at Floridablanca and answered questions about that research.

This project was also enriched by the feedback that I received during a number of presentations, among them the fourth annual Rio de la Plata Seminar at the College of William and Mary, Allison Games's Early Modern Global History Seminar at Georgetown University, the Atlantic World Workshop at New York University, and the PhD colloquium at George Mason University.

I want to thank my wonderful colleagues in Spanish literature, Betsy Lewis and María Laura Bocaz-Leiva at University of Mary Washington and Alison Weber at University of Virginia, who were always willing to help me with my translation questions. I could not do my research without the hard work and support of Carla Bailey, UMW's interlibrary loan librarian, and Lisa Patton, the history department's office manager. Suzanne Huffman, UMW's digital resources librarian, digitized the Vidal images. This is the third project for which I have had the pleasure of working with Stephen Hanna, who produced the maps. I always appreciate his cartographic skills, patience, and attention to detail. Rob Schwaller and Brad Benton made the months in Sevilla much more fun, and I was pleased to get to know Mariana Pérez while in Buenos Aires.

The time and energy of the staffs of the archives that I visited over the course of this project proved invaluable: the Archivo General de Indias in Sevilla; the Archivo Municipal in La Coruña; the Archivo Histórico de la Provincia de Buenos Aires in La Plata, Argentina; the Archivo General de la Nación in Buenos Aires; and the Archivo General de la Nación in Montevideo. The staffs at the Archivo General de Indias in Sevilla, the Museo Naval, and the Fundación Joaquín Díaz in Madrid were very helpful in providing images, and Claudia Jew at the Mariner's Museum in Newport News stepped in at the last minute to help me with the images of the ships. I especially want to thank the women who staff the LDS Family History Center in Fredericksburg, Virginia. Ever kind and professional, they went above and beyond to track down missing microfilms and even purchased a new chair to make me more comfortable during the months I spent at their film reader.

Having known Kris Lane since graduate school, it was a pleasure to be able to work with him as a series editor. This book is better because of his thoughtful editorial guidance. Clark Whitehorn at the University of New Mexico Press made the publication process remarkably easy.

I received funding for this project from the American Council of Learned Societies/National Endowment for the Humanities/International and Area Studies Fellowship. I was privileged to spend spring semester 2011 at the John Carter Brown Library as the Ruth and Lincoln Ekstrom Fellow and want to thank both the other fellows and the library staff for an intellectually invigorating, if very snowy, experience. A Waple Fellowship from the University of Mary Washington allowed me to finish my research and writing.

Part of chapter 2 previously appeared as "Campesinas transatlánticas: Las mujeres y la migración en el imperio español al fin del siglo XVIII," *Nuevo Mundo Mundos Nuevos*, Debates, 2012, 19 June 2012, http://nuevomundo.revues.org/63354. Part of chapter 3 appeared as "Public Health, Peasant Bodies, and the Spanish Colonization of Patagonia," *Social History of Medicine* 25, no. 2 (2012): 290–306, and part of chapter 4 appeared as "Babies on Board: Women, Children, and Imperial Policy in the Spanish Empire," *Gender and History* 22, no. 2 (August 2010): 269–83. Part of chapter 8 will appear as "From Peasants to Slave Owners: Race, Class, and Gender in the Spanish Empire," in Kimberly Lynn and Erin Rowe, eds., *The Early Modern Hispanic World: Transnational and Interdisciplinary Approaches* (forthcoming from Cambridge University Press).

During the many years of research and writing, Marcel Rotter and John Siegler have been wonderfully fun and patient friends, who regularly indulged me with fabulous food and drink. My long-standing friendship with Kit French continues to be important to me intellectually and emotionally. Finally, for more than twenty years Chris Kilmartin has been an unbelievably supportive partner, holding down the fort during research trips, making pancakes during chemo, and thoroughly proofreading every chapter. I could never thank him enough.

As the granddaughter of immigrant women, I dedicate this book to the millions of female migrants around the world who risk their lives in search of better futures for themselves and their families.

CHAPTER ONE

Rethinking Empire

Gender, Enlightenment, and the Patagonia Project

ON 20 MAY 1780, AFTER MORE THAN THREE MONTHS AT SEA, THE Spanish frigate *La Santísima Trinidad* dropped anchor in the port of Montevideo and Graciana Araque took her first steps onto American soil with a newborn baby girl in her arms. Months earlier, Graciana, her husband, Pablo, and their toddler, Cayetano, began a journey that took them from their home in northern Castile to the port at La Coruña and then across the Atlantic to Montevideo. They were not alone. Just two years before, José de Gálvez (1720–1787), the head of the Council of the Indies and longtime minister for King Charles III (r. 1759–1788), had promulgated an edict on behalf of the king, asking for two hundred poor families from northern Spain to volunteer to travel to the Río de la Plata to establish new settlements along the Patagonian coast. The response to the Patagonia project was enthusiastic. By 1784, more than 1,900 peasants had enlisted, making it one of the largest voluntary resettlements of free people of the colonial period. The 875 women and girls who volunteered were the largest contingent of Spanish women to cross the Atlantic before the mass migrations of the nineteenth century.

Graciana was one of thousands of women who emigrated from the Iberian Peninsula to the Americas during the colonial period; however, we rarely know much about them. Unremarkable in terms of wealth or status, their experiences as imperial migrants have been overshadowed by the often swashbuckling tales of the conquistadors, viceroys, friars, and merchants who made the same voyage. Yet, from a historian's perspective, Graciana and the other adventurous women who participated in the Patagonia project were particularly fortunate. The project's rich documentation describes the implementation of the colonization plan by Spanish authorities on both sides of the Atlantic and allows us to follow Graciana and the other women and their families from the moment that they left their native villages in northern Spain until the eve of independence in the Río de la Plata.

As the Patagonia project unfolds as a story of imperial reform and of female migration, it offers a prime opportunity for a transatlantic examination of sex and gender expectations. For decades, scholars of Spain and Spanish America agreed that the Mediterranean honor code was the dominant influence on gender norms around the Iberian world.[1] According to this paradigm, women derived their honor from their chastity and men derived theirs from the maintenance of the chastity of the women in their care. However, recent peninsular scholarship indicates that, beyond the nobility and aristocracy (and not even all of them), few women in either Spain or Spanish America acquiesced to this set of rigid social and sexual expectations.[2] Rather, the experience of gender in the Spanish Empire was much more complicated. With its transatlantic perspective, the Patagonia project reveals the complex interaction of prescriptive ideals and the realities of daily life that framed Spanish women's choices at the end of the colonial period.

Peninsular Women and Imperial Control in the Americas

From the beginning, the Spanish monarchy made peninsular women central to the formation of its overseas empire. As early as Columbus's second voyage, the Crown admonished settlers to bring their wives with them to the Caribbean. A few women accompanied Columbus in 1497, and prior to the departure of governor Nicolás de Ovando for Hispaniola in 1502, an effort was made to recruit two hundred married couples to accompany him. In the end, fewer than half that number made the ocean crossing, but they were only the first of a steady stream of Iberian women to settle in the Americas. In fact, at least one thousand peninsular women emigrated to the Americas between 1509 and 1538. By the middle of the sixteenth century, family migration, which usually included at least one woman, became quite common, so much so that by the end of the century female migrants outnumbered male migrants from Sevilla and Cádiz. In general, women made up between

20 and 30 percent of those leaving for the Americas, but it was a source of frustration for royal authorities that the majority of immigrants were single men.[3]

Over the course of the seventeenth century, Spain's European rivals relied increasingly on government-sponsored family migration projects to increase the numbers of white women at their settlements around the Atlantic world. In 1687 the Dutch East India Company resettled a group of French Huguenots to the Cape of Good Hope. Late in the seventeenth century, the Portuguese began to move families around their empire, sending some to Mozambique and moving others from the Azores to Brazil.[4] However, the Spanish Crown continued to count on personal initiative rather than government intervention as the basis of its colonization policy, and, as a result, the numbers of peninsular women and families leaving for the Americas remained flat.

It was not until the eighteenth century, with the ascent of the Bourbons to the Spanish throne, that the Spanish Crown began to employ government-sponsored family colonization projects as an imperial strategy. First, it engaged poor families from the Canary Islands to help secure San Antonio in the early 1720s. Then in 1726 (and again in 1729) the monarchy recruited more families, mostly from the Canaries, to establish the city of Montevideo. Slightly later, resettled families were key to reinforcing the Spanish presence in St. Augustine, Florida. By midcentury, José de Gálvez was pushing for families to colonize parts of northern Mexico and California, although in the end those initiatives, as well as others across the northern frontier, relied almost exclusively on colonists already living in the Americas.[5] These family colonization schemes were deeply rooted in more than two centuries of Spanish imperial policies and priorities; however, by the 1770s those endeavors, including the Patagonia project, had new intellectual underpinnings—they were clearly articulated as Enlightenment solutions to perceived crises across the Spanish Empire.

Without a doubt, a sense of crisis permeated the court of Charles III. Not only was the Crown concerned that Spain was being overtaken by its imperial rivals, especially England, but Enlightenment thinkers and royal authorities worried about an array of other issues, including population imbalance and the fact that Spain seemed unable or unwilling to industrialize at the pace of its European counterparts. Overpopulation and sluggish economic development in turn created a host of social problems, including vagabondage and crime. In response, Spanish intellectuals and bureaucrats formulated a series of policies aimed at improving the economy and increasing monarchical authority that would become known as the Bourbon reforms.[6] The Patagonia project was one Bourbon response to these perceived crises—one that was tightly bound to Enlightenment ideas about the utility of using peninsular women to solve some of eighteenth-century Spain's most intractable challenges.

Among their many concerns, Enlightenment thinkers believed that Spain was losing its dominance as an imperial power. Gálvez worried that "every day Spanish America is more exposed to the insatiable ambition of some European powers" and that "insatiable ambition" was particularly evident in the English threat to the Patagonian coast. The English and the Spanish had vied for control of the region for nearly two centuries, despite the fact that the harsh climate, poor soil, and unconquered Indians had thus far made it impossible to sustain a European settlement. In the late sixteenth century, the Spanish Crown attempted to close the Straits of Magellan to English corsairs by establishing an outpost there. However, the colonies of Nombre de Jesús and Rey Don Felipe, founded by Pedro Sarmiento de Gamboa (1532–1592), soon fell victim to the inhospitable climate and poor provisioning. When an English ship under the command of Thomas Cavendish (1560–1592) stopped at Rey Don Felipe in 1587, the twenty remaining inhabitants were in such a miserable condition that he renamed the place Fort Famine before rescuing the survivors. The specter of this disaster haunted the Spanish for centuries. Even as royal authorities planned the Patagonia project, one noted that they should be careful not to repeat the "lamentable" experience of Sarmiento de Gamboa.[7]

Despite the climatic and logistical obstacles, interest in the region intensified in the late seventeenth and early eighteenth centuries as the English increasingly viewed the Patagonian coast and the Malvinas Islands as strategic centers for their control of both the Atlantic and the Pacific. In 1670 Sir John Narborough seized Puerto Deseado on the Patagonian coast in the name of the English king Charles II (1630–1685), but this outpost was also quickly abandoned. As he circumnavigated the globe, Admiral George Anson (1697–1762) stopped at San Julián in 1741 and famously asserted that, supported by an alliance with the Indians, the English could expel the Spanish with a force of only 1,500 men.[8] Such threats grew more menacing once the English established an outpost at Port Egmont on the Malvinas Islands in 1765 (although they withdrew in 1776). Finally, the lack of a Spanish presence in Patagonia took on new urgency in 1774 with the publication of the ex-Jesuit Thomas Falkner's *A Description of Patagonia and the adjoining parts of South America*. He made the threat to Spanish control clear, noting that "if any nation should think proper to people this country it might be the cause of perpetual alarm to the Spaniards; as from hence ships might be sent into the South Seas, and their seaports destroyed, before such a scheme or intention could be known in Spain or even in Buenos-Ayres." Someone at the Spanish court took Falkner's warning seriously, arguing in the earliest of the Patagonia project's documentation that English ambitions in the region necessitated immediate Spanish settlement.[9]

In addition to the English, the Spanish Crown worried about the imperial agenda of the Portuguese. During the eighteenth century, the conflict between the two Iberian empires in the Río de la Plata was ongoing, and the establishment of the city of Montevideo in 1726 was a direct response to Portuguese westward movement beyond the border established by the Treaty of Tordesillas. After the Treaty of Madrid (1750) fell apart in 1763, an expedition led by Pedro Cevallos (1715–1778) took the town of Colônia do Sacramento and expelled the Portuguese from most of the eastern territories, although Spain returned Colônia in the subsequent peace treaty. A decade later, the Spanish Crown ordered Cevallos and the largest armada ever sent from Spain to the Americas to retake all Portuguese-occupied territory. With his victory, Spain gained control over Colônia, Misiones, and the entire Banda Oriental.[10] However, in his 1778 tract in favor of establishing colonies in the Río de la Plata, Galician intellectual José Cornide (1734–1803) reminded his readers of "the bad faith with which the Portuguese have conducted themselves in those countries [Paraguay, Tucumán, and the Río de la Plata]."[11] As they formulated the Patagonia project, Spanish authorities were still not convinced that their conflict with the Portuguese in the region had come to an end.

From the perspective of the Crown and Enlightenment intellectuals, the most effective way to exert and maintain control over these highly contested territories was to establish permanent settlements. Of course, towns had been central to the establishment of Spanish control since the early days of the conquest, but in more peripheral areas the Crown had relied on soldiers and missionaries rather than colonists to enforce Spanish authority. However, by the eighteenth century the Crown had grown increasingly distrustful of both clergy (the same sentiment that prompted the expulsion of the Jesuits) and creole soldiers.[12] Military outposts not only cost the government money, for decades missionaries in border areas had complained that soldiers were hard to control and that their violence compromised the clerics' work with native peoples. Moreover, from an ideological perspective, neither soldiers nor missionaries were effective extensions of Bourbon paternal power. The king was not a benevolent father figure to either missionaries or soldiers, whose ecclesiastical and military hierarchies were controlled by other central authorities.[13]

In contrast, towns were self-sufficient, generated new economies, and encouraged productive interactions with Indians. In his call for colonists, a priest in Sonora, Mexico, poetically noted, "Each individual is a fort, each family a trench, and each town an impregnable citadel."[14] The main difference between a fort or mission and a town was the presence of women. Women's ability to turn men into fathers and individuals into families made them the linchpin of the colonial project.

In making towns central to Bourbon imperial policy, authorities ascribed a remarkable amount of familial and social authority to peninsular women. Although in Spain lower class women's poverty often made them morally suspect, in colonial society their unblemished racial and religious lineage imbued them with considerable moral superiority and societal influence.[15] Most important, the presence of married white women on the frontier was believed to be able to tame the otherwise uncontrolled sexuality of Spanish men. Across the borderlands, Spanish political, ecclesiastical, and military authorities grappled with the sexual violence that Spanish soldiers perpetrated on native women. Sexual violence not only disrupted efforts at conversion and assimilation, it provoked violent response from native peoples that compromised Spanish territorial control.[16] Unwilling to acknowledge the role of power and dominance in these attacks, authorities naively assumed that men engaged in sexual violence only when they could not have sex with women to whom they were connected by the inalienable bonds of matrimony. They believed that Spanish women's potential to provide religiously sanctioned intercourse and moral pressure to ensure their husbands' fidelity would be enough to end Spanish men's sexual predation.

In addition to ensuring male monogamy, authorities argued that the presence of wives and children would stop Spanish men from deserting. During the 1774 Anza expedition in California, Viceroy Bucareli required the troops "to bring their wives and children in order that they become better attached to their domicile." Only a year before the decision to colonize Patagonia, Gálvez called on his brother, the governor of the Canary Islands, to recruit seven hundred soldiers to settle in Louisiana and to give preference to married men, hoping that the presence of women would provide some stability on that frontier.[17] At the beginning of the Patagonia project, he specifically acknowledged his hope that wives and children would help lessen men's temptation to abandon the new outposts.[18]

Authorities also expected peninsular women to serve as moral exemplars in frontier communities. The competing gender and sexual expectations of native groups and the more tolerant sexual norms of nonelite, and often nonwhite, creoles created a scenario in which authorities relied on peninsular women both to act out an idealized vision of Spanish femininity based on female chastity and modesty and to pressure other women to comply with that same ideal.[19]

Peninsular women bore other responsibilities as well. Ann Stoler and Frederick Cooper have argued that "colonial regimes faced—in different times and in different ways—the problem not just of reproducing people, but of reproducing ways of life and forms of power."[20] On the peripheries of the Spanish Empire, the task of "reproducing ways of life" would fall almost exclusively to peninsular women who would bring Spanish culture to Indians, mestizos, and other insufficiently Hispanized peoples. During the colonization of California, Junípero Serra acknowledged women's centrality in assimilating native women, writing to Mexican Viceroy Bucareli asking for industrious Spanish women to help train local Indian women in Spanish ways. Spanish women were expected to teach native women to cook, clean, sew, and perform other household duties in a Spanish manner to ensure their effective Hispanization and Christianization.[21]

Peninsular women's role as transmitters of culture was even stronger within their own families. On the edges of empire, educating their children in Spanish food ways, dress, and household management took on new importance. Pedro Rodríguez Campomanes (1723–1802), one of Spain's most illustrious Enlightenment thinkers, asserted the critical role of women in raising children in new colonies. Musing about the possibility of marrying Spanish women to foreign men in another colonial context, he declared, "The children learn the language and our customs well, as mothers are who principally take care of their education." This emphasis on the education of children also reflected a broader Bourbon concern with both education and child rearing.[22] Spanish mothers were the critical link between the Crown and the next generation of colonial subjects.

Finally, Spanish authorities valued peninsular women's reproductive potential. In the Americas, areas with insufficient white populations were vulnerable to foreign invasion and left large parts of the empire under the control of Indians. Based on their previous experience, Spanish authorities knew that, in the long run, they could not rely on immigration for population growth, thus the emphasis on family resettlement schemes and the insistence on women in their reproductive years. Although at times the Crown settled for the presence of Hispanized, mixed-race women, in general the preference was for white women, whose morality and cultural purity was unquestioned. Much was at stake. Any failure to fulfill these responsibilities could compromise Spanish colonial authority.[23]

Peninsular Women and Enlightenment Crises in Spain

Convinced of the importance of peninsular women to the imperial project, there was never any doubt in the minds of royal authorities that they would look to northern Spain to provide the female volunteers to go to Patagonia. By focusing their energies on that part of the kingdom, they believed that not only could those peasant women shoulder the responsibilities of imperial colonization, but their participation could also resolve a number of social and economic problems that affected the region. Most Enlightenment intellectuals agreed that by the eighteenth century, Spain suffered from a serious population imbalance—while many parts of the empire experienced a dearth of inhabitants, northern Spain (Galicia, Asturias, and Cantabria) was beset by overpopulation. Indeed, eighteenth-century censuses reveal large differences in population density across the peninsula. In 1752 Galicia was home to approximately forty-four persons per square kilometer and Asturias thirty-three, compared with Extremadura with only ten persons per square kilometer.[24] As Campomanes declared, "Galicia is very populated and has a true excess of inhabitants." According to José Cornide, the population of Galicia was "very numerous because of the extreme fertility of the women, the quality of the food, the proximity to the sea, and the temperateness of the seasons."[25] The consequences of this population imbalance were far-reaching. While large tracts of land went uncultivated in the south, the combination of dense population and partible inheritance progressively impoverished families in the north.

Both foreigners and Spaniards alike lamented the poverty of northern Spain, particularly Galicia. After traveling through the region in 1779, American John Adams wrote, "I see nothing but signs of poverty and misery among the people. A fertile country, not half cultivated, people ragged and dirty, and the houses universally nothing but mire, smoke, fleas, and lice." Such a pitiful description was not merely the product of Anglo anti-Spanish sentiment. According to Enlightenment intellectual Benito Feijoo (1676–1764), "In these lands there are no people more starved or more naked."[26] Intense poverty left the population desperately vulnerable. Severe subsistence crises struck Galicia in 1769 and 1770, and epidemics hit in 1765 and again in 1768–1770.[27]

The relentless poverty aggravated by sporadic crises forced northern peasant men and women to leave their homes in search of work in other regions of Spain or in Portugal. In the first part of the eighteenth century, Feijoo argued that one of the most serious problems affecting Spain was that "many thousands of Gallegos [natives of Galicia] leave to dig up the vines and harvest the crops in various provinces of Spain. It is only just that each person might work in his homeland." Willing to undertake any work to survive, Gallegos became known as the "slaves" of others. As early as 1757 Englishman James Bruce declared the inhabitants of Galicia to be "indigent and miserable to a point difficult to imagine, slaves of the rest of the provinces of Spain and Portugal," and Enlightenment scholar and cleric Martín Sarmiento called Gallegos "the unhappy poor who are slaves of all and of the land." By 1769 the Junta of the Kingdom of Galicia was prompted to write to the Crown that Gallegos "certainly are the most enslaved of the Spanish world, there is no comparison between their misery and suffering and that of both Castiles."[28]

As a means to alleviate northern poverty, many thinkers pushed the government to redistribute the Spanish population. In fact, one utopian work from the period, *Descripción de la Sinapia, peninsula de la tierra austral* (Description of Sinapia, peninsula of the southern lands), made population redistribution central to the maintenance of the perfect community. Anonymous and undated, it has been variously attributed to Sarmiento, to Campomanes, and to an unidentified author of the earlier eighteenth century.[29] In the story, the author has discovered an account by Dutch explorer Abel Tasman that describes the utopia on the peninsula of Sinapia (the word is an anagram of "[H]ispania)" as "the most perfect opposite of our Spain." One aspect of that perfection was the prince's ability to manage the population according to need, sending away inhabitants when the population became too large and bringing new inhabitants when the population declined.[30]

In that context royal authorities implemented a series of internal resettlement schemes, usually for strategic purposes, including an attempt to move one hundred families from either Mallorca or Cataluña—or an equal number of foreign Catholic families—to the uninhabited island of Cabrera in the Balearics. These "poor, hardworking people" would supposedly stop North African corsairs and Menorcan smugglers from using the island as a refuge. In 1763 a similar project resettled a group of Genoese families who had been rescued from the North African island of Tabarca to the tiny island of San Pablo, off the coast of Alicante, which was renamed Nueva Tabarca.[31] However, the most significant attempt to manage the population imbalance was Campomanes's organization of the colonization of the Sierra Morena in 1767. In this case, rather than resettle Spanish families, the monarchy contracted with Bavarian Johannes Caspar Thurriegel to bring six thousand Flemish and German Catholics to establish colonies in that sparsely populated and largely uncultivated region of Andalucía.[32] But even then authorities attempted to integrate peasants from northern Spain into the project. To prevent the foreigners from disrupting local marriage markets, the authorities believed that it would be "useful" to admit Spaniards from the more densely populated regions, including the coast of Galicia, Asturias, and Cantabria. In addition to "uniting" foreigners with Spaniards through marriage, such a plan would ease some of the north's overpopulation and move the most fertile Spanish women to where their potential children would be most useful. Indeed, some of the earliest documentation of the Patagonia project suggests looking at the project in the Sierra Morena to see if what had been accomplished there might be adaptable to the South American effort.[33]

In addition to using poor northern Spanish women's reproductive potential to more effectively balance the population, royal authorities wanted to put them to work for the state. Nearly all of Spain's Enlightened economists believed that one of the main failures of the economy was its inability to make good use of the labor of the Spanish people. As the author of *Sinapia* proudly proclaimed, "In Sinapia, everyone works, from the prince to the least citizen."[34] However, that was not the case in eighteenth-century Spain, where large numbers of men and even more women had no regular employment. Of course, few peasant women had the luxury of idleness, but women's agricultural labor was largely invisible to most elite men, and it was somehow not defined as "work." So, in one treatise after another, Spanish intellectuals estimated the numbers of idle women and considered how their employment on behalf of the state might produce impressive windfalls. According to the Madrid Economic Society, in the capital alone twenty-five thousand women—nearly half the female population—lived in idleness. Economist

Bernardo Ward counted two million idle women and estimated that if women and girls would only spin more, the Crown would take in around 20 million *escudos* per year, "almost three times as much as the King collects from all of the Indies."[35] A decade later, Campomanes upped the ante, figuring that there were four million able-bodied adult women who could spin during their "free time." At 20 pesos per woman, this home industry could generate 80 million pesos per year—"more than the value of the Indies." He also argued that women had no less an obligation than men to work for a living and provided a list of artisanal occupations, including embroidering and painting fans, that women might undertake "for the general benefit of the State."[36]

Expanding opportunities for employment was critical, as both intellectuals and royal authorities believed that the masses of unemployed, impoverished men and women posed an imminent threat to social stability. As early as 1762 Campomanes suggested sending poor families to colonies in South America, where he believed that vanity alone would keep them from becoming vagrants. The threat was more than hypothetical. In 1766 popular protests erupted across the kingdom, in large part against a rise in grain prices, but also in opposition to other unpopular reforms, including sumptuary laws.[37]

Women's employment would help ease those social tensions by alleviating the poverty that beset tens of thousands of Spanish families. Putting women to work would also benefit the state by altering women's marital and reproductive choices. Ward argued that the state should "stop this impediment [unemployment] to marriage, [and] introduce industry such that all the women who want to work can earn one or two reales per day and each man five or six and they will marry by the thousands those who are now useless for the ends of the government and the state." He even advocated providing dowries for poor girls, but only as prizes for high productivity, such as for those who performed best at the spinning wheel. Campomanes concurred, arguing that working women would marry earlier and bear more children, content in the knowledge that they could care for them. Moreover, Ward argued that after giving birth everyone benefitted from women earning their own livings, "as [children] of one or the other sex receive their first impressions from their mothers."[38] Working mothers would serve as exemplars for the next generation of productive Spaniards.

Those same Enlightenment thinkers argued that northern Spanish women were by nature especially hard workers. Ward believed that "laziness was not generalized across Spain; in Cataluña, Valencia, Galicia, Asturias, and Vizcaya the people apply themselves pretty well."[39] Campomanes praised the women of northern Spain (in particular those from Galicia, Asturias, Cantabria, Vizcaya, and Guipúzcoa) who fished, sold fresh fish, cultivated the land themselves, and sold bread. Those women "did not disdain to apply themselves to however many tasks their ability might permit and make them able to sustain their families." They also cared for livestock, guided the carts, harvested and gleaned, and even worked the land when men were absent. However, physical labor did not in any way compromise their reputations: "Their customs, robustness, and modesty are worthy, and they give them a decided superiority."[40] In 1778 Cornide advocated for the use of Galician families as colonists, connecting these diverse ideas about demography, poverty, work, family resettlement, and women. He reminded Gálvez that Gallegos were poor but industrious and that Galician women were known for their "extreme fecundity"—all virtues that could be put to use on the Patagonian coast.[41] Gálvez clearly agreed.

Royal authorities formulated the plan to colonize Patagonia in order to manage a variety of crises on both sides of the Atlantic. Based on their Enlightenment understanding of poor women's place in eighteenth-century society, they looked to the resettlement of northern Spanish peasant women as a means to resolve demographic, economic, and social issues on the peninsula and to bring stability and security to the periphery of the Spanish empire. But first, they would have to convince some women to volunteer.

CHAPTER TWO

"It will be very advantageous to have some families"

Gender and the Recruitment of the Colonists

BY THE SPRING OF 1778 GÁLVEZ WAS READY TO PUT THE PATAGONIA project into action. As confident as he was in the project's ability to resolve some of Spain's most pressing problems, he was also certain that conditions among the northern peasantry were desperate enough that they would respond enthusiastically to the king's call for volunteers. However, recruitment proved to be much more difficult than authorities in Madrid ever imagined, and gender quickly became central both to the attempt to attract colonists and to their decisions to enlist. For the Patagonia project to succeed, the authorities had to convince peasant women that leaving behind everything that they held dear for the chance at a new life on the distant coasts of Spanish America was the best choice for themselves and for their families.

As Gálvez had decided to focus recruitment efforts in Galicia, the project's peninsular base would be the Atlantic port of La Coruña, which had been open to trade and limited passenger travel to Buenos Aires since 1767, and he appointed Jorge Astraudi (1715–1795), the interim intendant of Galicia, to head the peninsular side of the project.[1] As the Crown's representative in La Coruña, and as the royal official with authority over both the military and the treasury, Astraudi was in the best position to muster the resources necessary for this transatlantic endeavor.

His first task was to distribute nearly four thousand copies of the royal edict asking for volunteers to cities and towns across Galicia:

> In the provinces of the Río de la Plata, it will be very advantageous to have some families from Spain who are well versed in all types of field work and other similar labors, suitable for the best instruction in domestic things, so that by their example the natives of that region might achieve the desired perfection in everything that makes a good citizen. For these reasons, the King has charged Your Lordship with bringing together some poor families of this kingdom [Galicia] capable of fulfilling that objective, negotiating with them the terms under which they might go obediently to the destination determined by the Viceroy of Buenos Aires, of course offering that the cost of the voyage on the mail ships from that port will be paid by the His Majesty. I charge you to make the arrangements to carry out the King's order, notifying me of the number of families who present themselves to make this journey and the number of persons who make up each one [family].
>
> [Signed by José de Gálvez Aranjuez 22 June 1778]

> I send this to all the cities, towns, and places of this kingdom for the general knowledge of all the inhabitants, for the use that each might deem appropriate. Individuals who are inclined to pursue this prospect should present themselves to me to discuss the clear advantages that will come from the new establishment and hope for the great, innate piety of His Majesty and his paternal love for his Vassals:
>
> [Signed by D. Jorge Astraudi Coruña 29 June 1778].[2]

Once city officials received the edict, Astraudi expected them to post the copies in public and use any means possible to get word to their citizenry. What they did with the first edict is unclear, but a letter from the city of Pontevedra in Galicia—in reference to a second attempt to attract volunteers in the spring of 1779—describes the process that those officials undertook to implement the monarchy's plan. Having received two copies, the city council posted one "in the customary place" and reported that the other remained with the council "so that they might convoke the citizens of the town." The council then called a town meeting on a Sunday at 10:00 a.m. to read the edict aloud. That morning they rang the church bells to call the inhabitants to the main plaza and waited patiently for them to arrive; however, much to their disappointment, no one showed up. The councilors waited until noon, but still no one appeared, so they disbanded.[3] City councils across Galicia presumably took similar steps and experienced the same dismal lack of enthusiasm. In all, only 36 families and 11 single men (a total of 168 people) answered the first call for colonists, a far cry from the 200 families that Astraudi needed to recruit.

In addition to being few in number, the first group of volunteers bore little resemblance to the type of colonists that royal authorities desired for the new outposts. Although the edict called for Gallegos, at least five of the families were headed by men from other parts of Spain, including Matías Lagarreta and his wife, Ana María Castellanos, from Vizcaya and Antonio Berdonces who hailed from Andalucía. All of the married couples had children, but the average age was more than thirty-eight years old for the husbands and thirty-six for the wives. Rather than attracting young families whose reproductive potential would be useful in the Americas, the edict had brought in mature couples. All of these women were already mothers and most were at the end of their childbearing years. Moreover, although soldiers were not supposed to be enlisted in the project, the very first volunteer, Marcelo Mendián, was a retired soldier who had made the transatlantic voyage to Montevideo once before in 1772 as a member of the Mallorcan regiment.[4] Few of the men described themselves as either farmers or artisans.

Not only were the first volunteers disappointing, the fact that the cohort consisted of only thirty-six families was a serious setback for Astraudi. So, why did so few inhabitants of poor, overpopulated Galicia answer the call from the king? According to Enlightenment economic theories, Gallegos, who were the "slaves of all," should have been eager to leave their tragic circumstances for a brighter future in the Americas. However, the feeble response to the royal edict revealed how little the Italian-born Astraudi and the other authorities knew about the people they governed. Although the economic situation in Galicia may have seemed dire to economists, a variety of other factors, many of which were connected to the gender expectations of the region, hindered Gallegos's participation in the project.[5]

First, in Galicia long-distance migration was purely a masculine, not a family, endeavor, so much so that both single and married Galician men felt a certain cultural imperative to migrate. In Galician peasant society, women inherited as much as (or more than) men, engaged in nearly all of the same agricultural tasks, and were accustomed to heading households. In some parts of the region, couples lived with the wife's family (uxorilocal residence), leaving young husbands subject to the authority of their mothers-in-law. In this context, many men felt that they could make a more substantial contribution to the household by leaving. Gradually, long-distance migration became so associated with masculinity that men who stayed at home were viewed as weak or even effeminate.[6]

Moreover, by the time that Gálvez announced the Patagonia project, the migration routes followed by Galician men were already well established. For at least a century, Gallegos had been following in the itinerant footsteps of their fathers, brothers, and cousins. Skilled men, especially stonemasons, found work in Madrid and other expanding cities, while those with few skills worked the harvests in underpopulated Castile or found employment as menial laborers in expanding port cities, including Oporto and Lisbon in Portugal and Sevilla and Cádiz in the south of Spain. These peninsular migration routes were also influenced by the region's gender expectations. Generally, Gallegos intended their migrations to be temporary, as the permanent abandonment of family was associated with neglecting one's masculine responsibility. Thus, no matter how far they traveled (Lisbon was a good ten days from Santiago de Compostela, Madrid was at least twelve days away, and Cádiz was a distant twenty days from coastal Galicia), as long as they remained on the peninsula, men could maintain the cultural fiction that in time they would return home to their families. As a consequence, prior to the middle of the eighteenth century, the numbers of Gallegos leaving for the Americas remained low.[7]

In addition, Gallegos' access to land clearly discouraged family migration. Most rented property through long-term leases, known as *foros*. These leases generally provided the owner with fixed rents for the lives of three kings and allowed peasants to work, pass down, and sublease the land as if it were their own.[8] Partible inheritance, in which all siblings inherit equally, also helped ensure that most Galician peasants had enough land to cultivate a small vineyard or grow some grain and raise a little livestock. Few would ever become rich, but as José Cornide noted, there were very few Gallegos who "did not have land to cultivate or industry capable of subsisting."[9]

Most Gallegos may have had access to land, but the small size of their parcels may have actually encouraged men to migrate. As a result of partible inheritance, 50 to 60 percent of the peasants of western Galicia cultivated plots of only around one-half hectare. In 1750, on average, Gallegos cultivated fewer than one and a half hectares (slightly more than three and a half acres) per inhabitant. Some men viewed these tiny farms as too small, as they were manageable for women to work with or without male labor. Thus Gallegas (women from Galicia) generally migrated within the region, to work as wage laborers or domestic servants while they were single, but once married, they expected to remain at home and tend the family farms.[10]

The project's emphasis on married couples, which may have been a somewhat scarcer commodity in Galicia than in the rest of Spain, further complicated the recruitment efforts. The intensity of male migration was such that many parishes were left with as few as eighty-five men for every one hundred women, and half of all parishes had some dearth of men. In parts of the region, more than one-third of households were headed by women, some of whom were married but whose husbands had migrated and many others who had remained single their entire lives. During the eighteenth century, at least 14 percent of Galician women never married and in some areas 20 to 30 percent remained single. Of course, just because these women remained unmarried, they did not necessarily refrain from relationships with men. Cohabitation was common, as marriage offered little stability for women if their husbands intended to migrate.[11] However, the Patagonia project was not open to couples living in such informal arrangements.

By the end of September, Astraudi was seriously concerned about the lack of volunteers and tried to redirect the project in ways that would attract potential colonists. He suggested to Gálvez that they include military men and foreigners among the enlistees (having already contracted the retired soldier Marcelo Mendián). The inclusion of military men was critical, not so much in La Coruña but in nearby Ferrol, where the expansion of the military base meant that there was a large population of soldiers, soldiers' families, and military veterans. According to Astraudi, military officers had contacted him and said that "there were an infinite number of married couples with children and many of them had six or eight young children." Not only did these men have many useful skills, but allowing them to enlist in the Patagonia project would relieve some of the pressure on housing in the area and help alleviate their poverty.[12] However, Astraudi's desire to include former soldiers in the project conflicted with the Crown's goal of ending the use of military men as settlers on the frontier, and Gálvez firmly rejected his proposal.

By mid-October 1778 Astraudi was eager to get the project underway, and he rushed to arrange for the first volunteers to set sail. As he had not made prior arrangements for their passage, he was forced to rely on the regular

Figure 2.1. *Galician Farmer from Betanzos,* by Juan de la Cruz Cano y Olmedilla. *Colección de Trajes de España tantos antiguos como modernos que comprehende todos los de sus dominios.* Madrid: Casa de M. Copin, 1777, n073. Reproduced courtesy of the Fundación Joaquín Díaz.

Figure 2.2. *Galician Peasant Woman*, by José Rivelles (Juan Carrafa engraver). *Colección de Trajes de España*. Madrid: Calcografía Nacional, 1825, cuaderno 6/No22. Reproduced courtesy of the Fundación Joaquín Díaz.

mail ships that traveled between La Coruña and Montevideo. Mail service between the two cities had existed since 1764, and the ships carried some passengers; however, between 1770 and 1777 an average of only twenty-nine passengers per year traveled by mail ship to Montevideo. The trip was expensive—around two hundred pesos—and was permitted only under certain circumstances to soldiers, clerics, and a few merchants.[13] The next ship to depart was the mail frigate the *Princesa*, but most of the passages had already been booked by the newly appointed bishop of Buenos Aires, Sebastián Malvar y Pinto, and his entourage; a judge appointed to the *audiencia* of Charcas; and some other passengers. As a result, Astraudi could only find accommodations for twenty-one colonists.[14] On 21 October 1778, the *Princesa* and its small band of six peasant couples and their nine children departed for Montevideo.

As soon as the *Princesa* set sail, Astraudi began the process of preparing the passenger list for the second ship, the frigate *Nuestra Señora de los Dolores*. He quickly reached a deal with ship owner Juan Pablo Genovés for a much cheaper passage. The royal treasury had paid 165 pesos per passenger (including the cost of rations) on the *Princesa*, while an adult passage on the Dolores cost only 120 pesos per person over the age of six and 117 pesos per child between the ages of two and six. Infants traveled for free. Driving a hard bargain, Astraudi later negotiated the fares down to 110 pesos (for those over age six) on the ships acquired by Miguel de Goyeneche.[15]

By the end of October the number of volunteers for the second voyage had grown to 146, and as the authorities took stock of them, these peasant colonists were more like what they envisioned for their new establishments. At least sixty-six of the seventy-four adults were Gallegos, and there were twenty-nine married couples. The married men in this group were slightly younger on average (thirty-five years old) and a number were quite young. Benito Seoane was only twenty-three years old, and he and his nineteen-year-old wife, María, were parents of a one-year-old daughter. There were also a number of young couples without children, like Manuela Espinosa and her husband Amaro Fernández. At twenty-four and twenty-seven years old, respectively, they were exactly the kind of colonists whom Astraudi hoped to attract.

To understand why these peasants decided to volunteer for the Patagonia project, it is important to remember that migration was more than just a reflexive response to harsh economic circumstances. Across Europe, peasants were remarkably mobile, and to different degrees single men and women, as well as entire families, were willing and even expected to relocate at some point in their lives.[16] Certainly poverty, taxation, population pressure, and access to land influenced many peasants' decisions to migrate; however, a wide range of other social, cultural, and personal factors also came into play.[17] Even peasants moved for adventure, in response to interpersonal conflict, and merely out of a sense of restlessness. For some, migration was a part of broader family strategies, while for others, the decision to leave reflected purely individual motivations.[18]

Although the project piqued the interest of few Gallegas, many of those who did answer the call for volunteers were already experienced migrants. The first two ships carried thirty-eight adult women, at least one-third of whom already had some documentable migration experience before coming to La Coruña, and their itineraries demonstrate the role played by short-distance migration to the port cities of La Coruña and Ferrol in preparing the women for participation in the project.[19] For instance, the first enlistee, Marta Muñiz Villar, from San Martín de Lestón (22 kilometers southwest of La Coruña), had moved to La Coruña well before the inception of the Patagonia project. Perhaps she accompanied her first husband to the city or maybe she went there in search of work as a young widow. She must have met her second husband, Marcelo Mendián, there, as he was from a village east of La Coruña. Their son was then born at the port in 1776. Antonia Armada, a passenger on the *Nuestra Señora de los Dolores*, also had prior regional migration experience. She was from the parish of Santa María de Castro in Narón, about 55 kilometers north of La Coruña, while her husband hailed from San Vicente de Lagoa, 130 kilometers to the east. Her eldest child, José, was born in her native village, but then she and her family migrated to the port city of Ferrol, where her two younger sons were born.[20]

Typically, Galician women migrated to the region's expanding port cities enticed by the possibilities of work as domestic servants.[21] La Coruña served as a magnet for single working women and became quite the city of women. Between 1752 and 1787 the population almost doubled and women far outnumbered men.[22] The situation in Ferrol was much the same. With a rapidly expanding population, only about 20 percent of women who married there were natives of that city.[23] Although most female migrants were single, these burgeoning urban economies provided new opportunities for married women as well.

Whether alone or accompanied by husbands and children, short-distance migration offered critical new experiences for women.[24] Consider, for instance, the experience of Josefa López, who moved to La Coruña at least thirteen years before the Patagonia project. Her native village of San Esteban de Morás sat just outside (twenty-two kilometers) of the city. When she made the short journey to La Coruña, she did not encounter significant cultural or linguistic changes; however, the differences between the busy port city and the sleepy village of her childhood were considerable. San Esteban de Morás was a smallish town of 830 inhabitants compared to La Coruña's nearly 14,000.[25] The quiet homogeneity of the village would have contrasted with the busy, cosmopolitan nature of the port, where she would have seen sailors and soldiers from around the world and heard dozens of languages. From a gendered perspective, La Coruña offered more possibilities for women than she would have known at home. The city was teeming with young women much like herself who had journeyed from their tiny villages in search of work. Women ran boarding houses, owned shops, sold fruit and fish in the public market, and worked in a variety of professions, including as bakers and cloth makers.[26] It is likely that there she met her husband, Ramón, who was from Frades, just to the north of La Coruña. Thus, in her initial move from a small town to a big city, Josefa acquired new knowledge and experience that would be foundational for her decision to enlist in the colonization project and make the transatlantic journey.

In addition to acquiring their own migration experience, some of the peasant women came to understand the complications of resettlement and adjustment to new cultures through their spouses. Twenty percent of the women on the first two ships had married men from other regions of Spain, including Aragón, Valencia, and Andalucía. As they learned to cook their husbands' favorite foods or sing the *refranes* of their hometowns, they acquired the tools for cultural adaptation that would prepare them for life in the Río de la Plata.

For many of the women, the move to Galicia and the potential transatlantic journey were just the next phases in an already peripatetic life. Eight of the earliest women to volunteer were from outside Galicia, including Josefa Sermilo, the wife of Vicente Estevan. At thirty-two years old, she came to the Patagonian project with extensive migration experience. She was from the diocese of Santander, where she must have met her Gallego husband, as her two eldest children were born there. At least seven years before the project, the family migrated to Ferrol, where her two youngest children were baptized. Her younger sister, María Sermilo, had also traveled extensively before coming to Galicia. María had married Cristóbal Martí from Valencia, and like her sister, her two oldest children were born in Santander. Her third child, María, was born in Valencia, and the three youngest in Ferrol. By the time María's family boarded the *Nuestra Señora de los Dolores* to make the transatlantic journey, they had already traveled across most of the Iberian peninsula.[27]

No doubt unaware of the experience that these women brought to the project, when Astraudi wondered why so few Gallegos volunteered, he saw women as the crux of the problem. He was concerned that women were being deterred by people who tried to dissuade them with tales of danger and even death. He became suspicious when, in the process of obtaining the consent of some of the married female volunteers, some of the women were timid or slow to respond to his queries.[28] Upon investigation, he found this to be the case with Feliciana López, the wife of Rafael Corbella, a Gallego farmer and stonecutter. Evidently, Feliciana had lost her resolve to enlist after her parish priest told her that "they were going to be captured by Indians, that it was all a trick and that they would perish in the sea or in the fury of the fires upon landing." This information infuriated Astraudi and he communicated his displeasure with the priest to ecclesiastical authorities. He then used his powers of persuasion to calm Feliciana's fears. She, Rafael, and their son left on the *Nuestra Señora de la Barca* one year later.[29]

Concerned about the dearth of colonists, Astraudi allowed two widows, one widower, two single women, and eleven single men to enlist on the second expedition. The unmarried women were mothers or sisters of the married couples, and the widower's wife had succumbed just prior to the ship's departure. Astraudi's willingness to accommodate these individuals, particularly the older women, may have been due to his desire to see that the project did not get stalled at this critical juncture.

The presence of so many single men on the second ship's passenger list also reveals some of the authorities' ambivalence about the decision to prioritize families. Although families would provide the kind of stable households that the Crown desired, few of the married men had the artisanal skills necessary to aid in the construction of the outposts in Patagonia. In contrast, in the first cohort of single men, more than half claimed to be artisans of one sort or another. The two Troytiño brothers and their cousin, José Corral Troytiño, all told the royal notary that they were farmers and had experience with beehives and as wax makers. Antonio Beres claimed to be a shoemaker; Bartolomé Vázquez was a mason; and in addition to being a farmer, Vicente Vázquez was a carpenter and a weaver. The other five men did not indicate that they had particular skills; nevertheless, they were placed on the passenger list. Although ostensibly the Crown did not want to add to the population of single men in the Río de la Plata, it clearly could not envision the construction of these frontier outposts without them, so along with the married couples, the single men boarded the *Nuestra Señora de los Dolores* in early December 1778. However, delayed by weather, the ship did not depart until the 28th of the month.

Contracting the Volunteers

Once a person, typically a married man, came forward to local authorities to volunteer, he and his family were swept into the complex bureaucracy of the Spanish Empire in general and the Patagonia project in particular. As was true of all transatlantic migrants, the applicants had to request licenses to emigrate to the Indies; however, as participants in this royal colonization project, these volunteers would be vetted not by the Casa de Contratación in Sevilla, but by the bureaucrats in charge of the project in La Coruña. Although there is no mention of such a process in any the documentation, according to Castilian law all of the men had to prove that they were of pure Christian lineage and that they were not emigrating to evade the payment of debts or other legal entanglements.[30] If the man was accompanied by a woman, the couple had to prove that they were legally married. It was up to local secular and ecclesiastical authorities to do all the initial investigations, including finding witnesses and copying paperwork, such as baptismal and marriage records. Then, armed with the necessary documentation, the volunteers were supposed to make their way to La Coruña, where Astraudi would give his final approval and they would be enlisted in the project.

In rural areas, the fact that the quality of documentation did not always match the expectations of the royal bureaucracy sometimes complicated the vetting of the colonists, as happened to Feliciana López and her husband, Rafael Corbella, the couple who were almost scared away by the prospect of being taken by Indians. During the process, a priest claimed that the couple was not legally married. Nevertheless, they presented themselves to Astraudi as ready to enlist. When Astraudi became aware of the complication about their marital status, he contacted the bishop of Mondoñedo, who then conducted his own investigation. After some searching, the bishop reported that Rafael and Feliciana were indeed married in January 1774 in Mondoñedo and that their daughter, María, was baptized in May of that year (an interesting fact in itself!). The confusion stemmed from the fact that Feliciana used the name Rossa both in her marriage record and in her daughter's baptismal record and that there were difficulties finding evidence of Rafael's baptism.[31] Moreover, the priest in question was not even their parish priest. Such bureaucratic miscommunications are not surprising, as clerical literacy was poor and record keeping weak in rural Galicia. Indeed, as we will see, as the project progressed many volunteers appeared in La Coruña without all the necessary documents, and not all of the more than 1,900 colonists actually went through the vetting process. Many men and women merely picked up and moved to La Coruña and successfully insisted on being added to the passenger lists.

Upon the peasants' enlistment, royal authorities carefully orchestrated the formation of the contractual relationship between them and the Crown in ways that emphasized the gendered nature of Castilian legal responsibility. The first volunteers to participate in this ritual were Gallegos, Marcelo Mendián (or Mandiá), and Mendián's wife, Marta Muñiz Villar, who were accompanied by their son and a son from Marta's first marriage. On 5 October 1778, in the presence of Astraudi and the project's legal advisor, Bernardo Herbella, the notary Cayo Acha de Patiño created the contract between Marcelo's family and the Spanish Crown that would be the formula upon which all the colonists' contracts were based.

The agreement began with the basic biographical material on each passenger and a physical description of the senior adult male:

> D^{n} Marcelo Mandía [Mendián] and Dª Marta Muñiz Villar de Francos, his wife, citizens of this city, and Don Marcelo, by trade a farmer, 40 years old of the Galician nation, son of Don Antonio Mandía and María Benita de Neyra, born in the parish of San Julián de Soneyro, in the jurisdiction of Miraflores of this province, of regular stature, a swarthy face, pitted from smallpox, brown eyes, black eyebrows, hair the same color interspersed with white and Doña Marta, 30 years old, born in San Martín de Lestón in the jurisdiction of Bergantiños of this same province, daughter of Don Antonio Muñoz Villardefrancos and of Doña Josepha Reymondez Figueroa and they have for their legitimate children Luis Vicente de Mandía, 2 years old, born in the parish of San Jorge of the said city, and Joseph Malín, son of Esteban Malín, deceased, and the same Doña Marta Muñiz from a first marriage, 9 years old from the aforesaid parish, and Don Blas González, aged 18, their nephew who is accompanying them.[32]

The contracts reveal the Crown's desire to accurately identify male transatlantic passengers by their relationship to parents, place of birth, and physical characteristics, all of which had been a critical part of the bureaucracy of emigration since the sixteenth century.[33] In a world where the name pool was relatively small, neither a Christian name nor a surname was a particularly good way to identify someone; there were lots of men named Juan Rodríguez. Moreover, the move to the Americas allowed for individual refashioning, and men frequently changed their names or adopted aliases. Royal authorities wanted to be able to identify any of the male colonists for any of a variety of reasons, including trouble with the law, family business, and military conscription.

As far as the contracts for the Patagonian expeditions went, the need for detailed physical descriptions of one adult male in each "family" denoted a particularly masculine responsibility for his relatives and his relationship to political authority. Interestingly enough, when unaccompanied widows enlisted with their children, the notary did not provide any physical description of them. Even though they were independent heads of household, royal authorities had little interest in registering them as individuals subject to state regulation and surveillance.[34] Indeed, over the course of the project some women made it onto the passenger lists with very little if any identification, even early on. For instance, in all of the documentation on both sides of the Atlantic, the wife of Manuel Martínez, who embarked on the third expedition, is merely identified as Ana María, without any surname, parentage, or place of origin.[35] Notarial lapses such as these indicate that some combination of laziness and inefficiency worked in tandem with bureaucratic misogyny to marginalize women's presence in imperial record keeping. However, although the authorities may not have always noted women's native villages or ages, they did undertake "the rigorous examination" of the "qualities" and "conduct" of the female enlistees.

It was no accident that the contracts gave physical descriptions of the men but required an examination of the conduct and qualities of the women. Because the Patagonia project placed so much responsibility on the female volunteers, royal authorities were anxious to ensure that they upheld the rigorous moral standards prescribed by the Spanish upper classes. Presumably, their greatest concern was sexual conduct, although it is difficult to know exactly what kinds of behavior Astraudi and the other bureaucrats would have viewed as problematic. While it was clear that women of truly loose morals, such as prostitutes, would not make desirable colonists, it is unlikely, for instance, that having had a child out of wedlock would have disqualified a female volunteer. Large numbers of women in northern Spain bore children out of wedlock. According to Castilian law, those children were legitimized once their parents married, as happened frequently, and single mothers do not seem to have had problems integrating their natural children into their families once they married someone else.[36] Bigamy may have also been a concern. When it came to transatlantic migration, authorities were always concerned that migrants used the ocean voyage to escape one relationship only to enter into another. In Galicia, they may have worried that abandoned wives, known in the region as *viudos dos vivos* (widows of the living) would attempt to flee their parishes with men other than their husbands. Yet the need for women seems to have trumped any of these concerns. There is no evidence that any women were rejected as a result of the "rigorous examination."

Having assured themselves of the general morality of their female volunteers, royal authorities proceeded to formalize the women's participation in the project. According to Castilian law, married women had to swear that they entered into any contract of their own free will and without coercion, and the authorities involved in the Patagonia project took this injunction very seriously. Astraudi noted that the "free will of the married women in order to accompany their husbands before swearing on the contracts is one of the principle cares that requires time due to the different places and provinces of which they are residents."[37] He wanted to make absolutely certain that the married women were volunteering for no other reason than "to suit their interests and family." As the project proceeded, Astraudi made sure that if the women could not so swear or decided not to participate, they (and their families) were allowed to return home at the expense of the royal treasury.[38]

After the identifying passages, the contracts specified that the couple agreed to embark on the next ship and submit to the wills of the viceroy and intendant in Buenos Aires. Once settled in the Río de la Plata, *tanto marido como mujer* (both the husband and the wife) agreed to cultivate and care for the land, cattle, and government-issued farm implements. The contracts clearly indicate that women bore equal responsibility as men for fulfilling these contractual obligations. Indeed, in the next section, as was the norm in the Castilian legal system, the wives waived the rights and laws "in their favor" that prohibited them from engaging in contracts and taking on any legal responsibilities. By waiving those rights, these wives became contractually bound to the Crown just like their husbands.[39] The equal obligation of both men and women was critical, as unlike other migrants who crossed the Atlantic on their own or as a part of official entourages, these colonists' place in colonial society would be defined by these contracts, and their rights, including their freedom of movement and their ability to marry, would be constrained by this contractual relationship often for the rest of their lives.

The Second Edict

By early 1779 Astraudi realized that without significant changes to the project, he was not going to meet his goal of two hundred families anytime soon, and he believed that women's anxieties were at the heart of the recruitment problem. In February he wrote to Gálvez that not only had few families volunteered, but that some had come to La Coruña only to return home because their wives did not want to make the journey. Astraudi said that he had found "some scattered voices of inconsiderate and ignorant people" that frightened the women with stories of the dangers of leaving Spain and of the ocean voyage. He would later report that some men had enlisted, and when they returned home to get their wives, the women no longer wanted to go. In the hope of combating these rumors and augmenting the number of volunteers, Astraudi circulated a much more detailed call for volunteers, which focused more strongly on mitigating women's anxieties.[40]

The new version of the edict began by emphasizing the obligation to volunteer for such a project and with a nod to the expected reciprocal relationship between the king and his subjects. Since the late middle ages, Spanish kingship had been built upon an understanding that support from the populace was to be reciprocated with benevolence.[41] Taking that relationship a step further, the Bourbon kings emphasized their paternal devotion to their subjects. Thus, the edict lauded the king for his "innate paternal love for the care and aid of poor families." Then, tinged with the utilitarian vocabulary of the Enlightenment, it asserted that the project would make poor Gallegos "useful to the state." The message was clear. Poor families should volunteer both out of respect for the king and to help the nation. Such appeals were meant equally for men and women. The edict then restated the desire for farmers and people who would make "un buen pueblo," a good town or citizenry, as well as the preference for married over single people. The edict clarified that in addition to paying the cost of transportation, the Crown would provide housing, land, seeds, farm tools, and maintenance for the first year.

Both as an advertisement of the project's initial success and as a means to counteract any negative rumors about the expeditions, the new edict recounted the departure of the first two ships. It assured its audience that the first families had left on 20 October "with all possible comforts." The description of the second expedition is even more detailed. It noted that the Crown also paid the costs of the baggage and clothing of the volunteers on the *Nuestra Señora de los Dolores*, that each person received alms "in cash," and that they all had been given housing in La Coruña. On board ship, they were accompanied by a chaplain, a surgeon, and a pharmacist and had been provided with beds and food.

The marketing continued with the edict assuring the audience that by "royal order" Astraudi had made certain that "the families do not suffer" and that during the voyage they would have everything that is necessary to "live well." Not only was the voyage itself going to be comfortable, but life on the other side of the Atlantic was utopian. The colonists who had left on the first two ships were becoming "happy . . . hacienda owners in prosperous, fruitful lands situated in a benign, healthy climate." The Río de la Plata would be the perfect place for these peninsular families, despite what he called "the inconsiderate influence of some less educated people" who attempted to dissuade them from taking advantage of "these benefits." It is important to note at this point the edict's critical omission: the actual site of the settlements. Patagonia was not mentioned anywhere.

Astraudi then described the provision of food and the conditions of transport in great detail and in a manner clearly aimed at mollifying women's concerns. From the day they boarded the ships until they disembarked in Montevideo, each person over six years old would receive a food ration equal to that of the crew of the mail ships, and each person between two and six years old would get one-half ration. In European peasant society, food was women's responsibility. Women not only planted and harvested but also cared for kitchen gardens, gleaned fields, tended farm animals, and prepared meals. To convince peasant women to relinquish one of their most critical tasks, the feeding of their families, to male authorities, Astraudi had to provide explicit information about his ability to provide in their stead. To reassure them, he detailed both the content and distribution of each ration.

In addition to 18 ounces or more of wheat biscuits, each volunteer over six years old would receive

> on Sundays, Saturday and Wednesdays, 12 ounces of meat; on Mondays and Thursdays, 10 ounces of bacon; on Wednesdays and Fridays,

> 10 ounces of cod, every day 4 ounces of garbanzos, favas or other vegetables; on Tuesdays and Fridays, 11½ ounces of oil, and on the rest ½ ounce; also on Tuesdays and Fridays, 4 ounces of vinegar and always the necessary firewood so that they might make themselves three hot meals each day, one in the morning of soup with garlic and pepper, and for those who want it, two other soups with meat or fish at midday and afternoon.

The sick would be provided with chicken stew and any other condiments appropriate for their cure, as well as brandy for humid times and when necessary, noodles, rice, butter, and a larger portion of sardines. Royal authorities in La Coruña would ensure the quantity and quality of the foodstuffs.

If the peasant women were concerned that they were also being asked to surrender their control over household goods, Astraudi reassured them that they would be able to bring along their personal possessions, including "mattresses, bedclothes, clothing, chests, trunks, seeds, and tools." As the edict called for poor families, Astraudi made it clear that he would also provide for those who did not have basic supplies. He boasted that "those who do not have a bed will be given one to sleep on. On the last voyage, I made them supply twelve new mattresses, twelve blankets, twelve pillows, and twenty-four sheets for the sick and for pregnant women."

Finally, Astraudi promised to take "spiritual and bodily care of the families" by providing chaplains, surgeons, and pharmacists, as well as all the necessary adornments and implements to fulfill their jobs. Each paragraph carefully assured any wives and mothers who might be interested in volunteering that their families would in no way suffer as a result of their participation in the project.

In the midst of recruiting new volunteers, the third expedition, the frigate *Nuestra Señora del Socorro*, set sail in April 1779 with eighty-three colonists on board. Among the thirteen families, twenty-one single men, and four widowers, was Antonia Seijas, who had made the transatlantic voyage once before. Born just outside of La Coruña, she married Francisco Torres, a soldier from Lérida. She then traveled to Montevideo with him, where he served as a drummer in the Fourth Company of the Twenty-Ninth Battalion of Mallorca. They crossed the ocean with their son, José, who seems not to have survived, but Antonia and her husband had four more children while living in Montevideo. The family returned to Spain with the regiment in 1772, but quickly volunteered as colonists in 1778, along with their two surviving children, Pedro, age nine, and María Francisca, age ten. This family's experience reminds us that by the eighteenth century it was increasingly common for men, women, and children to travel to and from the Americas, as international conflict led to the deployment not just of troops but of military families across the empire. In the case of the two battalions of the Mallorcan regiment that traveled to Montevideo, the 1,268 men were accompanied by 11 spouses and 9 children of officers and by 36 wives and 32 children of sergeants, captains, and soldiers.[42] The American experiences of women like Antonia were strong counterpoints to the frightening rumors that rumbled through the colonists' ranks.

Unfortunately for Astraudi, even after the publication of the second edict he still had not reached his quota of two hundred families. Only forty-nine families and thirty-four single men had embarked on the journey to Montevideo. So, despite Gálvez's rejection of his earlier requests, Astraudi made the unilateral decision to publish the edict seeking volunteers across northern Castile and Asturias. As we will see, that decision would bring an entirely different kind of volunteer to the project and make gender central to its administration in new and complicated ways.

Astraudi's decision to extend the project to Asturians and northern Castilians changed the project profoundly. The response was overwhelming. Beginning in the spring of 1779, large groups of poor peasants began to make the long trek from the peninsula's interior to the port at La Coruña. Some traveled as far as four hundred kilometers in horrible weather for the opportunity to begin a new life in the Americas. There was no doubt in anyone's mind why these peasants were willing to undertake such an unpleasant journey. The majority of the Asturian volunteers came from small towns outside of Gijón on the north coast and from the mountainous areas outside of Oviedo. Although some were probably involved in the fishing industry, most were peasant farmers who rotated grains (spelt, rye, corn, some wheat) with beans and raised a few head of sheep, goats, and cattle. These areas were very densely populated and seigniorial dues weighed heavily on the peasant population.[43] The captain of the militias in La Coruña, José Moscoso, wrote to Gálvez that the Asturians were "fleeing from the calamity of the weather and looking for the paternal aid of the King."[44] Moscoso was right. Severe subsistence crises had struck Asturias between 1763 and 1773 leaving its population weaker and hungrier than ever.[45]

The situation was much the same for the Castilians, most of whom came from an area bounded by the cities of Astorga, León, Palencia, and

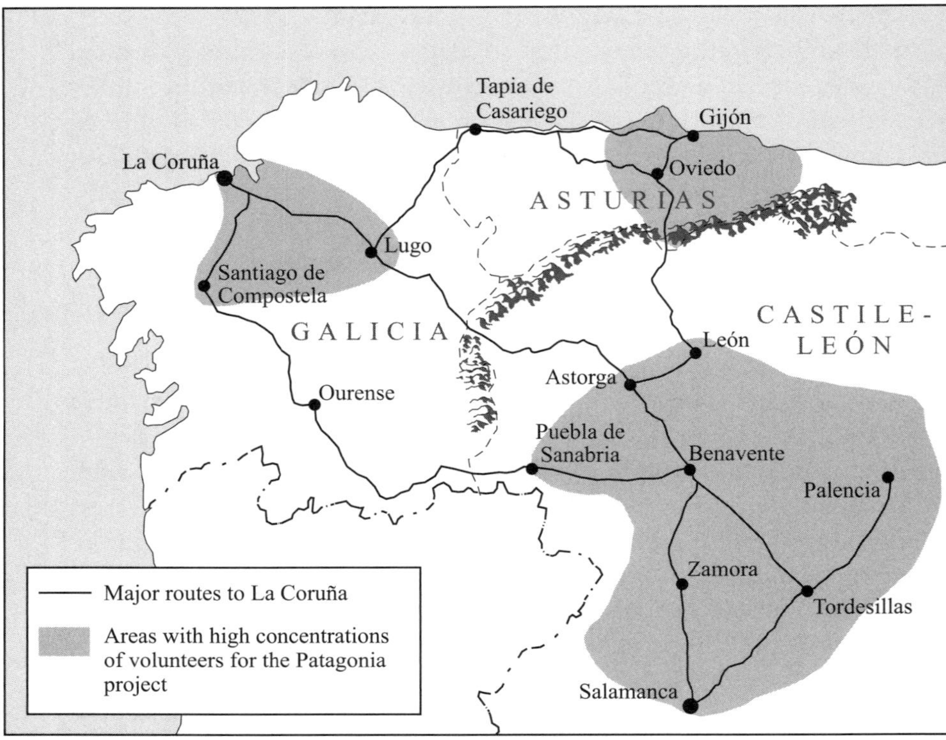

Map 2.1. Northwestern Spain, showing major routes to La Coruña and areas of high concentrations of volunteers for the Patagonia project.

Salamanca.[46] This northwestern sector of Castile-León was also home to mostly small farms of mixed agriculture and small livestock. However, the region was much more sparsely inhabited and dotted with depopulated villages. Yet here, too, the situation among the peasantry was dire. Across northern Castile, poor harvests in the mid-1760s were aggravated by bouts of heavy rain followed by a damaging drought that lasted through the next decade.[47] These crises were accentuated by the burdens of high seigniorial rents and depressed wages. For subsistence-level farmers, as long as harvests were good, they could survive, but the ongoing crises of the mid-eighteenth century pushed many into poverty.[48] For many Asturians and Castilians, the Patagonia project offered a lifeline out of their economic misery.

Nevertheless, the project had to overcome some cultural obstacles to long-distance migration in those areas too. Although in general Asturians were

Figure 2.3. *Asturian Peasant Woman*, by José Rivelles (Juan Carrafa engraver). *Colección de Trajes de España*. Madrid: Calcografía Nacional, 1825, cuaderno 6/No21. Reproduced courtesy of the Fundación Joaquín Díaz.

Figure 2.4. *Asturian Peasant Man*, by José Rivelles (Juan Carrafa engraver). *Colección de Trajes de España*. Madrid: Calcografía Nacional, 1825, cuaderno 6/No21. Reproduced courtesy of the Fundación Joaquín Díaz.

Figure 2.5. *Woman from León*, by Juan de la Cruz Cano y Olmedilla. *Colección de Trajes de España tantos antiguos como modernos que comprehende todos los de sus dominios*. Madrid: Casa de M. Copin, 1777, no19. Reproduced courtesy of the Fundación Joaquín Díaz.

more likely to have some experience with migration than the Castilians, based on the available evidence, few of the Castilian and Asturian women came from villages with histories of male migration and few had traveled far from their native villages prior to enlisting in the project.[49]

For instance, only 3 of the 159 women from Castile-León had documentable migration experience. By 1774 Dominga Carvallo and her husband had already emigrated from their home in Salcedo de Bierzo to Galicia, where she bore a daughter before the project began. In contrast, María Antonia Labié had moved around quite a bit. Born in Zamora, she married a Catalan and bore two children in two different Galician towns. Finally, Paula de Vega from Rioconejos in León married and had her children in the larger town of Benavente before coming to Galicia.[50] These women were clearly the exception to the norm.

In a report to Gálvez, Astraudi worried about these less experienced women. He could not imagine "the torture" of having "abandoned their homes and families," "especially the women" who had done so "ingenuously and without full understanding of what being expatriated requires." From his perspective, some of the colonists had volunteered "dazzled by the hope of ambitiously enriching themselves, others in order to leave their miseries and travails."[51] Either way, they were bound to be disappointed.

On some level he was right to be concerned. For these women and their families, the decision to leave was different than for their more experienced Galician counterparts. However, the colonization project, with its emphasis on familial migration and the economic incentives offered by the Crown (paid passage, as well as the promise of land, houses, and farming equipment), created a scenario that was attractive to these inexperienced female migrants. As married men could not participate without their families and there was no expectation of return, there was no need for women to remain at home. And in fact the power of the project's emphasis on the family is clearly evident: at least thirty-five women enlisted along with their brothers, thirty-one mothers accompanied their adult daughters, and fourteen pairs of adult sisters volunteered. Other women arrived in La Coruña in the company of uncles, aunts, cousins, and stepsiblings. Indeed, many of the women enlisted in the colonization scheme along with a host of relatives. To give just one example, Rosa Duarte, from the parish of San Sebastián de Quintes in the bishopric of Oviedo, traveled to La Coruña and eventually the Río de la Plata accompanied by her husband, their five children, her brother and his wife, a brother-in-law and his wife, a sister-in-law, her mother-in-law, and ten nieces and nephews, not to mention some neighbors and friends from the same village.[52] For women like Rosa, family migration mitigated a host of obstacles to their relocation. In addition to freeing them from their responsibilities at home (as the family presumably sold all of its land and possessions), the presence of family members alleviated anxieties about physical safety, morality, and loneliness. These women would have the same type of support network during their travels and resettlement that they would have had at home.

The migration of other family members could be central to a woman's decision to emigrate, as was true of the case of Isabel Peláez. Isabel had enlisted along with her husband and four children; however, during the long wait at port, her husband died, and in November 1781 her eldest son Felipe, then eighteen years old, was seriously ill in the Buen Suceso hospital. (He later died.) In the midst of these crises, Isabel obtained the necessary medical release from the doctors and asked to be freed from her contract.[53] Astraudi granted her request and she was given money to return home. However, by April 1782 she had changed her mind. She asked that she be reinstated as a colonist since her deceased husband's brother José and her own brothers, Felipe and Juan Peláez, had already left on the *San José y San Buenaventura*. Otherwise, she asserted, she would be left "without aid or kin."[54] Such a decision made sense. It is not clear what other options this forty-two-year-old woman would have had. If she and her husband had disposed of their property before enlisting, it is possible that she had nothing to go back to, as at least some of her immediate family had already made the journey. Whatever future she had with them seemed better than remaining behind without them.

Moved either by economic necessity or a powerful sense of adventure, a few widows bravely enlisted as the heads of their own households. Forty-year-old Asturian widow María Antonia del Monte decided to continue on the voyage even after her husband, Francisco Antuña, died in La Coruña. She made the journey with four children ranging in age from two to twelve years old. The widow Gerónima Salso, from Ponferrada in Astorga, enlisted along with her five children ranging in age from two to seventeen. María Rubiera enlisted along with her five children, her mother, and her eldest son, who married in La Coruña just before embarking.[55] Maybe these widows felt safe among close friends or neighbors from their native villages, or they may have hoped to move to a part of the world where their chances of remarrying were improved.

The Patagonia project got off to a shaky start. The first edict called on Gallegos to volunteer, but few responded. In Galicia, despite the region's poverty, gender norms dictated that men and single women migrated, not families. As a result few married women and their families volunteered. Their lack of cooperation forced Astraudi to issue a second edict, in which he made the project more attractive to women. Even then he failed to get the desired two hundred families and was forced to extend the call for volunteers to neighboring Asturias and northern Castile. This expansion brought large numbers of women without migration experience into the project, many of whom enlisted along with their extended families. The decision to volunteer, however, was only the first step in their transatlantic journey. They would have to make the often long journey to La Coruña, where the presence of women and children would define the wait at port.

CHAPTER THREE

Women and Children at Port

HAVING DECIDED TO ENLIST, PEASANT WOMEN AND THEIR FAMILIES from across northern Spain sold their possessions and began the perilous trek to the port at La Coruña. Carrying only some food and clothing on their backs or in small carts, the initial stage of the journey proved to be particularly challenging. A number of women gave birth and many children fell ill along the side of the road. Fortunately, their situations improved once they arrived in La Coruña. Astraudi quickly established a relatively efficient bureaucracy to provide for their basic needs until their ships departed. However, international politics often led to long delays between departures and left hundreds of people milling about the city. The large numbers of women and children offered new challenges for Astraudi and the other authorities; yet, despite the costs, he worked hard to ensure a happy, healthy cohort of colonists.

The first challenge that the families faced was the grueling journey from the Spanish interior to the Galician coast. There were only three main roads from Asturias and northwestern Castile to La Coruña. The first went from León to Astorga through Ponferrada, across the Sierra de Ancares to Lugo, then on to Betanzos and La Coruña. The southernmost route followed the medieval Camino de Santiago from Salamanca to Zamora to Benavente, then into Galicia through Ourense to Santiago de Compostela and north to La Coruña. Most of the colonists from Asturias probably came via the coastal route, through either Oviedo or Gijón to Tapia de Casariego, then to Lugo and on to La Coruña (see map 2.1).[1] Although all three routes were regularly traveled, there was very little available in terms of services. An early nineteenth-century traveler noted that along the road from Astorga, "foodstuffs are scarce and the inns are miserable; and thus, the traveler who wants to make the journey less uncomfortable must take along his own bed and arrange for foodstuffs in Astorga until he leaves Bebimbre." The journey was, by all accounts, terrible. Passing through the Asturian town of La Robla, statesman and Enlightenment intellectual Gaspar de Jovellanos wrote that he could not accurately describe "how bad, how dirty, and how uncomfortable" the roadside inn was. "Far from offering a traveler asylum from the discomforts of the road, it makes one anxiously desire to return to the road in order to flee from a shelter so uncomfortable and disagreeable."[2] Of course, unlike the king's minister, who was accustomed to better accommodations, the peasant women generally came from poor farming households; they were presumably accustomed to a certain level of discomfort and physical hardship and might have found the accommodations provided by the shabby roadside inns quite acceptable.[3]

Peasant travelers faced other obstacles along the routes. The high sierras in eastern Galicia were often impassable for months at a time due to mud and snow, and washed-out or heavily damaged bridges regularly stranded travelers. From Benavente to La Coruña the recently constructed royal highway provided some relief, but the harsh weather frequently challenged travelers who took that route. Moreover, banditry was always a threat, and these travelers, many of whom carried all of their worldly possessions, were particularly vulnerable to thieves.[4]

In addition to rough roads, miserable inns, and lawlessness, the peasant families experienced a world of physical complications during the journey. Blas de la Madera's wife, Francisca Prieto, gave birth on the road from Asturias. Another husband left his pregnant wife and their two young children in a town just outside of La Coruña while she gave birth. He went on to the port alone and requested additional aid from Astraudi to bring them to the city.[5] All along the route, children fell ill. Some died, forcing parents to bury them far from any place that they might call home.

Astraudi detailed for Gálvez the trials of one group of peasants from Salamanca and Toro who had traveled more than four hundred kilometers through excessive heat and storms over the course of three weeks, remarking that their circumstances provoked in him "the most tender compassion." Later, another cohort of colonists arrived from Asturias, "some on foot, others in carts and on mules, full of children of all ages totally soaked from the continuous cold rains, miserable, and naked."[6] (They were not literally naked, but inadequately clothed.) Astraudi tried to alleviate some of their suffering by asking local officials along the way to provide them with aid and by authorizing payments for portage of their goods and families, but the reality was that he could do little to mitigate the vicissitudes of climate and the misery of their poverty.

As difficult as the overland journey could be, a group of Asturian families had a particularly traumatic experience during their travels to La Coruña. In August 1779, having heard the call for colonists, three families from the tiny village of San Juan de Muñoz in the mountains of Asturias decided to volunteer: Domingo de la Infiesta (thirty-three), his wife, María Manuela Blanco (twenty-six), and their three children; Adriano de la Infiesta (forty-three), his wife, Manuela Vigil (forty-two), and their four children; and José Labandera (forty-two), his wife, María Vigil (thirty-nine, the sister of Manuela), and their six children, who ranged in age from three to fifteen. According to their own account, as required, the families went to the authorities in their town to be processed as colonists, but because of various pregnancies and illnesses among the women and children, their departure was delayed for two years. Finally, in early 1781 they traveled the twenty-two kilometers to the port city of Gijón, where they bought passages to La Coruña on the schooner *San José*, which left on 3 February 1781. Suddenly, near Cedeira on the northwesternmost tip of Galicia, the ship was overtaken by English corsairs. Just before the men from the pirate ship boarded the *San José*, four sailors and one passenger fled in the launch, leaving the ship's owner, a boy, and the Asturian families to be taken prisoner. Quickly, thirty armed Englishmen boarded the ship, confiscated most of the food and the sails and rigging, and stole everyone's money.[7] Fortunately, the terror was short-lived as the next day they were all safely released. The schooner then sailed to the Galician port of Vivero, where the Asturian families disembarked and made the rest of their journey by land. They arrived in La Coruña about ten days later and presented themselves to Astraudi. Not surprisingly, they were cold, destitute, and weary from the journey. He let them stay temporarily in his home, gave them a hot meal, and made sure that they were provided with basic clothing, including pajamas for the children.[8]

Many other peasant families arrived in La Coruña in terrible condition. When a group arrived on 18 April 1779, Astraudi was so distraught by their state that he personally searched for beds and other provisions. He eventually acquired eighty used blankets and sheets from the military, as well as some used clothing and underwear. He was particularly worried about the state of the children and of the three women who were about to give birth. Later that year, a group of families appeared in La Coruña in even more serious straits. Among the families were eighty-one young children and infants, some of them still breastfeeding, all described as completely naked. There were so many that Astraudi could not handle them all himself, and he enlisted his aides to help feed and find beds for them. Five of the children were sick, and two had to be sent to the hospital. Eight women were about to give birth, and one woman had given birth on the road. They finally found a place for these expectant mothers to rest; however, the next night around eleven o'clock, twelve more families arrived from Asturias and Castile. These poor people had survived on nothing but bread for days. They brought with them twenty-eight children and seven infants. One woman had given birth five days before on the road, but the child had died in Betanzos. As it was late in the evening, Astraudi fed them and let them spend the night at his home.[9] Similar scenes would play out at Astraudi's residence dozens of times during the summer and fall of 1779.

Just as the enthusiasm for the project intensified, international politics brought it to a standstill. The ongoing war with England meant that Miguel de Goyeneche, with whom Astraudi had negotiated the acquisition and outfitting of the ships, could not find any ships to transport the colonists, forcing Astraudi to temporarily suspend the project in July 1779. The decree that put the project on hold noted that the king had decided to stop the expeditions for the safety of his loyal vassals. Therefore, anyone who wanted to return home temporarily could do so at the cost of the royal treasury, and they would be notified by edict when they should return.[10] However, there is no indication that any of the colonists took Astraudi up on his offer to go home, presumably because they had nothing to return to, having already sold their homes, lands, and other possessions.

No ships left for the next seven months, but that did not stop the flow of peasants to La Coruña. By the end of October 1779, there were 658 peasants at port and by 3 November that number had swollen to 826, all of whom were milling around waiting for ships to take them to Montevideo. This backlog of passengers transformed Astraudi's administration of the project. Now, in addition to finding and outfitting ships, his work revolved around providing for the basic needs of such a large influx of poor peasant women and children.

The Basic Necessities: Lodging, Diapers, and Marriage

As the families arrived, the first order of business was to find them a place to stay. Astraudi housed them in a variety of settings, generally in the newish neighborhood known as the Pescadería (the parishes of San Nicolás and San Jorge), on the hill overlooking the port. Relying on both his military experience and his access to military resources, he placed most of them in barracks. In the hope of maintaining order, he tried to organize the barracks by province, as he believed that people from the same region were more likely to get along with one another.[11]

The barracks were not comfortable. The peasants complained about the cold, especially since they could not afford to buy more firewood. Enduring the discomfort of pregnancy in the barracks was so difficult that at one point a group of pregnant women petitioned Astraudi to be housed in private homes. They were looking for quieter places to stay, where they could "avoid the scuffles and scandals" that regularly riled the barracks. When Juan Martínez's wife, Antonia, fell ill, he too asked that they be moved from the barracks to a private house.[12]

As they were accustomed to doing when troops were quartered in the city, royal officials contracted with city residents to house the colonists in private homes. Astraudi even paid one hundred reales to the city constable, Juan Sánchez, for having helped find housing for some of the families. The relationships between the authorities and the landlords varied. Sometimes the project's treasurer paid rents directly to the landlords, while at other times he provided rent monies to the colonists. It seems clear that at least some of the colonists paid all or a portion of their own rents, possibly in order to have better housing. After her son was born, Margarita Ramos and her family were living in a private home, but once they fell ill, her husband, Vicente Beade, asked that they be moved to one of the barracks, as he was two months behind on his rent.[13]

The project was a boon for the local real estate market and particularly for female landlords. Reading through the accounts, I found it striking how many women earned money by housing the colonists and their families. To give just a couple of examples, in the summer of 1779 Astraudi approved the payment of 102 reales 12 maravedis to doña Ana Caamero for having provided housing to Pedro Díaz and his family. The project also paid 30 reales to doña María Ygnés Rodríguez for the families that she housed.[14]

If the barracks were crowded and unpleasant, it is not clear that private lodgings were any more spacious or comfortable. Often as many as four families shared houses or even rooms. Narcisco González, his wife, Isabel Santos, and their three children all rented one room in a private home. Others rented ranchos—small, poorly constructed, one-story habitations that were common in the Pescadería. Although soldiers were regularly housed in ranchos, in 1785 military engineer Antonio López Sopeña described them as "very uncomfortable and derelict." When the need for lodgings exceeded the available real estate, some families were housed in a warehouse rented out by Antonio Bentura.[15]

In addition to housing, each family received regular rations of bread, oil, firewood, and one real per day per person.[16] However, as the crowds at port grew larger (and poorer) and their waits grew longer, the families grew restless. In August 1779, on behalf of a group of colonists who had been there since the end of April, seventeen men had the notary compose a petition to Astraudi complaining that the daily real and the ration of bread did not provide even a half day's food. Moreover, they had already consumed all the foodstuffs that they had brought with them from home. They asked him to double the real, as well as to provide some extra funds to purchase shoes, shirts, and other necessities. Astraudi agreed to increase their subsidy by half.[17]

Almost daily Astraudi and the other bureaucrats received petitions from the peasant colonists asking for additional funds to help them through difficult times. Although most of the requests came from men, women—even wives—petitioned on their own behalf, and Astraudi granted them the funds directly. As most of the peasants were illiterate, Cayo Acha de Patiño, the project's official notary, or other professional scribes were evidently readily available to write these petitions, as the project's documentation includes hundreds of individual requests. Of course, the use of notaries was a central part of Spanish culture, even at the village level, and Spaniards were accustomed to delegating their writing to professionals. This system allowed pregnant women to regularly ask for additional alms. Astraudi approved twenty reales for María González, the wife of Julián Rodríguez, to "attend to her nakedness" as she was pregnant, and twenty-four reales for Andrea Gómez, the wife of José Vázquez, who was in a similar situation.

One of the most frequent requests from female colonists was for diapers or money to purchase them. Living solely off the daily real, mothers could not afford the necessities that came with childbirth and believed that, as volunteers for the Patagonia project, it was the Crown's obligation to provide them.

María Gómez made a plea that was typical: "At the feet of Your Lordship . . . she finds herself pregnant and close to giving birth and without diapers, shirts, or blankets with which to swaddle the child when it arrives . . . and she does not have anything to buy them with on account of the extreme poverty in which the supplicant finds herself." Two other women had similar memos composed over the next two days. These petitions are often formulaic, indicating that Acha de Patiño or the other notaries may have helped the women formulate their requests; however, it is also likely that these women consulted with one another regarding Astraudi's willingness to provide such aid. In fact, Astraudi approved twenty reales for each of them.[18]

In addition to food, shelter, and diapers, Astraudi found himself in charge of the general safety and policing of the colonists. In the fall of 1779 he dismissed two couples and three single men upon having discovered their "bad conduct." A few weeks later, two single men, whom he described as "libertine and incorrigible," were pressed into naval service. He hoped they would serve as examples to the rest. This strategy does not seem to have had the desired effect. At one point, he had to pay eighty reales to the city jailer when four of the male colonists were arrested.[19]

Lots of people living in close quarters meant that scuffles and quarrels were common in the barracks, often among people from different provinces. There were also problems with people leaving the barracks late at night to frequent taverns and being arrested by soldiers, despite the fact that Astraudi had ordered them not to detain his charges. The notary Acha de Patiño must have been in charge of dealing with local authorities, as he complained that the frequent robberies among the colonists often kept him up until two in the morning. In fact, the "scandals" in the two main barracks were serious enough that Astraudi eventually reached an agreement with the commandant general to put a captain and six soldiers in each barrack. In addition to maintaining order, they would also assist with the distribution of oil and firewood.[20] In late 1780 Astraudi decided to form two militia companies, made up of seventy-three male colonists each, that would protect La Coruña during the war with England (if necessary) and then defend the new outposts in the Río de la Plata. Astraudi headed up the militias, which provided yet another mechanism for him to exert control over the increasingly restless men.[21]

Astraudi also had to intervene in conflicts between the colonists and local merchants over unpaid debts. Juan Lamar, a master shoemaker, claimed that he had advanced 386 reales to Domingo Irigoin, who had been working in his store. However, Irigoin had fled one night and Lamar had heard that he was in La Coruña, ready to leave for the Río de la Plata. Lamar asked that Irigoin be put in jail until the debt was satisfied. Francisco Salgado complained vociferously that the colonist Roque de Castro and his family were leaving on the next ship without having paid their debt to him. Unable to find Roque, the judge had Roque's wife, Rosa de Cruces, arrested. After much litigation, the conflict was resolved, but the complaints delayed the family's departure by nearly a year. Salgado made trouble for other colonists as well, calling Antonio Gómez and others "thieves and vagabonds." However, Astraudi was suspicious of Salgado's motives and zeal, "due to his advanced age," and dismissed his complaints, noting that it was "very common among the poor to be debtors."[22]

Clearly Astraudi went above and beyond in terms of providing for the colonists during their wait at port; however, such activities pale in comparison with his determination to enforce a strict morality among them by ensuring that as many as possible were married and by creating "families" where none had existed before. His attempts to control both male and female sexuality would have long-term implications on the other side of the Atlantic.

Although other contemporary colonization projects, such as those formulated to extend Spanish control over California, had included some single women, Astraudi went to considerable lengths to prevent women, even the daughters and sisters of colonists, from leaving the port unmarried. His concerns about single people clearly had a transatlantic component. On his side of the Atlantic, young single women complicated his efforts to maintain sex segregation at port and, as we will see in the next chapter, on board ship. On the other side of the Atlantic, single women caused other problems. Among the documentation of the expeditions is an anonymous tract from 1774 describing Buenos Aires. In this work, the author laments the packs of young Spanish men who arrived full of dreams and pretensions, but who were also lazy and ended up just hanging out on ranchos and in houses that he says are "full of European young men that do nothing more than be there without work or learning a skill that might be useful to the Republic." He added that "those same men live without marrying." Interestingly enough, this same author believed that Buenos Aires was full of single women, at least a dozen for every man, who were as or more dangerous than the single men. (Based on census data we know that this sex imbalance did not exist.[23]) According to the author, these women would do anything to get the men they desired. Single men and women were so disruptive to colonial society that the author suggested that they either marry or return to Europe immediately. Astraudi seems to have been influenced by the anonymous text and told Gálvez that marriage would prevent neglect and mendacity among the colonists.[24]

As a result, during the vetting process the authorities rejected many single men, and the publication of the edict, with its preference for married couples, seems to have encouraged many to formalize long-standing relationships or to form new ones to improve their chances of being approved for the project. Andrés Martínez married his cousin María Martínez (who was five years his senior) in November 1779, just prior to setting off for La Coruña. Escolástica Cordero married her relative Pedro Prieto just before they left for the port. Bartolomé Barredo had enlisted as a single man, but during one of the long waits between departures he went home to his natal village in Asturias to marry a local girl, Francisca Menéndez. She returned with him to La Coruña and was placed on the passenger list. Similarly, José Antonio de Arce came to the port, enlisted, and then returned home to Asturias to marry. He then brought his new wife to La Coruña to wait for their ship to depart.[25]

Despite these measures, close to one hundred single men and at least sixty-three single women over the age of eighteen traveled to La Coruña and were placed on the passenger lists. Most of the women were grown daughters traveling in the company of their parents, but eleven were sisters, cousins, or in-laws of the colonists, and at least two of the women had no clear relation to any of the colonizing families. Based on Astraudi's understanding of the situation in Buenos Aires, the arrival of these single women in the Río de la Plata would only further destabilize an already difficult gender dynamic. So he would have to take action.

As is evident from the anonymous text, the concerns about single men and single women were different. Single men needed to work and to be "useful," whereas the threat from single women was not laziness but their unsupervised sexuality. Since Astraudi believed that marriage would both encourage men to work and constrain women's sexual activity, he focused his energies on finding spouses for as many single women as possible.[26] Indeed, the willingness of authorities to intervene to facilitate marriages fell easily into line with other Bourbon reforms that gave the state increased authority in the marriage process.[27] That Bourbon enthusiasm was evident when Astraudi wrote enthusiastically to Gálvez of his successful engagement of a young woman who had traveled to La Coruña to enlist in the project under false pretenses. At seventeen or eighteen, she had latched onto a family as they traveled from Zamora, telling the authorities that she was their niece. Upon arriving in La Coruña, Astraudi dutifully checked to ensure that she was, as she claimed, an orphan. When he investigated the whereabouts of her parents, he discovered that she was not related to the family with whom she had arrived; rather, they had found her destitute along the road and had allowed her to join them.[28] Astraudi then asked the family to be responsible for her during the transatlantic journey, but they refused, as they already had children of their own. Concerned about her safety, Astraudi took her into his home temporarily to protect her from "the risks that her liberty presented and even more so where there were troops." He then found her a husband, also an orphan from Castile, using "loving persuasion" and other inducements to get the young man to marry her. Astraudi was even the godparent at the wedding, where he sang and danced along with the other colonists.[29]

Due to Astraudi's intervention, thirty-four couples married in La Coruña before embarking on the transatlantic voyage; however, these shotgun weddings were quite unlike ordinary northern Spanish peasant marriages. Had they remained at home, the average Gallega would have married at nearly twenty-six years old. In some villages, women typically waited until they were twenty-seven or even thirty to marry. Their Asturian counterparts married slightly earlier, around twenty-four and a half, and women from Castile-León still younger, at just under twenty-four. Moreover, across northern Spain, their husbands married at more or less the same age, although brides with younger husbands were quite common in some areas of Galicia. Thus, typically, Spanish peasant brides were mature women, many of whom had already experienced some economic independence and most of whom had already engaged in sexual intercourse. From a social and sexual perspective, wives and husbands entered marriage as relative equals.[30]

However, the couples matched by Astraudi were very different. The mean age of these new brides was barely nineteen years old.[31] Three were only fourteen years old, even though the average age of their husbands was a more typical twenty-six and a half years. It is difficult to untangle the reasons behind the sudden drop in the age at marriage among the colonists' daughters. There was no obvious economic incentive to quickly marry off children of either sex, as all of the colonists were equally provided for during their stay in La Coruña. Indeed, there was some disincentive, as once the new couple married, the parents lost the child's daily real. Considering that these were supposedly some of the poorest peasants in eighteenth-century Spain, the parents' willingness to give up both their daughters and the extra real per day seems particularly surprising.

Concerns about young female sexuality may have been at the core of these decisions. Some parents may have seen certain benefits in conforming to Astraudi's more rigid sexual expectations. Marrying off their daughters at such young ages would have ensured that they did not engage in premarital sex and did not in any way compromise the families' opportunities in the project by becoming pregnant. Some parents may have felt vulnerable in their new surroundings and potentially unable to protect their adolescent daughters from rape in the barracks in which many of the families were housed or on the streets of the bustling port city. Finally, marriage ensured that the girls would be cared for if anything should happen to the parents during or after the transatlantic voyage.

As per Astraudi's plan, all of the youngest brides were married off to men from their same region or even the same hometown. The most youthful bride, Francisca Antonia Riera, was barely fourteen when at port she married seventeen-year-old Juan Peláez, also from Asturias. Two of the youngest girls were from the bishopric of Zamora. María Antonia Tamame was only fourteen when she became the wife of twenty-seven-year-old Ignacio las Heras, also from Zamora. María Mata, age fifteen, married twenty-five-year-old Lorenzo Pinto, who presumably had traveled with them from their hometown of Almeida de Sayago.[32] One has to wonder what these girls thought as they married these older men, some of whom they had just met—a situation that their mothers and other female relatives were unlikely to have experienced.

For the slightly older brides, a complex array of factors taken in combination with Astraudi's enthusiasm for married couples may have led them to marry (or their parents to marry them off) before they boarded the ships for the Río de la Plata. Some of these women may have used marriage as a way to extricate themselves from obligations to their families, especially those who traveled to La Coruña with uncles, aunts, or other more distantly related family members, rather than with parents. From a bureaucratic perspective, once married, the new couple became "independent" from any relatives with whom they had enlisted, and the daily real and other provisions were then distributed directly to the husband. Catalina García had enlisted along with her uncle, but once in La Coruña she married Miguel Mallada from the same village near Oviedo. Similarly, María Antonia Rivero (twenty-eight) came with her aunt and uncle, but married Juan de la Fuente (twenty-one), also from Asturias, before she sailed for Montevideo. Ángela Ortega (nineteen) described herself only as the "relative" of a family from Palencia. She married

Tomás Centeno during the long wait at port, and the couple enlisted independent of her relations. Marriage also provided some women with the opportunity to separate from stepfamilies. Teresa Muñiz had made the journey with her mother, stepfather, and six stepsiblings. Marriage changed her status from babysitter to independent woman. Similarly, María Muñiz (no relation to Teresa) and her sister Isabel came with their father, his second wife, and their two young children.[33] Both married at port, Isabel only days before the departure of the *Santa Ana* 2, allowing them to make the journey independent of their fathers' new families.

As was true of the younger brides, many of the women who married during the wait at port found husbands from their home villages or one nearby; sometimes they had traveled to La Coruña with their future husbands. Casimira Fernández (seventeen) and her sister Clara (nineteen) married José Cordero (twenty-one) and Antonio Caballero (twenty-four), who had come from nearby villages in Astorga. Two weeks after Antonio married Clara, his sister María Caballero (twenty) married Clara's father, Pascual Fernández (forty-three), who had traveled with the Caballero family from Astorga to the port. Marriage also created tight connections among Asturian families. The recently widowed María Antonia Santurio married the widower Juan Arce (who died before leaving for the Americas), and three weeks later, Juan's daughter Manuela (eighteen) married María Antonia's son José Nava.[34] Marital bonds among these neighbors no doubt helped ease the anxieties that accompanied the decision to enlist in the project.

The few truly unattached single women found love or at least good traveling companions among the colonists. Juliana Pérez (twenty-five) had enlisted along with another family, but then met Pedro Martín Gallego (twenty-five). After getting engaged, he also enlisted for the voyage. The most surprising bride was Antonia Solibán, whom the notary described as "neither family nor head of household." She was from Guipúzcoa, had arrived seemingly unaccompanied, and was only fourteen years old. She married Juan Alonso, a thirty-year-old farmer from Zamora. He had traveled to La Coruña with his uncle, who had been forced to resign from the project due to illness. By marrying, both solidified their chances of ending up on the passenger lists and probably of finding success in the Americas.[35]

A few single women found spouses among the widowers who had come to enlist. Having arrived at port poor and pregnant, María Castañeda (twenty) faced double tragedy. She was quickly widowed and bore a posthumous son who died soon after birth. Undeterred by her personal losses, she was determined to leave for the Río de la Plata, and authorities enlisted her along with her sister and brother-in-law. She then met and married Antonio Constanzo (twenty-six), a widower who had enlisted along with his cousin and his wife. Juana de Pintos (eighteen) suddenly became stepmother to two young children by marrying forty-eight-year-old widower Francisco Zurdo. Such marriages were critical for Francisco and other single fathers like Fabián Cerrón, who desperately needed helpmates to care for their young, motherless children.[36]

Despite his best efforts, Astraudi could not convince all the single people to marry. Two of the single women joined the expeditions in the service of other families. Ramona Villamil, twenty, had already moved to La Coruña from Mondoñedo when she came to be employed by the family of Juan Francisco Buela. The couple had four children under eight years old, and Buela, a farmer from the town of Padrón near Santiago de Compostela, requested that the authorities enlist Ramona to "assist with the education of his daughters" and teach them to sew. Francisca Lamela was hired as a wet nurse for colonist Margarita Ramos when it was found that she could not nurse her newborn child. Francisca then agreed to accompany the family to the Río de la Plata at the royal treasury's expense.[37]

In fact, despite his initial reservations, Astraudi allowed a few young single women to enlist as a means of joining other family members. At least two young women decided to migrate after having been recently orphaned. María Josepha Pidal, nineteen, had enlisted along with her parents; however, they both died before the family embarked. María Josepha then asked Astraudi to allow her to be added to the family of her aunt and uncle, Manuela Pidal and Manuel Torre. She argued that, poor and orphaned, she could help them work the land in the Río de la Plata.[38]

María Díaz Fernández, also recently orphaned, enlisted as a colonist so that she could join her brother in the Río de la Plata, where he and his family were already settled. She asked that she be added to the family of Juan Martínez, her neighbor, and that he be charged with getting her to her brother.[39] At the same time, Antonia Mosquera also requested that she be allowed to enlist and that Juan Martínez take her to her father. She had been listed as a passenger for the second voyage, but her mother died before they were ready to embark. According to her request, some people had counseled her to remain in La Coruña, where, in their opinion, she would have a better chance of getting ahead. However, now, approximately two years later, she felt deceived and "repentant" and wanted to join her father in the Río de la

Plata.[40] Juan Martínez actually agreed to take both women, but for reasons that are unclear he never boarded the ship, and neither María nor Antonia appears on the passenger lists.

María Gregoria Abad did join her relatives in the Americas. When her father, his second wife, and their son left in April 1779 on the *Nuestra Señora del Socorro*, María Gregoria remained on the peninsula in the care of her grandfather. In June 1782, after his death, María Gregoria, now nineteen, asked to be reunited with her father and stepfamily. The authorities consented and placed her in the care of Manuel Antonio Gándara and his wife for the voyage. Gándara's wife had been too ill after giving birth to leave on an earlier ship, and María Gregoria may have been tasked with helping care for the family's three young children.[41]

When all else failed, Astraudi created families where none had existed before to ensure that single people did not arrive in the Americas unsupervised. Single adult cousins, brothers, sisters, and sisters-in-law were *agregado* (added or attached) to nuclear families, even when they enlisted separately. As often as possible, young single men were attached to or noted as "traveling in the company of" older couples. For instance, although he had no connection to them, Domingo Echevarría, a twenty-two-year-old farmer from Pamplona, was agregado to the family of Benito Macías and Josefa Domínguez, both from Galicia. It seems clear that Benito, more mature at forty-six, was expected to supervise the younger man. Pedro and Vicente Mayo, twenty- and twenty-three-year-old brothers from Astorga, were agregado to the family of Manuel Ortiz and María Marcos. José Guerrero from Toro was agregado to Francisco Vázquez, a thirty-five-year-old widower with three young children.[42] Presumably, in the company of married couples and more mature men, these single men would be less likely to desert or misbehave. Moreover, this bureaucratic manipulation allowed Astraudi to maintain the fiction that there were close to two hundred total families long after he had exceeded the quota.

Healthy Colonists

Finally having taken care of their basic needs, married off as many single people as possible, and created an array of new "families," Astraudi used all the resources at hand to ensure the health and physical well-being of the colonists, an endeavor that had serious ramifications for the women and children. The peasants arrived in La Coruña malnourished and with a remarkable array of physical ailments. Many required immediate medical attention. In the fall of 1779 a group of families from Zamora arrived infected with smallpox. Astraudi responded immediately, allowing them to spend the night at his home and providing them with food, blankets, and basic medical care. Recounting the events in a letter to Gálvez, he noted that he "feared that many would continue to fall ill due to the excesses that they had suffered from the weather and such a long journey, especially those who came on foot."[43] In the moment, he and his servants undertook to diagnose and triage these patients. According to Astraudi, some suffered from colds, while others were just sickly. A few children required immediate hospitalization.

No doubt as a result of the influx of new arrivals, a smallpox epidemic spread through the population of colonists. By the eighteenth century, smallpox was a common, survivable childhood illness, and families would rarely seek medical intervention.[44] However, for Astraudi, it was important to control the outbreak in order to ensure calm in the barracks and the orderly embarkation of the ships. The sick colonists taxed the limited resources of the local health providers. By the end of November 1779, there were sixty-nine children, thirty-eight men, and forty-six women in the city's Buen Suceso hospital, which usually only handled ten indigent patients at a time.[45] In addition to smallpox victims, Nicolás Tixera, a doctor from the royal military hospital, noted that three men and ten children had died in the hospital from the weakness and depression that he believed resulted from the harsh journey to La Coruña and from a lack of proper food and clothing. In just the first year or so, colonists and their children spent 324 days in Buen Suceso. Some recovered, like Magdalena Gutiérrez, who entered the hospital on 3 March 1780 and left eleven days later.[46] Others were not so fortunate and they took their last breaths in the tiny hospital cots.

At the height of the project, Astraudi appointed Dr. Vicente Antonio Posse Roybanes to oversee the provision of healthcare to the colonists and to supervise the other four or five doctors, surgeons, and interns. These healthcare providers made regular visits to the barracks, as well as to the private homes and apartments. At the beginning of July 1781, Posse Roybanes made a list of the patients whom he had visited, noting how many times he had seen each over the course of the previous month or so. He reported seeing Isabel Pelaéz's child twenty-eight times, and the wife and daughter of Francisco Nava on fourteen different occasions.[47] He had an informal consultation with Juana de Jesús and saw more than a dozen other patients at least twice. His work was complicated by the outbreaks of smallpox and dysentery that sprang up with each group of new arrivals from the interior.[48] Nor was he the only doctor being worked to the bone. In December 1779 the surgeon Juan Manuel Sobrino recounted that at one point, there were as many as eighty people sick. He complained that his colonist patients often lived far from one another and that he was forced to make house calls at night and at other inconvenient times.[49]

The doctors employed the full array of medical techniques and remedies to try to heal the colonists. As was typical of the era, most of their treatments relied on diet or a combination of diet and medication. When Bernarda Caldelas suffered from a stomach ailment accompanied by fever, Dr. Tixera asked Astraudi for additional funds to continue her dietetic regimen and her medications. When Felipe Arce Fresno, a colonist from Asturias, his wife, and his child all fell ill, he requested that Astraudi grant him some alms so that he could purchase chicken soup, chocolate, and biscuits, as recommended by the doctor. Pascuala García, the wife of Lázaro Fernández, wrote to Astraudi saying that her bedridden husband had been under the care of the doctor and the surgeon, who had applied "all the remedies conducive to the reestablishment of his health." She needed an additional fifty reales to help pay for pork fat, linseed, and brandy for his care.[50]

The medical professionals took a holistic approach to healing that required other types of interventions by Astraudi. For instance, a doctor recommended that Francisco Méndez and his family be provided with different housing as his current lodging was too humid and was making his two children sick.[51] Dr. Tixera wrote to Astraudi about the terrible situation of Isabel Blanco. According to Tixera, "among the other sick that I attended and visited in the mill [another site where colonists were housed], there is a poor woman whose husband is very sick in the hospital and for some days she has been suffering from fevers produced by a strong attack of erysipelas [a skin infection] on her face and her two infants are also sick in the same bed. I am filled with the greatest tenderness and pity to see my miserable patient with her two children in great despair as there is no sibling or relative to kindly care for her." Astraudi granted him forty reales, presumably to hire someone to help care for Isabel and the children.[52]

Astraudi invested extensively in treating pregnancy-related illnesses and providing postpartum care, an indication of the degree to which women's fertility was central to the success of the colonization scheme.[53] As they waited to embark, the female colonists continued to conceive and give birth. Approximately 17 percent of the women gave birth at port, and the births seemed to come in waves. In January 1780 six women delivered babies. In June 1780 another seven gave birth. March 1782 saw the largest number of documented births by female colonists at port in a single month—eight. Assuredly, many more women became pregnant. Although I have found evidence of the births of thirteen children who did not later appear on passenger lists (and thus must have died), it is likely that many other children died soon after birth or were stillborn and thus were not recorded in the documentation of the project. In any case, by 1 July 1783 there were at least 112 children under two years old among the colonizing families.[54]

For the most part, the births themselves did not require action by Astraudi or his medical staff. Despite detailed medical records, I found no documentation that either the project's medical practitioners or midwives were present at the births of the colonists' babies.[55] Either local midwives' fees were low enough to be affordable to the colonists on their daily real, or women relied on female friends and relatives to help them through labor.[56]

On the rare occasions when childbirth became a medical crisis, the project's administrators provided extraordinary care for the mothers. Francisca Prieto, who gave birth in December 1779, spent more than twenty days in the Buen Suceso hospital with complications from the delivery of her child, all at the expense of the royal treasury. A doctor visited María Herrero four times in the barracks after she gave birth in the spring of 1781. Another surgeon cared for Josefa Domínguez, who suffered from some type of postpartum illness.[57]

Without a doubt, the most surprising medical intervention that took place during the wait at La Coruña was what was either a caesarean birth or episiotomy performed on Marina Margarita Arroyo. According to her husband, on 11 August 1781 there was a problem with the way that the baby was situated in the womb and medicine had not resolved it. So the surgeon at the royal hospital, "opened up the said woman and took the baby from her body."[58] The infant appears to have died, but Margarita accompanied her husband to Montevideo on the *Santa Ana 2*, which left La Coruña on 2 October 1782.[59] In fact, not only is her recovery remarkable considering the invasive surgery involved, but I found evidence that only one enlisted female colonist died of pregnancy-related illness before leaving La Coruña—a testament both to the quality of medical care provided by Astraudi and to the women's physical endurance.[60]

After the births, Astraudi also found himself taking a role usually reserved for fathers—paying wet nurses.[61] When Margarita Ramos, who had recently given birth, found that she was unable to lactate, she and her husband hired a wet nurse and asked that she be allowed to accompany them to Montevideo; Astraudi agreed. Similarly, when Ángela Marcos fell ill with a serious fever for more than a month, her husband, Francisco Rodríguez, requested additional monies to pay her medical expenses as well as the costs of a wet nurse to care for their three-month-old child. Astraudi gave him forty reales.[62]

The project's administrators also intervened to help children afflicted by disease. In November 1779, during the outbreak of smallpox, forty-six women and sixty-nine children from among the colonists were being cared for at the Buen Suceso hospital, and more than two dozen families requested additional alms to help care for their children.[63] Moreover, when children died during the waits at port, Astraudi and other royal officials were always willing to help mitigate the family crises that followed. While Antonio Menéndez's wife was still suffering from some illness, presumably smallpox, his twelve-year-old daughter died. He had to ask Astraudi for additional alms to pay for burial and other expenses. Fernando Quevedo lamented that the cost of burying his infant daughter left him with nothing to support his wife and family. He needed extra alms to make ends meet. The infant girl of Miguel Prieto and María Herrero died after a three-week illness in January 1780. To bury her in a local church, Prieto sold some of the family's clothing. He then asked Astraudi for some alms to cover the cost of new clothes.[64]

During the wait at port, health problems caused some potential colonists to have changes of heart, and Astraudi willingly released petitioners from their contracts and usually gave them some money to pay for the return trip home. As early as December 1778, Antonio Martínez and his wife Rita Gómez decided that, considering their health, the expedition was too risky and asked to be released from their contracts. Astraudi agreed.[65] Domingo Baquero from Castile asked to be allowed to return home because neither the "continuous medications" nor the "rigorous diet" of the hospital had cured his illness. He asked to return home "to take the airs of that land." Dr. Tixera added a note that said that from the moment they had arrived, Baquero's wife had been ill with periodic fevers and jaundice. Although he had administered the necessary remedies and her illness had subsided somewhat, "the healthy and free native airs" of their home village was the best hope for a cure.[66] Over time, approximately 168 people became too ill to make the voyage, and either they petitioned on their own or the doctors recommended that they be released from their contracts.[67]

At times, the doctors referred directly back to the goals of the project when deciding that colonists could no longer fulfill their contracts. The wife of Diego Corral had convulsions, and the wife of Tomás del Río was paralyzed in her right leg, leaving her "unable to exercise the functions and labors of her sex." The doctor also declared that the sexagenarian Andrés Delgado, who suffered pleurisy, was "in a state of health so weak and debilitated that he would be unable do the hard labor to avoid necessity and poverty."[68] Such chronically ill patients would not be useful to the new settlements in the Río de la Plata.

In addition to illness, the death of a spouse impelled some women to ask to leave the project. Catalina Martínez had enlisted with her husband, their seven-year-old son, and an infant. However, when her husband died, she no longer wanted to make the journey and asked to be released from her contract and return home. Her request was approved. The same was true of Antonia Carvajal who after having been widowed asked to return home with her young son to the care of her brother. In total, the notary reported that 111 colonists died at port.[69] Some of their family members continued on to the Río de la Plata, while many others gave up their dreams of new lives and returned home to grieve.

As it seems to have been relatively easy to get released from the contracts, it is surprising that sixteen "families" just deserted.[70] The documentation provides no other information about them. Some may have been scared off by the rumors of the dangerous voyage; others may have found work or love in La Coruña. Still others may have fallen into legal trouble. However, at least at this stage of the project, by far and away the majority of the volunteers were committed to starting new lives in the Río de la Plata.

To that end, over the course of 1780 five more ships departed, carrying nearly 700 passengers. Four left in one convoy: the *San Felipe Neri* with 128 volunteers, the *Santísima Trinidad* with 137, the *San Joaquín y Santa Ana* with 12, and the *Nuestra Señora de la Barca* with 193. The *Real Carlos* departed in May with another 264 colonists. By that point, in the spring of 1780, Astraudi had met his quota of two hundred families (using his broad definition of "family"). However, he still had hundreds of people waiting at port and was determined to get them all to Montevideo as quickly as possible.

Unfortunately, no ships left during the following year due to war with England. The Atlantic was far too dangerous and it was difficult to find ships to engage for the project. Finally, by the spring of 1781 Goyeneche was able to hire a Portuguese frigate to make the voyage. In April the *San José y San Buenaventura* would help relieve the burden at port, taking 586 passengers.

Even after the *San José* departed, there were still 185 people waiting at port, and they would not be able to leave for some time.[71] Another fourteen months passed before the next ship, the Portuguese brigantine *Santa Ana*, departed with 57 colonists in June 1782. By October 1782, when Francisco Fernández Pello, his wife, and their two children finally embarked on the *Santa Ana 2* along with 186 other passengers, they had been waiting since September 1779. Moreover, although Gálvez regularly reminded him not to exceed two hundred families, Astraudi continued to accept new volunteers. Even Pascual Jordán, a retired soldier who had been among the first to apply but had been rejected, eventually was placed on the passenger list along with his wife and five children.[72] As the last babies were born, the sick grew well enough to travel, and random relatives appeared at port, Astraudi always agreed to allow just a few more to enlist, including a group of poor families who appeared at the port in February 1783.

The peninsular side of the project was finally drawing to an end by 1783, in large part because Astraudi was transferred to the intendancy of Jaén, leaving the lawyer, Bernardo Herbella, to deal with the last volunteers. Despite his misgivings (mostly surrounding the exorbitant costs of the project), Herbella found passage for 119 colonists on the *Nuestra Señora de la Lapa* in July 1783, including a single woman and her illegitimate daughter. When a final group of Asturians appeared nearly a year later, Herbella rejected them, but they appealed directly to the king for permission to embark and were admitted by royal order.[73] These last few stragglers set sail on the *El Buen Jesús de Familia, San Antonio y Ánimas* in June 1784.

After a dismal start, over the course of nearly six years, approximately two thousand peasants volunteered for the project to colonize Patagonia.[74] Gálvez was determined to populate the new outposts in the Río de la Plata with women and families, and the passenger lists reveal how effectively Astraudi met that goal. Not only was he able to create families where none had existed before, but he invested extensively to make certain that they were well cared for, spending lavishly on everything from diapers to doctors. His focus and investment paid off. In the end, at least 875 women—426 adults and 449 of their nieces, sisters, and daughters—made the transatlantic crossing headed for new lives in the Río de la Plata.

CHAPTER FOUR

Women, Children, and the Transatlantic Voyage

JUST AS THE COMPLICATED EFFORTS TO RECRUIT, FEED, HOUSE, AND otherwise provide for the colonists at the port of La Coruña revealed how central gender was to the implementation of the Patagonia project, the preparations for the voyages themselves were clearly influenced by the desire to see that the women and their families made it safely to the Río de la Plata. From the refurbishing and provisioning of the ships to women crying out in labor and toddlers running across the decks, the colonists' experience of the Atlantic crossing was marked by the presence of women and children.

The royal officials who oversaw the outfitting of the ships that had been hired to carry the peasant colonists to Montevideo proved to be quite conscientious about assuring the safety, comfort, and even morality of their passengers. Indeed, these priorities required officials to significantly alter most of the vessels before any of the colonists could embark. First and foremost, Spanish and Portuguese brigantines and frigates were not made to transport large numbers of passengers and certainly not families. The mail frigates that made the crossing usually carried fewer than a half dozen passengers, and much of the space on the brigantines was devoted to weaponry and cargo.[1] So, to transport the colonists, the interior of the ships had to be reconfigured, with the space below decks divided into small compartments that would serve as their living spaces during the voyage.

The safety of the passengers was the primary issue in terms of the configuration of the ships. Even at the end of the eighteenth century, the Atlantic

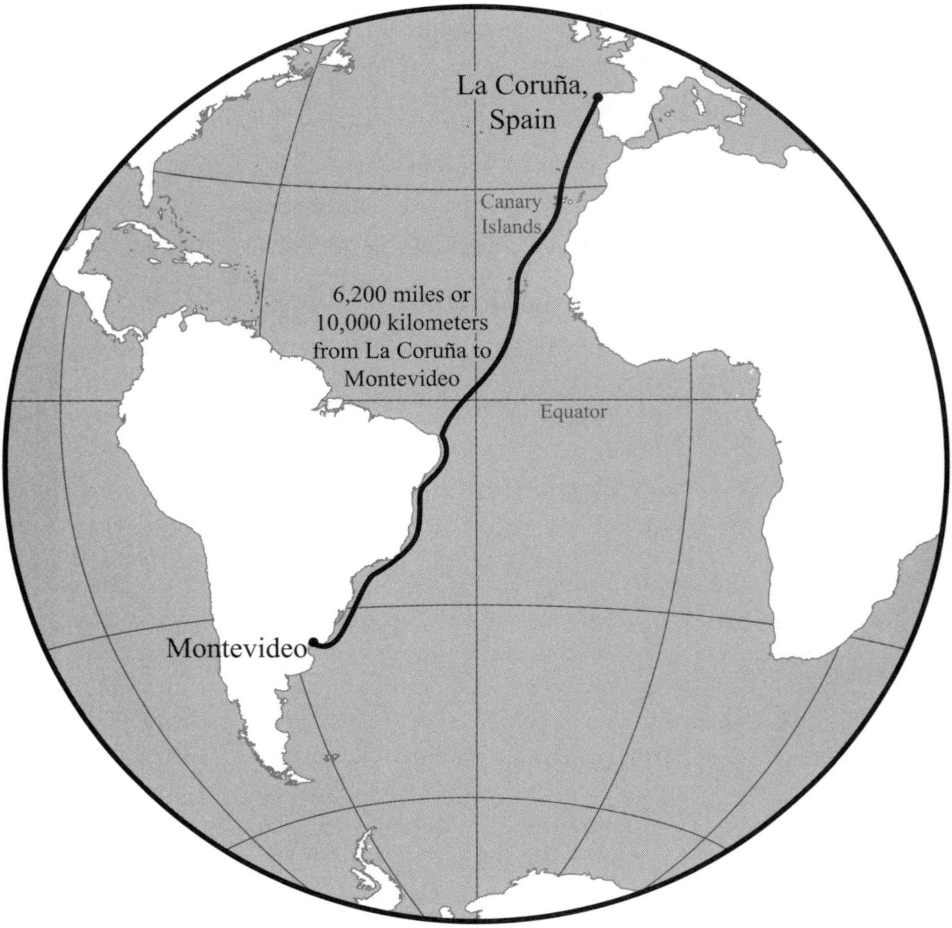

Map 4.1. The transatlantic journey from La Coruña, Spain, to the Río de la Plata.

could be dangerous. Those aboard faced the possibility not only of rough seas and inclement weather, but also of skirmishes with pirates and even naval warfare. To reduce the chance of injuries, Astraudi reported to Gálvez that ship owner Juan Pablo Genovés had put up nets and grillwork on the *Nuestra Señora de los Dolores* so that children would not accidentally fall into the sea. On the *Real Carlos*, the ship was arranged so that if a battle ensued, the passengers would be protected "so that no one might suffer the misfortune of falling into the water." To prepare the brigantine *Santa Ana* for the colonists,

Figure 4.1. Spanish frigate like those that carried the colonists from La Coruña to Montevideo. Fragata española del porte de 40 cañones vista por la popa navegando a un largo. Dibo. Por D. Agustín Berlinguero, Grabo. Por Rodríguez y por Gasco (ca.1790). Reproduced with permission from the Mariner's Museum. Newport News, Virginia.

Figure 4.2. Spanish brigantine like those that carried the colonists from La Coruña to Montevideo. Bergantin español del porte de 16 cañones ciñendo el viento mura estribor vista por la aleta de sotavento con viento fresco y mar llana. Dibo. Por D. Agustín inguero, Grabo. Por Rodríguez y por Gasco (ca.1790). Reproduced with permission from the Mariner's Museum. Newport News, Virginia.

damage done on its previous journey was repaired, and berths and other unnamed alterations were added for the "comfort of the families."[2]

As was true at port, sexual morality was an issue for royal authorities, and before the departure of the *Nuestra Señora del Socorro*, Astraudi checked to make sure that lodging spaces for the single men and the married couples were clearly separated. He may have been concerned about the sexual safety of the young women and girls; among the passengers were twenty-three independent single men and another handful of adolescent boys and young men attached to families. Or maybe he just wanted the young families to have some privacy. Whatever the case, this separation of single men from the rest of the colonizing families became the norm on subsequent voyages. On the *Real Carlos*, which carried 264 peasant colonists across the ocean, the ship's owner built compartments between the decks with separate spaces for married couples. On the *Santa Ana*, Astraudi boasted that the lodging for the passengers had been divided by marital status, age, and sex to their "full satisfaction and comfort."[3]

In addition to altering the ships to accommodate the colonists, Astraudi tried to ensure that the peasant passengers were treated well by the ships' captains and crews. He must have known from his own military experience that officers often did little to hide their disdain for ordinary soldiers and sailors, let alone peasant passengers. The contracts with the ship owners required the captains to provide the passengers with rations equal to those provided to ships' crews from the day they embarked until their arrival in Montevideo. Moreover, the captain was to "care for them," and the contracts specified special treatment for sick passengers and pregnant women, particularly those who might go into labor during the voyage. The earliest version of the contract with the owner of the *Nuestra Señora de los Dolores* also noted that the captain and crew were not to permit any verbal or physical mistreatment of the sick. Interestingly enough, that clause did not survive the negotiations. The final version more generally asserted the ship owner's responsibility for the "good treatment of the families and anyone else."[4]

After the crew loaded the ship's supplies, the passengers' possessions were carried on board. The petitions for relief from Domingo de la Infiesta and his companions, who had been intercepted and robbed by corsairs on their way to La Coruña, provide what is probably a typical list of the goods that the peasant families packed for the voyage. Each of these three families left their homes with some money, a trunk or two, and some basic foodstuffs for the journey, including pork and bread, as well as shirts, shoes, and household

TABLE 4.1. The ships

SHIP	DATE OF DEPARTURE	DATE OF ARRIVAL	NUMBER OF COLONISTS*	DEATHS ON BOARD	BIRTHS ON BOARD
La Princesa	21/10/1778	28/12/1778	21	0	0
Nuestra Señora de los Dolores	27/12/1778	10/4/1779	146	5	1
Nuestra Señora del Socorro	21/4/1779	12/7/1779	83	0	0
San Felipe Neri	14/2/1780	8/5/1780	128	1	0
La Santísima Trinidad	14/2/1780	20/5/1780	137	0	2
San Joaquín y Santa Ana	14/2/1780	27/5/1780	12	0	0
Nuestra Señora de la Barca	14/2/1780	27/5/1780	193	4	1
El Real Carlos	24/5/1780	15/8/1780	264	12	1
San José y San Buenaventura	15/4/1781	19/7/1781	586	36	15
Santa Ana	20/6/1782	29/9/1782	57	0	2
Santa Ana 2	2/10/1782	30/12/1782	186	4	1
Nuestra Señora de la Lapa	1/7/1783	26/10/1783	119	2	2
El Buen Jesús de Familia, San Antonio y Ánimas	15/6/1784	4/10/1784	23	0	1

* It is difficult to get an exact number of passengers on board. Not everyone on the passenger lists created in La Coruña embarked and the lists created in Montevideo do not always match those created in La Coruña. Moreover, Juan Alejandro Apolant's numbers in *Operativo Patagonia* contain some errors. These are my best counts having examined the many versions.

linens. Adriano de la Infiesta also brought a hatchet and some silver buttons.[5] It seems likely that most of the other passengers brought similar goods, although the food would have been consumed prior to the ships' departures. Typically, crew members were allowed only one trunk or piece of luggage for clothing and maybe a small mattress;[6] however, the basic contract with the ship owners required that the colonists be allowed to bring aboard their personal possessions, including beds and mattresses, clothing, household goods, farm and artisanal implements, seeds, and trunks. The passengers and their possessions were ferried to the ships in small boats that Astraudi contracted for that purpose.

One of Astraudi's greatest challenges was getting the colonists on board the ships, so he made each occasion into a spectacle less focused on efficiency than on alleviating the anxieties of both the passengers and those who remained at port. The embarkations were highly choreographed festivities that were, depending on the number of passengers, sometimes relatively calm, at other times chaotic, but always dramatic.

The events began with a Mass in the parish church of San Nicolás, close to where many of the colonists had been housed and not far from the port. At the departure of the *Nuestra Señora de los Dolores*, Fray Manuel de la Concepción gave a "most efficacious" speech about the "obligations of Christians to obey their contracts and the piety of the king" that was to "inspire" his "children." The crowd prayed for the happy parturition of the princess and for the safe travels of the loyal vassals. The sermons and prayers whipped the crowd into a frenzy. According to Astraudi's account, the families and the multitude of citizens who had gathered "demonstrated much fervor and tears of joy." Everyone then left the church in procession carrying the standard of *Nuestra Señora de los Dolores* to the pier where, "conquering the hustle bustle and confusion with kindness," the 146 passengers boarded the ship to the sound of bagpipes, drums, flutes, and tambourines. The musicians had been paid for by Astraudi, and with a nod to the regional culture, he specifically noted that these instruments were typical of Galicia.

Adding to the excitement at the departure of the *Nuestra Señora de los Dolores*, two women gave birth just hours before the embarkation, and to Astraudi's glee they decided to continue on the journey anyway.[7] Úrsula Riobo was already mother to a teenage son, but the birth of Ventura (whose name means "good fortune") as they were ready to depart infused the ceremonies with special meaning and gave the crowd more reason to celebrate.[8] Astraudi had placed his hopes for the project on the reproductive potential of these peasant women, and Spain's security and prosperity rested in their ability to bear healthy children at the new outposts. The fact that Úrsula was strong and determined enough to make the transatlantic journey not only confirmed to Astraudi that his plans for the new colonies were correct, but also reminded the other female passengers of the tenacity that they could bring to the project.

While the passengers made their way onto the ships, on the dock the townspeople were dancing and shouting, "Long live the king!," their enthusiasm enhanced by the wine that Astraudi provided to toast the health of the monarch and Gálvez. At some of the departures, these events were followed by another round of prayers and a gift of five reales to each colonist in the name of the king. In another attempt to connect the colonists to the monarchy, Astraudi required that in return for the money, each recipient was obligated to pray the rosary daily "for the happy success of the sovereign intentions of His Majesty."[9] As one might imagine, these ceremonies became quite expensive, and after Astraudi left La Coruña for the intendancy of Jaén, the predeparture spectacles declined considerably as the thrifty lawyer Herbella reined in the project's soaring costs.

Generally, it took a few days or even longer to get everyone onto the ship, and once everyone was on board, the departure was often delayed due to bad weather or the threat of piracy. As a result, there was much coming and going between the ships and the dock. In the winter of 1780, when the four ships were waiting at port to leave in convoy, small boats carried people back and forth to land on a daily basis. Most of these impromptu returns to the port dealt with women and children. According to the project's comptroller, on 26 January, a small boat made five trips to ferry to the ships families who had arrived late. The following day they made another four trips to transport families who had stayed on land for a variety of reasons and to let some husbands who had already boarded return to fetch possessions that had been left behind at their lodgings. A couple of days later, some heads of families went back to the port to buy things for their children. On 30 January Pedro Sastre and his family had to be removed from one of the ships when it was discovered that his son had smallpox, and another family and their possessions were ferried to the ship to replace them. Additionally, Astraudi allowed ten or twelve women at a time to return to land to wash clothing, presumably to conserve the ships' water supplies.[10] It is easy to forget that in the midst of this massive transatlantic project, wives and mothers still had to do their daily chores.

Officials also made regular visits to the ships. A request for payment by the owner of one of the small boats notes that officials came to the ships searching for one Mariano Pose, the nephew of an enlisted couple, whom they believed might have come aboard fleeing arrest. He was not found. Doctors conducted medical inspections, and the accountants and notary double-checked both the provisions and the people on board. Juan de Ponte, the comptroller, reported boarding the *Real Carlos* along with some of the heads of the families. The colonists hurried to get their possessions on board and arrange them on a day that was so hot that Ponte fell ill enough to require last rites.[11]

The colonists must have felt a range of emotions as they boarded the ships. Some would have been excited about the adventure that lay before them. Others were frightened by the rumors of danger on the high seas and the tales of fierce Indians on the other side of the ocean. Many would have been tired and frustrated by the long wait at port, and some had barely recovered from illness and childbirth at the moment of embarkation.

The festivities, drinking, and intense emotions that accompanied the embarkations could be a potent combination. A serious incident that took place during the long, slow boarding of the *San José y San Buenaventura* in the spring of 1781 reveals the tensions that were simmering among those passengers involving the rations for small children. From the beginning of the enterprise, officials had decided that children between the ages of two and six received a half ration, and children under two years old would receive no rations. In theory, this policy made sense. Eighteenth-century elites were preoccupied with maternal breastfeeding, and presumably most peasant women also preferred to breastfeed for an extended period for financial if not nutritional reasons.[12] Earlier shiploads of colonists had not complained about the policy, but at this point, some combination of the long delays at port, crowded onboard conditions, and anxiety over the impending ocean voyage prompted new concerns about the rations.

The crisis was already looming as the notary created the passenger list. It had been nearly a year since the last ship had departed, and this vessel would transport the largest group of colonists across the ocean—586 peasants, including at least 46 children who were two years or younger. Unlike the passenger lists for the other ships, parents expressed their anxiety over infant rations by declaring that their children were more than two years old. Parents of fourteen children strategically declared their sons and daughters to be "more than two years old" or "two and a half" or "two plus months old." In no other age group and on no other passenger lists did parents or the notary take such pains to provide such detail about their children's ages. However, at least in the minds of these parents, clarifying their children's ages could make the difference between hunger and starvation, sickness and health, on an already potentially dangerous journey.

As the embarkation was slow and parents got a glimpse of conditions on the ship, they became increasingly frustrated with the policy on infant rations. They did not dispute the benefits of breastfeeding; rather, they claimed that the infants needed the same rations as the older children, as breast milk alone was not sufficient. Moreover, due to seasickness the breast milk of some mothers was drying up when they boarded the ship.[13] A group of fathers petitioned Astraudi to have the ration for infants increased.

The project's legal advisor, Herbella, investigated, and in his report to Astraudi he responded that, indeed, children older than eight months needed some additional soup or light food. Having spent time aboard the ship, he also noted that children older than one year needed to eat at all hours, and if they did not have food, they screamed and cried, disturbing the other passengers. In addition, the different quantities of rations were causing quarrels and anxiety among the parents, who were becoming jealous of one another. Herbella reported, "We have seen in this embarkation that these infants cause more problems than the adults and they cause problems for the ship with their frequent emergencies that require more medicine. Making them comfortable makes the rest much more uncomfortable."[14] To keep the peace, and for the safety and well-being of all involved, the request to provide extra rations was approved.

During that same embarkation, the project's notary, Cayo Acha de Patiño, was checking the passenger list when he heard shouts that something had caught fire on board ship. Panic ensued and the mothers raced to grab their children, whom they started tossing from the ship to a nearby barge. The notary tried to calm everyone, but to no avail. According to his account, the boat captains attempted to rescue him via a hanging cable; however, he ended up in the water, losing his hat and cape in the process. Fortunately, no one was seriously injured.[15]

This difficult embarkation hardly prepared the families for the difficulties that they would face once the ships set sail. The first moments after the ships sailed out of the harbor must have been particularly difficult for the peasant colonists. As they watched the shore recede from view, it became painfully clear that these would be their last glimpses of their native lands. Some might have felt a pang of regret about the decision to leave as they waved good-bye to their friends and neighbors who remained at the dock. Compounding the mental anguish, the first few days of the voyage were generally very rough, as the weather off Spain's northwestern coast is notoriously bad.

Certainly the voyage of the first ship, the *Princesa*, did not begin auspiciously, as within a few hours of departing a sailor fell into the ocean and had to be rescued. After that, the ship was beset by almost continuous storms. For an entire month the weather was so severe that the captain was forced to sail closer to England than he would have liked, ultimately reaching the island of Madeira. According to the bishop of Buenos Aires, who was also a passenger, it took twelve days for the ship to get around Cape Finisterre due to the "horrible and dangerous" seas. Strong winds and high waves battered the ship. Conditions improved briefly, but then deteriorated again. As they crossed the equator, the ship continued to be plagued with heavy showers and violent currents. Similarly, the captain of the *Real Carlos* reported "ugly storms," full of lightning and thunder, harsh winds, and "angry waters" during much of the journey.[16] The violent motion of the ship made it nearly impossible to do anything, as everything was tossed from side to side. Food and dishes tumbled from the tables, and the sleeping were thrown from their beds. The rain and waves left everything and everyone cold and drenched. At the height of the storms, passengers could neither eat nor sleep and, when caught off guard, some might be injured. Of course, some of the first peasant passengers hailed from Galicia's fishing villages and a few others from the Asturian coast, and they would have had some experience on the water. But as the project progressed, most of the colonists were from the interior of Asturias, León, and Castile and would have been much less familiar with the ocean, ships, and the physical demands of seafaring.

On many of the voyages, the rough seas and violent storms were only sporadically punctuated by calm, during which the crew could repair battered equipment, and the passengers could settle their stomachs and wash their clothes. However, the calm seas created their own anxieties. Passing through the doldrums, captains and crews worried that a dearth of winds would unduly prolong the voyage and tax the rations.

Over the course of the voyage, the peasant passengers also experienced the dramatic change of the seasons as they moved from the northern to the southern hemisphere. Most of the ships left during the chilly, damp months between October and May. On English and French ships, crews performed a carnivalesque hazing ritual known as the "baptism of the tropics" as they passed the Tropic of Cancer, dousing anyone who had not yet made the crossing with seawater, but there is no evidence that the Spanish engaged in the bawdy and often violent test.[17] The journey then carried them through the warm, wet tropics and across the equator. More so than the cold, the heat was greatly feared by transatlantic passengers, as there was no escaping the tropical stickiness that made their unventilated berths into ovens.[18] Luckily, for most of the passengers the worst of the heat did not last long, with the temperatures gradually falling as they continued southward. The ships that set sail from La Coruña in February, at the height of the northern hemisphere's winter, arrived in Montevideo just in time for winter in the southern hemisphere; however, the passengers who left Spain just as the cold set in during the fall made it through the tropics only disembark in the heat of Montevideo's summer.

Even when the weather was fine, international conflict and the persistence of English privateers disrupted navigation and endangered the lives of the colonists. Spain's intervention in the American Revolution had brought it into fierce conflict with England, especially on the high seas. The war with England forced Gálvez to suspend the expeditions for nearly a year between spring 1779 and winter 1780, as the seas were just not safe enough for passenger travel. The probability of conflict was great enough that after the departure of the *Nuestra Señora del Socorro*, Astraudi asked permission for the colonists to be armed.[19] Then, in response to the ongoing warfare, the decision was made to send four of the ships in convoy; the *San Felipe Neri*, the *Santísima Trinidad*, the *San Joaquín y Santa Ana*, and the *Nuestra Señora de la Barca* would leave along with some other ships, including the *Cortés*, on 14 February 1780. The plan was somewhat successful, although the *Nuestra Señora de la Barca* got separated from the rest of the convoy after only about a week at sea.[20] In addition to the convoys, Astraudi relied more heavily on Portuguese ships. In 1782 Astraudi wrote to Gálvez about the rumors that the newly independent United States might declare war on the Portuguese, further disrupting the project. Indeed, Astraudi made a personal visit to the French consul to review the situation. They decided to translate the colonists' passports into French, "as the Americans are not versed in our language." The monarchy also looked to Benjamin Franklin to reassure them that the Americans would not intervene.[21] When the peace agreement with the English was reached in 1783, the danger subsided, but by that point only a few stragglers remained in La Coruña. Those last few colonists who left that summer on the *Nuestra Señora de la Lapa* travelled with a safe-conduct promise and passports signed by the English king.[22]

In addition to formal conflict on the high seas, Astraudi complained to Gálvez about the "many enemy corsairs that pass boldly along these coasts."[23] Indeed, the captain of the *Real Carlos* reported an encounter with English corsairs at the beginning of the journey and had a skirmish with an English ship on its return voyage to La Coruña. Fortunately, his ship was well armed with twenty-eight cannons and fifty muskets for the crew of fifty-two.[24] Only one ship, the *San José y San Buenaventura*, was actually detained by English corsairs. Upon being boarded, the captain of the ship, Juan da Costa, panicked and threw all of ship's paperwork, including the passengers' passports, into the water.[25] But the corsairs left empty handed, as the poor passengers had nothing worth confiscating. The expeditions were lucky that they did not encounter more problems with corsairs. Having made the trip to Montevideo without incident, the surgeon on the *Nuestra Señora de los Dolores*, Pedro Garzes, was returning to La Coruña on the frigate *El Gallego* when it was surprised by English corsairs and taken to Ireland.[26] Word of these encounters caused an uproar at port. Astraudi reported that some of the colonists were so afraid of the voyage that they had left and were hiding from authorities.[27]

The trip from La Coruña to Montevideo lasted as few as seven and as many as fifteen weeks, depending on the weather and piracy. Unfortunately, the available documentation provides little indication of daily life on board ship during those weeks and months.[28] Certainly, royal officials painted a rosy picture of the conditions. The largest ship, the *San José y San Buenaventura*, was, according to Herbella, outfitted so that the passengers "could not enjoy more ease and comfort . . . The floor boards are in the best proportion and between the divisions are sufficient spaces in the form of cloisters for the free movement of people from one side to the other without falling. The rooms are proportioned so that two people occupy as much space as in earlier embarkations was occupied by three." The *Nuestra Señora de la Lapa* also seems to have had some extra room. The ship, which Herbella reported was large enough to carry 145 to 150 passengers, only transported 119.[29] However, his cheerful reports aside, it is likely that the passengers would have been uncomfortable in the small spaces provided for them. According to historian David Northrup, on British ships of the era that had been refitted for passengers, the berths were only two meters long and about half a meter wide. On German ships, entire families crossed the Atlantic in two-meter-square berths that were only one meter high.[30] If these tiny spaces were at all like those built for the colonists, there was probably only enough room in each compartment to hold passengers' personal possessions and for them to lie down.[31] Moreover, there is no indication that larger families were assigned larger berths than smaller ones. So, for the widower Diego Gordon and his son, José Antonio, who crossed the Atlantic on the *Santa Ana 2*, the living situation may have been quite suitable; however, consider how crowded it must have been for Serafina Fernández, who was accompanied by her husband, four young children, and two young adult cousins. Even on calm days, it is hard to imagine how anyone got any sleep.

Despite the fact that the ship's captain and crew knew how important it was to keep the ship, the people, and the linens clean to prevent outbreaks of disease, it is likely that lice, fleas, and/or rats infested the ships.[32] Moreover, the stench below deck must have been intense. In addition to the urine, vomit, and feces produced by the passengers, the ship reeked from the bilge water that accumulated in the bottom of the ship and from the live animals that each ship carried as a part of the food supply. The air was further fouled by the smell of animal waste and the stench associated with their slaughter. The colonists were also provided with wood for cooking, so a layer of smoke must have hung over many parts of the ship.

Although none of the peasants recounted their shipboard experience in print, we can get a sense of how filthy conditions were from a letter from an Asturian immigrant who made the voyage to Buenos Aires by steamship about a century later:

> It was the most evil and most disgusting thing that God has loosed on the world. I continue believing that for an individual who might have committed half a dozen crimes, the best punishment would be to send him by steamship to Argentina. One night we tried to sleep in those disgusting bunks, but it was impossible due to stench of urine and poop; one could not breathe.[33]

As a result, passengers spent as much time as possible on deck where the air was fresh and they could move around, weather permitting. In fact, generally passengers preferred to sleep on deck, even during bad weather, rather than put up with the smell.[34] On the nicest days, they probably aired out their clothing and bedding and sprinkled the areas below deck with vinegar to diminish the odor.

Although their sleeping spaces were tight and their living spaces smelly and dirty, the passengers' access to food was remarkably generous. As promised in the edict calling for volunteers, Astraudi provided the colonists with the same rations that were considered appropriate for the crews of warships and mail ships.[35] Treatises from the era reflect a combination of military reform efforts and eighteenth-century concerns about health and hygiene. Experts on mariners' health specified the importance of the basics: vegetables, vinegar, and oil.[36] Water, wine, and some protein, usually salted

TABLE 4.2. Daily rations on board ship (in ounces)

	MONDAY	TUESDAY	WEDNESDAY	THURSDAY	FRIDAY	SATURDAY	SUNDAY
Meat			12			12	12
Bacon	10			10			
Dried cod		10			10		
*Menestra**	4	4	4	4	4	4	4
Oil	½	½	½	½	½	½	½
Vinegar		4			4		

* Menestra is a mixture of dried fava beans and chickpeas

fish or pork, filled out the passengers' diets. According to their contracts, every day each passenger received eighteen ounces of biscuit, five *cuartillos* of water, and two pounds of firewood. Other rations were distributed on alternate days.

The ships also carried a variety of other foodstuffs including sardines, rice, hams, and chocolate.[37] Adding to the smell and the chaos on ship, the *Nuestra Señora de los Dolores* also transported 36 live sheep, 8 lambs and pigs, and 250 chickens.[38] Passengers on the *San Felipe Neri* also had cheese, spices, 1,200 eggs, and coffee. Astraudi reassured Gálvez after the embarkation of the *Santa Ana* that he had gone over all the provisions and that they were of the best quality, sufficient for a voyage of four months, and most important for the project's mission, healthy for women and children. Of course, the animals did not always survive long enough to be consumed, as many were swept into the Atlantic's stormy seas.[39]

Whatever the quality of the provisions, for the most poverty-stricken peasants, the mere access to so much meat was novel. Benito Feijoo described the diet of northern Spanish peasants as "a little black bread, accompanied by some milk or some vile vegetable, but all in such sparse quantities that there are some who only get up from the table full once in a lifetime."[40] English traveler Joseph Townsend noted that Asturians "eat little flesh, they drink little wine; their usual diet is Indian corn with beans, peas, chestnuts, apples, pears, melons, and cucumbers; and even their bread, made of Indian corn, has neither barm [brewer's yeast] nor leaven, but is unfermented and in the state of dough. Their drink is water."[41] Moreover, peasants from the interior would have drunk more milk and eaten less fish than their coastal neighbors.[42] Considering these regional differences, it is likely that some of

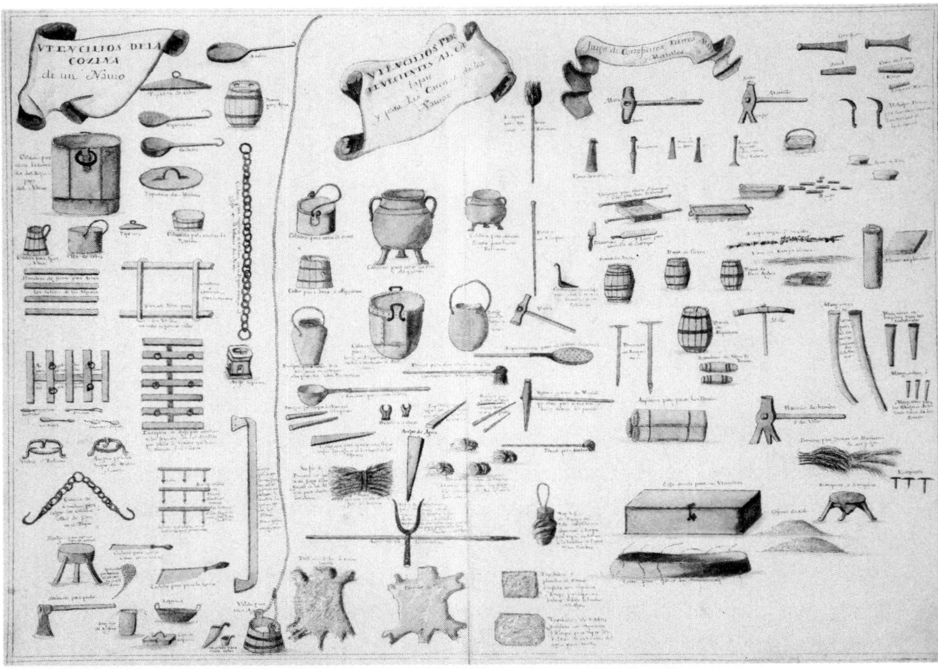

Figure 4.3. Ship's cooking utensils. Diccionario de Construcción Naval del Marqués de la Victoria. España. Ministerio de Defensa. Archivo del Museo Naval. AMN.MV.98.

the women were forced to cook traditional products in new ways as well as learn how to cook unfamiliar products from their shipmates.

Although ostensibly the colonists received no more food than the crew members on a typical voyage, it appears that as a result of Astraudi's careful planning, they were considerably better provided for than other transatlantic passengers. For instance, on her voyage from the Canary Islands to Havana in 1789, the Marquesa de la Real Proclamación, in addition to noting how frightened she was throughout the voyage, complained about the lack of food and water on her ship.[43]

In fact, the colonists only complained about poor treatment on one ship, the *San Felipe Neri*. According to the passengers, the captain, Francisco Xavier García, had unacceptably reduced their ration of water. After a month at sea, some of the men confronted the captain, who taunted and yelled at them in response. The captain then placed them in chains, giving one woman

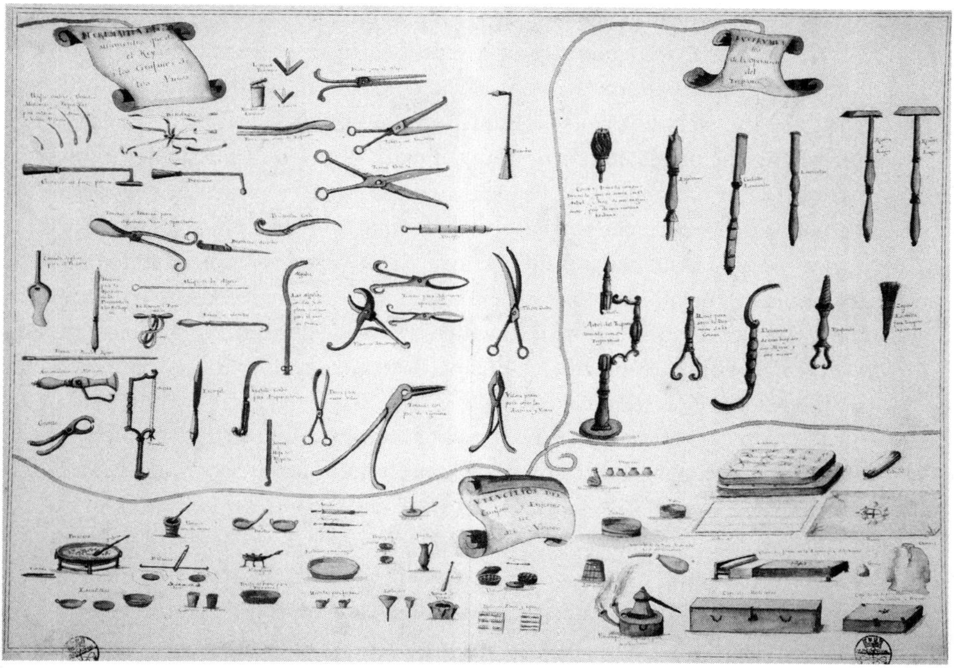

Figure 4.4. Ship's surgeon's tools. Diccionario de Construcción Naval del Marqués de la Victoria. España. Ministerio de Defensa. Archivo del Museo Naval. AMN.MV.100.

such a fright that she miscarried. When the passengers arrived in Montevideo, they filed a formal complaint with royal authorities about his actions.[44]

Just providing healthy food and clean water was not enough to ensure the successful transport of the peasant colonists. Disease was a constant threat on board ship and after the departure of the *Princesa*, Astraudi ensured that each ship had at least one doctor as well as a pharmacist and a full array of medications. His decision to provide medical care during the voyage was not only the sensible next step after having supplied such extensive care at port, but it was also clearly in line with an array of eighteenth-century naval medical and sanitary reforms.[45] Since 1748 naval surgeons had been trained at the Real Colegio de Cirujanos de la Armada in Cádiz, and it was common for merchant vessels to have a trained medical professional on board. As La Coruña was home to one of the main military hospitals in the Spanish Empire, it is likely that the practitioners who accompanied the colonists were experienced naval surgeons.[46] Pedro Garzes cared for the passengers on the *Nuestra Señora de los Dolores*, and Joseph Benito Vázquez was the surgeon on the *Nuestra Señora del Socorro*. Their responsibilities included not only caring for the sick, but also maintaining the box of surgical implements, supervising the meals, and overseeing the distribution of medicines by the pharmacist. Although they had been trained as military surgeons, they probably had some experience working with women and children. While at port they not only worked at the military hospital (which was not limited to military patients), naval surgeons also commonly supplemented their meager salaries by working in the towns in which they were quartered.[47] Others may have treated women and children during the transport of military regiments and their families across the ocean.

Each ship carried an extensive array of medications and a pharmacist to concoct the remedies. The list of medicines on the *Nuestra Señora de la Barca* included 115 different oils, balms, tinctures, spirits, pills, and other assorted pharmaceuticals and was somewhat more extensive than the list of medications on the *Nuestra Señora de los Dolores*. In general, the choice of medications was determined by naval regulations. Indeed, the lists are closer to what would become the naval norm in 1789 than to the earlier 1770 list.[48] From marshmallow syrup, cinnamon water, and rose oil to scurvy grass, the medical providers had everything they needed to help manage the array of ailments that might befall the peasant passengers.

When it came to disease on ship, the illnesses that plagued the passengers did not discriminate based on gender. Throughout the voyage, the captain of the *Princesa* reported that eight or ten passengers and crew were regularly sick with dysentery and constipation. Dysentery, which is highly contagious, could be quite dangerous, as victims easily became dehydrated and ships had limited supplies of fresh water. In addition, both Vicente de Lardizábal in his *Consideraciones político-médicas* (1769) and Pedro González in his *Tratado de enfermedades de la gente de mar* (1805) noted that first-time passengers, more so than mariners, often suffered from painful constipation.[49]

Seasickness was endemic on all voyages, and although not life threatening, it traumatized even the most stalwart of men.[50] Passengers often believed that they were going to die. Writing home from Havana in 1764, one Canary Islander described his transatlantic experience as a "happy navigation, the hardship of seasickness notwithstanding."[51] Pedro González's description of the progression of symptoms from which passengers suffered makes even the modern reader cringe:

> Just as the vessel begins to move, impelled by a favorable wind; just as mother earth flees from the view of those who always leave it with grief and sorrow, is when the new sailors are attacked by an uncomfortable and unknown illness. . . . they begin to yawn and stretch; their faces grow pallid and discolored. Soon they are afflicted by a grievous pain in the head, in whose interior something seems to spin, and soon after they often feel violent throbbing in their temples. Their eyes almost cannot bear the light, and if they had to testify, they would assure that all objects that they face are in continuous circular motion.

After describing the stomach pains, spasms, vomiting, and muscle weakness that followed, he reminded his readers that little could be done to relieve the victims' distress: "The sick are not well except lying down; and even in this position the vomiting, pain, dizziness continue." The situation was worse for women who, "on account of their daintiness, suffered much more, as their imagination is too often terrified by the multitude of symptoms that accompany seasickness."[52] During storms, many passengers would be violently ill, vomiting into whatever bin was available. As we have already seen, the colonists also believed that women experienced seasickness differently than men, blaming the malady for causing women's breast milk to dry up even before the ships left the port. If seasickness was already wreaking havoc on the colonists while the ships were docked, how much worse it must have been for them once the ships set sail in the rough waters and harsh storms of the Atlantic! Passengers on other eighteenth-century voyages reported that just as they recovered from their initial bouts of seasickness, a storm would hit and the agony would return. Although the ships' doctors were supplied with the usual medications, including laudanum and broth spiked with saffron, in reality little could be done to relieve the endless nausea.[53]

For the most part, scurvy was not an issue for Spaniards during the Atlantic crossing. The typical Spanish diet had a high enough concentration of vitamin C to protect voyagers, and the ships carried a number of potential remedies for the disease, including scurvy grass and lemon syrup.[54] Nevertheless, believing that his ship had been struck by an outbreak of the disease just as they reached the Río de la Plata, the captain of the *Nuestra Señora de la Barca* decided to disembark 62 of the 193 passengers at the port of Maldonado before carrying the rest to Montevideo. However, not all of those taken off the ship were ill. As Uruguayan historian Juan Alejandro Apolant has pointed out, parents would have had to disembark with sick children and vice versa. It is unlikely that the illness was scurvy. There were plenty of healthy provisions on all of the ships, and the 109 days at sea was quite typical. Moreover, scurvy is not contagious and none of the passengers died.[55]

Although gender was not much of a factor in the diseases that struck during the Atlantic crossing, youth was, and smallpox proved to be as dangerous to children at sea as it had been at port. On the *Real Carlos*, on which 12 children died, the captain described all but one as dying of smallpox.[56] Accidents and gastrointestinal illnesses were the likely causes of the other deaths.[57] The youngest passengers were the most vulnerable. Nearly half of the children who died during the crossing were less than one year old. In addition to disease, seasickness may have contributed to the deaths of some of these infants, as it may have left mothers unable to care for them. Overall, at least 401 children under the age of six embarked in La Coruña, and another 26 babies were born on the ships. Of those 427 children, 37 died during the crossing, a child mortality rate of approximately 8.5 percent and about 50 percent of the total shipboard deaths. Slightly more boys died than girls. Surprisingly, these mortality rates are quite in line with those on the few other passenger ships that have been studied. As was true of everyone who died during the voyage, the bodies were committed to the sea with the appropriate rites and prayers led by the ships' chaplains.[58]

Despite the relatively low loss of life, for a handful of families the trip was devastating. Santiago Sastre and Inés Martínez lost both of their children during the crossing. María Tudela's only daughter María Antonia died after only three weeks at sea; her son, who had been born in La Coruña, died two months later, two weeks before the ship arrived in Montevideo. Gerónima Salso, a widow, lost two children on the voyage about a month apart and had to manage both her grief and her other three children alone.[59] On many of the ships, the last few days of the journey were particularly difficult, with a number of children dying just prior to or on the day of arrival. Even so, it is important to remember that most of the young children, many of whom were only days and sometimes hours old, survived the journey.

One of the most striking features of these expeditions is the large number of female passengers who were pregnant and gave birth during the crossing, and Astraudi was particularly attentive to their needs. Based on the number of births soon after arrival in Montevideo, many women set sail having already conceived. As noted earlier, Astraudi made sure that ships were properly outfitted with additional beds and linens for pregnant women. The *Santa Ana* had six additional beds and the *Santa Ana 2* had sixteen.[60] Even on the final voyage, during which the ship carried only three families and a single man, the official in charge noted that one of the women was soon to give birth and that there was an injured child aboard, so he provided extra linens for these passengers.[61]

In addition to making expectant mothers as comfortable as possible, the surgeons were supplied with medications that could help alleviate some of the discomfort associated with pregnancy and childbirth. Some of the medications had multiple uses, including those for pregnant women. Pedro Vidart, in his *El discípulo instruido en el arte de partear* (1785), recommended that new mothers take chocolate or drink a concoction of viper-root and couch grass in the first days after birth. Vinegar served an array of medical purposes related to childbirth, including coagulating blood, and mallow helped relieve constipation.[62] The remedies for seasickness mentioned above could be critical for pregnant women as their inability to keep food down could lead to complications, including miscarriages.[63]

Astraudi's efforts to ensure the health and safety of pregnant women and their infants paid off. In total, twenty-six women gave birth during the Atlantic crossings, no doubt in very stressful and very unhygienic circumstances.[64] When Rafaela Guerra went into labor on the *Nuestra Señora de los Dolores*, everyone in the vicinity heard her cries, as there was little if any privacy. Some of the women in labor were surrounded by extended family members—sisters, sisters-in-law, and even some mothers and mothers-in-law—but there were also plenty of strangers close at hand. Some might have been helpful, caring for older children and calming frantic husbands, but others may have just tried to ignore the excitement as they had their own children and families to tend. To ensure the salvation of the newborns' souls, the chaplains baptized the babies immediately, although Rafaela's baby, María de la Encarnación, who was born just prior to reaching port, received the sacrament upon arrival in Montevideo.[65]

On the *San José y San Buenaventura*, fifteen children were born during the four-month voyage, meaning that childbirth was always on someone's mind. The ship departed on 15 April with 586 passengers. A child was born two days later, and another was born during each of the next two weeks. Francisca Prieto and Antonia de la Infiesta both gave birth on 3 May. Three more children were born on consecutive days 23, 24, and 25 May. June was relatively quiet, with only one birth, but five more children were born during the last two weeks of the trip before arriving in Montevideo on 19 July.[66] Just as at port, there is no mention in the documentation of midwives, leading me to assume that women acted as midwives to each other and called on the ship's doctor for medical interventions when necessary. Whoever attended the births had excellent skills. None of the mothers who gave birth on ship died in childbirth during the crossing, and only three of the children born on ship died on the high seas. The voyage seems to have been harder on mothers who had given birth prior to setting sail. Of the seven mothers who died during the Atlantic voyages, two had borne children within six months of embarking.[67]

Overall, such careful attention to the health of the passengers paid off. Only 15 adults (6 men and 9 women) died during the ocean voyages.[68] More than half the deaths came on the crowded *San José y San Buenaventura*, which lost 36 of its 586 passengers (8 adults and 28 children). Twelve of those children died in June 1781 after about eight weeks at sea. Nevertheless, the overall shipboard mortality rate for the project was only about 3 percent, in line with the evidence from the few other passenger ships for which there are data.[69] No one died on six of the ships.

When death struck, it was devastating for these young families who had mustered such courage to move to the Americas. The family of Manuela de la Torre and Francisco de Génova suffered a double trauma when their father and then their mother died on the high seas. Fortunately for their three youngest children, Juan (age fourteen), Manuel (twelve), and Francisca (six), their older brother, also named Francisco, and his new wife had joined them on the journey. The young couple, both only eighteen years old, then took charge of their younger siblings. Tomás Pérez was left alone after the death of his wife and infant son. Even the happiest moments, like the birth of a child, could be tempered by the loss of another. María Aparicio gave birth to a son on the high seas in May 1781, but lost her one-year-old son a month later. The same thing happened to Francisca Prieto and her husband Blas de la Madera.[70] The family members with whom they had begun the journey would not be the same as those with whom they started their new lives in the Americas.

To assist these families both in their joyous moments and during their times of need, at least one priest sailed on most of the ships. Not surprisingly, not all were motivated to volunteer by purely spiritual concerns. A priest named Manuel Riguero agreed to travel along with the passengers on the *Nuestra Señora de los Dolores* in return for his free transportation, as some of his neighbors and relatives were among the colonists and he wanted to settle in the new outposts along with them. He was willing to perform religious duties on ship but asked to be paid for his spiritual services at the same salary as the surgeons. In a rare moment of thrift, Astraudi denied his request, but Riguero made the voyage anyway. Generally, it was the ship owner's responsibility to find a cleric. For the *San Felipe Neri*, Goyeneche went to the rector of the convent of San Agustín in Santiago de Compostela in search of candidates. Astraudi was especially concerned that the passengers on that voyage have a priest on board, as it would take place during Lent. On the *Santa Ana*, the priest was a Franciscan, Francisco García.[71] These priests were expected to lead all spiritual activities, as the seas permitted, including performing baptisms, saying mass, preaching, taking confession, and administering last rites. As seasickness and smallpox left many believing that they were about to die, these men were kept quite busy. To facilitate the administration of the sacraments, all of the ships also carried a basic array of religious ornaments, but the *Nuestra Señora de los Dolores* was fully outfitted with chalices, fonts, crosses, missals, and wafer irons that would be used in the new outposts.[72] The clergy were also charged with some nonspiritual tasks, including ensuring the correct provisioning of food, water, and medicine.

In the documentation of the project, the presence of children on the ships looms large. Scholars know almost nothing about the experience of traveling with children or how children experienced the transatlantic voyage, although by the eighteenth century children regularly made the Atlantic crossing.[73] Clearly, the authorities understood that ships posed particular dangers for children. As we have seen, they were concerned about the possibility of children falling overboard and made the necessary alterations to ensure their safety. However, the large numbers of very young children on some ships must have affected the experience of the crossing for everyone on board. The *San José y San Buenaventura* transported more than two hundred children under age ten, and as noted above, fifteen babies were born during the four-month crossing and twenty-eight children died. So many young children meant large numbers of diapers. As it is unlikely that diapers could be washed every day, depending on access to water, the sheer quantity of dirty diapers would have significantly added to the already putrid smell of the ship. Moreover, the noise and energy of so many children must have been trying at times for both the crew and the other passengers.

The rest of the onboard experience remains somewhat of a mystery. The ships' logs almost exclusively describe the seas and the weather, and the mostly illiterate passengers left no written descriptions of their voyages.

Figure 4.5. Ship's religious ornaments. Diccionario de Construcción Naval del Marqués de la Victoria. España. Ministerio de Defensa. Archivo del Museo Naval. AMN.MV.101.

Moreover, although many collections of letters from either sailors or other emigrants during the period exist and have been published, they rarely mention the voyage itself. Thus, we do not know exactly how the colonists passed the long days and nights on ship. Daily chores like cooking, cleaning, and childcare must have taken up a considerable amount of time and energy, as did caring for the sick. As Stephen Berry has pointed out, the rhythms of shipboard life were completely different than those on land.[74] Although the crews' lives were regulated by work and shift changes, the passengers had no such rhythms to mark the passage of time. On other eighteenth-century transatlantic voyages, when the weather was good and morale high, passengers and crew entertained themselves with music.[75] Although it is possible that the peasant passengers also used music to pass the time, teaching each other the folksongs of their respective regions, in general, they must have grown increasingly bored with every passing week at sea.

By examining the colonists' relationships over the long run, it is clear that some people found companionship and/or love during the crossing. María Fernández Porley married Cristóbal Brunet, who had also been a passenger on the *Santa Ana 2*, only six months after arrival. Asturian Blas Álvarez married Francisca González, with whom he had travelled on the *San Felipe Neri*. Similarly, Tomasa de la Hera, one of the few independent single women, married her shipmate, Pedro Mayo, soon after arriving in the Río de la Plata. It is likely that other relationships formed during the long voyage, but those connections are difficult to see in the extant documentation.[76]

As the ships finally sailed into the Río de la Plata, the navigation up the estuary presented the ships' captains with one last set of difficulties. As the vessels made their way up the Río de la Plata, the shoals and currents rendered entry into the port at Montevideo particularly dangerous. Many ships foundered or sank. In fact, on the last day of its journey the *Princesa* faced serious storms and winds so strong that the ship had to wait in the bay overnight until it was safe to drop anchor.[77]

In addition to the dangers of the Río de la Plata itself, the excitement of arrival was tempered by exhaustion, illness, and death. As the *Princesa* arrived in late December 1778, both pilots had been sick for days. In fact, the second-in-command was so ill that the captain did not think that he would survive the voyage. The captain of the *Real Carlos* also arrived "pretty sick."[78] The last few days were hard for some of the passengers as well. Having survived the crossing, their health gave out just before they disembarked. Rosa de Viñas, a forty-nine-year-old mother of two, died four days before the ship docked. Francisco Pardo, husband, father, and grandfather of colonists, died the day before his ship arrived in Montevideo. Little Ramón Riestra had been born on ship a little more than two months earlier, but he did not live to see his family's new home in the Americas.[79]

At the same time, other families found reasons to celebrate, as a number of women carried newborn babies onto American soil. Graciana Araque took her first steps in the Río de la Plata with her newborn daughter, Francisca Agueda, whom she delivered just before the *Santísima Trinidad* arrived at Montevideo. María González gave birth to her son José Antonio as the *San José y San Buenaventura* came into port.[80] Conceived in Spain, these truly transatlantic babies took their first steps in the Americas.

Many passengers must have felt a sense of relief as they disembarked. They were tired and dirty. Some were sick, and others were grieving. Some had left their homes as many as four years earlier and had still not arrived at their final destinations. However, all in all, the great lengths to which authorities went to make the transatlantic crossing safe and healthy for the peasant colonists were successful. In the midst of storms and pirates, women gave birth to healthy children, no toddlers fell overboard, and nearly all the passengers arrived safe and sound. No doubt, many of the women and children were as thankful as the captain of the *Princesa*, whose last words in his log upon arrival were "Long live the Virgin!"[81]

CHAPTER FIVE

"A Nursery of Vices"

Masculine Crisis in Patagonia

DURING THE SAME MONTHS OF 1778 AND 1779 THAT ASTRAUDI WAS organizing and overseeing the recruitment, care, and transportation of the first few hundred volunteers in La Coruña, preparations were underway on the other side of the Atlantic for the construction of the outposts in Patagonia. From the outset, the project faced significant challenges. The proposed site of the nearest outpost was nearly one thousand kilometers south of Buenos Aires in a region that more than two hundred years after the arrival of the first Spanish explorers remained largely unknown. The Spanish had not yet even completed a systematic exploration of the coastline. As a result, maps of Patagonia were still dotted with mysterious places only minimally explored since the sixteenth century, like Bahía sin Fondo (Bottomless Bay) into which they (incorrectly) believed the Río Negro flowed. They also knew nothing specific about the land, the climate, or the peoples who lived in the region, as there were no permanent Spanish settlements south of the Río Salado. In fact, from there to the Straits of Magellan, Spanish knowledge of the territory was almost nonexistent. In Patagonia, the entire project, from exploration to housing, started from scratch.

Not surprisingly, given the long distances and incomplete understanding of the region, much could and did go wrong. Far from the center of authority, the officials in charge of the project fought among themselves, nearly compromising the entire enterprise from the outset. These conflicts were intensified by shortages of water, the onset of disease, and contacts with Indians.

The construction of the outposts in Patagonia also exposed irreconcilable gender expectations among the men, from the viceroy down to the slaves, often with tragic results.

Early on, a misstep by King Charles III made conflict among the project's leaders almost inevitable. While Astraudi was excitedly issuing the royal edict and waiting for the arrival of the first volunteers in La Coruña, the king was busy appointing the men who would head the Patagonia project on the other side of the Atlantic. In the spring of 1778, he named Juan de la Piedra as *comisario superintendente* and Antonio de Viedma as treasurer of the soon-to-be-constructed outposts at Bahía sin Fondo and San Julián. However, in a confusing turn of events, the king also named Antonio's brother, Francisco de Viedma (1737–1809), as comisario superintendente of San Julián.

Each of the king's appointees had extensive experience in both the military and in royal colonization projects. Juan de la Piedra, who hailed from Santoña, Cantabria, had served as accountant for the navy in Ferrol, Galicia. In 1772 he was sent to the Malvinas Islands to serve as a treasury official; however, after only four years, deteriorating health forced him to return to Spain. His experience in the Malvinas no doubt made him an attractive choice as superintendent, as he would have some general knowledge of the Patagonian climate and the logistical issues that would face the outposts.

Francisco de Viedma, from Jaén in southern Spain, was a desirable candidate in other ways. Along with his brothers Antonio and Andrés, Francisco joined the navy, and the brothers' exemplary service attracted the attention of the king. Francisco became known as an expert in agricultural techniques and had worked with Pablo Olavide on both the colonization of the Sierra Morena in Andalucía and the colonization of Sonora.[1] His brothers would also apply their military and bureaucratic experience to the Patagonia project. In addition to Antonio's appointment as treasurer, Andrés would be appointed interim superintendent at San Julián, although he would be unable to fulfill his responsibilities due to illness.

With their appointments in hand, Juan de la Piedra, Antonio de Viedma, and their entourages set sail from La Coruña for Montevideo on 20 June 1778 on the mail ship *La Diana*. For reasons that remain unclear, Francisco de Viedma did not depart along with them, and his ship, *La Diligencia*, did not leave Spain until the other men had nearly reached Montevideo in August.[2]

Just as the superintendents were making their way across the Atlantic, key political changes were taking place in the Río de la Plata. In June 1778 Juan

José Vértiz y Salcedo became the new viceroy. American born (ca. 1718), his father had been governor and captain general of the Yucatán. Juan José followed in his father's footsteps, devoting his life to a military career that first took him to Italy, Portugal, and Germany. He arrived in the Río de la Plata in 1769 as the inspector general of the troops and oversaw the Spanish assault on the British settlement at Port Egmont in the Malvinas. He rose quickly through the ranks, becoming interim governor of Buenos Aires in 1771, but was passed over in favor of Pedro Cevallos as the head of the new viceroyalty when it was established in 1776.[3] Vértiz succeeded Cevallos two years later, but just as his appointment came through, as a part of the Bourbon reforms, the Crown divided royal authority in the Río de la Plata between the viceroy and the intendant, a decision that would have important implications for the administration of the Patagonia project. The new intendant, Manuel Ignacio Fernández, would be in charge of supplies and finances, and Vértiz would have authority over the military and other basic administration. Unlike on the peninsula where Astraudi had singular authority over nearly all aspects of the project, on the American side the authority over the project was tenuously divided among four men: the viceroy, the intendant, and the two comisario superintendentes.[4]

Tensions among the project's leaders surfaced soon after Piedra presented his commission to Vértiz.[5] Piedra was very assertive with the officials in Buenos Aires. His orders commanded the viceroy and the intendant to facilitate the provision of whatever supplies and people that he might need, and Piedra pushed for as much as he could.[6] He asked for five armed vessels and two launches to carry supplies and 227 men (including 100 soldiers). He also requested sixteen cannons and munitions for the soon-to-be-constructed fort. However, Vértiz was determined to assert his authority over Piedra and did not immediately authorize Piedra's supplies; instead, he had Piedra submit a detailed accounting of what he would need for the venture to the intendant, which Piedra dutifully provided. But rather than order its fulfillment, in another move intended to remind Piedra of his place in the bureaucratic hierarchy, Fernández sent it to a committee for consideration, further delaying the expedition's departure. In addition, as had been true on the Spanish side of the Atlantic, it was difficult to find ships during the war with England. The committee agreed to provide a mail ship that had recently been seized from the Portuguese, two schooners (also Portuguese), and a frigate, all of which were in need of repair and had no crews.[7] Piedra was furious. He had been led to believe that he would have access to better equipment than war-ravaged leftovers. This initial confrontation between Piedra and authorities in Buenos Aires foreshadowed much more serious problems to come.

Throughout the spring of 1778, authorities continued to give Piedra the bureaucratic runaround. In October Piedra went to Montevideo to prepare his ships, but the official in charge claimed that he had not received approval from Fernández to pay for the repairs and supplies. Piedra then attempted to play one official against the other, complaining to Vértiz about the state of the ships and the fact that some of his crews were unhappy with the provisions and were already deserting. That tactic also proved unsuccessful. Besides, he had to wait for Francisco de Viedma, who did not arrive in Montevideo until November. Further aggravating Piedra was the fact that during those four long months, he received no pay for his services.[8]

When Francisco de Viedma finally arrived, Vértiz proceeded to establish a clear hierarchy among himself and the two comisario superintendentes. In a letter to Gálvez, he named Piedra as the "principal" superintendent, commenting positively on his leadership skills, noting that Piedra had "more aptitude and knowledge of these situations" as the result of his experience in the Malvinas.[9] After explaining his decision to Gálvez, Vértiz provided extensive instructions to Piedra that clearly defined the scope of the endeavor and the roles of all involved.[10]

Vértiz charged Piedra with establishing an outpost "capable of subsisting on its own" that could serve as a stopover point or provide support for other outposts. If during the voyage down the coast they encountered foreign ships, they were to "kindly" assert Spanish authority over those waters. The instructions further outlined the reconnoitering expeditions that would occur upon reaching Bahía sin Fondo. Once ashore, if they encountered any Indians, they were to treat them kindly as well. They should then search for the appropriate place to establish an outpost, ensuring that the air was good, the land was fertile, and the site was defensible. Upon accomplishing these tasks, Vértiz instructed Piedra to leave his second-in-command (Francisco de Viedma) and one of the accountants (Francisco Igarzábal) to supervise that site while Piedra and the crew continued on to San Julián. Francisco de Viedma would then be responsible for additional explorations and the mapping of the area around Bahía sin Fondo. The military officers and troops were expected to help the superintendent in any way necessary. When Piedra and the crew reached San Julián (or an appropriate site farther south), they were to follow the same instructions when establishing that outpost over which Piedra would be in charge. Thus, prior to departure, the project's leaders had clear instructions and well-defined hierarchies through which to implement them; however, once they got to the Patagonian coast, those carefully delineated relationships would quickly fall apart.

After many delays, in December 1778 the expedition was finally ready to depart for Patagonia. Despite the emphasis on women's participation in the project, this first cohort to leave for the southern coast was made up entirely of men. In addition to the ships' crews, Piedra was joined on the expedition by the Viedma brothers, two warehouse supervisors, two scribes, four Franciscans as chaplains, four surgeons, one pharmacist, one Indian interpreter, twelve volunteers, seven carpenters, two plumbers, three masons, two coopers, two blacksmiths, one lantern maker, two bakers, fifty convicts, and sixteen royal slaves. The military contingent included seventeen officers and eighty-six soldiers from the Regiment of Buenos Aires.[11] The men in charge of constructing the new outposts in Patagonia included quite a cross section of early modern male society—elite/poor, literate/illiterate, skilled/unskilled, free/enslaved, law-abiding/criminal, military/civilian, white/black, and European/American/African.

The social, economic, and racial differences among the men who set out for Patagonia were evident from the beginning and would only be accentuated as the project progressed. Both on the peninsula and in Spanish America, class divisions subjected men to different and often competing gender expectations. According to the prescriptive literature, Spaniards expected men, particularly aristocratic men, to be of untarnished lineage, protective of their honor, temperate but willing to employ violence when necessary, protective of women and children, and to be good providers for their families. A man was also expected to capably fulfill his *oficio*—his trade or office—whether he was a farmer, a shoemaker, or a city councilman.[12]

Although most men would have agreed on those aspects of Spanish masculinity, popular culture and the prescriptive literature of the period often presented contradictory expectations of masculine behavior.[13] For example, popularly men felt pressure to prove their masculinity through sexual promiscuity, while prescriptively men were supposed to be respectful and protective of female chastity. Men were also given conflicting messages about their places in the social hierarchy. On the one hand, a Spanish man was supposed to expect appropriate deference from those below him in status and to be appropriately deferential to his social superiors. On the other hand, men were expected to demonstrate that they had control over their own destinies and were not subject to anyone else. Of course, this last expectation was especially difficult for lower-class men to meet, as they were always subject to the authority of someone above them in the social hierarchy.

Soldiers made up the largest group of men on the expedition and brought their own priorities for masculine behavior to the project. Not unlike today, regiments in the eighteenth century were, as Cristina Borreguero Beltrán has referred to them, a "microsociety" bonded by discipline, obedience, loyalty, and camaraderie. However, such a homogenized view of the Spanish military obscures the very significant distinctions that pervaded the ranks. The troops were divided according to the official military hierarchy, which in this expedition was headed by a lieutenant and two sublieutenants. These men likely came from more elite sectors of society and had some education.[14] The medical staff was also made up of military men, including Diego Garrido. A native of Jaén, Garrido arrived in 1777 as a surgeon's assistant on the hospital ship *La Limeña*. He later worked at the new military hospital outside of Montevideo, eventually becoming chief surgeon for the army.[15]

The majority of the troops were lower-class men who had come to their military duty through a variety of channels. Some of them had volunteered to serve in the regiments, as the military potentially offered social mobility but more importantly provided some protection against hunger and poverty.[16] Most, however, had been conscripted by regional and local levies in Spain and the Americas. Still others were rounded up as vagabonds and forced into military service as an alternative to jail.[17] In addition, as a result of a royal order from 1773 that sent one-time military deserters to serve in the Americas, five hundred deserters from the peninsula arrived in Buenos Aires in 1775 to join local regiments.[18] Therefore, some of the troops may have been loyal, duty-bound soldiers, while others were merely poor men who had been thrown into the military against their wills. Although these men otherwise had little in common, they quickly became acculturated to the notions that masculinity was based on martial skills and that the masculinity of men outside the military was suspect—ideas that would have profound consequences at the new establishments on the Patagonian coast.[19]

Criminals made up the second largest group of men on the initial expedition, but if the first group of criminals was similar to later cohorts sent to the colonies in Patagonia, the majority of them were also former soldiers. Later, at San Julián, at least half of the convicts were former soldiers who had been convicted of crimes from drunkenness and desertion to robbery.[20]

The sixteen royal slaves who accompanied the expedition had been taken from Santa Catalina in Brazil and were identified as coming from Congo and the Mina coast. Royal slaves were owned by the state for use on government projects. Some had been captured or purchased by royal officials, but others may have been troublesome slaves who had been donated to the state by their owners.[21] These men may have had more control over their persons than we might expect. As will be discussed in more detail later, in the Río de la Plata, slaves had extensive physical freedom and often lived and work alongside free men (both black and white) with no perceptible difference in their conditions or mobility.

The Franciscans who joined the expedition frequently took on the role of mediators among these very different types of men. They came to their involvement in the Patagonia project quite accidentally. At least three, Antonio Comajuncosa, Tomás Nicolau, and Jerónimo Escárigas, were Catalans from the Colegio de Misiones de Escornalbou. The colegio had been founded at the end of the seventeenth century to train friars for missions in the Americas, but they also had a strong missionary presence in rural Cataluñia.[22] In 1778 Comajuncosa and fourteen other Franciscans sailed to Montevideo on *La Diana*, the same ship that carried Juan de la Piedra and Antonio de Viedma. They were making their way to their mission in Tarija (present-day Bolivia). According to Comajuncosa, during the voyage they asked permission from the captain to preach and take confessions from the crew, and they instructed the sailors about how to make a proper confession. He joyfully proclaimed the power of their mission to "disarm" the fury of the winds, seas, and storms during the Atlantic crossing. Upon arrival, three of the friars remained in Montevideo preaching to the masses while their colleagues arranged for the next phase of their journey. Their zeal so moved Vértiz that he detained four of them to act as chaplains on the expedition to Patagonia. They enthusiastically accepted the charge.[23]

The rest of the men were artisans with a variety of skills. These men filled an uneasy place in the social hierarchy between the educated elites and the soldiers and convicts. As Lyman Johnson has persuasively demonstrated, working-class men viewed themselves as having honor in ways comparable with elites, generally based on their ability to fulfill their oficios and to exercise authority over the apprentices and laborers in their employ. However, at the same time, their masculinity was constantly being challenged both by elite men who were prejudiced against manual labor and by other lower-class men who saw their pretensions to honor and authority as unjustified.[24]

The expedition finally set sail on 15 December 1778, with the *Santa Teresa* leading the flotilla out of Montevideo harbor. In the end, royal authorities had provided Piedra with four ships and two launches. He also took a full array of weapons, tools for artisans and engineers, religious ornaments, food for fifteen months for the troops and colonists, medicines, twelve oxen and twelve horses, and a variety of seeds. The journey down the coast took twenty-one days and was complicated by the fact that the ships quickly became separated. Nevertheless, on 6 January 1779, the *Santa Teresa* entered Bahía sin Fondo, and on the shore of a small, sheltered bay that they named San Matías, the Spanish established the first of the new Patagonian settlements, San José.

Immediately, Piedra sent parties out to search for fresh water; however, these lands were far from hospitable. Thomas Falkner, the English Jesuit whose writings had, on some level, prompted the expeditions, described the desolation of the region: "All the seacoast from about twenty leagues south of the second outlet [Bahía sin Fondo] is a dry barren country with very little pasture and uninhabited by man or beast. . . . It has no water for a great part of the year."[25] Piedra was, no doubt, familiar with Falkner's account, but he seems to have willfully ignored the Englishman's negative assessment of the coast and decided to go ashore anyway.

The inability to find a source of fresh water provoked the first of many disputes among the leaders of the expedition, as they publically questioned each other's ability to fulfill their oficios. Francisco de Viedma reported to Vértiz that, without consulting him, Piedra ordered that all of the supplies be unloaded on to the shore, including those intended for the second settlement at San Julián. Despite the "misgivings" of those around him, he also insisted on disembarking everyone on the pretext that the ship was overrun by rats that were destroying everything. The Viedma brothers and others complained about the lack of fresh water until finally Piedra agreed to send out more search teams; however, conflicts about precedence and authority also complicated these efforts. When Piedra put Lt. Pedro García in command of the schooner the *San Antonio la Oliveira* to reconnoiter the Río Sauce, the pilot, Manuel Brunel, at first refused to go, saying that it would result in his dishonor and claiming that he should be in charge of the expedition.[26]

Desperation, Desertion, and Disease

By the second week of February, the situation really started to unravel at the encampment. Francisco de Viedma found that nine of the convicts had deserted. Desertion was common among soldiers both on the peninsula and in the Río de la Plata. The conditions of life were so poor and the work so onerous that soldiers often viewed desertion as the only means to escape their obligations and find a better life. For men fleeing problems on the peninsula, desertion was also a mechanism to avoid being sent back to Spain with one's regiment.[27] However, no matter how dismal life was at the encampment at San José, the decision to desert was very risky. This territory was completely unknown. By leaving the encampment, they placed themselves at the mercy of the climate, the topography, and the ever-changing relations between the Spanish and the nomadic Indian groups who traversed the region. Considering how dangerous it was to leave the outpost, these desertions were a strong defiance of authority and an equally strong assertion of the expectation that a man should be free to come and go as he pleased.

Despite the dangers, another three sailors deserted soon after. From there, the floodgates opened, with soldiers and sailors deserting nearly every night. On 13 February, three more sneaked away, as did another three soldiers from the Regiment of Buenos Aires two days later.[28] The desertions cost the outpost dearly. Each time, Francisco de Viedma and Juan de la Piedra had to organize search parties to track them down, using men and supplies that could have been put to better use searching for water or constructing the fort.

Often the same forces that made life at San José unpleasant conspired to force the deserters back to the Spanish outpost. On 16 February, three of the sailors who had deserted reappeared, forced by hunger and thirst to return to the camp. One of their group had drowned. In an act reminiscent of seeking sanctuary in a church to evade prosecution, the men asked for the protection of the Franciscans so that Francisco de Viedma would not make examples of them in an attempt to prevent further desertions. Over the next couple of days, more deserters returned, but Viedma decided to punish only the one whom he perceived to be "the most guilty." His leniency was not unusual. Although in principal military desertion was a serious crime, in reality the constant need for soldiers meant that deserters often received little or no punishment. For instance, in 1776 the Crown ordered a royal amnesty for one-time deserters. Rather than face imprisonment or other punishment, they would be returned to their regiments and their service extended another six years.[29]

Hoping to reassert his authority and stem the flow of deserters, Piedra sent the ships' pilots Basilio Villarino and José Ignacio Goicochea up the Río

Negro in search of water. They left on 12 February and about twenty miles upstream found fresh water and wood and received meat from some Indians (probably belonging to groups whom the Spanish called the Pampas Indians). While they were away, conditions deteriorated and tensions rose at the encampment. Francisco de Viedma later described a settlement crippled by the lack of fresh water, a dearth of portage animals to get them to the fresh water, and poor supplies.[30] The Franciscans called on their spiritual resources to try to keep the men calm. Every night they taught Christian doctrine to the "blacks, criminals, and ignorant soldiers, as well as the sailors," soothed the anxious, mediated disputes, and generally kept the peace. Most importantly, they consoled the sick who filled the hospital and buried the dead.[31] Scurvy was beginning to rear its ugly head.

The onset of scurvy led the medical men to take sides in the conflict between Piedra and Francisco de Viedma. In their analysis of the health conditions at the outpost, there was no doubt in their minds that this site was too unhealthy. Not understanding the source of the illness, the surgeons and the pharmacist believed that the water was causing diarrhea and vomiting among the men. As a result, the surgeons clearly aligned with Francisco de Viedma, who wanted the encampment moved, and against Piedra, who did not.[32]

Piedra's leadership was also challenged by the troops, who refused to cooperate with him. Vértiz's *Instructions* ordered the officials and troops to aid in the expedition, and their commander was expected to maintain the most exact discipline and ensure that they did whatever work was necessary for the project.[33] However, Francisco de Viedma reported back to Vértiz the "great reluctance" with which the soldiers completed the assigned tasks, instead preferring to spend the day entertaining themselves. Such problems with military discipline were not unique to the Patagonian outpost or necessarily a product of Piedra's poor leadership. A decade before, Vértiz, who was then military inspector general, noted that the troops were "accustomed to not receiving any punishment for their crimes" and that they were forming "conspiracies and uprisings under any pretext." Certainly, far from royal authority, soldiers had little incentive to comply with the viceregal orders. Hoping to restore order to the camp, in early March Francisco de Viedma requested that Vértiz send him thirty more workers and that those workers either be black because they are "docile and easier to govern" or at least convicts who had committed less serious crimes and were "more robust." Or, put another way, he asked for men who could not successfully challenge the authority of the comisario superintendente.[34]

Also by early March, the conflict between Piedra and the Viedma brothers had reached a breaking point. Part of the problem was the unwillingness of the Viedma brothers to submit to the leadership hierarchy formulated by Vértiz. From Piedra's perspective, he had the direct charge from the king and the viceroy and therefore was the singular source of authority on all aspects of the project. From Francisco de Viedma's point of view, he had been given the same title and charge as Piedra; as such, he believed that Piedra should consult with him and that he had the right to challenge Piedra's decisions. Moreover, a general sense of Piedra's incompetence frustrated Francisco de Viedma and was compounded by the conflict between his brother, Antonio, and Piedra. In his position as accountant and treasurer, Antonio de Viedma played a significant role in the supervision of the project on behalf of the Crown. He was personally responsible for disbursing all funds, keeping daily ledgers, and providing information on expenditures back to both Buenos Aires and Madrid.[35] According to Antonio de Viedma, Piedra would not allow him to do his job. On 2 March, Antonio de Viedma wrote to both Gálvez and Vértiz, explaining that he was unable to look after royal interests as his charge required and accusing Piedra of acting despotically. He had asked Piedra for the lists of supplies that were being loaded onto the ships and for information about disbursements, but despite repeated requests, Piedra had not provided him with the necessary documentation. Piedra continued to refuse his requests during the voyage and once they reached land, Piedra became irritated and threatened to send him and his brother back to Buenos Aires. In a moment of staunch but quiet defiance, Antonio de Viedma responded by standing there silently with his arms crossed. If he had to continue in his position, he asked that Vértiz dispatch an order that Piedra treat him as was appropriate for a representative of the king, undeniably challenging Piedra's authority and impugning his reputation.[36]

Then Piedra panicked. Unable to maintain control at San José and fearing that Villarino and Goicochea, whom he had sent in search of water, were lost, he made the sudden and surprising decision to leave the outpost. He would later argue that he had only left to obtain more supplies, but for all intents and purposes he abandoned the settlement. On 4 March, he departed for Montevideo on the *Nuestra Señora del Carmen*.

When Piedra arrived in Montevideo, the viceroy immediately accused him of dereliction of duty. According to both Gálvez's and Vértiz's instructions, once the first site was established at Bahía sin Fondo, Piedra was supposed to leave his second-in-command and one of the accountants in charge and continue with the exploration of the coast toward the Straits of Magellan. Vértiz told Gálvez that "Piedra is not fit for this vast charge" and went on to assert that Piedra fulfilled his duties "fraudulently and superficially" and was "principally concerned with his own comfort: qualities that are totally contrary to this type of operation." The viceroy grew even angrier when he discovered that Piedra had been opening the correspondence from San José that was addressed to Vértiz. He called Piedra's act "a very reprehensible and abominable excess against society" that "civilized nations detest and that our laws punish severely." Vértiz took it as a personal affront, saying that Piedra denied him the "respect and honor that is rightly owed to me."[37]

Piedra's flight settled at least one of the conflicts at San José, as it left Francisco de Viedma solely in charge. Fortunately for him, the most pressing issue, a lack of fresh water, was resolved when Villarino and Goicochea returned on 13 March with the news that they had found water and a more habitable site up farther up the Río Negro. Francisco de Viedma decided to move most of the inhabitants to the new site, although he felt obligated to maintain the precarious outpost at San José in case Piedra returned and as a means to supply any future outposts. On 16 April, guided by Villarino, Francisco de Viedma and two ships moved twenty-one miles upriver to a site on the right bank where there were fertile plains and plenty of willow to serve as fuel. He left his brother Antonio at San José with the men and supplies slated for the second outpost at San Julián.

The men began construction of the new outpost they would call Fuerte de Nuestra Señora del Carmen y Pueblo de Nueva Murcia, known as Fuerte del Carmen. This site too was short-lived, as only two months later it flooded. Thankfully, no lives were lost and most of the equipment remained safe on the vessels, but in response, Francisco de Viedma decided to move the settlement to the north bank of the river, which was at a higher elevation.[38]

By the end of May, just as the site at Fuerte del Carmen was taking shape, a new conflict emerged. Francisco de Viedma and the commander of the troops, José Martí, began to lock horns. In a letter to the Viceroy, Francisco de Viedma complained that Martí denigrated his authority. Martí insisted that he [Martí] was the only one who could give orders and that Viedma was just there to look after the Crown's interests. Francisco de Viedma appealed to Vértiz to ensure that both the commander and the troops understood that they were there to help with the expedition and that they had to "respect and obey him."[39] These tensions between the civilian and military administrators of the outpost festered throughout the winter. Martí and Francisco de Viedma could not even agree about what time to close the door of the fort each evening.[40] It would take nearly two years to resolve their issues. Eventually, Francisco de Viedma was named "governor at arms" to "avoid disputes between the troops and the Superintendent of the establishment."[41] The decision was quite a blow to Martí, who was forced to cede his military authority to his civilian counterpart.

While those tensions simmered at Fuerte del Carmen, the situation in San José worsened, with ten men falling victim to scurvy.[42] As man after man fell ill, the surgeons at the site mulled over the possible causes for the onset of the disease, agreeing on some level that the lack of fresh water was at fault. We know now that the real cause was vitamin C deficiency. However, although the Scottish doctor James Lind had asserted a relationship between a lack of fresh fruit and vegetables and scurvy, his hypothesis had not yet been widely accepted, even by the British admiralty.[43] Moreover, the doctors on the expedition may have been unfamiliar with that correlation, since scurvy was relatively rare on Spanish ships as typically symptoms did not appear until the patient had gone six weeks without any ascorbic acid. In general the ships on the Atlantic crossing were well stocked with onions, garlic, and other vegetables, and most Spaniards would have had some ascorbic acid built up in their systems allowing them to go as long as six months without augmenting their diets.[44] However, the encampment at San José had already exceeded those limits. By June 1779 it had been nearly seven months since they had left Montevideo, and their rations of fresh fruits and vegetables would have long since run out.

The men suffered horribly. Scurvy exhibits an array of progressive symptoms, including ulcerated gums, jaundice, black spots on the body, muscle pain, intense lethargy, difficulty breathing, and finally death.[45] Helpless before the growing numbers of patients, the Franciscans tried to provide spiritual consolation, never leaving the bedsides of the stricken. Comajuncosa remembered "consoling the afflicted, interceding for the guilty, suffering hunger and thirst with the needy, and eventually falling ill with the sick."[46]

At this critical juncture, someone at San José gave voice to the fear, frustration, and anger that was building among the men, tacking a poem to the door of the makeshift chapel:

M and P have to live
A and V have to die
There's no way around it.
Let them pay half
and the horses the other half.

Everyone wants this to come out well,
and if this doesn't happen, all will die.
Friars and troops
Have to embark
For another port there is no doubt
Stay if you like
everyone else will be prudent.

The Rudder is finished
As is well verified
Twenty-one men buried
By this illness as they say
Scurvy has broken out.

Already lacking the medicine
To stop this contagion
The medical staff is heading off to another port
To get out of this destruction.

The total loss of all
is the best medicine
Let the government remain alone

If we do not leave here
for another port
You can be certain
That all here will die.

If the embarkation is delayed
For false reasons
One will see the troops rise up
And for very just reasons.[47]

Someone, possibly Antonio de Viedma, either took the poem off the door and saved it or saved a copy as evidence of the danger that threatened the outpost. It was clear to him that the author was a soldier and not one of the convicts. He told Vértiz that "although don Nicolás García offered his help, I could see that the troops were exceedingly disgusted with the site . . . and with the slightest insinuation of any bad intention I think that they will revolt, especially when I saw the couplets that they tacked to the door of the church." The threat of revolt was real. Soldiers in the Americas had rebelled at least nine times since 1760, although not so far in the Río de la Plata.[48] Antonio de Viedma did not want it to happen on his watch.

Unaware of the growing crisis at San José, authorities in Montevideo prepared to send the first colonists to the site. This stage of the project had also been plagued by delays, and after nearly six months of waiting at the port, on 6 June 1779 sixty-nine of the peasant colonists who had arrived on the *Princesa* and the *Nuestra Señora de los Dolores* set out for San José on the *Visitación*. There were fourteen families, including twenty-nine children, one grandmother, and six single men. The passenger list had been altered numerous times since April, as three single men who were set to depart on the *Visitación* had already deserted by early May.[49] For at least two of the families, the fact that they had to leave at that very moment must have been heartbreaking. Vicente Estevan and his wife, Josefa Sermilo, had to leave behind their daughter María de la Cruz (age eleven); and Alberto Espinoza and his wife, Manuela Martínez, had to leave without Alberto's sister. Both were too sick to travel. Presumably, there were promises that they would be transported to Patagonia at a later date. In addition to the colonists, the ship carried quite the Noah's ark, with twenty horses, a number of oxen, forty head of cattle, twenty mules, twenty-four donkeys, fifty sheep, forty pigs, an array of birds including six hundred hens, as well as other supplies and furniture for the new establishment.[50]

However, disaster struck almost immediately. On 12 June, while the *Visitación* was still in the middle of the Río de la Plata, a strong wind came up. By the next morning, the winds were so violent that they lashed the ship against the rocks. The crew of the ship fired shots asking for help; however, the winds and waves prevented launches from making their way out to the stranded ship. The only aid that Joaquín del Pino (1729–1804), the governor of Montevideo, could provide was to send a small detachment of soldiers to prevent any looting of the supplies that might wash ashore and to rescue anyone who might try to swim to land. To make it easier to see the disaster unfolding before them, soldiers built three large bonfires on the shore and kept them lit all night long. The next day the weather improved and the launches could finally get to the ailing ship and retrieve the colonists and crew. Governor del Pino then sent fifty convicts to fetch the supplies from the beach and to bring ashore anything that had been left on ship. When they got there, they found that the hull had been completely flooded, killing some of the animals. The ship was impossibly wrecked and had to be destroyed. Amazingly, no human lives were lost and most of the supplies were recovered.[51]

While authorities in Montevideo regrouped from this catastrophe, the officers at the outpost at San José, including Antonio de Viedma, the military leaders, the Franciscans, and the medical men, had decided that the situation was hopeless. The intensity of the outbreak of scurvy and the lack of supplies were leading the outpost toward disaster and they agreed to abandon the site. As it was the middle of the winter, it took them more than a month to load the ships and depart. During that period, the deaths continued. Juan Carmunda, Domingo Anima, Antonio Congo, and Francisco Mina, four of the outpost's sixteen royal slaves, died.[52] In August, as the *Santa Teresa* was ready to transport 113 sick men back to Montevideo, 43 men had already died, leaving only a skeleton crew of troops at San José. By the time the ship anchored in Montevideo's harbor, 4 more men had died and Antonio de Viedma was dangerously ill.[53]

Soldiering On

One would think that a project so beset by problems would be quickly put on the back burner; however, despite the resounding failure of Piedra's leadership, the sinking of the *Visitación*, and the abandonment of San José, Vértiz moved forward with the venture. On 16 September a vastly smaller group of colonists left Montevideo for Fuerte del Carmen. Two brigantines carried five families and six single men, one person fewer than expected, as during the interim one of the single men, Andrés Martínez Vázquez, had deserted. The voyage went off without incident and the two ships carrying the colonists arrived safely at Fuerte del Carmen on 2 and 11 October, where they encountered the foundations of a relatively stable colony.[54] The inhabitants had survived the first winter; the land was fertile, although they were experiencing some drought; the air was healthy and the climate "more benign." There were

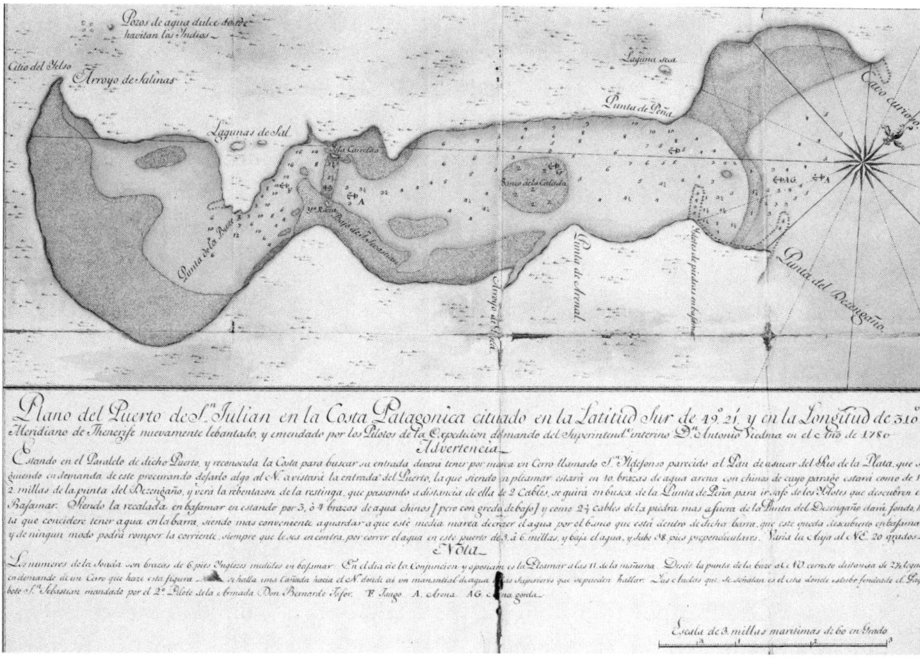

Figure 5.1. Map of the harbor at San Julián (1780). España. Ministerio de Educación, Cultura y Deporte. Archivo General de Indias. AGI, MP-Buenos Aires, 133.

plenty of cattle around and Indians had assured Francisco de Viedma that there was abundant wood for fuel and construction.[55]

At about the same time, Vértiz named the barely recovered Antonio de Viedma as superintendent of the soon-to-be-established outpost in San Julián, replacing the disgraced Piedra. The viceroy provided him with three ships, food for one year, water for three months, artisan's tools, eight mules to use as pack animals, and around one hundred men, including twenty-five sailors, a Franciscan, a new accountant, forty-one soldiers, five carpenters (one of whom was a convict), three plumbers, two masons, a blacksmith, a baker, a doctor, two bloodletters, and sixteen single men. The new expedition set sail on 3 January 1780. After forty-eight days they explored the Gulf of San Jorge and paused briefly at the bay of San Gregorio before finishing the journey south to the bay of San Julián.[56]

As always, the first task upon dropping anchor was to find fresh water, but initial attempts came up empty. Fortunately, within a couple of days the pilot

Goicochea encountered an Indian, who preceded a much larger group of two hundred Tehuelche Indians. By the mid-eighteenth century, family-based bands of Tehuelches roamed Patagonia, hunting guanaco, plundering, and trading livestock. The bands were led by two caciques (chiefs) called Julián Gordo and Julián Grande. Goicochea accompanied the Indians back to their encampment, where they gave him meat and showed him a permanent, good water source not far from the ship. Cacique Julián Grande did not hesitate to aid the Spanish pilot. He was familiar with but distrustful of the Spanish, having spent time in Buenos Aires.[57]

Back at the base camp, Antonio de Viedma then faced a dilemma about where exactly to establish the settlement. If it were situated on or near the beach, it would be far from the water source and the best land for agriculture. If it were inland, it would be close to the Indians and difficult to transport supplies from the ships. Unlike Piedra, Viedma refused to make a unilateral decision, preferring to consult the authorities in Buenos Aires, carefully tending his relationships with his superiors before settling on a location. While he awaited a response, he explored the regions farther north toward Puerto Deseado. They unloaded the ships and began to build homes out of hides and wood and set up an oven. Viedma also took the opportunity to smoke the rats off the brigantine, the *San Francisco de Paula*. By the beginning of May, they had begun work on the warehouse, the chapel, and the homes for the medical practitioners.[58]

From the beginning, it was clear that Puerto Deseado was not as promising a settlement site as San Julián. The topography was difficult and there was a lack of fresh water. Nevertheless, Antonio de Viedma was intent on staying there, at least for the winter. In early June he wrote to Vértiz with suggestions about how to improve the situation. It was clear to him that they needed more portage animals, as too many had died during the voyage. To improve their chances of survival, he suggested that they corral the animals for a few days before embarking them and feed them the same food that they would eat on the voyage.[59] More seriously, disease was starting to take a toll. After reassuring Vértiz that "the people have been and are robust," he noted that seven were sick, six with syphilis. Three of them were also afflicted with scurvy. He wanted to send them back to Montevideo, but three of the sick men were soldiers and their commander refused to let them go.

As had been true at the other outposts, once scurvy appeared, its wrath was incessant. In July four men died, and in August nine more died. Eleven were dangerously ill. Antonio de Viedma saw signs of discontent and to avoid the uprising that seemed inevitable, he decided to transport the unhappy and the sick to Buenos Aires along with Goicochea, who would explain the situation to Vértiz. Viedma remained with twenty-two men at Puerto Deseado. Goicochea returned with the *Carmen* on 12 November with instructions from Vértiz to go back to San Julián and establish an outpost near the water source. He also brought more supplies, some artisans, peons (free unskilled wage laborers), two soldiers, and five sailors. They quickly dismantled their tiny outpost and returned to San Julián.

Upon entering the bay on 24 November 1780, Antonio de Viedma and his men happily encountered two ships that had just arrived from Montevideo. Onboard were a detachment of soldiers, around seventy-five colonists, and an array of supplies. However, their hopes were quickly dashed when the brigantine, the *Nuestra Señora del Carmen*, ran aground. The crew and colonists were saved, but they were unable to rescue the horses, mules, and other supplies.[60] Antonio de Viedma quickly regrouped and with the help of the troops established the new outpost near the springs, a colony that would come to be known as the Nueva Población y Fuerte de Floridablanca, or just Floridablanca, after the king's minister and early advocate of the colonization project.

Taking stock of the efforts to this point, it is clear that the establishment of the outposts had been very costly, with at least two ships sunk and another wrecked, thousands of pesos of supplies and animals lost, and dozens of men dead. By the end of 1780, two sites, San José and Puerto Deseado, had been abandoned. Only 55 colonists were living at Fuerte del Carmen and 81 at Floridablanca/San Julián. Of the 136 colonists in Patagonia, at least 45 were single men in addition to more than 100 soldiers, sailors, convicts, and peons.[61]

The continued reliance on single men to maintain the outposts perpetuated and even accentuated the problems that had afflicted the forts since their foundation. At both of the remaining forts, interpersonal conflicts exposed problems of authority and control engendered by the different expectations of masculine behavior. Not surprisingly, the population of soldiers, convicts, and peons demonstrated very little willingness to follow the orders of either the superintendent or the lieutenants. They engaged in minor acts of defiance like illicit sex and card playing, as well as more serious crimes including desertion, murder, and mutiny. In January 1781 the friars bemoaned the state of affairs. Despite their best efforts to provide "perfect and public spiritual instruction to the faithful," there were too many inhabitants who "disturb

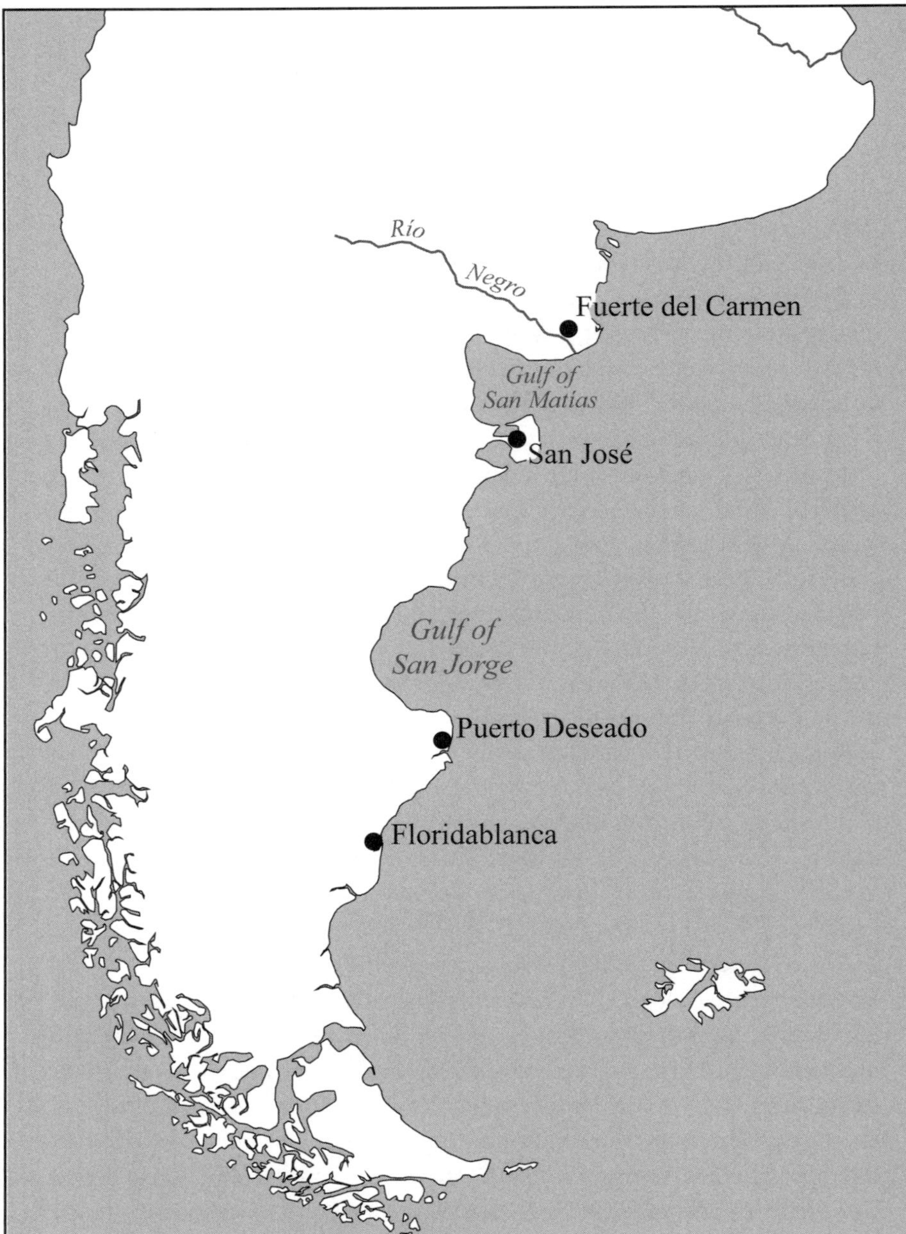

Map 5.1. Attempted and actual sites of eighteenth-century Spanish colonies in Patagonia.

the peace" and "completely resist our advice, as well as the superiority and justice of our Lord Superintendent."[62]

More than just resisting advice, the soldiers, peons, and convicts eschewed both religious and military injunctions against a number of activities, including sex with indigenous women. Lust posed a serious challenge not only to Viedma's authority, but also to efforts to Christianize the Indians and to improve Spanish/Indian relations. Despite issuing orders to refrain from such interactions, Francisco de Viedma reported finding his men sleeping with Indian women. Offenders faced fines and wage garnishment and the penalties were doubled if the perpetrator was caught a second time.[63] Here we clearly see the differing expectations of upper-class and lower-class men in terms of sexual activity. For a man in a position of power like Francisco de Viedma, sexual self-control was the epitome of masculinity, while for the men in his charge, sexual promiscuity was both an indicator of virility and an assertion of independence from religious, civilian, and military control.

Alcohol, which was central to the social interactions among lower-class men, was implicated in a range of problems. At Floridablanca, where the food supply was already limited, the theft and illicit sale of alcohol demonstrated Antonio de Viedma's inability to control the outpost's provisioning and was an implicit challenge to his ability to carry out his oficio.[64] The black market in alcohol also had other consequences, as soldiers and the other noncolonist men used the bottle to drown their fears. At least one inebriated worker accidentally drowned, and another worker nearly died when his rancho outside the fort at Fuerte del Carmen caught fire. When some of the men tried to extinguish the flames, they had a difficult time rousing the inhabitant because he had been drinking.[65]

Alcohol also fueled violence among the soldiers and workers, particularly when combined with card and dice playing. Scholars have shown that lower-class men's reputations often hinged on their ability to perform well in such competitions.[66] As the games were often punctuated by fights, the superintendent tried to outlaw them, fining both the players and the overseers of the establishments in which the games took place. Those who were caught betting suffered additional penalties, including hard labor without pay. These attempts at control were for naught. In 1782 Francisco de Viedma complained to Vértiz that the outpost was more a "nursery of vices than a Catholic settlement."[67]

These low-level vices were nothing compared to continual threat of mutiny at these outposts on the fringes of the Spanish Empire. The first evidence of trouble came in February 1781 at Fuerte del Carmen. Four soldiers attempted to mutiny to prevent the arrest of one of their own, one Juan Bonell. A month later more soldiers attempted an uprising.[68] On 17 April at five in the afternoon, don Francisco Xavier Piera, a cavalry officer, imprisoned three soldiers, Josef García, Victoriano Guevara, and Juan González, for insubordination and sedition. Hoping to isolate the troublemakers, the men were transferred to the brigantine that was anchored in the bay, *El Belén*. However, Piera heard rumblings that one of the prisoners was innocent and that another soldier, Zeferino Martínez, was the ringleader of the group. He subsequently took Martínez prisoner. These arrests only increased the defiance of the troops, as other soldiers stepped forward in support of their imprisoned colleagues. According to Francisco de Viedma, a soldier, Miguel García, stood before his commanding officer and told him that if those men were going to be held on the ship that he wanted to go with them. The officer then asked, "You want to go?," to which García replied, "Yes sir," and he was taken into custody. At the same time, Francisco de Viedma had Juan Bonell arrested for his involvement in the February uprising and to prevent further disturbances.[69] However, these sporadic attempts to impose order had little effect, as many men decided that it was easier to desert than to mutiny.

The desertions that plagued the forts were clear evidence of the rejection of the superintendents' authority. We have already seen how the regular flow of desertions affected both forts during the first few months of their existence. However, even the onset of winter did not stop men from leaving. In mid-May 1781 a peon and a convict deserted from Fuerte del Carmen. The convict was definitely determined to get out from under royal authority; he had also made an attempt to desert in March but had been quickly apprehended. His luck was no better this time. Three soldiers and two peons set off toward the Río Colorado in search of the men. A few days later they found them hiding out in a nearby Indian camp. Eighteen new convicts arrived in early November 1781 and began work first on the hospital and then on the construction of new and better houses for the colonists, but this new group proved to be no more reliable than the last. On 4 November, two of them, José Ignacio Arroyo and José León Godoy, deserted, taking with them five mules and eleven horses. Their departure spurred others. Less than two weeks later, a peon deserted. This time Francisco de Viedma attempted to use deception to find them. He sent two peons dressed as Indians out on horseback, hoping to trick the men, who might be hiding nearby, to come out to join the "Indians." The ploy was not successful.[70]

In Spanish culture, elite men often criticized lower-class men for their spontaneous violence, and at the colonies the men in charge were at a loss for how to control the outbursts.[71] At Fuerte del Carmen on 6 April 1781, one peon, Antonio Gil, hit another peon, Pedro Grueso, in the head with a stick "for seemingly no reason," landing one in the hospital and the other in jail. Even as the living conditions improved in the spring of 1781, the colonies saw an uptick in violence among the men. On 10 October a soldier named Asencio Molina threw a rock at a hunting dog belonging to the pilot Basilio Villarino. When confronted, the soldier said that if it were necessary he would also hit Villarino, and then in an act of defiance he turned his back to the officer in charge. The next morning the dog went missing. Officials suspected that it had been killed by Molina, but after an investigation they found that another soldier, Manuel García, had killed it with his bayonet. To prevent more violence, Viedma sent García on a reconnoitering expedition. Nevertheless, Molina continued to cause problems at the fort. In December he was caught hitting Francisca Xaviera, the maid of the outpost's treasurer, don Francisco Igarzábal, with a shoe and violently choking her, and he was again taken prisoner.[72]

Conflict between the troops and the male colonists at Fuerte del Carmen also disrupted life at the colony. Evidently, one night Alberto Espinoza, a tall Gallego blacksmith, got drunk and hurled insults at some soldiers. In response, Juan González, a soldier from the Regiment of Buenos Aires, had lain in wait and assaulted Espinoza, presumably in defense of his reputation. González was promptly arrested, but the troops were outraged and when their commander appeared to complain, Francisco de Viedma criticized him for the troops' lack of discipline. The troops pressed Espinoza to take back his words, but he refused. González then confronted Francisco de Viedma, arguing that he was in the right and that it was wrong that he had been arrested while Espinoza went free.

Hoping to end the conflict, Viedma decided to send Espinoza and his family back to Montevideo. He expressed his relief to Vértiz: "It presents me with a great opportunity to get rid of two of the greatest good-for-nothings, particularly Alberto." He went on to compare Alberto to a useless drone that disturbs the "well ordered republic of the bees" and called him a sponger. According to Viedma, Espinoza devoted his time to discouraging the other colonists and now was unable to work because of the incident with González. When Espinoza arrived in Montevideo, he was immediately imprisoned, much to his dismay, as he feigned that he had no idea what the charges were.[73]

Compounding the tensions between the inhabitants of the colonies were the complicated relationships between the outposts and the Indians who inhabited the lands south of Buenos Aires. These relations were often cooperative because the outposts were dependent on the Indians for survival; however, the colonies' reliance on Indian leaders for food challenged the Spaniards' expectations about their dominance over the territory and provoked tensions about masculine power and authority on the Patagonian frontier.

By the 1780s the viceroy and other officials had considerable experience with the Indians around the Río Negro and the Río Colorado and were familiar with their caciques; however, royal authorities had no knowledge of what kind of peoples, if any, lived in the regions farther to the south. From the initiation of the project, Vértiz was emphatic about royal policy in terms of dealing with any Indians that the expeditions might encounter. His *Instructions* for Piedra admonished him to treat any Indians "with the greatest kindness" and provide them with the many gifts that the expeditions carried for that purpose, "taking great pains to hug the children in the presence and absence of their parents." The superintendents were supposed to "persuade them to peace" and make them understand the purpose of the outpost, which was to "teach them to know God and his holy law so that they might be saved." They should not do them harm or take their homes. If possible, they were to try to get one of their leaders, cacique Negro, who headed some bands of Pampas and Tehuelches, to come to Buenos Aires to make a peace treaty. He also encouraged the men to be amateur ethnographers. Vértiz had heard that there were other more reclusive Indians on an island in Bahía sin Fondo. He directed the Spaniards to learn more about those Indians, including where they came from, how many there were, what religion they professed, and whether they subsisted on livestock or agriculture. Again, he pushed them to "assure them of our good friendship" through gift giving.[74] Of course, Vértiz had little choice but to cultivate good relationships with the Indians. The Spanish had only a minimal presence in the area and exerted no control over the territory. He also knew that provoking the Tehuelches and other Indian groups would only jeopardize the lives of Spaniards living on the frontier outside of Buenos Aires.

At both colonies supplies arrived only irregularly during the first few months, and the inhabitants were largely unable to provide for themselves, leaving them vulnerable to hunger and disease. Argentine anthropologist Lidia Nacuzzi has argued that this situation led to a more equitable distribution of power between the Spanish and the Indians.[75] Certainly at Floridablanca the need for food forced Antonio de Viedma into a subordinate position vis-à-vis the native caciques and compromised any assumptions about the Spaniards' dominance.[76] The caciques' ability to give meat to the Spanish made them the main providers for the colony and positioned them to control the terms of trade and negotiation with the Spanish. Moreover, when caciques came to the forts with "gifts" of meat, they were, in fact, demonstrating their masculine skills as hunters and warriors to inhabitants of the colony.[77] In this context, it is not surprising that the Pampas and the Tehuelches eagerly showed the Spanish to sources of fresh water and firewood and provided them with guanaco meat.

In sharp contrast, the goods that Antonio de Viedma gave to and bartered with the Indians were generally not necessities. By conducting regular exchanges with the Indians, he hoped to level the playing field with his Indian counterparts and maybe eventually assert his authority over them, an intention about which the caciques presumably were not unaware.[78] Despite his cheerful description of these economic interactions, the Indians generally had the upper hand. The irony could not have been lost on both parties that most of the horses and other goods that Indians were selling or trading had been stolen during attacks on other Spaniards.

The Indians' relationships with the forts reasserted their dominance over the territory. At Floridablanca, especially in the winter months, the Indian encampment, the *toldería*, was adjacent to the fort and the fort's warehouse provided some supplies to the Indians. Antonio de Viedma interpreted the Indians' presence and their eagerness to trade as signs of their dependence on the Spanish; however, from the native perspective, the decision to set up their *toldos* around the forts reminded Viedma that Indians controlled the land outside their doorsteps and that Spanish access to Patagonian territory came in exchange for food and other goods.

As they documented their relationships with the Indians for royal authorities in Buenos Aires and Madrid, the Viedma brothers struggled to describe to their superiors a scenario in which they were at least the equals of the caciques. Antonio de Viedma called the Indians "obedient" and noted that "generally, these Indians have a very sweet and innocent nature and they treat me with so much affection." He also claimed that cacique Julián Gordo had such affection for him that "when the *toldos* are near here he doesn't leave my room." However, that is not necessarily how the Indians understood the cacique's incessant proximity to Viedma. His unwillingness to leave

Antonio de Viedma's side might have been more about control or distrust than about the "affection" that Antonio de Viedma believed he sensed.[79]

For his brother at Fuerte del Carmen, the situation was somewhat different. Spaniards and Indians had long-standing relations on the Buenos Aires frontier and one of the caciques had even spent time in the capital, so that the terms of association and commerce were already clear. However, on a day-to-day basis there were actually greater tensions between the Indians and the Spanish at Fuerte del Carmen than at Floridablanca. Francisco de Viedma noted in June 1779 that the Spanish went armed to their meeting with the cacique to "instill some fear" in him. The colonists also indicated that they were afraid to move beyond the immediate confines of the fort, as it would expose them to the "rigor of the Indians."[80]

Spanish encounters with Christian captives were a constant reminder of their lack of control over even other Spaniards on the frontier. In July 1781 Francisco de Viedma reported meeting two Christian women, sisters-in-law from Luján. The Indians had killed their husbands during a raid and they were caring for a nephew whose mother had died in captivity. In the same Indian encampment, there were at least two other relatives, a toddler named Pedro de la Rosa and another young boy who had been taken captive from near one of the forts outside of Buenos Aires. Their mother had died, but their surviving sisters were living at the camp of Guchulap, a Puelche (eastern Pampas) cacique. According to the women, there were other Christians also living at the camp. Francisco de Viedma then attempted to arrange a rescue of or trade for the captives, an act that forced the Spanish to submit to the rules of exchange dictated by the Indians.[81] These captives were vivid indicators of the Spaniards' failure to protect their women and of the Indians' dominance over both the land and the people.

A combination of ethnic hatred, fear, miscommunication, and masculine frustration sometimes led to violence between the inhabitants of the outposts and the Indians. Francisco de Viedma reported that on 23 June 1781, the cacique Talquaquia and another Indian came to tell him that a colonist, Domingo Antonio Cañas, had shot and wounded a relative of the Indian's in the face. Apparently Cañas had fired at the Indian for having brought horses onto his land. As soon as it happened, the Indians became afraid that the Spaniards were going to kill them all and confronted Francisco de Viedma about punishing the offender. To ease the tensions, Viedma made a spectacle of going to get Cañas, accompanied by two soldiers with bayonets, and having him taken to Viedma's room where he gave him a "terrible scolding" and ordered him put in the stocks. Viedma also insisted that the Indians bring him the wounded man to be healed at the fort. Despite his quick work to calm the situation, the incident had serious ramifications. A few days later some of the fort's livestock disappeared, and Viedma bemoaned the fact that the Indians may have stolen the animals in retaliation. He successfully dispatched eighteen men in search of the missing animals.[82] Disaster was narrowly averted.

On the far edges of the Spanish Empire, fear, hunger, and frustration both provoked and exacerbated conflicts among the men at the Patagonian outposts. The leaders of the expedition fought among themselves, men deserted, the troops rejected the authority of the civilian leadership, and soldiers fought with colonists. Spanish dependence on nearby Indians only intensified the pressure on individual men to assert their masculinity. The authorities believed that the presence of peninsular women would help to calm these tensions. However, as we will see, the arrival of female colonists caused as many problems as it solved at the two outposts.

CHAPTER SIX

Gendered Lives at the Edges of Empire

THE INSUBORDINATION AND VIOLENCE THAT PLAGUED THE Patagonian outposts during their construction came as no surprise to royal authorities. Indeed, the entire project was predicated on the ideas that, left to their own devices, soldiers, sailors, and convicts would misbehave and that peninsular women were necessary to tame them and bring order to the new communities. Unfortunately, the failure of the outpost at San José, the sinking of the *Visitación*, and the onset of scurvy among other problems significantly delayed the women's arrival, and once they disembarked, their presence complicated life at the colonies in unpredictable ways. Although the female colonists did bring some sense of normalcy to the outposts, their sexuality and fertility became the focus of attention for both the families and the superintendents. Moreover, the presence of women and children put pressure on the inhabitants to become self-sufficient. As their survival came to depend on male colonists' ability to farm, the failure of agriculture would have disastrous implications for both Fuerte del Carmen and Floridablanca.

The First Spanish Women at the Outposts

On 1 October 1779 five peasant women stepped off two ships at Fuerte del Carmen. A Basque (Ana María Castellanos) and four Gallegas (Josefa Longuera, Manuela Martínez, Pascuala do Campo, and María de Aneyros) became the first white women on the Patagonian coast in nearly three hundred years. It is hard to imagine that they were anything but anxious. They had already survived the transatlantic crossing and two had experienced the wreck of the *Visitación*. All the while, they continued to fulfill their household duties, caring for their children and their husbands, laundering clothes, and preparing meals. The tenuousness of the circumstances at the outpost must have been immediately evident. Although most of the inhabitants at Fuerte del Carmen had survived the first winter, there were few signs of normal life. When they looked around, they would have been overwhelmed by the fact that they were they only women among more than one hundred unhappy and poorly supervised men.

Worse yet, they had no place to live. The colonists had been promised housing, but Francisco de Viedma had decided to postpone construction of their homes until after the fort was completed. In the interim the colonists would live in makeshift habitations made from hides and chaff, structures that left them exposed to the weather and Indian attacks as well as to the potential predation of soldiers, peons, and convicts.[1] Viedma quickly realized the precariousness of these habitations and sent word to Vértiz to stop transporting colonists until proper housing had been constructed, effectively putting the establishment of the colony on hold.[2]

As a result, it would be more than a year before the next cohort of colonists arrived at the fort, and that group included only one family, that of Francisco Centeno, a baker, who was accompanied by his wife, Rafaela Guerra, and their three children. It is unclear why this family was sent to the outpost unless Francisco de Viedma had specifically requested someone with Francisco's particular skill. The rest of the new colonists were single men who could help with the construction of the outpost. So, for two years, in addition to the soldiers, sailors, convicts, and peons, the outpost was home to only six women and nine children. Rafaela Guerra had a son and two daughters, Josefa Longuera had two young sons, and María de Aneyros was the mother of three little girls, María, Teresa, and Antonia Juana, and a son, Benito. The documentation is painfully silent about their lives at the outpost, but the work must have been hard and life must have been dreary. The women must have relied heavily on one another as they learned to make do at the encampment. Indeed, the sex ratio at Fuerte del Carmen did not change significantly until September 1781, when the next set of families arrived, including fifteen women and girls; and it changed even more around the new year of 1782, when a large contingent of colonists disembarked that included seventeen adult women and thirteen girls. Until then, a colony envisioned for families remained primarily a military outpost for the first three years of its existence.

Although these women were supposed to tame the tensions and violence at the outposts, within months of her arrival one of the female colonists had the opposite effect. Colonist Ana María (Palacios) Castellanos was at the center of a dramatic series of events that rocked Fuerte del Carmen during that first year. She and her husband, Matías Lagarreta, both from Vizcaya, were one of the first couples to volunteer for the expeditions and were among the first to be sent to Río Negro in September 1779. However, once at Fuerte del Carmen, their lives began to unravel. Matías became an inveterate drunk, such that it caused him "infinite" problems. Among other issues, in February 1780 Matías stabbed a master mason, and Francisco de Viedma punished him by shackling him and putting him to work as a peon. Despite the restraints, he escaped and deserted to the Indians. After he was recaptured, the comisario superintendente imprisoned him for twenty days, but he still did not learn his lesson. According to Viedma, a combination of his drinking and "the craziness of his wife" left him a "fool."[3] Ana María also caused plenty of trouble. In February 1780 Viedma punished her with a fine of ten pesos for mouthing off to Corp. José Michan.[4] However, soon her difficult personality was compounded by her obsession with the fort's blacksmith, Domingo Basiga.

Matías may have been a drunk, but Basiga had a fiery temper. On 14 March 1780 he shot and killed a relative of the cacique Chulilaquin. Evidently the Indian had ridiculed him, as Basiga said, "No Indian was going to make fun of me," before shooting the young man.[5] As Lyman Johnson has pointed out, teasing and taunting was a critical feature of masculine relationships and helped defined the hierarchy among men.[6] For Basiga, the fact that he was teased by an Indian (his social inferior) was an insufferable insult to his masculinity.

Francisco de Viedma knew that the murder would aggravate tensions between the inhabitants of the fort and the Indian's relatives, so he had Basiga arrested and taken to the brigantine *Carmen*, which was anchored just offshore, as much for safekeeping as for punishment.[7] His suspicions proved correct, as two days later the mother of the deceased came to the fort to find his murderer and kill him. Viedma tried to calm her, placating her with food and drink, and the incident seemed to be over; however, Matías Lagarreta came to Viedma to warn him that his wife was determined to kill the murdered man's mother. After a preliminary investigation, Viedma arrested Ana María to prevent further bloodshed. As he came to find out, Matías's denunciation had interrupted more than an attempted murder. The next day, Viedma was brought a letter from Ana María to her imprisoned lover, Basiga, that revealed a much more extensive plot. Addressing the letter to "my dear love of my heart," she tells him that Matías, whom she refers to as "the drunk," had ratted on her and that she had been put in the stocks. Then, in between breathlessly unpunctuated words of love and longing, she describes a plan to have him escape and for the couple to run off together:

> I cannot stop this heart from sighing and although I can't see you there is no comfort for me . . . I want to go with you if you can leave by the stable there is a fellow countryman who says that he can hide you . . . because they say that they are going to hang you by God I ask you that you don't leave me I want to die with you there is no comfort for me until I see you in my arms . . . I hope that you can do this favor I ask you for the love of God that while the people are sleeping you can escape you can ask Pepe to accompany you so that you can escape with the guitar I did not send it to you because we are going to take it with us write me and give me this comfort for the love of God you see how full my belly is I want to go to give birth with you I won't bother you anymore until I see you with me, you who the heart esteems and longs for your dear Ana Maria de Palacios.[8]

This letter is remarkable in a number of ways and reveals how quickly the situation had deteriorated at the fort.[9] First, although she had only arrived at the fort a few months earlier, her "full [pregnant] belly" indicates that she had been engaging in an adulterous relationship with Basiga under her husband's nose, undermining both the sacrament of marriage and Matías's authority. Moreover, the letter shows Ana María at the center of a larger plot to circumvent the authorities at Fuerte del Carmen. She found other accomplices like Pepe who were unhappy enough at the outpost that they were willing to risk their lives to help the couple escape.

Francisco de Viedma arrested all those implicated in the letter and took extra precautions to ensure that they did not escape. Eventually he set everyone free except for Ana María, whose case he remanded to the viceroy in Buenos Aires. In his letter to Vértiz, he described Ana María as "bad tempered" and "capable of doing damage and losing it all." He kept her imprisoned so that she would not instigate "worse evils."[10]

To maintain any semblance of order at the fort, Viedma felt obligated to remove both Matías and Ana María from the outpost, as they were, in his words, the "very opposite" of what a settler family should be. Yet, once they arrived in Buenos Aires, the authorities refused to release them from their colonist contracts despite their potential to disrupt the project. Rather, they sentenced Ana María to two years in a house of reclusion (presumably in Buenos Aires), where she would have time to think about what she had done under the careful supervision of a matron of good morals. Matías was instructed to have a stable household ready upon her release.[11]

In sharp contrast to the fits and starts of family life at Fuerte del Carmen, the arrival of the first women at Floridablanca was carefully orchestrated. In September 1780 Governor Joaquin del Pino was instructed to determine the colonists for this distant outpost according to a clearly delineated list of priorities. First, he was to choose colonists from that region of the peninsula most represented among the colonists waiting in Montevideo, presumably so that as many of the colonists as possible would be bound by blood relationships, culture, and language. The next priority was to transport those poor souls who had been aboard the *Visitación* when it sank in Montevideo harbor. Finally, he was to choose "those who have single daughters or married couples of the right age for an increase in the population."[12] For Floridablanca to succeed, it would need women capable of bearing children.

Governor del Pino completed his task as ordered and sent twenty-four adult women to the colony at Floridablanca in the spring of 1780. Nearly all of these women met the criteria of being "the right age for an increase in the population." Nine were recently married women in their late teens and twenties who had not yet borne children. A number of those, including María Mata, had been among the very young brides married off by Astraudi at La Coruña. Three more were in their twenties with young children and two were single. Other than one widowed mother, the rest were slightly more mature mothers of young children. Their reproductive abilities were readily on display.

As per the instructions, Governor del Pino took advantage of the extended families from northern Castile who had enlisted together to create a support system for the colonists at the new outpost. Two families from Almeida de Sayago in Zamora came with their newly married adult children and three other families from the area. Six of the couples were from Palencia and eight from Astorga. Thus, nearly all of the women settled at Floridablanca along with mothers and/or sisters-in-law, or at least with other women who spoke their dialects, wore similar clothing, and prepared the same foods. In addition, many of the colonists had crossed the Atlantic on the same ships. No doubt, those bonds would help the women persevere at one of the most distant outposts in the Spanish Empire.

After a three-week voyage, the first families arrived at Floridablanca at the end of November. During that first summer, the colonists lived on the beach in tents, although as we saw in the previous chapter, a dearth of fresh water at that location forced Antonio de Viedma to move the settlement approximately ten kilometers inland. The move also allowed him to establish some spatial segregation at the outpost between the women and families and the soldiers, sailors, and convicts. As Argentine archaeologist Silvia Buscaglia has argued, Viedma created a designated space for the single male sailors and other men whose behavior was difficult to control. To reinforce the separation, he restricted the female colonists' access to the coast.[13] Such separation was a critical aspect of maintaining order, as the arrival of the colonists meant that some men (the colonists) had regular sexual access to women, while other men (the troops, convicts, and peons) did not.

Like his brother at Fuerte del Carmen, Antonio de Viedma prioritized the construction of the fort. The wooden fort at Floridablanca was fifty meters square, surrounding a large internal plaza. It had bastions at each corner and was encircled by a moat. At the front were the communal living spaces of the troops, convicts, peons, and tradesmen. The rear housed the chapel and the individual living spaces of the superintendent and other officials. A communal kitchen was located in the center of the plaza. The bastions were used as warehouses and as a temporary hospital. On either side, the spaces were divided into nine identical rooms to house the families, allowing them greater privacy and defining the nuclear family as the central organizational structure of the colony. Each family, no matter how small or large, lived in one room that was approximately five meters by two. By all accounts, these spaces were dark and humid. Francisco Gavarri described them as unlivable and said that spending time in them was like being buried.[14]

It took more than three months to build the fort, and luckily Antonio de Viedma moved the settlers into the fort in April while the days were still warm, although the nights were getting cold. At the end of the month, the outpost suffered a heavy snowstorm and conditions worsened with each passing week. By the first week in June Viedma noted that it was too icy to work, and within a month they were battered by snow, ice, rain, and freezing temperatures. Although it is impossible to know the exact climatic

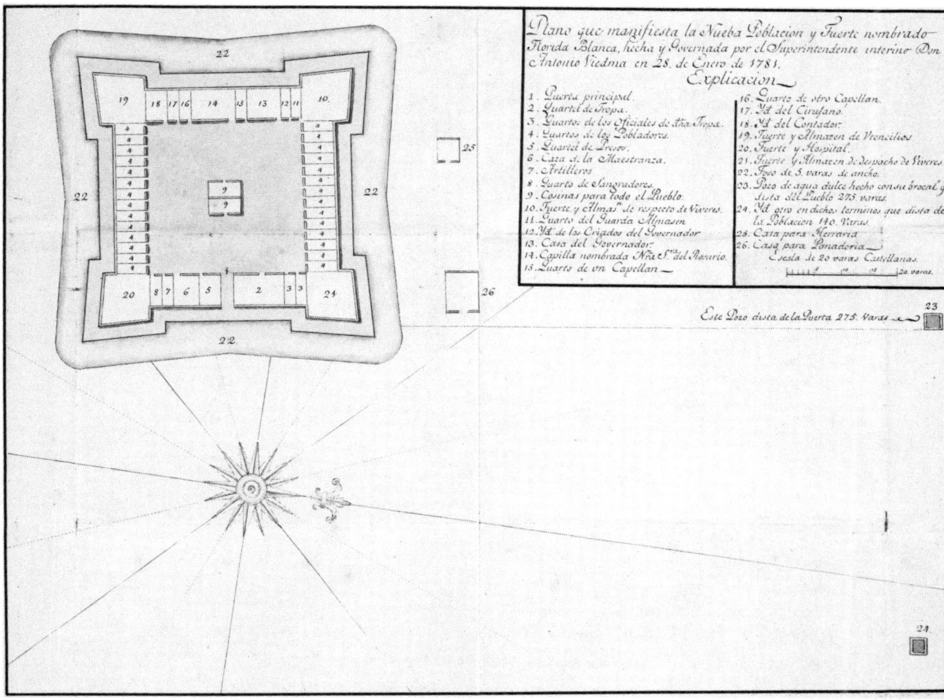

Figure 6.1. Plan for the colony and fort at Floridablanca (1781). España. Ministerio de Educación, Cultura y Deporte. Archivo General de Indias. AGI, MP-Buenos Aires, 138.

conditions that the colonists experienced in the late eighteenth century, the bitterness of the Patagonian winter is undeniable. The average temperature in July is around zero degrees Celsius with twenty-seven-kilometer-per-hour winds making it feel like minus six to minus ten degrees.

Once the winter weather abated, the plan was to build three sets of nine connected houses for the colonists. Although not all of them were completed, the homes that were finished were all identical—thirty square meters, with a kitchen and a bedroom. The walls were made of mud and adobe and the roofs were tiled.[15] The rows of houses faced each other in front of the fort, a layout that not only made it easier for authorities to supervise the women and children but also reinforced the ability of the colonists to watch over one another.

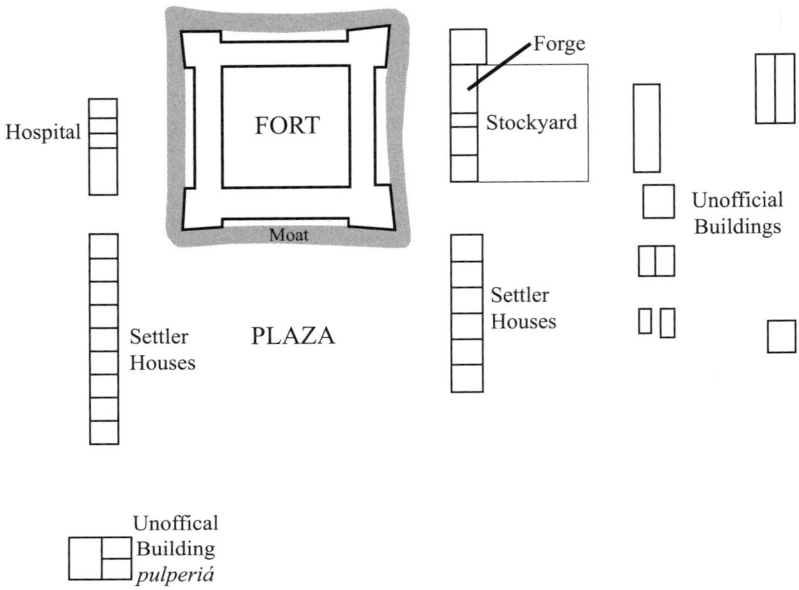

Figure 6.2. Excavations of the colony at Floridablanca. With permission, based on the drawings provided by Silvana Buscaglia.

Marriage, Death, and Birth at the Outposts

Much as we saw at the port at La Coruña, at both Fuerte del Carmen and Floridablanca marriage became central to the colonists' family strategies, as they married off their adolescent daughters as soon as possible. Certainly at these distant outposts marriage took on new urgency, as the large population of men with little or no access to women left the unmarried female colonists vulnerable to sexual predation. In this precarious situation, the rapid marriage of the single girls, usually to older men, protected them from unwanted sexual advances by the soldiers and convicts. Marriage also helped the families conform to the expectations of the authorities, who wanted young families willing and able to bear children as quickly as possible. In addition, the new couples eased the pressure on the girls' families. Not only would their new husbands, rather than their fathers, care for and provide for them, but older married siblings could care for the younger ones if something should happen to the parents. Finally, neither the authorities nor the other colonists doubted the power of the sacrament of marriage to control the girls' behavior and the behavior of men toward them.

Of course, initially there were no Spanish single women at Fuerte del Carmen, and the authorities in Montevideo seem to have been cognizant of the dangers for young women. Even as more families were allowed to settle, only four families with unmarried adolescent girls were sent to the fort, and all of those girls were married within weeks of arrival. Within a month, fourteen-year-old Francisca García was married to her Astorgan compatriot, twenty-four-year-old Pedro Méndez. Just a few weeks later, thirteen-year-old María Pita was married to a single colonist, Manuel Fernández. The other two single girls arrived just after the new year of 1782. Only a month later, fifteen-year-old Gerónima Rita Crespo married sixteen-year-old Andrés Araque, and seventeen-year-old Francisca Sánchez married José Rial. The speed with which these marriages took place indicates that it was just too risky for the girls to remain single, even under the supervision of their fathers.

At Floridablanca, no doubt for the same reason, by the time they arrived all but three of the adolescent girls were already married, including María Mata (seventeen), María Antonia Tamame (sixteen), María Verde (fifteen), and Antonia Solibán (sixteen). Casimira Fernández was the oldest of the recent brides at only nineteen. Their husbands were all in their mid to late twenties—on average, thirteen years older than their brides.

Surrounded as they were by soldiers and convicts, the safety of the three unmarried girls—Bárbara Pérez (twenty-two), Rosa (fifteen), and Josefa (thirteen) Hernández Cuenca—must have been on everyone's minds. Bárbara, the eldest, was the first to marry at the colony. In September 1781 Francisco Ortiz, a caulker from the brigantine *San Francisco de Paula*, asked permission to marry Bárbara. He was duly informed that the decision to marry one of the colonists came with conditions. Ortiz had to remain at the outpost working at his trade for six years. He also had to reimburse the royal treasury the cost of her Atlantic voyage (150 pesos fuertes), which he did, and they were married at the beginning of 1782.[16] Bárbara's marriage must have come as quite a relief both to her father (her mother had recently died) and to the authorities, as her physical safety was no longer their concern.

Although the colonists believed that they could count on marriage and family ties to protect their daughters, the Floridablanca colony's most sordid incident took place not between a soldier or convict and a female colonist but within a family. Rafaela Bedoia (twenty-seven) had come to San Julián with her older brother, Santiago (forty-one), with the first group of colonists in November 1780. Ostensibly, the tall, fair-haired Santiago was supposed to watch over his sister; however, within six months he was suspected of engaging in incestuous relations with her. As soon as he was apprised of the situation, Antonio de Viedma intervened. First, he sent Santiago to the outpost at Río Negro to get him away from Rafaela. Then, to protect her from further abuse, he married Rafaela off to Manuel García, the baker, and changed his status to that of a colonist.[17]

In 1781, with the turn of the season from summer to fall, the colony at Floridablanca began to experience the regular rhythms of life and death. On 8 February it lost its first female colonist, María Ortiz, although the documents do not indicate what cut short her life at only forty years old. On the brighter side, two months later the colony celebrated the birth of the first baby, a girl named Vicenta, born to María Mata and Lorenzo Pinto. Vicenta's birth brought new intimacy to the relationship between the colonists and their Indian neighbors. Soon after giving birth, María fell ill and her milk dried up. Fortunately for her, an Indian named Patricio, whose wife had also recently given birth, was visiting the fort along with cacique Julián. The Indian couple remained after the other Indians had departed so that the wife could serve as the wet nurse for Vicenta.[18]

Whatever joy Vicenta's birth promised was quickly quashed when at the end of April Floridablanca endured a massive snowstorm. The early onset of winter proved to be a very bad omen. Antonio de Viedma reported that the same day the storm hit another female colonist died.[19] From that point on, disease wreaked havoc on the colony. Even Viedma fell ill and was confined to his bed for most of the winter.

The devastation was quick and intense. Within weeks a variety of ailments wiped out the family of Pascuala Fernández. The young woman from León may have died of complications from pregnancy; her son Simon died two weeks later and her husband soon after.[20] Dionisia Garabito would lose both her son and her husband during that same two-month period. The tragedies seemed not to end for the Descosido-Quintana family from Astorga. They had already lost their daughter Paula during the Atlantic crossing. Then on 14 May 1781 the mother, Melchora Quintana, died, possibly from complications from pregnancy. A week later her nine-year-old son, Fabian, died, and her husband and newborn succumbed a month after that. An older Astorgan couple, the widower Andrés Prieto and his new wife, the widow Pascuala Rojo, kindly took in their surviving child, Felipe, orphaned at the age of twelve. During that winter other children would be left without parents. After María Herrero died in April and her husband, Bartolomé Tamame, died in July, their older daughter, María Antonia, and her husband, Ignacio las Heras, took in her younger sister.[21]

A letter from one of the colonists, written only a few months later in the summer of 1781–1782, describes the tragic circumstances in the colony that previous winter. Santiago Morán, a farmer from Palencia, had come to Floridablanca with his wife, Lorenza Aparicio.[22] His lengthy letter began with a poignant plea about the "necessity" in which the colonists found themselves and appealed to Vértiz as "the pious father of some unhappy children." According to Morán, in June, July, and August, thirty-four people, both old and young, had died of the "*mal de Luanda*" (scurvy). He then gave an agonizing description of the progress of the disease, which began with "pain in the calves, hamstrings and thighs until they are hard as rocks and covered with black spots," leaving the patient prostrate in bed and putrefying until he or she was taken to the cemetery.[23]

His heartbreaking description was confirmed by others. By September the accountant Gavarri felt obligated to remind Vértiz of "the very lamentable state in which these colonists find themselves." There was little food, nothing to drink, no wood for fires, and no medicines. He reported that the colonists were so terrified by the state of medical care that they said that entering the hospital was the same as preparing for death and that the medical staff "authorized one's dispatch to eternity." He pled with Vértiz to send some artisans and workmen to build sturdier homes and to send additional supplies of wood, cattle and other animals, and, above all, more wine. Between May and September 1781, fourteen colonists, nine soldiers, and four peons died.[24]

As he described the toll that illness was taking at Floridablanca, Santiago Morán also indicated that the outbreak was causing a rift between the colonists and the authorities. According to Morán, Antonio de Viedma refused to send the sickest of the colonists back to Montevideo, although he had done so for some of the sick troops. When they made their request, "he gave no other response than that they were colonists" and thus had to stay. Santiago wondered whether the colonists had "committed some crime in coming to colonize" and whether they had been deceived. He told Vértiz that it could not be "the royal will of this Lord our sovereign to send these vassals (although poor wretches) to be sacrificed."[25]

Just as supplies were dwindling and all seemed lost, two ships arrived from Montevideo with food, clothing, and other necessities that would keep the colony going for another ten months. Antonio de Viedma reported that the ships' arrival had eased the anxiety of the inhabitants and that the sick began to recover. Even he felt well enough at the beginning of October to take a walk using a cane.[26] Life on the Patagonian coast was beginning to improve.

Fortunately for the inhabitants of Fuerte del Carmen, scurvy was not really a problem as they had better access to fresh fruits and vegetables, and generally the health of those colonists seems to have been better than at Floridablanca. However, the soldiers, slaves, and other workers still suffered from an array of illnesses. Fevers were the most common ailment, but wounds and work-related injuries also kept hospital beds full. The small wooden hospital, pretentiously named the Royal Hospital of Our Lady of Carmen, San Cosme and San Damien, was staffed by Manuel Aguilera, a surgeon who dutifully kept lists of the members of the colony who were treated at the hospital from March 1781 until March 1782. Ventura Chapaco, the colony's black translator, spent much of the spring and summer with an inflamed leg and other health problems. One of the few colonists to enter the hospital was Santos Gaspar, a young man from Zamora who spent considerable time receiving care for fevers. It is most telling that during the winter and early spring, when illness ran rampant at Floridablanca, the hospital at Fuerte del Carmen saw much less activity, and in July, September, and October no colonists were admitted. They may have been healthier than the peons, soldiers, and convicts, or they may have stayed away from the royal hospital, having the same sense as their counterparts in San Julián that entering the hospital was a death sentence. If that were the case, then family members, and in particular female family members, must have taken on the burden of caring for the ill at home.

The cold, hunger, and threat of disease made the experience of pregnancy and childbirth at the forts particularly taxing. Escolástica Cordero, a twenty-seven-year-old from Astorga, conceived soon after she and her husband arrived in Floridablanca, and she spent much of her pregnancy watching other colonists and their children fall victim to disease. The October birth of her son, Santiago, was an omen of better health and fertility for the weary inhabitants. In February 1783 Antonio de Viedma cheerfully reported that from the fifteen married couples, there had been eight "quite robust" births.[27] In addition two other women, Antonia Solibán and Dionisia Garabito, left the outpost while pregnant and gave birth only a few months after returning to Montevideo. However, Antonio de Viedma's account and his upbeat tone were a bit deceptive. Despite the remarkable youthfulness of the brides at Floridablanca, not even half of the adult female population gave birth in the first three years. (Two women gave birth twice.) Yes, there were positive signs of fertility among the female colonists, but there were also reminders of the tragedy of infant mortality in general, and of the difficult Patagonian environment more specifically. Three babies were born, but Escolástica Cordero's second child and four other young children died. María Mata gave birth to two children, only one of whom survived. Each death provoked considerable anxiety, as the perpetuation of the outposts was at stake.

The improved conditions at Fuerte del Carmen led to more births, despite the fact that most of the women at the outpost were well into their childbearing years. According to a census done at the fort on 1 October 1784, fourteen of the twenty-five married women had given birth since arriving. Two sets of twins had been born and four women had given birth twice.[28] In addition, the authorities allowed an Indian girl to leave her newborn at the fort. The girl had shown up at the fort with an infant whom she claimed was hers by someone at the outpost. After her Indian husband threatened to kill the baby, she decided to leave the child to be cared for by the Spaniards. The colonists willingly took the baby in. They baptized her, named her María de la Asunción, and gave her to a female colonist to be fed cow's milk.[29] Clearly, the colonists believed that their health and well-being was secure enough to take on the additional responsibility.

The emphasis on fertility made life difficult for women whose husbands died, as they faced conflicting pressures from authorities, especially at Floridablanca. On the one hand, widowhood did not abrogate their colonist contracts; as such, they had the right to remain and struggle on with life at the colonies on their own, they could try to find new husbands, or they could ask for permission to return to Montevideo and be resettled elsewhere. On the other hand, widowhood seemingly left them unable to fulfill their prime responsibility as colonists since they would bear no more children.

The authorities left no doubt that widows with children were no longer wanted, declaring them "useless" for the establishment of the outpost.[30] Both Manuela Herrero and Dionisia Garabito were widowed by the outbreak of disease at Floridablanca in the winter of 1781. At only twenty-three, Manuela was left to care for her twelve-year-old stepdaughter, and Dionisia had three children of her own. It is unclear whether the women were pressured to leave the outpost or went willingly, but both returned to Montevideo in March 1782. It is possible that Dionisia did not go of her own accord. In October 1782 she gave birth to a son in Montevideo, noted in the parish register as the legitimate and posthumous son of her husband, José Fernández; however, as José had died fifteen months earlier, this child had certainly been fathered by someone else, and authorities may have sent her back to Montevideo to manage the scandal associated with her nonmarital relationship. The likely father was Tomás García, a soldier who had been stationed at Floridablanca and whom she later married in Montevideo.[31]

In contrast, Lorenza Aparicio decided to stay at Floridablanca. Her husband, Santiago Morán, who wrote that heartfelt plea to Vértiz about the horrific conditions at the outpost, promptly died, leaving Lorenza widowed at only twenty-nine. It is curious that she did not return to Montevideo along with Manuela and Dionisia. The only evident difference between Lorenza and the other two widows was that she did not have children. It is possible that the authorities believed that without children she was better positioned to remarry than the other widows. In fact, a couple of years later she married Ignacio Fernández, the overseer of the livestock at the colony.[32]

Only one of the widowers at the fort remarried. Andrés Prieto (fifty-three) had volunteered for the project as a widower, and in 1781 he married his cousin, Pascuala Rojo (also fifty-three); however, soon after they were both sent back to Montevideo, having also been deemed "useless" due to their age.[33] Back home on the peninsula, the labor provided by older adults was central to the functioning of the household. They worked in the fields, tended livestock, and cared for their homes as long as they were healthy. This notion that older, but not infirm, men and women had nothing to offer the Patagonian colony could not have made sense to the peasant colonists.

The overall stability of the colony at Fuerte del Carmen also meant that widows fared much better than their counterparts at Floridablanca. Women who were widowed at the fort were not pressured to leave, and all seem to have found new spouses. For instance, two years after her husband died, Josefa Lorenza remarried, this time choosing a soldier from the Buenos Aires Regiment, Andrés Zerezuela.[34] In 1787, after losing her husband, Tomás Tejedor, Luisa Marcos married José Blim, from Pisa in Italy. What the Italian was doing at the fort is not evident from the documentation, but he was evidently a desirable spouse for the widowed colonist.[35]

One widow manipulated her status so that she continued to receive the benefits afforded to her as a colonist even after her remarriage to a soldier. María Ventura del Río arrived in the Americas on the *Nuestra Señora del Socorro*, along with her husband and two children, but both her husband and her son died during the wait in Montevideo. Soon afterward she began a sexual relationship with a soldier from the Savoy regiment, Fulgencio González, who promised to marry her, but his military superiors denied his request to wed. María Ventura then appealed to the bishop of Buenos Aires, arguing that she had allowed him "as much as a loving woman might permit he whom she chooses as her spouse." The bishop granted her petition and the couple married in June 1781. However, only a month later, in a review of the colonists waiting to depart Montevideo, she was listed without her second husband and as having two children, one by her first husband and another who must have been fathered by González prior to their marriage.[36] In December 1781 she and the two children left for Río Negro and González arrived in Fuerte del Carmen a month later. By this point, the authorities had no problem sending a widow to the outpost, but it is not clear that María and Fulgencio ever lived together as husband and wife. All of the documentation at the fort refers to her as a widow, and when she died in 1812 in Montevideo, her will referred to her as the widow of Andrés Gómez.[37] Why the deception? Despite the fact that marrying González in Montevideo would have legitimized their child, she nevertheless decided to hide her marriage from the authorities associated with the Patagonia project. It is possible that Fulgencio was not allowed to bring a new family to the outpost or that maintaining her status as a colonist may have given her access to better rations than were available to her husband.

At the Patagonian outposts, female sexuality and fertility took center stage. All the young women were quickly married off to older men to protect them from the unruly soldiers and other inhabitants and to begin the process of perpetuating family life at the establishments. Especially after scurvy took its toll at Floridablanca, women who could not or would not fulfill that expectation were deemed useless for the project and returned to Montevideo.

"For the Love of God," Send Food

While the women bore responsibility for family life at the outposts, the superintendents looked to the male colonists to fulfill their obligations as the heads of household; their most important role was to provide food for their families. Initially, royal authorities provided almost everything. The colonists were supposed to receive basic food supplies daily, including bread, dried legumes, salt, oil, salted meat, bacon, and rice. However, the cost and the distance from Buenos Aires and Montevideo made provisioning the forts a logistical nightmare. Fuerte del Carmen was more than one thousand kilometers and a two-week voyage, and Floridablanca was approximately

1,800 kilometers and *at best* a three-week voyage from Montevideo. (Strong headwinds often made the return trip much longer.) Besides, the colonists had been transported across the ocean to become farmers, because without a successful agricultural base, the outposts could not survive.

As most of the women had been relying on rations for at least of two years at this point, they were already accustomed to cooking the unusual combinations of foods and distributing the rations across the day. Some of the foods were familiar. Archaeological evidence indicates that they ate mussels and fish and consumed the pigs and cattle that had been brought to the site, but the women also learned to integrate local foodstuffs into their diets in order to survive. For instance, the regular ration of yerba mate, a native infusion that contains caffeine, was a new taste for the peninsular families.[38] The women also learned to cook the local fauna, in particular the guanaco, a camelid that roamed the Patagonian plains. Indians regularly provided guanaco meat for the colony; however, preparing the meat was often a challenge. Colonists regularly complained about the lack of firewood at both outposts, which left them cold and unable to cook.[39]

Of course, even these unusual foods were better than no food at all, as the colonists at Floridablanca suffered regular food shortages. The irregularity of supply ships meant that in the first two years, the quality and quantity of rations distributed at Floridablanca varied from month to month. For instance, during the first, harsh winter, there was more meat and oil but no bacon, and the rations of legumes declined compared to previous months. The arrival of supply ships in mid-September 1781 was "very opportune" and revitalized everyone. According to Gavarri, "We had found ourselves submerged in a terror, almost panic," but the arrival of those two ships "had opened the hearts of the poor [colonists]." The ships brought tastes of home, including Spanish wines and lentils.[40]

Before his untimely death, Santiago Morán provided a much less cheerful account of the supply ships, complaining that they did not bring what the colonists needed, in particular chocolate, sugar, and ham to "refresh their bodies" and help heal the sick. Moreover, they needed more wine. Morán was concerned enough about the provisions at the outpost to ask permission to leave his wife in Floridablanca and take five hundred pesos that he and another colonist had saved to come back to Montevideo and purchase some food. If not, "for the love of god," he pleaded to Vértiz to send soap, sugar, chocolate, vinegar, and wine to help get the colonists through the winter, which had "punished us rigorously."[41] His petition seems to have gone nowhere. By the summer of 1782, the situation was even more desperate. Other than guanaco, bacon was the only meat available, and there was a significant decline in the rations of oil and legumes. They did receive some wine and brandy, but not as regular rations.[42]

Of course, the colonists were expected to provide for themselves as quickly as possible, as the success of the agricultural enterprise was critical from a number of perspectives. The Enlightenment creators of the project were convinced that agriculture was a key means to secure the territory and form the basis of a local economy. For the superintendents, self-sufficiency was a key indicator of success and order at the colonies. For all involved, without an independent food supply the colonies could not survive.

To that end, each family had been given the necessary tools and seeds, and special plows had been designed and shipped on the first voyage from La Coruña.[43] However, at both sites these provisions proved to be largely useless. The soil was poor, the water too salty, and the rains irregular. The colonists recounted working hard, but to no avail. As one sad soul at Fuerte del Carmen noted, "This land was not capable of sustaining such an innocent vassal." Even when they were able to get something to grow, flocks of birds against which "it was impossible to defend" destroyed their efforts. At other times, plagues of grasshoppers and locusts "annihilated" everything.[44]

Seemingly oblivious to the climatic and other issues, Francisco de Viedma believed that the poor harvests at the colony were due to laziness among the male colonists, a charge that not only impugned the peasant men's reputations, but also aggravated the increasingly uneasy relationship between him and his charges. Juan Gómez de la Pinta, Francisco Segurado, Damaso Marcos, Esteban Valer, and Antonio García complained that after they told Viedma that the land was useless for farming, he threatened them. They also reported that he swore that he would kill colonist Vicente Vázquez, who supposedly had voiced similar complaints.[45] Vázquez, who really wanted to be allowed to return to Buenos Aires, countered Viedma's charges by disputing his authority and fairness. In a letter to the viceroy, he asserted that Viedma resented him for having defended a peon, José León, after León had killed an Indian. Vázquez also claimed that although he lived alone far from the fort, Francisco de Viedma had come to his house to threaten him.[46]

Viedma knew that, as the comisario superintendente, the failure of agriculture at the colony would reflect poorly on his leadership, but his efforts to resolve the problems only sowed dissent among the inhabitants. In an attempt to provide each settler with cultivatable land, he subdivided the lands that had originally been designated for the first settlers. Thus, the first settlers who had toiled so hard to clear and plant lost part of the fruits of their labor to the new arrivals. This decision caused rancor among the colonists such that "one could not raise a chicken without doing harm to someone else."[47] Rodulfo Trigueros complained to the viceroy that Viedma had redivided the plots so that he had one of inferior quality. For that reason he wanted to return to Buenos Aires. Viedma reacted by accusing him of laziness and trying to influence the other colonists not to work, and he eventually retaliated by exiling Rodulfo to San José.[48] The colonists were further insulted when, after their crops failed, Viedma also took some of the fields from the colonists and gave them to peons to cultivate, to see if "the land is good and the petitioners bad."[49] Nothing could have been more emasculating to the peasant men than to be unable to provide for their families and to be incapable of fulfilling the primary task assigned to them by the Crown.[50]

Much later, in February 1783, the authorities brought together all the colonists at Fuerte del Carmen and asked them to report on their harvests. Those reports reveal the severity of the agricultural problems. Most had planted wheat, and some had more success than others. Manuel Fernández, from Zamora, had planted three-and-a-half *fanegas* of wheat and had harvested thirty-one, but he then lost half of it to locusts and floods. In contrast, Manuel Román, from Astorga, planted slightly less than three fanegas and harvested nineteen. His crops had only suffered a little damage from the locusts.[51] Other issues impeded the agricultural success of the colony. Climate, soil, and pests aside, these families had not been successful farmers on the peninsula, and it was unlikely that they would suddenly become thriving agriculturalists in the difficult new setting.

At Floridablanca, although the yields were no better, the attitude of the colonists was generally more upbeat. Antonio de Viedma was intent on cultivating a variety of products, including wheat, barley, corn, leeks, and peaches, and he reported that they harvested some grain and vegetables in the summer of 1781. However, that success was short-lived. During the late fall and winter, not only did disease decimate the population, but the harsh conditions made it impossible to sow again for more than three months. Finally, by late August and early September the inhabitants were ready to try again. Each family received twenty fanegas of land. They later reported that although the land seemed fertile enough, they lacked oxen and tools, and the plows that had been constructed specifically for the outposts were not strong enough to break up the rocky soil. However, most believed that with enough animals and the right tools, they might be able to make a go of it.[52]

Their cautious optimism aside, by early 1783 it was clear to many, especially to Viceroy Vértiz, that the outposts were nowhere close to becoming self-sufficient. Moreover, the costs of maintaining the Patagonian outposts were too high and would only continue to rise. He explained to Gálvez that due to the costs of the Tupac Amaru and Katari rebellions in Peru, maintaining the colonies was not financially viable. He had done due diligence and asked for reports from all the interested parties, including the colonists, and found only misery. One colonist described himself as "a poor, miserable, cold and forsaken man." The colonists at Fuerte del Carmen pleaded for aid, arguing that the King would never want his vassals to be so unhappy and that it was impossible such a pious monarch would "deceive" his subjects.[53] From those painful letters (which he included along with his own missive to Gálvez), Vértiz determined that the outposts were not useful. In addition to the high seas and the difficult climate, the soil was poor and the area lacked fresh water and wood. Neither Puerto Deseado nor San Julián offered opportunities for commerce. As a result, he advised that they should abandon all the settlements other than Fuerte del Carmen, whose population should be reduced.[54] Without hesitation, the Crown agreed and issued the royal order to close the settlements in August 1783.

The decision to abandon the settlements came very quickly; however, bringing this phase of the Patagonia project to a close would not be easy. Evidently, the decision to abandon the project did not reach officials in Montevideo in time, and more ships loaded with artisans, construction materials, and other supplies arrived at Floridablanca in November just as the colonists were ordered to pack up everything, including any wood that might still be useful.[55] The only evidence of Spanish control would be a column with the royal arms on it and an inscription that indicated that these territories pertained to the Spanish Empire.[56] To prevent "foreign powers" (i.e., the English) from taking possession of the site, the superintendent was ordered to demolish all of the buildings, reducing the homes and the fort to ashes.[57] By January 1784 everyone was ready to leave, and all but one of the colonists from Floridablanca were transported back to Montevideo, arriving in April. Only Rafaela Bedoia and her husband, the baker, remained in Patagonia, opting to move to Fuerte del Carmen.[58]

The process of abandoning the colony was further complicated by the fact that between July 1783 and May 1784 the American side of the project experienced a complete change in leadership. The comisario superintendente at Floridablanca, Antonio de Viedma, asked to be allowed to return to Spain. The intendant, Manual Ignacio Fernández, was given a new commission and was replaced by Francisco de Paula Sanz. Viceroy Vértiz resigned and, having turned over the reins of the viceroyalty to the Marqués de Loreto, also retired to Spain. Ever so briefly, the new viceroy considered restarting the colony at Floridablanca, as Juan de la Piedra and other supporters of the project had the viceroy's ear and renewed their efforts to keep the outposts alive.[59] Even Francisco de Viedma presented a strong defense of the outposts, arguing that they were still valuable as centers for the whaling industry and salt production. If those arguments were not enough, he reminded the viceroy of their Christian duty to convert the large numbers of Indians who lived in the region.[60] However, the authorities had very different plans for the Pampas Indians. After the abandonment of the colony at Floridablanca, the Crown ordered their extermination.[61]

The Crown decided only to maintain the colony at Fuerte del Carmen, not to expand it. In August of 1783 Francisco de Viedma was removed from his position at Río Negro and in 1785 became the intendant of Santa Cruz de la Sierra (Bolivia).[62] He was replaced by his former rival, Juan de la Piedra, who after a vigorous campaign had been officially cleared of all charges against him and declared a "good, faithful, and zealous minister."[63] Piedra did not, however, learn his lesson, and his independent nature soon got the best of him. A year later he and the pilot Villarino were killed by Indians during an unauthorized expedition in the area.[64]

Despite the danger, most of the colonists who had been transported to the colony at Fuerte del Carmen remained there. At the end of the century, when their contracts were liquidated, forty-four inhabitants were party to the document, thirty-three of whom were the original families.[65] A small contingent of troops remained at the fort at San José until 1810, when it was destroyed by an Indian attack.

The abandonment of Floridablanca did not quash the Crown's enthusiasm for family colonization. Only three years later, the Spanish attempted to stave off the English in Central America by colonizing the Mosquito Coast of Guatemala with nearly one thousand Gallego and Asturian peasants and three hundred Canary Islanders transported under the same contractual conditions as the Patagonia project. The project was an unmitigated disaster as hundreds died en route and many more fell victim to tropical disease and violence from both Indians and the British. Those outposts too were quickly abandoned.[66] The Crown had learned nothing from the experience in Patagonia.

The Patagonia project had been a disaster. All the carefully laid plans and great expense employed to bring women and children to the farthest coasts of South America came to nothing. For their part, the women fulfilled their contractual obligations despite the fact that nothing in their pasts could have prepared them for the experience of eating guanaco and drinking yerba mate in hide tents in the brittle wind and cold of Patagonia. In the worst of conditions, both physical and mental, they bore children, fed their families, and cared for the sick and dying. However, the presence of women exacerbated other problems. The only way to protect them from the hundreds of sex-starved men at the outposts was to marry them off as quickly as possible, because women who did not conform to the sexual expectations of the authorities compromised their efforts to bring order to the outposts. The male colonists faced their own challenges. When they proved to be less than successful farmers, they were emasculated by their social superiors and could do little more than beg for the mercy of the authorities. However, once most of the colonists were transported back to Montevideo, an entirely different set of gender dynamics emerged during the next phase of the colonization plan.

CHAPTER SEVEN

Far from Patagonia

Gender on the Spanish Frontier

WHILE THE VIEDMA BROTHERS WORKED TO ESTABLISH AND STABILIZE the outposts and the first groups of colonists struggled to survive on the Patagonian coast, ship after ship full of peasant colonists continued to drop anchor in Montevideo's harbor. As they stepped off the ships, they had no idea that their futures were still in limbo. Nearly all of the colonists would spend an extended period in the port city, awaiting transportation to other sites. Then, some of them would then spend most of the next few years fending off Indian attacks in the countryside outside of Buenos Aires, while most of the rest would be settled in new communities on the eastern side of the Río de la Plata, known as the Banda Oriental, where officials expected them to bring Spanish ways and Christian morality to that newly acquired frontier. For the most part, they did their best. They married early and bore plenty of children; however, in a few cases, the flexible gender expectations they had been accustomed to on the peninsula clashed with the more rigid expectations of the authorities and the other colonists with tragic results.

The colonists' first moments on American soil were fraught with mixed emotions. They were weary, excited, and anxious. Some women stepped onto the beach with newborn babies in their arms, eager to begin their new lives, while others trudged into the city mourning the loss of husbands, wives, mothers, fathers, and children who had not survived the crossing. For a number of the colonists, their arrival at the port of Montevideo was truly the end of an epic journey, as the voyage took the ultimate toll on some of the women and children. Antonia de la Infiesta's baby boy, Ramón, who had been born aboard the *San José y San Buenaventura* during the crossing, died just as the ship pulled into the harbor. Dominga Carvallo, who had traveled all the way from the village of Salcedo de Bierzo in Astorga, also died that day and was buried far from home at the church in Montevideo. She left her husband, Ambrosio, to care for three children, one of whom was still a baby. The widower Blas García found himself mourning the death of his older son, Antonio, the day that the *Real Carlos* anchored in the harbor.[1]

Although most of the colonists survived the ocean voyage, the physical and mental stress of the transatlantic crossing continued to affect them during their first few weeks in the Río de la Plata. Francisca Fernández arrived on *Real Carlos* on 15 August 1780, but died soon after, having given birth to a child who also did not survive. One indication of the lingering effects of the voyage was that an additional fifteen passengers on the *San José y San Buenaventura* died within six weeks of arrival in the Americas. Among the dead were Josefa de la Vega. She had given birth only months before the ship departed and suffered the loss of her infant son less than a month into the crossing. The ship arrived on 19 July 1780 and she was dead by September. María Manuela Blanco came ashore on the same day, but both she and her four-year-old daughter died within the next few weeks.[2]

As the ships dropped anchor, the colonists may have been surprised at how small Montevideo was. Situated on a thin peninsula with long slender coastlines, the walled city was very compact, still a frontier town with fewer than five thousand people living within the city walls and about as many scattered across the countryside. The hustle and bustle of the port would have been familiar even to colonists from the interior of the Iberian Peninsula, as most had spent significant time in La Coruña before embarking for the Americas; however, unlike the well-trodden medieval streets of the Galician port, Montevideo was relatively new, having only been founded in 1726. Moreover, in terms of sex ratios, Montevideo was the opposite of the ports of northwestern Spain in which women made up the majority. Among the white adult population, men outnumbered women by nearly two to one, and single white men were almost 20 percent of the population. The city was also racially diverse, with small but visible populations of both free and enslaved Indians, blacks, and mulattos.

At the end of the 1770s, Montevideo was booming. Diego de Alvear (1749–1830), a Spanish military official, called it "the happiest era for Montevideo" and extolled the "new energy" that filled the town. This dynamic city was

Figure 7.1. Montevideo harbor. Montevideo desde la aguada. Fernando Brambila (1793). España. Ministerio de Defensa. Archivo del Museo Naval. AMN, ms.1726 (59).

focused on commerce: "There is no house where they do not sell something, causing no little admiration that they can subsist in such an expensive land and with such a small number of inhabitants."[3] If Montevideo was any indication, the future for the immigrants looked bright.

As they wandered the streets, the peasant colonists were probably most struck by the same two things that always prompted comment from visitors to Montevideo: the decaying cattle corpses that were strewn across the beaches and the packs of wild dogs that prowled the city and harassed the inhabitants. Slightly later, Englishman Thomas Kinder reported that "the cattle are mostly slaughtered by the beach close by the wall to the east of the town and the remains left to putrefy causing the stench perceptible for a mile when you happen to be leeward of it." Those smelly corpses fed an ever-growing population of wild dogs. Another Englishman complained about "the immense number of dogs that keep garrison in every habitation and which post themselves under the windows where they howl incessantly till day-light. . . . They often attack foot passengers and sometimes even horsemen."[4] Outside the city walls there would be much more in terms of local fauna that was unfamiliar to these peasants—parrots, rheas, jaguars, and swarms of hummingbirds; however, at least at first, the packs of wild dogs must have been particularly disconcerting if not downright frightening.

The pace of arrival of the ships from La Coruña meant that the city was inundated with peasant colonists very quickly. About 1,000 colonists (and eight of the thirteen ships) arrived between December 1778 and August 1780.[5] During that same period, only 136 people were sent to Patagonia. As a result, in only eighteen months the new arrivals increased the population by nearly 20 percent (from 5,000 to 6,000) and enlarged the white population by even more (33 percent).

One would think that so many new people would tax the resources of the city; however, just as in La Coruña, the colonists' basic needs, including housing, rations of bread, meat, salt, and firewood, and daily real per person, were provided by royal officials. Local merchants seem to have had no problem supplying the required products, as despite the rapid growth of the population, the city council never indicated any issues with provisioning the town during those months. However, the costs to the royal treasury were substantial. In November 1780 the Crown spent 2,372 pesos 6 reales on housing and the daily real for the 497 colonists in the city. In the royal accounting books, those expenditures may account for the huge increase in what are referred to as the "extraordinary" expenses of the royal treasury. These expenses jumped as the population of colonists increased, from 46,337 pesos in 1779 to more than 90,000 pesos in 1780. This figure nearly doubled again in 1781 to 178,446 pesos, making up nearly 70 percent of the total expenditure of the royal treasury in Montevideo.[6]

As had been true in La Coruña, city officials had nothing to do with the project. Despite the fact that hundreds of immigrants swarmed the city between 1779 and 1784, the city council never made any mention of the peasant colonists; rather, it focused on the mundane issues of city governance—planning the festivities to honor patron saints and the births of royal children and managing the slaughter of cattle. The records indicate some concerns about a rise in prices at about the time that the colonists arrived and note a need to reinforce the city jail, but never in the context of the influx of new residents.

The task of managing the colonists and fulfilling their contracts fell to military officials. José Francisco de Sostoa, the military official in charge, complained to Intendant Fernández in January 1779 that he was having problems with the provisioning system. The meat rations for colonists were too large, so half went bad, and the dried legumes were inedible. Moreover, they were supposed to house as many colonists as possible in government-owned buildings, but there were none available.[7] A month later, Sostoa again voiced his frustration about the inability to find housing for the peasant colonists for the four *pesos* allocated for each family, making him the object of the "continuous clamor of these poor people." The problem had still not been resolved in April 1779 when he informed Intendant Fernández that the *Nuestra Señora de los Dolores* had arrived but that he had still not found housing for the families who had arrived on the *Princesa* three months earlier.[8]

Despite these complications, the peasants adapted quickly to their new surroundings. Don Pedro Garzes, the surgeon who had accompanied the colonists on the *Nuestra Señora de los Dolores*, wrote to the authorities in Spain in August 1781. He reported that the colonists had disembarked "completely happy" and had immediately looked for lodging, which he noted was not difficult to find (contradicting Sostoa's reports), and for work appropriate to their skills. He also said that they were quick to adopt colonial fashions. They "abandoned the clothes that they had from Spain because it was so ordinary and bought others that were finer." When Garzes asked them how things were going and if they liked it there, they had responded that all they wanted was to be given permanent homes so that they could work their own land.[9]

During the next year, as so few colonists left for Patagonia, the numbers of colonists living in the city at the cost of the royal treasury continued to grow, especially in the spring of 1780 when the convoy of four ships arrived from La Coruña. At this point, officials felt pressured to find a new solution to their maintenance, at least in the short term. Noting the ongoing problems in Patagonia, Intendant Fernández suggested to Gálvez that they send the families to the new town of San Carlos, just outside of Montevideo, which had recently been abandoned by the Portuguese. The colonists could "replace and augment the population and also watch over the few Portuguese who have remained there with the goal of extinguishing as much as possible the contraband in blacks and twisted tobacco from Brazil." The colonists could be useful in other parts of the Banda Oriental as well. The towns of Maldonado and Colonia del Sacramento also needed people both for their defense and for the development of commerce and agriculture. On the other side of the Río de la Plata, he suggested that they send the families to the new frontier forts of Chascomús, Monte, Luján, Salto, and Rojas, where their presence would protect the merchants traveling from Peru who presently were "very exposed to falling into the hands of Indians." To help ensure the success of the interim settlements, the authorities were to "make the heads of the families understand that their destiny is to increase and to perfect the populations that they form in this jurisdiction in the shelter and protection of the forts situated in the countryside in order protect the road from Mendoza and Córdoba." Vértiz concurred, telling Gálvez that rather than allow 658 people to live "uselessly" in Montevideo at government expense, they should be moved to San Carlos. Besides, if the colonists lived in homes abandoned by the Portuguese, the government could keep costs down.[10]

At first, these moves were meant to be temporary and were not, as officials regularly pointed out, *destinos fixos* (permanent destinations). The authorities were ever hopeful that the colonists would only remain at these sites until the problems in Patagonia were resolved and they could be permanently settled there. Keeping in mind the considerable stress that the colonists had already endured, officials in charge of them were also reminded that "these people must be treated with kindness and gentleness so that they maintain their enthusiasm and will embark without reluctance when we order them to the outposts on the Patagonian coast."[11]

Thus, in the spring of 1780, the process of moving the colonists to their temporary homes began. At the end of October, thirty-five families (about 138 people) were transported to the frontier forts outside of Buenos Aires. Authorities also engaged corps of Indians to move others to the towns in the Banda Oriental, so that by the end of the year, 121 colonists had been transported to Maldonado. These moves, combined with a nearly yearlong lull in departures from Spain, gave authorities in Montevideo a bit of a reprieve; however, the process of transporting the colonists was slow and in December 1780, there were still 496 newly arrived peasants cooling their heels in Montevideo.[12]

When the ships began arriving again in the winter of 1781, Viceroy Vértiz was once more faced with backlog of colonists in Montevideo. To resolve the "inconveniences" that resulted from maintaining so many immigrants, he and Fernández began to strategize about how to avoid paying them their reales and other expenses. They decided to move fifty Castilian families to Maldonado, where they could find housing and land to work.[13] In September he sent sixty-nine families (310 people) to Buenos Aires to work on the ranches outside of the city, but sixteen of those families (89 people) immediately went on to the Guardia de los Ranchos. This initial dispersion of the

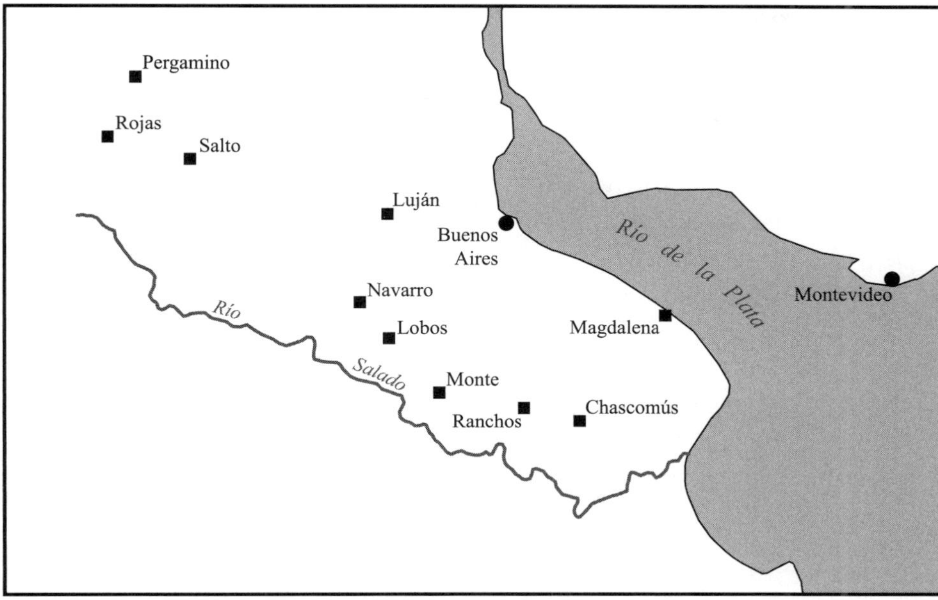

Map 7.1. The line of forts outside of Buenos Aires.

colonists around the region served its purpose. By the end of November 1781, only forty-five families and some single men (a total of 155 people) remained in Montevideo, some of whom would later depart for Fuerte del Carmen, as we have already seen. Over the course of the next year, the numbers of colonists in Montevideo would fluctuate, but by the end of 1782, all but the last two ships with about 145 aboard had arrived. By the end of January 1783, 350 colonists (eighty-one families and a few single men) remained in the city.[14] A year later, with the abandonment of Floridablanca, the numbers of colonists in Montevideo briefly increased again, but with time, all but a few would be resettled and the colonization scheme would take a definitive turn away from Patagonia.

On the Buenos Aires Frontier

The need to find temporary settlement for the colonists came on the heels of Vértiz's decision to expand a line of forts situated to protect the Buenos Aires countryside from Indian attacks. Late in the eighteenth century, officials

TABLE 7.1. Destinations of the colonists

FORTS OUTSIDE OF BUENOS AIRES	NUMBER OF COLONISTS IN AUGUST 1781*
Guardia de Chascomús	28
Guardia de los Ranchos	89
Guardia de Luján	36
Guardia de Rojas	30
Guardia de Salto	13
Guardia del Monte	23
SETTLEMENTS IN THE BANDA ORIENTAL	NUMBER OF COLONISTS IN 1788*
Canelones (Nuestra Señora de Guadalupe)	51
Colonia del Sacramento	85
Concepción de Minas	171
Pando	30
San Carlos Maldonado	295
San Fernando de Maldonado	320
San José de Mayo	213
Santa Lucía (San Juan Bautista)	157

* Exact counts are difficult as colonists (especially children) died, married outside of the colonist cohort, bought out their contracts, and/or moved to other settlements. Additionally, some colonists remained in Montevideo or spent extended periods of time there. Sources: AGNA, Sala IX, Montevideo 2.4.1, fol. 819ff; and Apolant, *Operativo Patagonia*, 199.

were still concerned about security, as the Spanish exerted little control over the territory outside of Buenos Aires. The line of new forts that Vértiz had established from Chascomús in the south to Pergamino in the north, manned by *blandengues* (lancers) were the focus of his strategy to increase Spanish authority over the region, but he believed that settlers would help solidify the Spanish presence. This decision would prove to be exceptionally dangerous, as Vértiz placed the colonists right in the middle of ongoing conflict between the Spanish and indigenous peoples in the area.

There were few permanent Indian settlements in the region, but Araucanians regularly crossed the Andes to raid Spanish settlements to the north and west of Buenos Aires, and Pampas and Patagonian peoples controlled much of the territory to the south. Some of these groups, especially those living south of Buenos Aires, had longstanding relationships with the Spanish. At one point Intendant Fernández provided a list of goods that he needed sent from Spain to provide gifts to Indians in order to protect Spanish livestock. The very detailed list included Catalan red wine, anise-flavored liquor, and an array of boxes and bells of specific sizes and colors. Fernández went on to warn his counterparts on the peninsula that there was no use sending other things, as the Indians did not like them.[15] In this and other interactions, the Indians, not the Spanish, controlled the terms of the exchange.

Although trade was common, so was warfare between Spaniards and various bands of Indians. Generally, the Spanish were on the defensive, as their periodic expeditions against the Indians were largely ineffective. There was much territory to cover, and the companies of blandengues at the rural forts were often small and plagued with desertions. Worse still, attempts to use the inhabitants of the countryside to augment royal defenses against the Indians met with resistance. For instance, the 1777 military orders requiring that all able-bodied inhabitants of the countryside appear immediately when called to take up arms against the Indians noted that often men responded too slowly, giving the Indians a window during which they could commit more robberies, kidnappings, and murders.[16]

With such poor defenses, the Indian attacks, known as *malones*, continued with impunity. The attacks generally began at night, led by scouts on horseback who collected information about the targeted white settlement. The warriors then attacked on multiple fronts to confuse the settlers, shouting, killing the men, and stampeding the livestock. They retreated quickly, taking as many cattle and horses as possible, as well as some captives, and setting fire to the fields behind them. A crushing blow to the Spanish military came on Christmas 1778, when Indians launched a surprise assault on the Guardia del Monte (where some colonists would soon be settled), wiping out the entire fort.[17]

In fact, the situation only worsened in the weeks just prior to the colonists' arrival. On 22 and 23 August 1780, the caciques Negro and Calpisqui attacked the line of forts, including Chascomús, Rojas, and Melincué. The offensive culminated later that week when over one thousand Indians led by cacique Linco Pagni assaulted the fort at Luján, the strategic center of the Spanish defenses. During that assault the Indians made off with 10,000 horses, 321 mules, and more than 170 head of cattle.[18] At least fifty soldiers and settlers were killed in the raid, and an unclear number were taken captive. The event so traumatized the survivors that the parish death register includes a letter from the priest, Cayetano de Roó, to Viceroy Vértiz and Juan José Sardén, the commandant of the frontier, describing the raid: "Having broken the peace with the Indians on the frontier of Luján by order of his Excellency his Lord the Viceroy that was maintained for many years in this district without committing hostilities, beginning at early evening yesterday they [the Indians] came to avenge themselves." According to the priest the attack involved at least two thousand Indians who, "after having robbed all the haciendas in the area," attacked the estancias and ranchos, "where with the most inhumanity they killed them [the settlers], leaving each man a martyr and they took the women and children captive." The Indians then attempted to enter the town, "which had no defense whatsoever." It was home to the venerated Our Lady of Luján, "who on this occasion defended her sad children from the hands of their cruelest enemies." Responding to Spanish prayers, the Virgin mercifully delivered a dense fog that left the Indians confused and unable to find the town. The priest blamed the disaster on military officials who, he said, did not realize how large the Indian force was until it was too late.[19] Then, as if to punctuate his frustration, he solemnly entered the burials of forty-four white men into the register, followed by the burial of a group of mulattos and vagrants found dead in the countryside. That night haunted the survivors. Ana María Rodríguez was taken captive by the Indians in that *malón*, and once she was freed, she dedicated her life to serving Our Lady of Luján until she died suddenly in 1786.[20] Her presence in the church kept the memory of that terrifying night alive long after the last body was buried.

As a result of the malones—just as the colonists arrived at the forts—conditions outside the forts were deemed too dangerous. From Buenos Aires, one royal official acknowledged that that attack on Luján had been "the most barbarous and audacious [attack] that the Infidels had committed in many years." In response, Vértiz ordered all of the families, including those whom he had just settled, to move within cannon shot of the fort for their own safety.[21]

Indians continued to raid in and around many of the forts during the colonists' first summer on the frontier. Within a couple of months, during late 1780 and early 1781, Indians attacked near Luján again. Although no colonists were kidnapped, some of their neighbors were. Juan Josef Bravo later described being surprised by three Indians on horseback, two dressed in purple ponchos and the third in a blue one. Around the same time, a former captive, Nicolás Romero, appeared at the Guardia del Monte. He told how he was taken by around twenty Indians while he had been off searching for some missing horses. In 1781 Indians attacked the home of María Paula Santana's family near the Guardia de Zanjón. After capturing María and her two daughters, "they set fire to the fields, herding the captives and the little booty that they had in front of them."[22]

These incidents were just the tip of the iceberg. Throughout the Río de la Plata, the taking of captives was very common, and Indians took both Spaniards and Indians from other ethnic groups. They often used captured Spanish women as barter in exchange for cattle, liquor, and other Spanish goods. Former captives declared that the Indians had "many" and "more than fifty" captives living among them. Blas Pedrosa, a Gallego from La Coruña who was captured and lived among the Indians for ten years, reported that the Indians had "infinite captives."[23]

Even having heard these stories of Indian attacks, nothing could have prepared Isabel Carreira and her family for the tragedy that would befall them. She had volunteered for the Patagonia project along with her husband, Silvestre de Puente, a carpenter and farmer, and their three children. They settled near the fort at Monte and led a relatively quiet life until 1784. Then one night Indians suddenly attacked their farm and took the couple (but not their children) captive. They quickly released Silvestre, ostensibly to care for his family, but kept thirty-two-year-old Isabel. Another colonist met an even more tragic fate, possibly as part of the same malón. One of the first families to enlist, Juana de Seijas and her husband, José Bedoia, both from Galicia, had been sent to the Guardia del Monte in 1780. José "perished at the violent impulses of those barbarians" while trying to protect his family.[24]

It is not surprising that the Indians kept Isabel and released Silvestre or that they killed José Bedoia. Gender was central to the taking of captives, and male captives were less desirable because of their potential for violence and their general unwillingness to adapt to Indian society. Some Indians may have used their female captives as a wives, as it was a cheaper than paying for wives in societies that required a bride price. Spanish women not only offered new childbearing possibilities to clan-based groups, but Spanish women living among Indians were quickly integrated into their economy, either as agricultural workers or herders or domestic helpers. Moreover, women rarely tried to escape, preferring to remain with their captors, especially if there were children involved.[25]

If Isabel remained alive for any length of time, we can discern little about her experience in captivity. Unlike their North American counterparts, Spanish captives (either male or female) did not publish accounts of their experiences once they returned to Christian society.[26] It was usually military officials who took statements from former captives and, as a result, the interrogations focused solely on military intelligence. They asked about the circumstances of the kidnapping (to make sure that the interviewee had not deserted to the enemy), and sought strategic information about how many Indians he or she had seen, about their leaders and settlements, and whether the captive had heard of new plans to attack.[27] They never inquired about life among the Indians.

The Spanish also understood the utility of taking Indian captives, whom they used to redeem Christian hostages like Isabel. Indeed, the colonists may have had some contact with Indians who were held at the forts for this purpose. For instance, some Indians were being held at the Guardia del Monte in the early 1780s around the time that the colonists arrived. A former captive, Pedro Zamora, appeared along with two Indians sent by the cacique Lorenzo to arrange the release of two relatives of the cacique's in exchange for Zamora's wife and daughter, who remained as hostages.[28]

When trading hostages was not an option, the Spanish offered Indians goods in exchange for Christians. In 1779 the redemption of one captive cost an array of riding related goods, including three flannel blankets, one sombrero, a saddle pad, stirrups, two pairs of spurs, a bridle without bosses, and a halter. They also demanded three ponchos and fifty mares. Thus, captives became part of the extensive trading networks of the Pampas. Although officially Spaniards could only trade with Indians with whom they had made peace, the reality was that the frontier was quite permeable, and people and goods went back and forth over the contested borders with little or no interference from authorities.[29]

However, such attempts at redemption did not bring back Isabel Carreira, a fact that frightened and angered the other colonists. In later documents, representatives of the colonists pointed specifically to her capture and the murder of José Bedoia, complaining to royal authorities about the colonists "living exposed to repeated invasions of Indians" whom they described as "fiery and indomitable people" who "destroyed families." Moreover, the failure of the authorities to adequately protect them left "the Indians absolute masters of their *ranchos* and fields."[30] The authorities' response demonstrated little concern for the colonists' plight. Fifteen years later, as the colonists fought for the compensation promised to them by their contracts, Silvestre requested the *diario* owed to his captive wife. Although the authorities acknowledged this "mournful and painful occurrence," they pointed out that it had not taken place at the colonists' final destination but at their "provisional or interim"

Figure 7.2. Pampas Indians outside of a store selling goods produced by Indians. Emeric Essex Vidal, from *Picturesque Illustrations of Buenos Aires and Monte Video* (London: R. Ackerman, 1820).

placement, "where they frequently experience such terrible tragedies as this." Without evidence that Isabel was still alive, they argued, they could not grant his request. Every effort should be made to rescue her and should she be rescued, Silvestre then had the right to her diario from the day that she was taken captive.[31] She was never heard from again.

Authorities in Buenos Aires believed that the best way to tame the violence and general lawlessness of the countryside was through the introduction of Spanish families. As early as 1774, the Buenos Aires city council lamented that the frontier population included "a multitude of men who live by what they steal, without knowing God or the King." They argued that new towns would "clean the countryside of these abandoned families by reducing them to Christian and Civil conduct, gaining for God many souls and for the King many who might truly be his vassals." Indeed, in his reflections on his tenure as viceroy, Vértiz acknowledged that he had created the new settlements "to reduce the many dispersed people of these countrysides to a Christian, civil, and sociable life."[32] Although they had been unable to bring civilization to Patagonia, the peasant women's ability to create a safer, Christian countryside could be put to good use on the Buenos Aires frontier.

Interestingly enough, despite the negative perceptions of the authorities in Buenos Aires, the countryside was already home to a significant number of women and children, even before the arrival of the colonists. Although this seemingly uncontrolled region would, in the nineteenth century, be romanticized as the world of the gauchos (migratory horsemen and ranch hands, usually of mixed race, who roamed the Pampas), in the 1780s it was not yet the masculine frontier that it would become. In fact, as early as 1744, only a slightly larger number of men than women populated the region, and among the white population, by far the majority, there were even more women. By 1778, just prior to the arrival of the colonists, the Buenos Aires countryside was home to more men than women, but nothing like the lopsided sex ratios of the nineteenth century. Despite the dangers, plenty of families settled there, as well as some single women and widows who worked the land on their own.[33] However, although the majority of those women were white, or at least identified as white, they were not Spaniards, but creoles. Thus, for the purpose of hispanizing the countryside, they were invisible to the authorities.

The conditions of life on the frontier bore little resemblance to Spain and made it nearly impossible for the colonists to change the rural culture in any meaningful way. Their new homes, called ranchos, were fairly basic habitations, constructed only of hide or earth, with straw roofs.[34] According to Félix de Azara, who traveled the countryside on behalf of the Crown during this period, many homes had neither doors nor windows. The entrances were covered only by hides to protect them from the elements. Exposing his elite sensibilities, Azara proclaimed his amazement at how sparsely the homes were furnished, often with only a barrel for water, a horn to drink from, a barbeque, and a *chocolatera* to warm the water for the ubiquitous yerba mate. The colonists had little in terms of personal possessions, and furniture like beds seem to have been a rarity in the area. Like their neighbors, the colonists may have slept on the floor, perhaps on straw mats or, as Azara says, on animal skins. Even the colonists were disappointed by their circumstances. In later complaints to authorities, they noted that they had been left without "even the small comforts to which we were reduced in our homeland."[35]

It must have been some consolation that, as was true at Floridablanca, at least the authorities settled families and compatriots together. For instance, a group of Asturians became the founding families of Ranchos (now General Paz), where María de la Iglesia and her husband, José Duarte, were settled near his sister, Rosa Duarte, and her family.[36] Nearby were other families from Quintes and Siero in Asturias. At least as they struggled to adjust to their new homes, they could work with and complain to other women who understood what they had left behind. There were mothers, sisters, and in-laws who spoke the same dialect, who tried to replicate beloved meals with strange new foods, and who missed the same mountain villages that were now an ocean away.

They needed all the support they could muster to overcome the challenges of living on the Buenos Aires frontier. In addition to Indian raids, they found it difficult to provide for themselves. According to the colonists' contracts, the Crown was supposed to give them land, houses, livestock, seeds, and farm tools, but the colonists in the Buenos Aires countryside later claimed that the authorities did not provide them with houses or title to their lands and most did not receive the daily real. They must have built their homes themselves or rented from others. Moreover, the authorities had not considered whether the sites were appropriate for small-scale agriculture. Not only was the soil different from what the colonists were accustomed to in Spain, but many did not have access to sufficient water to maintain their crops during the long, dry summer. Their situation was made even more difficult as the entire region experienced an intense drought during these years. As early as 1780, the viceroy had called upon all of Buenos Aires to attend special masses to implore the heavens to bring rain.[37] There was no way that the colonists could eke out a living on the parched land that the Crown had provided them. To make matters worse, so many wild dogs roamed the countryside that officials at the forts sent teams of soldiers out regularly to kill them. There seemed to be no immediate resolution to their situation. As long as they were considered to be there temporarily, "*sin destino fixo*," royal officials were not interested in making their lives more tolerable.

Nor did these problems prevent the authorities from moving more colonists to the area. In 1781 sixty-nine families crossed the Río de la Plata to work on farms outside of Buenos Aires owned by local oligarchs. Like their counterparts at the forts, the landowners were supposed to provide them with homes and land to work, but they do not seem to have done so. The colonists complained that not only had the landowners not complied with their contracts, but they also collected "everything," leaving the colonists unable to earn a living. As a result, over the next few years most of them demanded that they be resettled elsewhere.[38]

As had been true for their counterparts in Patagonia, this untenable situation forced the families into a state of dependence that compromised the men's status as providers. On the peninsula, they had been poor but independent, earning their meager livings off small plots and day labor. Now they were reduced to working lands owned by others and relying on the government subsidy (which was rarely paid) to feed their families. At the fort at Ranchos, these frustrations erupted in violence. Skinny, bearded Adriano de la Infiesta skirmished with his Asturian countryman Francisco González. According to the fort's captain, the two got into a brawl over a piece of land, and both suffered serious head wounds.[39] Having recently lost his wife, Miguel Castellote from Teruel in Aragón reacted differently. He was settled at the fort at Luján where he married a local widow. However, within a year he complained that he was suffering and that he wanted to be sent to Santa Lucía on the other side of the river where some of his relatives were living. When he did not get an immediate response, he deserted his wife and four children. Others must have had similar thoughts, as Sardén, the commandant of the frontier, asked the authorities to make an example of Castellote in order to deter others from deserting. In later documents, representatives of the colonists expressed how compromised they felt. Ygnacio Otero, a settler at Rojas, and Antonio García, from Chascomús, described their "pain and great grief" at having to ask for the monies owed to them by the Crown.[40]

Some women just felt too vulnerable to stay, having heard the story of Isabel Carreira and other abducted women, and they knew that life would be easier in the Banda Oriental. María García, from the bishopric of Salamanca, volunteered for the Patagonia project at age thirty-one along with her husband and two young daughters. The family arrived in Montevideo in

May 1780 and was sent to Chascomús in October of that same year. The couple settled in and she bore two more children on the frontier; however, in September 1785, when her husband Manuel died, she then asked to be moved with her four children to Colonia del Sacramento, safely on the other side of the Río de la Plata.[41]

Relocated temporarily to the forts outside of Buenos Aires, the peasant colonists were dumped into circumstances that allowed little opportunity for success. Ongoing Indian attacks left the women vulnerable to abduction and endangered the lives of the men. At the same time, their attempts to farm were compromised by exploitative landlords and drought. María García was right—their best hope was to be moved to the Banda Oriental.

Creating Spanish Families in the Banda Oriental

The experience of the colonists who settled on the other side of the Río de la Plata, known as the Banda Oriental, could not have been more different. In the Banda Oriental, royal authorities were much more attentive and invested more substantively in their well-being. They assigned some colonists to expand towns already in existence and constructed new communities for others. In terms of the existing towns, the largest group of colonists would be settled at Maldonado (later San Fernando de Maldonado), about 115 kilometers from Montevideo. Situated at the entrance to the Río de la Plata, the port was strategically important to the control of the waterway and had been home to both civilians and a garrison since 1755.[42] Many of the rest were sent to nearby San Carlos, founded in 1763 by Pedro Cevallos to discourage Portuguese settlement in the region. Finally, a few were settled at Colonia del Sacramento, a Portuguese town taken by Cevallos in 1777 that became Spanish as a result of the Treaty of San Ildefonso that same year.

In addition to augmenting the populations of these already populated towns, Rafael Pérez del Puerto, an official of the royal treasury, was appointed to supervise the foundation and construction of five new towns in the Banda Oriental in which to settle the colonists: San José de Mayo (1781), San Juan Bautista (now Santa Lucía, 1781), Pando (1782), and Concepción de Minas (also known as Minas, 1783). The fifth, Canelones, was already home to a small population of Canary Islanders and Gallegos when Viceroy Vértiz officially established a town there, renaming it Nuestra Señora de Guadalupe in 1783. Before the project was completely abandoned, the colonists founded at least three other new towns: Rocha (1793), Rosario de Colla (which had been populated off and on since 1777), and San Gabriel de Batoví (today São Gabriel, Brazil, est. 1800).

In the Spanish Empire, the process of establishing towns had been formalized since the sixteenth century with the compilation of the *Ordenanzas de descubrimiento y población* (1573). According to the *Ordenanzas*, the chosen site must be in a healthy place with fertile soil, an abundance of land for farming and pasturage, fuel and wood for building material, fresh water, a native people, comfortable surroundings, and a main road open to the north wind. The instructions described the size and location of the central plaza, the laying out of streets in a grid pattern, and the positioning of the major buildings of the city, including the city hall, the church, and the marketplaces. The Crown also detailed the placement of polluting industries like tanneries, fisheries, and slaughterhouses so that the waste could be easily disposed of. Finally, the *Ordenanzas* spelled out the manner in which housing lots were to be distributed to the initial settlers.[43]

Two hundred years later, Rafael Pérez del Puerto relied on the *Ordenanzas* to guide his founding of the new town of Minas. First, he took some of the male heads of households out to scout for the best location. He then carefully laid out plans for the streets, plaza, and parish church. The spot they chose had plenty of trees and easy access to fresh water.[44] On this bureaucratically "perfect" site, they would build forty stone houses and kitchens, each with two doors and one window. Lt. Eusebio Vidal undertook more or less the same process for the establishment of San José.

Both Vidal and Pérez del Puerto relied almost exclusively on Indian labor to construct the colonists' homes, and the use of conscripted Indians turned the peasants' understanding of the labor hierarchy on its head. On the peninsula, the peasants built their own homes and those with artisanal skills worked on the homes of others. In the new settlements, Indians did all the work. In May 1783, approximately 150 Indians, members of the 1st, 2nd, 3rd, 4th, 5th, and 6th Compañías de Naturales, left Montevideo under the supervision of Sargent Rondeau with carts full of materials for the construction of Minas. These Indians were not slaves; each worker was paid four reales per month. They then began construction, first on their own ranchos just outside of town, and then on the homes for the colonizers. Pérez del Puerto found the conditions under which the Indians worked disturbing, and he worried that they were suffering due to inadequate clothing, disease, and lack of food. In October 1783 he finally received a delivery of clothing for the Indian

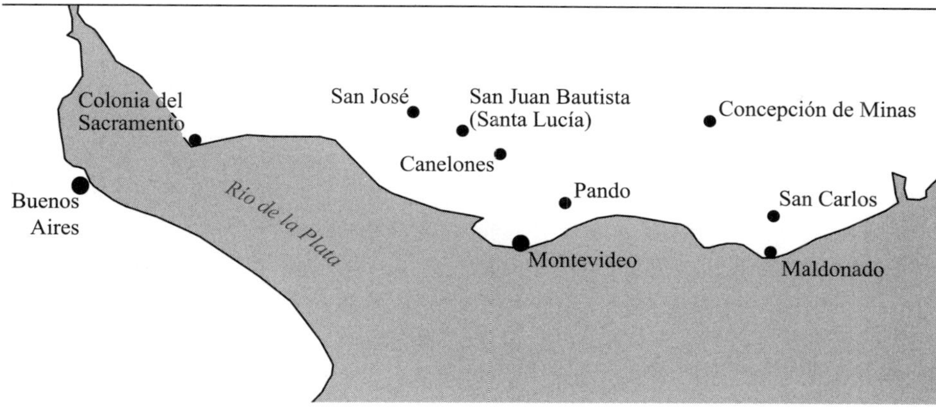

Map 7.2. The colonists' communities in the Banda Oriental.

workers, including shirts, vests, socks, ponchos, and three hundred pairs of underwear. Progress improved, and by December 1783 the walls of thirty-six homes were finished as were twelve kitchens. By Easter 1784 the colonists had settled into their new homes, and the Indians began constructing a jail, a small fort, and a church. In what was probably the first community celebration, Pérez del Puerto suspended work during Holy Week 1784 to allow the Indians to participate in the religious festivities.[45]

As construction came to an end, the colonists began settle into the patterns of daily life, doing the work for which they had been sent: creating new families in the Río de la Plata. At San Carlos, one of the first colonists to give birth was Agustina de la Puente, who bore a daughter, María Lorenza, in August 1780. This family had been one of the first to settle the town, as they had been removed from the *Nuestra Señora de la Barca* at Maldonado due to the illness that swept through the passengers. Within a month, they were transported to San Carlos. At Maldonado, Francisca García was the first female colonist to deliver a baby in October 1781. Francisca, her husband, and their three other small children had only just arrived, meaning that Francisca was very pregnant during the journey from Montevideo and the setting up of her household. Isabel Suárez must have become pregnant soon after she settled in her home in Canelones in the spring of 1781, as she had a daughter, Ana María, baptized the following July.[46] She was not alone. That winter the parish priest baptized three of the colonists' children in a row, indicating that many couples quickly acclimated to their new circumstances.

Childbirth and its aftermath was one of many ways that life was easier in the Banda Oriental. As they had throughout their migrations, women relied on their female friends and neighbors to help them through labor. At San Carlos, the baptismal registers indicate that Florentina Alonso served as the midwife for some of the women, including Anastasia Canela in 1786. Florentina, a widow in her midtwenties, joined the project with her parents. Soon after arriving in San Carlos she married a fellow colonist, Domingo González, and began delivering the community's children.[47] The infants had better spiritual care as well. Outside of Buenos Aires, there were very few parishes. When María García at gave birth to a son at Chascomús, a month passed before they could take the child to the closest parish to be baptized because it was about seventy kilometers away at Magdalena.[48] The inhabitants of San Carlos, Minas, and Colonia del Sacramento had much more regular access to the sacraments, even if facilities were poor and clergy sometimes hard to find.

The parish registers reveal another change that these immigrant families underwent as they settled in the Americas. In general, late marriage in northern Spain meant small peasant families with an average of only two surviving children.[49] Even among the women who volunteered for the project, very few had more than three children. However, the families expanded considerably as they settled in the Americas. A number of the young women who began their married lives in Floridablanca were later settled at Minas and proved to be remarkably fertile. Between 1783 and 1803, Escolástica Cordero (who, as we have already seen, twice gave birth in Patagonia before the abandonment of the outposts) had eight more children baptized, meaning that she was pregnant nearly every other year for most of two decades. Her neighbor María Herrero bore at least six children, María Mata bore nine, and Agustina Bartolomé gave birth to seven. At Colonia del Sacramento, Ana María Carbajal had at least seven children with her much older second husband, Antonio Palacio.[50] Overall, in Maldonado and San Carlos the colonists' families had nearly twice as many children as did their peninsular relatives.

That being true, children had quite a presence at the new settlements, making up around half of the population. In 1783 the forty-six families who founded San José had ninety-nine children of all ages. At San Carlos in 1790, nearly two-thirds of the population were children, making the new communities much like those that surrounded them, as youthfulness of the population was characteristic of the region as a whole. How these large numbers of children affected the new communities is hard to decipher. Scholars have written extensively about Spanish ideas regarding raising children during this period, and we know much about orphans, foundlings, and urban children;[51] however, we know almost nothing about the lives of rural kids. While alive, healthy, and out of trouble, they rarely appear in archival documentation. There were few schools in the region, so it is unlikely that many if any received a formal education. It is even unclear in the first decade if they learned the basic catechism, as many of the parishes were served only by itinerant clergy, who did little more than administer the sacraments. They presumably did chores that were appropriate for their age and size, but they must have also played together in town as their mothers and fathers shopped, prayed, and worked. Only one document out of the thousands that discuss the colonists gives any indication of how children entertained themselves in the new communities. As a part of a lawsuit between Ana María Olmos, a colonist in Maldonado, and a local military official, Ana María testified that she had been "playing with an eleven year old girl, dancing with her." The child then witnessed the brawl that ensued between Ana María and the official.[52] Such spontaneous moments of fun (at least before the brawl) were probably not unusual.

Not surprisingly, the deaths of infants and children are scattered throughout the parish registers. At Maldonado, Benita, the daughter of Francisco González and Ana Lobato, died at age six having survived the transatlantic journey at only fifteen months old.[53] At San Carlos, Bernardo Sánchez and Cayetana Louredo lost one-year-old daughter Gabriela in May 1784 and a six-day-old infant named Gertrudis Josefa in November of that same year. At Minas in 1784, Miguel Prieto and María Herrero, a young couple from Astorga, lost their son Tomás. Born while they waited at the port of La Coruña and having survived the ocean crossing, the child suffered an unknown illness and died. Both younger and older women grieved the loss of infants. At more than thirty years old, Costanza Pinto gave birth to a daughter, named Jacinta de los Ynocentes, who died only a few days later; the same fate befell the newborn of eighteen-year-old María Herredor. As physically and mentally tough as these women had proven themselves to be over the course of their journeys, the birthing process opened their bodies to the dangerous world of postpartum infection with often tragic results. Among others, at San Carlos Juana Ramos died after giving birth to twins, and a few years later Francisca González died after childbirth. Her baby died a few months later.[54]

While some of the colonists were busy bearing, caring for, and sometimes burying children, a slightly younger group of their peers were looking for some combination of love, companionship, and economic stability. By the time the colonists began their journeys, across the Atlantic Ocean women's marriage choices were increasingly constrained by the Royal Pragmatic on Marriages (first promulgated in Spain in 1776), which regulated "unequal" marriages and prevented young women from marrying against their parents' wills. Argentine writer Mariquita Sánchez remembered her childhood at the end of the colonial period when elite fathers arranged marriages and only told the girl a few days before the wedding. According to Mariquita, "Few marriages are made from love and those were in spite of the parents." She added that to speak about love was "a devil's farce." However, at the lower levels of society, there were few if any constraints on spousal choice. As was true around the Spanish-speaking world, some parents negotiated the marriages, but just as often couples made their own commitments and often brought neither goods nor money to the marriage. Although in Spain the adult women colonists had likely chosen their own spouses, in the new communities, as parents they played a much more central role.[55]

The clearest evidence that the first generation of brides among the colonists had little independence in their choice of husbands was that, as we have already seen, from the initiation of the Patagonia project girls married much younger than they would have on the peninsula. In the Río de la Plata, 90 percent of girls married between fourteen and twenty-two years old,[56] and as the colonists were resettled around the Río de la Plata, this pattern proved to be equally true for settlers who went to Patagonia, those settled outside of Buenos Aires, and those in the Banda Oriental. The women were on average only nineteen years old. Such a precipitous drop in the age at first marriage indicates a rapid change in attitudes toward marriage and premarital sexuality from those of their native villages on the peninsula.

In fact, not only did girls marry early, but the number of exceptionally young brides is shocking. Within a year of disembarking with her family, thirteen-year-old Antonia Caneda was married to a much older Maltese resident of Montevideo, Pablo Afonso (thirty-four years old). A few months later, fourteen-year-old María Antonia Fabra married fifteen-year-old Manuel Rocha. The youngest of the brides, María Francisca Duarte, was only nine years old in 1783 when she married her relative and fellow colonist Manuel Génova, who was only fourteen at the time. Both youths were part of a group of Asturian families from the parish of San Sebastián de Quintes who were sent to the new establishment at the Guardia de los Ranchos. On the other side of the river, in 1785 Pascuala Caballero at thirteen married the widower Francisco González (approximately twenty-eight) and became a mother to his toddler.[57]

Some families quickly latched onto early marriage. Although the average age at marriage in Zamora was 23.6 in 1787,[58] both of Ignacio Mata's daughters, María and Magdalena, married very young. María married before the family left La Coruña at fourteen. Magdalena, who was only six years old on arrival at Montevideo, married a fellow colonist at the age of eleven. The family had known her future husband, fellow Zamoran Agustín Ramos, during their stay at San Julián in Patagonia. When that settlement failed, the Mata family was sent to the new establishment at Minas and the couple married soon after Agustín arrived. Similarly, all the children in the Nieto family married young: daughter Josefa at thirteen, Manuela at thirteen, and the eldest sister, Matilde, at eighteen. Even their eldest son, Esteban, married at nineteen, much younger than other young grooms, who were typically in their midtwenties.[59]

At San José, where nearly all of the first colonists were from Asturias and there was considerable intermarriage among the families, the rapid adoption of the practice of early marriage for girls is even more remarkable. The average age at first marriage was in line with their American neighbors rather than their peninsular relatives. One would have thought that in such a culturally homogeneous community the colonists would maintain at least some of their peninsular ideas about women, sex, and marriage; however, clearly this was not the case. Moreover, the trend toward early marriage was evident whether the girl married another colonist or the son of a colonist (which they did about half the time) or a man not associated with the project.

As the families looked for spouses for their daughters, financial stability must have been a key concern. A man who was not a part of the Patagonia project had to petition for permission to marry the girl and pay the cost of her transport across the ocean, so potential husbands had to be willing to submit to the colonial bureaucracy (therefore, they could not be military deserters or criminals) and have some money. The parish registers from Canelones include some of the *expedientes matrimoniales*, in which parish priests investigated the prospective grooms to ensure that the young men were not already promised to someone else. Such investigations were particularly important in places like the Río de la Plata, which was full of young, single migrant men in search of new lives and, sometimes, new wives, and they provide some insight into the men who became husbands of the female colonists. For instance, in 1793 nineteen-year-old Isabel Castro, whose Galician parents had volunteered for the Patagonia project when she was six, was betrothed to Jacinto Nogeira (age thirty-three). Although not a colonist, he was also a Gallego, from Figuiera, in Ourense. According to a witness, Jacinto had worked in Cádiz for five or six years before making the voyage to "this America" nearly fifteen years before. If, in fact, that was true, he and his friend had made the crossing when he was only a teenager, presumably in search of work or adventure. A witness on behalf of Pedro Álvarez (twenty-five), another Gallego, told a similar story about having been neighbors back in Galicia and then working in Cádiz before coming to the Río de la Plata. Now Pedro wanted to marry the colonist María Bergues, who was no more than fourteen years old.[60] Although immigrants themselves, these men were established in the region and financially stable enough to have some savings or be able to borrow on credit to repay the Crown. Juana de Pintos, who had been married in La Coruña at only eighteen, was widowed again by 1786. Records indicate that she found a wealthy man, receiving a substantial bridal gift (an *arras* of four thousand pesos) from her second husband, a blacksmith in Montevideo.[61] Although it is unlikely that many of the girls found such prosperous husbands, the contrast between the poverty that the colonists left behind in Spain and the futures that these men promised might have been strong enough to provoke the change in attitudes toward marriage.

Another significant change was the difference in age between spouses. Among the generation of the girls' parents, most couples were relatively close in age, around three years apart on average. Moreover, as was common in northern Spain, in nearly a quarter of the couples the wife was older than her husband, and in another 20 percent the spouses were very close in age, within one year of each other. In contrast, in Buenos Aires, at least among the upper classes, significant age differences between husbands and wives were common. Susan Socolow has shown that upwardly mobile bureaucrats and merchants in Buenos Aires waited until they reached a certain stage in their careers to marry and may have been deeply invested in the virginity that young brides promised. Large age differences between spouses were also quite common among the Spanish immigrant population across the Río de la Plata.[62] The colonists quickly assimilated to this new expectation about marriage; among their children, the age difference between spouses (7.8 years [17.9 years old for women and 25.7 for men]) was more than double that of their parents. The large age difference had long-term implications for the colonists. As girls their own age married, the young men then had to wait until their midtwenties to marry and had to choose from among their peers' younger sisters for their wives. By doing so, they perpetuated not only early female marriage, but also significant age differences between husbands and wives beyond the end of the colonial period.[63]

This combination of very early marriage for girls and large age differences between spouses indicates that a radically different set of sexual expectations evolved during the Patagonia project. The mothers among the colonists came from communities in which honor was not necessarily tied to chastity, and, as a result, they had substantial freedom to develop physically and emotionally. Yet they did not hold late marriage and the sexual independence, emotional maturity, and economic autonomy that came with it as central to their sense of regional or gender identity. Rather, they seem to have easily adopted a different set of priorities that emphasized the benefits of early marriage for their daughters. By marrying earlier, young women (and/or their families) would have had greater choice of spouses.[64] They also presumably would have had their first sexual experience within the bounds of matrimony. However, early marriage also restricted these women's choices. Most importantly, as they reached puberty, these girls had little choice but to marry. There were no convents in eighteenth-century Montevideo, and at any rate peasant women rarely took the veil. For better or worse, each woman probably had only one sexual partner rather than the series of nonmarital relationships that many of their mothers had experienced. Finally, these young women would not have had the same authority in the household that their mothers had. Not only were they new to frontier society, but they were far from being the socio-emotional equals of their much older, more established husbands.

Interestingly enough, the changes in ideas about marriage that were so evident among the young female colonists did not affect their male counterparts. Although parents quickly married off their daughters, the single men among the colonists were not as enthusiastic about marriage, despite the availability of marriage-age women (both within the colonists' cohort and among the rest of the white population in the Río de la Plata). Not only did the sons of colonists wait until they were almost twenty-six years old on average to marry, of the 119 adult men who left La Coruña unmarried, I can find evidence of only 21 who married, and those who did rarely married other colonists, even though there were plenty of marriage-age single women. At least 32 deserted soon after arrival and the remaining 66 seemingly remained single, becoming part of what one author described as the "packs of unmarried men" who roamed the region. They joined hundreds of other men from northern Spain who migrated to Buenos Aires during the same period outside the scope of the colonization project and who remained single despite the availability of potential spouses. Coming from regions in northwestern Spain where women had considerable authority, many of these men were attracted to the independence and the masculine authority that came with migration, especially transatlantic migration.[65] As a result, their unwillingness to marry may be directly related to their decision to emigrate rather than to the circumstances in the Río de la Plata.

Beyond the common experience of marrying early and marrying men who were much older, the female colonists married all kinds of men. A few young women at nearly all the settlements married soldiers stationed at the local forts. For instance, Petronilla Herrador was betrothed to a Spanish dragoon at age thirteen. He would have brought a military pension and presumably some social stability to the marriage.[66] Daughters of colonists would have been attractive spouses for the soldiers, many of whom wanted to leave the military but remain in the area as colonists themselves. These women were not only white and from the peninsula, but had access to land, tools, and cattle. However, this choice was actually more complicated than just marrying any outsider, as all soldiers also had to get permission from their superiors to marry. The rules were complicated. To marry an officer, the woman had to prove that she was of the same social status as the man. For a lieutenant or lower to marry, the soldier had to prove that he had enough income to sustain the couple beyond his military salary, and the prospective wife had to be the daughter of an officer. If she was not an officer's daughter, the regulations required her to prove that she had income equal to her potential husband's salary. Soldiers who married without permission would be discharged. Not only did the Crown not want to be burdened by the pensions due to soldiers' families, but it was concerned that peninsular soldiers might purposely marry "inappropriate" women in order not to be sent back to Spain.[67]

In general, the girls were likely to marry men who came from the same region of the peninsula. Although a relatively small proportion of the colonists were from Galicia, they arrived to find a large number of potential spouses who had emigrated from the region in the previous decade or so. Jacoba López Fernández came with her parents at the age of seven from Betanzos. In 1788, at age sixteen, she married thirty-one-year-old Pedro Armida, who was from nearby Mondoñedo and had lived in Montevideo for about ten years at that point. Josefa Torreiro, the daughter of María Antonia

Agra and Blas Torreiro, from Galicia, was sixteen when she arrived. In Buenos Aires in 1787 she married Juan Carnero, a successful Gallego immigrant.[68]

Good arguments could be made for marrying either local or European men. In a play that was widely performed and circulated in the 1790s, *El amor de la estanciera* (The Rancher's Daughter's Love), a country girl, Chepa, must decide whether to marry Marcos Figueiras, a Portuguese, or Juancho Perucho, a gaucho. Although Chepa and her mother are drawn to the perceived wealth of the European-born suitor, Cancho, Chepa's father, advocates for Juancho, telling his wife, "Woman, those guys from Spain [*sic*] are all half rogues: one of our countrymen is worth more even if he only has four threads."[69] Nevertheless, most of the female colonists chose peninsular men over creoles.

Once a marriage was arranged, weddings on the frontier were not always the formal affairs that the church expected. In the 1779 visit to the parish at San Carlos, bishop Malvar y Pinto (who had arrived along with the first colonists on the *Princesa*), admonished the parish priest to stop holding weddings in private homes, as "the spirit of Our Mother Church" was that couples be joined in the church.[70] Rural weddings also faced unexpected disruptions. In May 1781, at Maldonado, an entry in the marriage register describes how the priest had pronounced the banns for the couple during mass one Sunday, but on the following Sunday, he said the banns twice on the same day in different masses, "being forced to make this decision with the notice of the immediate arrival of an enemy expedition [probably Indians] and so that the inhabitants could prepare themselves to abandon their homes."[71] On the frontier, sometimes one had to improvise.

Sex and Murder on the Frontier

Another striking difference between the colonists' lives on the peninsula and in these new communities was a decline in their tolerance for nonmarital sex. Well into the eighteenth century, northern Spain was known for its high rates of illegitimacy in comparison with other parts of Europe. Similarly, a number of scholars of the Río de la Plata have described a frontier society that was relatively tolerant of nonmarital sex. Félix de Azara famously said that there was not a girl over eight years old who was still a virgin. However, the demographic research tells a more complicated story. Before the 1760s and 1770s, white illegitimacy was low in most rural areas, although by the 1770s out-of-wedlock births had begun to increase.[72] According to María del Carmen Ferreyra, illegitimacy rates in the rural areas of Córdoba were as low as 2 percent in the 1760s but averaged around 7 percent in the 1770s. Bernd Schröter suggests that white illegitimacy in the Banda Oriental was low until the 1770s, when it began to rise substantially. Even with the increases, these white illegitimacy rates around 10 percent are dramatically lower than those in many urban areas of colonial Latin America, which ranged as high as 30 percent among white women.[73]

Certainly nonmarital sex was not unknown among the colonists. As early as July 1781, Antonia Seijas (thirty-eight), a recently widowed colonist from Galicia, wrote to the bishop of Buenos Aires that she had become pregnant by a much younger soldier, Juan Arencilla (twenty-nine). She told the bishop that she had engaged in sexual intercourse with him under the promise of marriage, but that his commanding officer refused to grant permission for them to marry. To remedy her situation, the bishop ordered that the couple be married as soon as possible.[74]

In San Carlos, the sex scandal at the time the colonists arrived revolved around a creole woman, Andrea Acosta. Andrea was from Rio Grande do Sul (Brazil) and had married a local man in 1773 at the age of only fourteen. Sometime around 1779, her husband returned to Rio Grande do Sul along with some other Portuguese. For much of the time since, Andrea had been having an adulterous affair with José Antonio Tabárez. The parish priest, Padre Amenedo, had attempted to end the relationship, even visiting the couple at Andrea's home. José testified that he had "been friends" with Andrea before he married, but since he married, they were no longer "friends." He also noted that he had been to her house lately and that she had five children born after the estrangement from her husband, but he did not know who the fathers were. Witness after witness testified to Andrea's scandalous life, but José Coello also noted that Andrea's children called Tabárez "father" and that Tabárez had conceded that the children could be his. However, when Andrea gave her side of the story, she testified that she did not know who the fathers of her children were. Despite the intervention of the authorities, Andrea went on to have even more children "of unknown father" and the astonishingly fertile Tabárez had fifteen children with his wife.[75]

Soon after their arrival in Canelones, the colonists must have been buzzing about fellow colonist Feliciana López. From the outset, Feliciana had not been certain that she wanted to come to the Americas. In chapter 2 we saw that she had nearly been scared off when told that she might be taken by the Indians. However, she found the necessary courage to continue, and after arriving in Montevideo she and her husband, Rafael Corbella, were settled in Canelones in March 1781. A year later, Rafael was murdered by a sailor who had deserted, Manuel Antonio Barbosa, alias "the tailor," who had been staying in the home of another colonist, Antonio Cid, under an assumed name. When Rafael's body was found two months later, hidden in the brush, Cid, Barbosa, and Feliciana were immediately arrested. Evidently, Barbosa and Feliciana had been having an affair and the three had plotted Rafael's demise. Antonio Cid died in jail in Montevideo in 1784. In the course of a long, drawn-out legal process, Barbosa escaped from jail and authorities declared that his flight was "the equivalent of a full confession." Feliciana was eventually sentenced to six years in reclusion in Buenos Aires, but she served only three and later returned to Montevideo.[76]

Such a sleazy affair must have been shocking to most of the colonists, who either were already less tolerant of nonmarital sex or were in the process of adopting a more rigid set of sexual expectations for women. As far as the documentary evidence indicates, only two women joined the colonization project with their illegitimate children, as the enlistment process clearly discouraged single mothers from volunteering. Twenty-three-year-old María Antonia Gómez, from La Coruña, had enlisted in the project as a single mother along with her parents and her seven-year-old natural daughter, María Lorenza. Presumably, the authorities deemed the presence of María Antonia's father to be essential to ensuring her proper conduct during the voyage and resettlement. She married an Asturian in Montevideo in 1784. The other single mother, Francisca Pérez del Prado, enlisted along with her mother and three-year-old daughter. However, two months before their ship departed, Francisca married a widower who was also on the passenger list, thereby resolving the issue of a sexually experienced woman traveling alone, no doubt much to the relief of the authorities. They later settled in Maldonado.[77] As mentioned earlier, the project's emphasis on marriage pushed many couples to wed even before leaving the peninsula, thereby resolving the issue of illegitimacy. According to Castilian law, as long as the parents of an illegitimate child faced no impediment to marriage, the child was legitimized once they were married.

Most of the adult female colonists were already married when they arrived, so at least initially there was little opportunity for premarital sexual relations; however, from early on in their resettlement it is clear that a least a few female colonists strayed from the project's stricter expectations about female sexuality. As discussed in chapter 6, a couple of women who had been settled initially in Patagonia had illicit relationships with single men, and the same was true in the Banda Oriental. In Colonia del Sacramento, María Manuela de la Fuente got caught up in a complicated situation. She had married Antonio Cid just before embarking in La Coruña. As just described, Cid was convicted in 1782 of killing Rafael Corbella and died in jail. María Manuela married again only six months after Cid's death, this time to a soldier from Gerona. Five months after her second marriage, she gave birth to a daughter who was baptized as the child of Antonio Cid (who had been dead for eleven months). Even the baby's death register refers to her as the daughter of Cid, in a clear attempt to disguise the unintended pregnancy. In San Carlos, two daughters of colonists bore illegitimate children in the first decade of settlement. María Rosa Rodríguez Maurente was only five years old when she arrived with her parents from Galicia in 1779. In September 1790, she gave birth to a daughter, Josefa Cypriana. It is likely that the father was Justo Gil, a soldier from Segovia stationed at Maldonado. In May 1791 he asked permission from his colonel to marry Rosa, and the request's approval noted that her family worked hard and was of "good conduct and integrity." I find no evidence of the baby, who may have died in the interim. Around the same time, Ventura Fabra, who was just a year younger than Rosa, gave birth to a baby boy, the son of Joaquín Benítez, from Salamanca. The ending was not so happy for Ventura. Soon after the baby was born, she and Joaquín were married. According to the marriage register, the wedding took place at home in private, as Ventura was gravely ill. They seemingly wanted to legitimize both their relationship and the child. Ventura died soon after.[78]

Although historical documentation rarely reveals the intimate details of good relationships, when relationships soured the resultant court cases overflow with evidence of how the colonization project provoked or intensified conflicts about the correct behavior of men and women. We have just seen how Feliciana López's illicit relationship led to the murder of Rafael Corbella, but he was not the only colonist who fell victim to domestic violence. Take, for instance, Marcelo Mendián's murder of his wife, Marta Muñiz Villar. This Gallego couple and their son were the first to volunteer for the Patagonian project and were on the first ship to leave La Coruña for Montevideo in 1778. Both were from Galicia; she was thirty and had been married before with a son from the previous marriage. He was forty and had traveled to Montevideo previously as a soldier in the Mallorcan regiment. At the point at which they enlisted, they may have been married only a couple of years, as the son they had together was two. They arrived in the Río de la Plata in December 1778 and eventually settled in Montevideo, but life was tough.[79] Within a year, Marcelo asked the authorities to give the daily real and the money for rent to his wife, as he was going to look for work in nearby farms "in order to clothe his children," as should any good father. Whatever his intentions, when he did not return his wife and children grew increasingly impoverished, and the authorities came to believe that he was trying to avoid being sent to Patagonia.[80] Marcelo eventually returned and the family acquired enough wealth to purchase a slave; however, relations between the couple continued to deteriorate as his wife's conduct further compromised his already shaken masculinity.

Marta's alleged misbehavior only began or became public in 1784. The year before—with a loan from a local *pulpero* (the owner of a corner store) Antonio Campos—Marcelo had bought out the family's contracts so that they would not have to go to Patagonia. Soon after, Marta began to go out in public without her husband, growing fatter and gaining her nickname, La Chispa, which translates as "Spark" or "Sparky" and has a connotation of drunkenness. As long as they had been colonists, she and Marcelo were expected to present themselves as a properly married couple. However, once he bought out their contracts, Marcelo lost the helpful surveillance of royal authorities, and he again appealed to authorities to intervene by filing for separation, having abandoned any attempt to control Marta himself.[81]

In November 1784 Marcelo went to the ecclesiastical authorities to accuse his wife of inappropriate behavior and to ask that she be put in reclusion. Around that same time, Marcelo attacked the pulpero, whom he suspected of having relations with Marta. In response, Marta accused Marcelo of abuse and asked for a divorce. The dispute wound its way to the bishop of Buenos Aires for five years. Just as it was ready to be resolved, the couple reconciled and neither followed up on their suits.

Then in August 1789, one night around midnight neighbors ran to the *alcalde ordinario,* saying that doña Marta had been stabbed. The official jumped out of bed and went immediately to the couple's house, where he found the body. The couple's black slave, Rosa María, and their two children told the alcalde that Marcelo had inflicted the stab wounds, and Rosa María presented him with the murder weapon. The alcalde then went in pursuit of Marcelo, who had already fled.

According to the testimony of Rosa María, the primary witness to the crime, after the couple had enjoyed a peaceful supper that evening, they spent the evening drinking and smoking. Marta then got a nosebleed, at which point Marcelo got angry and said that it was disgraceful that she was always bleeding like that, that she was living a bad life, and that around the neighborhood they called her "whore." She then called him an asshole, and Marcelo decided to go to bed. Soon Marta followed. In bed the fighting began again, with Marcelo saying that he just could not continue to sleep with a whore like her. Marta then smacked Marcelo with a shoe that she grabbed from underneath the bed. Marcelo told her not to hit him as, even though he was old, he was still her husband. Marta, who was described as very fat, then climbed on top of Marcelo, holding him down and almost suffocating him with her large body. Fearing for his life, he grabbed a knife and nearly decapitated her. Marcelo then ran out of the house, shouting good-bye to his screaming children, telling them, "What I wanted is done."[82]

Marcelo ran to a nearby church and was granted sanctuary, which prevented him from being arrested as long as he remained on church property. There he gave his own explanation to authorities about why he killed her. He described her as "extremely vicious with lust and drink" and as a thief who lived in concubinage, first with Antonio Campos and later with others. She was continually drunk, leaving her house and husband without permission and returning at all hours of the night from what he called her "infamous vices." Oddly, he also accused her of stealing and killing lots of hens and roosters. He wanted to reprimand her, but Marta was "manly and extraordinarily strong," so he kept quiet.

Unfortunately for Marcelo, the neighbors were unable or unwilling to corroborate his description of Marta's behavior. The next door neighbors, Juan de Amoedo and José de Cores, testified that they knew nothing about her concubinage or her dissoluteness or the chicken thefts. Marcelo ended up leaving sanctuary and stayed in jail for ten years in Montevideo. Just before his case was to be concluded, he escaped and was never heard from again.

The other case of spousal murder among the colonists was arranged by María Pose.[83] María and her husband, Mateo Suárez, were also Gallegos and among the first volunteers for the project. They made the transatlantic journey on the *Princesa* in 1778, along with Marta and Marcelo,[84] and survived the sinking of the *Visitación* in Montevideo harbor. After a couple of years in Montevideo, they were finally settled in San Carlos, where María bore a daughter. However, their lives took a turn for the worse, and in 1788 Mateo, a well-known drunk, was found facedown in a ditch on the road to Maldonado by another colonist, Manuel Rodríguez Sánchez. Rodríguez Sánchez, who described himself as a "surgeon in training," examined the body and, finding only minor contusions, told authorities that Mateo had drowned; however, when they fished out Mateo's body, they pressed on him, but no water came out, causing the authorities to consider the possibility that Mateo had been murdered.

The investigation then focused on Mateo's wife, María Pose, and two men, Manuel Gómez and Francisco García. According to the testimony of a number of witnesses, most of whom were other colonists, both Gómez and García had been peons working for Suárez and Pose, and there had been conflict between García and the victim. Moreover, colonist Andrés Rodríguez Morente testified that he had heard that prior to the murder, the couple had quarreled and that Mateo had hit María with a stick. He had also heard that María Pose was offering fifty pesos to anyone who would kill her husband.

In her testimony María denied offering money to kill her husband and claimed that the accused peons had never touched him. However, she added that she fought with Mateo just before his death and that he had hit her with a stick for having run away. María later described more violence at the hands of Mateo. Once with a stick in his hand, he paced across the patio, calling her a whore and a bad-living woman. Terrified, María begged him to come inside, so as to avoid any more scandal. However, María did not tell the whole story. The case also includes documents from 1787 in which Mateo Suárez accused his wife of having an affair with colonist Josef López. In those documents, a neighbor, Francisco Cancela, testified that he had seen María and López alone together while López's wife was out rounding up the animals. Evidently, Mateo had shown up unexpectedly and an argument with López ensued.

In the end, although Manuel Gómez received six years in prison and Francisco García got four, both of their sentences were commuted to military service. María was sentenced to six years of reclusion in Buenos Aires in the home of Cecilio Sánchez de Velasco. However, a year later, Cecilio decided to retire to the countryside and had María returned to jail. She was then placed in another *casa de residencia* where she made bricks. She died sometime after 1795.

These cases of spousal murder have much in common. Both women came from tiny Galician villages less than fifty kilometers apart. They grew up in places where there were many more women than men due to high rates of male migration.[85] Marta and María were among the first to enlist for a colonizing project that, in the long run, few Gallegos demonstrated any interest in. They crossed the Atlantic on the same ship. Upon reaching the Río de la Plata, they lived under the strict conditions of the colonists' contracts, under which they could not move about freely. More to the point, both husbands justified their interpersonal conflict and domestic violence as being the result of their wives' inappropriate sexual behavior. It is certainly possible that Marta the victim and María the murderess had been bad women on the peninsula and just continued their bad behavior in the Americas. Domestic violence was certainly common on the frontier.[86] However, considering the fact that the couples had been vetted by both municipal and royal authorities prior to their enlistment, it is more likely that these women, unhappy in their marriages, engaged in extramarital sexual activity that would have had different consequences back home on the peninsula. Women in Galicia had considerable sexual freedom, and although no one advocated adultery, rather than pressure couples to follow the ecclesiastical admonition that "what God hath joined together let no man put asunder," communities allowed for an array of irregular relationships, including concubinage. Unable to divorce, couples in conflict generally merely separated and took up with others rather than remain together in dysfunctional relationships.[87]

However, once these couples joined the Patagonia project, the rules changed. It seems clear that both Marta and María expected to have the same flexibility to move on to other relationships as they would have had at home, but neither Marcelo nor Mateo were willing to acquiesce to their wives' expectations of sexual freedom. Moreover, having spent years as a soldier, Marcelo would have been assimilated to a culture of masculinity based on patriarchal authority that was less dominant in Galicia. Thus, men like Mateo and Marcelo may have expected a degree of control over their wives that differed considerably from the expectations of their much more independent Galician spouses.

Intensifying the pressure for men to control their wives was the specter of official surveillance that came with their colonist contracts. As the authorities had a very specific vision of the type of colonist they wanted, they were highly interventionist in keeping couples together. For instance, when Ambrosio Rodríguez and his wife, María Bello, arrived in La Coruña from Astorga, their relationship was already in trouble.[88] According to documentation from Montevideo, they had never gotten along and he tried to leave her in La Coruña. Set on their desire for married couples, officials in La

Coruña forced the couple back together so that they might continue on as colonists. In the Río de la Plata, Ambrosio and María separated a number of times, but there too the parish priest did "anything possible to reunite them." In this case, both seem to have had a problem with alcohol. Caught up in the investigation of the murder of Mateo Suárez, María, who herself was described as often drunk, also noted that they would never have come to America if Ambrosio not been a drunk and had been "right in the head." Although Vicente Tarufo, the commandant of the fort at Maldonado, noted that while he had been in San Carlos, María had done nothing scandalous, Ambrosio wanted out of the marriage, and only four months after arriving in San Carlos, he abandoned María and their three children. Soon afterward their son José died, having been kicked in the stomach by a horse. María then asked permission to go to Montevideo to search for Ambrosio. She spent three years there, living off income she earned as a seamstress and washerwoman and leaving their farm untended. Finally, in 1784 the authorities tracked him down, put him in jail, and eventually forced the couple to reconcile.[89]

Rigid in their determination to make nuclear families the centerpiece of the colonization project, royal authorities proved to be impatient with men who attempted to flee their familial responsibilities. In 1786 the viceroy reminded a justice official in Maldonado of his responsibility to make sure that the community lived "honestly" and to apprehend men who had abandoned their wives. The desire to keep families intact sometimes led to remarkable leniency toward men's bad behavior. At Colonia del Sacramento, tall, brown-eyed Antonio Saura quickly got a reputation for "scandalous behavior" each time he got drunk. He was arrested and his wife petitioned for a separation. When the local military official sought to send him to another site, the viceroy intervened and ordered Saura released at Christmas. The viceroy was concerned that should the marriage end, Antonio would be evading his duties as a colonist and the care of his family would fall entirely to the Crown. The couple seems to have reconciled successfully.[90]

The colonization project's turn away from the outposts in Patagonia and toward resettlement in the rural areas outside of Buenos Aires and Montevideo forever altered the fates of the peasant colonists. Those who were resettled at the forts in the Buenos Aires countryside were exposed to dangers that had been unthinkable back in Spain and that made it nearly impossible to live as they had on the peninsula. Fortunately, daily life was safer for those who settled in the new towns in the Banda Oriental, where the younger generation adopted new sexual mores and marriage expectations. For some, this transition may have been easy, particularly as it was encouraged by royal officials; however, for others, the resettlement created a clash of gender cultures that on at least four occasions led to murder during the colonists' first decade in the Río de la Plata.

CHAPTER EIGHT

From Peasants to Slave Owners, from Colonists to *Vecinos*

DESPITE THE DANGERS THEY FACED AND THE ADJUSTMENTS THEY had to make, most of the peasant families settled into what they believed to be permanent homes and new lives in the Río de la Plata. Of course, most of their time and energies were devoted to establishing themselves economically, a task at which some were more successful than others. Particularly for women, that process was transformative in terms of their places in the complicated racial and social hierarchy of the Río de la Plata. But even as they became financially stable, they struggled to resolve their status vis-à-vis the Spanish Crown. To do so, they established the key institutions of Spanish life, parishes and city councils, through which both women and men could move away from their designations as colonists and assert their status as *vecinos* in the Spanish Empire.

As might be expected, despite the fact that all the heads of household among the colonists (both male and female) in the Banda Oriental received the same basic farming supplies from the authorities, some of the colonists proved to be less successful farmers than others. Many had not been particularly good agriculturalists on the peninsula, and in the Americas, they encountered all kinds of obstacles. Although travelers like José Manuel Pérez Castellanos waxed poetic over the "delicious valley" in which Minas was situated and the groves in and around Santa Lucía, many of the colonists had been assigned lands that were not very fertile. Moreover, the wealthy landowners who owned adjacent lands demonstrated little interest in helping their new neighbors. Throughout most of the 1780s, colonists in Santa Lucía complained that the livestock from the nearby estancia of Bartolomé Mitre (the grandfather of the future president of Argentina) constantly trampled their crops. Local authorities regularly issued fines, but Mitré refused to corral his animals.[1]

To no one's surprise, widows had a difficult time making a living on their own. At the end of the century, when Rafael Pérez del Puerto took stock of how the colonists across the Banda Oriental were faring, he noted Teresa Espinosa's troubles. Close to seventy years old in 1799, Teresa was already widowed when she came to the Río de la Plata along with her daughter and son-in-law. According to Pérez del Puerto, not only was she living in poverty, but her son had fled, having been implicated in a murder. Like a number of the female colonists, Josefa de los Santos was twice widowed by 1799, and Pérez del Puerto reported that due to her advanced age, she found herself in need, living on only the daily real. However, age seems to have been as much a factor as gender. Due to their "advanced age," a number of men, including Bernardo Sánchez and Manuel Durán (both fifty-nine years old), also lived in some distress and relied solely on the government supplement.[2]

Illness derailed the progress of some families. José Hernández, a blacksmith, did well enough initially to buy his family out of their contracts, but then he lost his sight and was living in San Carlos in great poverty. Juan Fabre made his living cutting hair but was later crippled and had to rely on the daily real. Pedro Mayo had to work especially hard to make his small farm work, as his wife had been ill for a long time.[3]

Others were just not meant for such a difficult life. Manuel Rodríguez Sánchez had become a "surgeon," but according to Pérez del Puerto, he was short on both intelligence and character, deficits that hindered his economic success. Pérez del Puerto did not know Ambrosio Rodríguez's occupation, but "he was often engaged in writing." A problematic man, as we have already seen, he must not have been very successful, as he too lived in some need. There were many others whom Pérez del Puerto described as "little dedicated to work."[4]

Pérez del Puerto distinguished between those who worked hard and those who failed to fulfill their oficio because they were lazy or poorly behaved or just less talented. However, in general, he sympathized with the challenges that his charges faced. He reported to the authorities that because of their "lack of liberty," few of the colonists were getting ahead, as they were still considered as being *en depósito* (only temporarily settled). Beyond that, "they were not and could not be equals," in part due to "that hidden hand known by the name of fortune that makes some similar people in some similar circumstances differ amongst themselves." He went on to remind the viceroy that the successes and failures of the colonists were as various as the "dispositions of men."[5]

Nevertheless, many of the colonists worked hard and found some success in their endeavors. José Mancebo had been a carpenter but was entrepreneurial enough to open a *pulpería*, a corner store. Francisco Osorio became the local pharmacist. A few quickly accumulated additional property. By 1799, Matías Alonso, a large, redheaded farmer from Astorga, owned an estancia and was doing pretty well. With the expanding economy, cattle ranching was more profitable than the agriculture that they had been brought to encourage in the region. In fact, Intendant Francisco de Paula Sanz complained that the colonists "plead for land only for estancias, thinking solely of cattle, and complain that the lands assigned to them are designated as *chacras* [small farms]."[6] The colonists already understood that livestock, not farming, was the key to success in the Banda Oriental.

From Peasants to Slave Owners

As they struggled to make their livings, the most dramatic change in the colonists' work lives and their status in colonial society was their integration into the region's slave-owning culture. Prior to their arrival in the Río de la Plata, it is likely that only those few colonists who had previously served in the military in the Americas would have had any direct experience with slavery. Rather, as we have already seen, from the perspective of Enlightenment thinkers, these peasants had been the peninsula's slaves—the workhorses of the rural economy, living in the worst of conditions, often barely able to survive. In their treatises, these intellectuals were talking about a figurative kind of economic slavery with which the peasant colonists were all too familiar. In colonial society, slavery had a very different meaning.

Although presumably none of the colonists had ever owned a slave, the intellectual framework surrounding slavery would not have been unfamiliar to them. For instance, they brought with them some knowledge of racial difference. By the eighteenth century, Africans had lived on the Iberian peninsula for centuries, and since the conquest of the Americas, Indians and mixed-race peoples made the transatlantic journey to Spain from time to time. As a result, Africans had both a physical place and a place in the minds of many Spaniards. However, unlike their counterparts in the south of Spain who lived among at least small populations of both free and enslaved Africans, sightings of nonwhite people would have been a rarity in the northern part of the peninsula. Until they arrived at La Coruña, it is more likely that they had either met with or heard about Africans through friends and relatives who had gone to the south in search of work. Large numbers of Gallegos and other northern Spaniards migrated to Cádiz, Sevilla, and Portugal, all of which had significant populations of Africans. In those diverse cities, they often worked in menial jobs like muleteers and porters, which brought them into regular contact with the nonwhite populations who worked in similar occupations.[7]

Most of the colonists had their first introduction to slavery with their arrival at the port of Montevideo. According to the 1780 census, people of color made up more than one quarter of Montevideo's population, more or less equally divided between enslaved and free people—70 Indians, 199 free mulattos, 327 free blacks, and 625 slaves—although the city was less racially diverse and less reliant on slaves than many other Spanish American cities. Having traveled extensively, Francisco Millau y Miraval reported that Montevideo had "a very small number of blacks and mulattos, which were only found in some families."[8]

Racial hierarchies were remarkably fluid in the Río de la Plata. Although Spanish law prohibited nonwhites from engaging in an array of activities, including holding public offices, receiving higher education, participating in many guilds, and becoming members in some civic societies, the enforcement of those laws and their application in daily life were often uneven. Among the lower classes, men of different races and statuses worked together, drank together, and even lived together with little difference in their material circumstances. In Buenos Aires and Montevideo, slaves, both skilled and unskilled, had considerable physical freedom and often worked for wages. The racial and socioeconomic hierarchy could be so complicated that European immigrants could be found working for creole and mixed-race masters and among artisans, and it was not unusual for black and mixed-race master artisans to supervise white apprentices.[9]

At least initially, once they were settled in their new communities, slavery played little or no role in the colonists' lives, in large part because in the early 1780s, the use of slaves in the regional economy and workforce was limited. At the forts on the Buenos Aires frontier, there is only sparse evidence of black inhabitants, either free or enslaved, as the unsettled nature of the frontier did not support the plantation-style agriculture that was associated with large slave populations. Historian Carlos Mayo found that of the sixty-six estancias on the Pampa, forty-one had a total of 164 slaves (90 men and 74 women), a median of only 4 slaves per estancia. In fact, as late as 1815, the area around Chascomús was 88 percent white and only 6 percent black. The situation was more or less the same around the city of Luján, and the civilian population in and around the fort where the colonizers lived was probably even whiter. The parish registers reveal only a few black residents. At Luján on 15 April 1781 Dominga Meneses, a black slave, married Salvador Correa, a free black. In 1794 the priest at Ranchos buried the natural daughter of Rita Martínez, the slave of Manuel Martínez, a lieutenant in the blandengues.[10]

In the Banda Oriental, the black population was also small. At the arrival of the colonists in 1781, Maldonado, with a population of 1,005, had only seventy-eight slaves, twenty of whom were younger than ten years old. In the rural area outside of Maldonado, permanently settled people of color were no more common. There were twenty Indian households, but only six free black households, in which twenty-four people lived. Only nine of the rural white families owned slaves.[11]

Despite the small population of people of color, daily life in their new communities created regular opportunities for interactions between the peasant colonists and their black neighbors, both free and enslaved. In Maldonado, five of the six male *pardos* (a racial term usually referring to a person of mixed African and European parentage) were artisans. Three were tailors and two were shoemakers, although there were also white tailors and shoemakers in town, as well as purveyors of these occupations among the colonists. Even if the colonists did not employ their services (preferring instead to rely on the services of their peninsular counterparts), these men who all worked in the same trade likely knew one another. In addition to meeting in the streets and markets, the races also mixed freely in the area's pulperías. By the end of the century, a number of colonists, including Domingo del Barrio in San Carlos and María Alonso and her husband in Minas, had opened pulperías of their own that served a racially mixed (and mixed-status) clientele.[12]

At first the colonists' ability to own slaves was limited by the fact that they were tied by their contracts to the Crown and lived in limbo for a number of years before being permanently resettled. Moreover, at least at the beginning, they were some of the poorest people in the region, almost entirely reliant on the government for their subsistence. In this way, they were much like other recently arrived immigrants, who were less likely to own slaves than more established residents. Not surprisingly, in Maldonado's 1782 census none of the colonists owned slaves, although a few of their noncolonist neighbors did.[13]

However, the colonists arrived at a critical moment in the history of slavery in the Río de la Plata. Many of the same Bourbon imperatives that underpinned the Patagonia project, in particular the Crown's desire to grow the region's economy, also led to the expansion of slavery. Although merchants imported only a few hundred slaves each year into the Río de la Plata before 1778, after the expulsion of the Portuguese from Colonia del Sacramento that year, Montevideo emerged as the region's slave entrepôt. By 1782–1783, more than 6,000 slaves were being imported into the city. Over the next decade, changes in colonial economic policy, including allowing Spanish colonies to trade with foreign colonies, expanded the legal slave trade with Brazil even further, bringing another 13,500 slaves between 1792 and 1799. In 1791 the port city received the royal monopoly for the introduction of slaves into the Río de la Plata, Chile, and Peru. The impact on the population was significant. Between 1778 and 1810, the slave population of Buenos Aires grew more than 100 percent, and the growth in Montevideo was even more intense. Between 1791 and 1810, the slave population of the frontier town increased 486 percent.[14] In addition to the official counts, slaves also entered the region illegally from both Brazil and the interior of the viceroyalty.

This influx of slaves occurred just as many of the colonists were gaining some economic traction. Therefore, once they were settled, the more successful and entrepreneurial among them began to use their savings in a way that would not have been possible on the peninsula. Although some complained about being cash poor (since the authorities did not provide many of them with their salary for most of the 1780s and 1790s), the fact that the government gave them houses, land, seed, and farm implements allowed some of them to accumulate enough savings to enter the market for slaves. Among the first to own slaves was Francisco Martínez, a farmer from Astorga, who settled in Maldonado in 1781 along with his wife, Francisca, and three children. In their new home, he farmed and worked as a carter. Only seven years later, he had saved enough to purchase a twenty-one-year-old slave named Ventura for 268 pesos fuertes. Francisco Osorio, the apothecary in San Carlos, purchased at least one female slave in the 1780s. By 1803 he owned eight slaves, three men and five women. He and his wife, Francisca Fernández, may have used the slaves to help prepare the medicines that he supplied to the community or to work as domestics or both. Moreover, skilled slaves frequently augmented family incomes through their wage labor. Vicenta Fortuna and her husband, Domingo Núñez, who had left their homes in Galicia where he was a butcher and farmer, settled in San Carlos in 1781. When Domingo died in 1811, he was a carpenter who owned four slaves. As Domingo suffered from some illness that curtailed his ability to work, his slaves may have been a major source of income. According to Pérez del Puerto, despite Domingo's physical problems, in 1799 the family was doing fine.[15]

There were significant differences in the colonist communities' integration into slave owning. In San José, where nearly all the inhabitants were from Asturias, the 1791 census indicates that few owned slaves. Even as the new community expanded, the 413 Spaniards owned only four slaves.[16] In contrast, at Pando the 34 Spanish and "foreign" (presumably Portuguese) married couples and 44 single men owned 3 married slave couples, 16 single men, 12 single women, and 6 children.[17] The difference might be attributed to the ratio of noncolonist slave owners to colonists. The noncolonists may have been more likely to own slaves and to own more slaves than the colonists, or their neighbors' slave owning may have influenced the colonists' decision to purchase African labor.

By the 1790s a number of farming colonists, including Matías Prieto, Cayetano Ignacio Huertas, and Francisco Pérez Brañas, could also afford slaves. Isabel Herrera and her husband, Matías Alonso, were very successful farmers, eventually coming to own a large estancia that they worked with the help of two slaves. Pascuala García was widowed in 1788 and in 1790 married a much younger noncolonist, Domingo Paredes, a farmer. They owned four slaves in 1803. In 1800 Francisco Aparicio purchased a sixteen-year-old female slave named Theresa for 250 pesos. That same year, Juan Antonio de la Fuente bought a male slave in his late twenties for slightly more money, 283 pesos corrientes, and José Rodríguez traded a middle-aged slave named Manuel for three hundred head of cattle.[18]

For poor people who had only recently come into their own land in the Americas, the decision to become slave owners indicates a rapid assimilation into colonial ideas about labor and status. In northern Spain, land was scarce and labor was easy to come by. In the Río de la Plata, the situation was the opposite; for the colonists the land was free, but labor required some capital investment either by paying wage laborers or by purchasing slaves. Moreover, slaves were a means to accumulate wealth, and slave owning was a sign of upward mobility. In fact, in Buenos Aires most slaves were owned by people of modest means who lived almost exclusively off the income produced by their slaves. Even poverty was not necessarily an obstacle to slave ownership. When María, the slave of Martín Pasqual, a neighbor of the colonists in Maldonado, died, the priest noted that her burial service was abbreviated and provided free because of the "recognized poverty" of her master.[19]

Female colonists also entered the world of slave ownership. In 1790, the parish registers note the death of the child of two black slaves owned by Ángela García.[20] Ángela and her first husband, Antonio Cantera, from Palencia, had enlisted along with their three young children. A farmer in Spain, Antonio also took up farming in Maldonado until he died in 1788. It is unclear whether they already owned the slaves and she inherited them or whether Ángela purchased them to help work the farm after his death. Either way, with the move to the Americas, her role as an employer was transformed. On the peninsula, she would have hired day laborers to help her with particular tasks, but the ability to own another person was a novel aspect of her experience in the Río de la Plata.

Slave owning became even more common among the younger generation of colonists and was definitely a sign of their commercial success and integration into the colonial economy. Antonia Menéndez arrived in the Río de la Plata along with her parents at age twelve. She married twice, but by 1836 she was widowed, living with a daughter, one male slave, and four female slaves. According to the 1803 census, Francisco Riestra, who had come to the Río de la Plata with his parents as a colonist at the age of thirteen, later lived in Montevideo with his wife, son, and one slave. At the same time, Cayetano Otero, who had arrived at age fifteen, was living in Montevideo with his wife and children. He owned a pulpería and three slaves, and he had three peons living with and working for him.[21] Many of the colonists who settled close to Montevideo were artisans, and presumably their slaves may have been at least semiskilled laborers who aided them with their work.

The relationship between slaves and masters in farm labor was complicated, as men of different races and statuses typically worked side by side in planting and harvesting, as well as caring for livestock. Prior to the great expansion of slavery in the 1790s, the Río de la Plata suffered from a general scarcity of workers, forcing landowners to employ whoever was available and willing to work, regardless of race or status. Thus, the workforce of the region's estancias included gauchos, peons, and slaves. When wages were high, gauchos took on more estancia work, but when wages were low, landowners relied more heavily on slaves as a response to the dearth of reliable paid laborers. In fact, the permanence of slaves in comparison with the rest of the workforce meant that black slaves sometimes supervised mixed-race and white peons.[22] Before coming to the Río de la Plata, many of the colonists had worked as temporary wage laborers, often traveling long distances during the harvest season, and some may have hired day laborers themselves. Therefore, it is possible that, at least initially, these poor settlers utilized slave labor to augment their own work on their farms with little differentiation between the work completed by themselves and their families and that done by slave labor.

The most striking effect of slave ownership on the peasant colonists was its transformation of the gendered division of labor, as slaves frequently took on work that peasant women had engaged in on the peninsula. In northern Spain, most peasants worked small plots, sometimes supplemented by small-scale animal husbandry. On those peasant farms, men and women worked side by side in the fields. Both Enlightenment thinkers and foreign travelers regularly commented on northern peasant women's field labor. Englishman Alexander Jardine remarked that "women in Galicia also drive the carts, steer the plow and spread manure, frequently by hand, instead of using a pitchfork." Moreover, in the parts of northern Spain that were marked by high rates of male migration, women did all or much of the agricultural labor and cared for livestock without male assistance.[23]

Once they settled in the rural Río de la Plata, the colonists quickly came to understand that slaves, not women, were expected to do much of that type of work. So, for instance, once Francisco Aparicio and his wife, Teodora de Plada, purchased slaves, it is likely that the slaves cared for the animals, freeing Teodora for other tasks. On the peninsula, it frequently fell to women to supplement family incomes by engaging in income-generating activities such spinning, selling surplus produce at market, or earning extra wages as harvesters, hoers, and weeders. In the Río de la Plata, slaves supplemented their owners' incomes by working as day laborers. In fact, the use of slaves as supplemental wage earners may have led Félix de Azara to criticize the laziness of rural women in the region. He described rural white women as dirty and foul pigs and dismissed their work as only "sweeping, [and] maintaining the fire to cook the meat and heat the water for the mate, without either spinning or sewing." Someone was working hard. Historian Donna Guy has argued that "women's cottage industries formed a mainstay of the provincial economies in the north, west, and center of the country," and Susan Socolow has asserted that women played a critical role in the rural subsistence economy.[24] If Azara did not see white women "working" in the rural Río de la Plata, it may have been that they left those tasks to slaves or hired free women of color.

The presence of female domestic slaves had the potential to significantly alter the work tasks of female colonists. On the peninsula, peasant women were accustomed to moving seamlessly between what Serrana Rial García has called the "floating frontier" between domestic and outdoor labor.[25] In the Río de la Plata, with slaves available to wash the laundry or cook or help tend the garden, they could engage in less rigorous work. Moreover, as colonial society viewed indoor work as more appropriate for women, the presence of slaves allowed the female colonists to restrict their tasks accordingly. In general, slave ownership gave peasant women some choices: they could decide what work they preferred and assign the less desirable tasks to slaves. Just as important, slave ownership gave these poor peninsular women some status in their new communities and clearly differentiated them from other poor white women.

Without any previous experience of slavery, the colonists had to learn what colonial society expected in terms of relations between masters and slaves.[26] Coincidentally, just as the first colonists were becoming slave owners, the Crown issued an edict on slave treatment, *Real Cédula de su Magestad sobre la educación, trato y ocupaciones de los esclavos* (His Majesty's Royal Decree on the Education, Treatment, and Work of Slaves [1789]), that may have been influential in this process. Twelve copies were distributed in Buenos Aires for the viceroyalty. For the most part, the decree was a compilation of previously issued royal edicts with few additions, promulgated in response to the French *Code Noir* and as another of the paternalistic reforms of the Bourbon kings.[27] Noting the failure of many owners to follow earlier laws, the preamble admonished slave owners to comply with the "principles and rules dictated by religion, humanity, and the good of the State, compatible with slavery and public tranquility." Owners were expected to baptize their slaves when necessary and to teach them Christian doctrine. They were not to work, either for themselves or for their masters, on holy days except during harvest time, and every day at the end of work, masters and or overseers were to pray the rosary with them. The decree asserted that the "primary" occupation of slaves was to be agriculture, and that they were to engage only in work appropriate to their ages and sexes. Owners were to house, dress, and feed them appropriately. To prevent fornication, owners

Figure 8.1. African women laundering on the shore beneath the fort at Buenos Aires. Emeric Essex Vidal, from *Picturesque Illustrations of Buenos Aires and Monte Video* (London: R. Ackerman, 1820).

were supposed to encourage their slaves to marry. The last seven sections of the decree attempted to regulate the use of punishment, especially violent punishment, by owners.

Authorities made no attempt to enforce the code, yet it faced significant opposition from slave owners across Spanish America. It was suspended in 1795 but never revoked.[28] Scholars agree that, in general, the decree had little impact on the treatment of slaves in the region. However, unlike other residents of the Río de la Plata, the colonists lived under the direct supervision of royal authorities. As a result, it is likely that they knew about the decree and that it had some influence on their behavior toward their slaves.

Beyond the expectations articulated in the decree, the easiest way to acquire knowledge of how to treat one's slaves was by watching other slave owners. A number of the shopkeepers in Maldonado owned a few slaves, and as the colonists went about their daily routines they would have witnessed how shopkeeper Domingo Almeda interacted with his slaves and could have chatted with the three slaves owned by the butcher, Pedro José Pérez, as they made their purchases.[29] They could use those interactions as a touchstone for their own experiences as slave owners.

The colonists also learned how to interact with their slaves from Padre Manuel de Amenedo Montenegro, a fellow Gallego and the parish priest of San Carlos. Beginning in the early 1790s, Padre Amenedo used slaves to help with the construction of the parish church. Among other tasks, his slaves Juan, Joaquín, and Pedro opened wells to catch rainwater. In 1799 Amenedo complained that he needed additional workers and wanted to purchase up to seven slaves for the purpose so that he would not have to pay wage laborers. On his behalf, Pérez del Puerto petitioned the viceroy for permission to import from Brazil "various blacks" to Maldonado to work on the church. During the construction, their work went uncompensated; however, Amenedo did not fail to pay them because they were slaves, but because he was short on funds for the construction. At the end of the project in 1801, Amenedo paid his slaves their back wages. In addition to these government-owned slaves, local owners also contributed their slaves' labor. A slave, Antonio Rodríguez, was provided by his master to work for six days for charity and then was paid four reales per day as a wage laborer. Still other slaves were lent to the construction of the church as payment for a debt owed by their master.[30] Thus, the construction of the parish church taught the colonists about the intricacies of slave and wage labor in the region.

The colonists' treatment of their slaves was also grounded in both their sense of duty to the Crown and their personal piety. As with all large groups of people, there might be considerable diversity in individual colonists' sense of obligation to comply with legal norms and religious ideals. Some colonists willingly fulfilled the expectations of the decree while others circumvented or ignored the demands made upon them as slave owners by the Crown.

In the parish documentation, we can see that many of the colonists did what was expected in terms of caring for the souls of their slaves, in particular having the children born to their slaves baptized. (Of course, the nature of the documentation does not allow us to know of the existence of children who were not baptized.) So, when Joaquín and Juana, both slaves of Matías Alonso, had a child, she was duly baptized. Slave owners were also expected to have any unconverted slaves that they might own baptized, as when José Borrego had the sacrament administered to two teenage male slaves who had

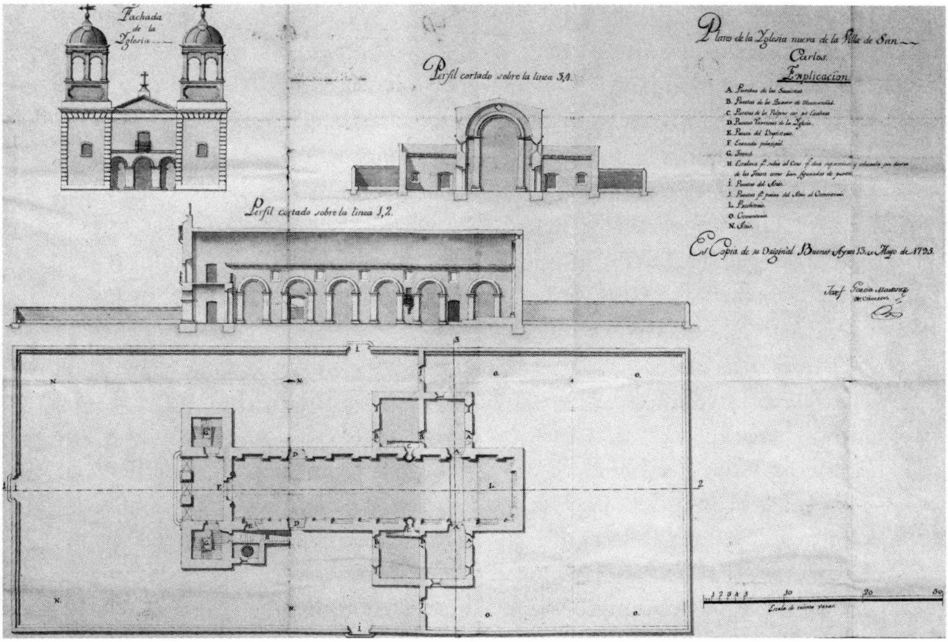

Figure 8.2. Plan for the church in San Carlos built for the colonists with slave labor. España (1795). Ministerio de Educación, Cultura y Deporte. Archivo General de Indias. AGI, MP-Buenos Aires, 190.

been born in Africa.[31] In doing so, the colonists took the first step to connect their slaves to the Catholic Church and to aid in their salvation.

A clearer measure of the colonists' investment in the spiritual lives of their slaves is the decision to allow them to marry. According to Castilian laws dating from the middle ages, all Christians, whether free or enslaved, had the right to marry, and they could marry either free or enslaved partners, although marriage to a free person did not change the enslaved person's status. Slaves were even allowed to marry when their owners opposed the marriage.[32] The 1789 decree urged slave owners to encourage their slaves to marry, even if it meant purchasing the spouse or potential spouse from another owner.

The decree's emphasis on marriage may have influenced colonist Domingo de Castro. He arrived from Asturias on the *Santa Ana 2* at the age of twenty-two and settled in Minas in 1783, where a year later he married the daughter of other colonists. Although it is unclear what profession he chose, by 1788 he was prosperous enough to own some slaves. In 1791 he had the parish priest administer the sacrament of marriage when his slave Antonio married another of his slaves, Juana. Among the witnesses were a slave of doña Bárbara Frontan and Isabel María, a free black woman. In 1798 Rosalia, the slave of Francisco Osorio, the apothecary, married a slave belonging to another owner. A few years later, a slave belonging to José Nava and his wife, Manuela, married the slave of another Asturian colonizer, Juan Santurio.[33] These married slave couples in turn produced legitimate, although enslaved, children. In 1800 a legitimate child was born to Juan (the slave of Astorgan colonist Antonio Revillo) and his wife, Cristina, the slave of one María Quadrado.

Other colonists did not seem to take as much care to ensure that their slaves' sexual activity occurred within the confines of marriage. Tomás Corbo's slave Juana had at least two illegitimate children, one in 1797 and another in 1802. The first child was baptized by fellow colonist José Borrego, who also appears in the baptismal record of another illegitimate child of a colonist's slave in 1805. When Joaquina, the child of María Morena, the slave of colonist Francisco Vicente, received the sacrament of baptism, her godmother was a slave belonging to José Borrego, and Borrego himself acted as a witness as did colonist Miguel Malo.[34]

Many factors militated against the colonists' ability or desire to regulate their slaves' sexual activity. They not only came from a peninsular culture that tolerated nonmarital sex, most came to slave owning with very little, if any, religious education. Even if they understood the religious implications of nonmarital sex, they were likely unable to articulate those spiritual concerns to their slaves. Moreover, the relative ease with which slaves moved around the region meant that they were often outside of their owners' supervision. And finally, the fact that many other slave owners did not encourage marriage among their slaves must have served as permission for the colonists to ignore both the civil and religious admonishments.

Although we will see that godparentage provided important connections among white women in in these communities, as was true in neighboring Brazil, masters generally did not act as godparents to their own slaves. Rather, other blacks, both free and enslaved, agreed to take spiritual responsibility for slave children. For example, the godmother of the illegitimate child of Tomás Corbo's slave was Rosa Recuero, the *morena* slave of another colonist, Manuel Recuero.[35]

Death provided the colonists with one last opportunity to see to the spiritual welfare of their slaves. Early on, Domingo de Castro made a somewhat halfhearted attempt. On the one hand, when one of his (unnamed) slaves died, Domingo paid for a Catholic burial and had his death registered in the parish register. On the other hand, the priest also noted that the slave had not received last rites before his death, as Domingo had not let the priest know of his impending death in time to administer the sacrament. However, with time, colonists like Miguel Malo in San Carlos took greater care to ensure a quality afterlife for their slaves.[36]

Beyond participating in the sacraments, as was their right as Christians, both slaves and free blacks engaged in community religious life alongside the colonists as members of the confraternity of the Virgin of the Rosary. In Spain those confraternities, founded by Dominicans, were common after the Catholic Reformation, and in the Americas they were often associated with people of color. When Ana Lobato, a colonist from Astorga, died in 1784, the parish register of Maldonado noted that she was a member of the confraternity of the Virgin of the Rosary. Four years later, when Antonio, a black slave, died, he was given the customary burial as a member of the same confraternity.[37] At least early in the history of these communities, religious activity also provided a forum for interactions between blacks and whites, free people and slaves.

As the colonists worked alongside and tended (or not) to the spiritual needs of their slaves, it is difficult to assess the degree to which the colonists engaged in sexual relations with blacks, either enslaved or free. Without a doubt, formalized relationships between blacks and whites were rare. By the end of the eighteenth century, although interracial marriages among nonwhites across the region became increasingly common, whites almost never married outside their race. Even in racially diverse Buenos Aires, Susan Socolow found that fewer than 10 percent of marriages were between social or racial unequals. Surely social pressure against whites marrying nonwhites increased when Viceroy Vértiz promulgated the Royal Pragmatic on Marriages in 1778, which allowed parents to prohibit marriages between their children and partners whom they deemed unequals, but all the evidence indicates that in the countryside marriages between whites and nonwhites were equally rare prior to 1778. For instance, in her study of San Isidro between 1731 and 1773, Sandra Olivero found only one instance of a white marrying a nonwhite.[38]

It is clear that a number of factors related to the colonists' contracts worked against their marrying people of other races. Not only were marriages between men of color and white women unheard of, but men of color in the rural areas were unlikely to have the funds necessary to compensate the Crown for a female colonist's transportation as required by authorities. Moreover, the fact that the colonists had to ask permission to marry outside of the colonist cohort may have made them even less likely to marry interracially, as it exposed them to the questions of social and racial inequality expressed by the Royal Pragmatic. Finally, the colonists lived among their families and neighbors, who brought with them certain sensibilities about not only racial endogamy, but also peninsular regional endogamy. As, at least among the colonists, Asturians were unlikely to marry Catalans, it was even less likely that they would marry Indians or Africans. The intraregional cohesion that characterized the project from the beginning served to reinforce interracial sexual sensibilities.

In that context, it comes as no surprise that only one colonist married a nonwhite woman and that she was Indian. José Ventura Echavarría, from Vizcaya, became a colonist at the age of nine along with his mother and his stepfather, Francisco Violeta. The family settled in San Carlos, where José Ventura did farm work and lived with his stepfather. In 1800 Echavarría married María Andrea Pereira, an Indian woman from Santa Teresa. When María Andrea died less than one year later, he then married another *india*, María Hipolita Carballo, from Misiones.[39] Unlike any of his counterparts, growing up in the Río de la Plata evidently influenced his spousal preferences.

Certainly marriage was not the only way to have relations with people of other races, and the rapid expansion of the mestizo and mulatto population during the last decades of the eighteenth century demonstrates that interracial sex was common. Although it is very likely that male colonists had illicit sexual relations with both free and enslaved nonwhite women, the evidence for those encounters in the colonists' communities is largely absent. We do know that the authorities worried about such relationships. In 1796 a military official outside of Buenos Aires complained about single women of color wandering through the countryside engaging in illicit sexual relations. According to the official, these women lived in rented rooms and were often drunk and disorderly. They "destroyed" families, stealing men from their wives and children.[40] However, despite the fact that these and other sexual encounters must have produced offspring, those children are not visible in the parish documentation, as in these communities, parish priests never designated the race of a foundling or child of an unknown father. Nor did these parishes keep separate registers for nonwhites, as was common in some urban areas. There are many explanations for the lack of racial indicators in these frontier parishes and the lack of specificity about the race of the participants. First, many of the priests were just sloppy in their record keeping. For instance, during his 1804 visit to the parish at Minas, Bishop of Buenos Aires Benito Lué y Riega had to remind the priest to keep to the prescribed form, including writing the date correctly and noting the age of the person being baptized.[41] Second, at least from the perspective of the church, a person's race was inconsequential in terms of the administration of the sacraments. Including that information, as well as free or enslaved status, was purely customary.

There is no documentary evidence that any of the male colonists fathered children by nonwhite women; however, as the colonists settled down, a close examination of the baptismal records in Minas and other communities reveals a very different and significant change in community norms. Although between the arrival of the colonists and 1806 the numbers of illegitimate children remained low, the parish at Minas saw a significant increase in the numbers of *expósitos* (abandoned children) in the second decade after settlement. During the first decade at Minas (between 1783 and 1792), only one or two abandoned children were baptized annually (out of approximately twenty to thirty total baptisms per year). However, beginning in 1793, although the numbers of illegitimate births remained steady at two or three per year, the numbers of abandoned children increased dramatically and faster than the birthrate generally. In 1797 six or more abandoned children were being baptized annually. By 1800 thirteen of the eighty-two children baptized were foundlings. The same was true at Canelones, where the growth in the numbers of foundlings far outpaced both the growth in the number of total baptisms and the numbers of illegitimate children.[42] Unfortunately, it is impossible to know how many of the parents of these foundlings were colonists or their children. Yet, considering the fact that the colonists made up the largest group of new inhabitants of these communities, it is likely they produced at least some of these foundlings. It is also interesting to note that colonists never stood as godparents for any of the foundlings (although one colonist, Juan Amor, was a godparent for the baptism of an Englishman converting to Catholicism). According to canon law, they could not be godparents if they were already the parents or grandparents of the children. Finally, in neither the parish documentation nor the extensive genealogical histories that have been completed for the Banda Oriental have any of the colonists' children or grandchildren born in the Americas been described as mixed-race. If the intention was to hide the children produced by interracial relationships, then these communities were particularly successful in that regard.

If indeed the colonists were the parents of at least some of these children, and particularly if one parent was not white, the growth in the number of expósitos could indicate the continued influence of the more rigid morality of imperial authorities. As the colonists remained under the supervision of viceregal authorities until the end of the century, they may have perceived some benefit in terms of that relationship in opting for abandonment over baptizing an illegitimate child. It is also possible that the parish priest influenced the decision in some way, possibly through his own stricter morality. Whatever the case, although illegitimacy rates and the toleration for nonmarital sex seem to have been more or less the same on the peninsula and in the rural Río de la Plata, the colonists may have faced more intense surveillance by imperial authorities than other inhabitants, prompting them to abandon their illegitimate children rather than raise them.[43]

Beyond work and sex, one particular case indicates that interracial interactions in the new communities could be complicated. Doña Ana María Olmos, the wife of Francisco Zeballos (both from Palencia), ran an unregistered pulpería out of the couple's home in Minas, probably to bring in some additional income. According to court documents, on 27 July 1802 she was enjoying a relaxing morning. A neighbor was inside the house playing the guitar, and Ana María was outside of her house dancing and playing with an eleven-year-old girl, when a *mulatillo* named Pedro Ignacio stopped by to purchase some pies. Ana María began dancing with the young mulatto when suddenly Juan Antonio Álvarez, the sergeant of the militias, angrily strode up to them wanting to know who was making fun of him. According to Álvarez, as he walked by, the mulatto had made a farting noise with his mouth, an offense made more insulting by Pedro Ignacio's youth and race. Without warning, Álvarez attacked Pedro Ignacio. Ana María grabbed Álvarez by the shoulder and told him to leave. According to Ana María, Álvarez hit her hard enough to throw her to the ground, and then he beat her with a stick. According to Álvarez, Ana María retaliated by pulling his hair and shouting insults at him. The little girl ran for help, and eventually neighbors arrived to separate them. Álvarez stormed off and then went around town around calling Ana María a "really big whore."[44] This incident shows that on one level, the races interacted comfortably, as Ana María not only sold goods to a mulatto child but also danced with him and stepped up to protect him from the sergeant's violence. It also reveals racial tensions that were serious enough to push Sergeant Álvarez to beat that same mulatto child over a rude noise and to call Ana María a whore for cavorting with her perceived social inferiors.

Having chatted and danced with people of other races, the colonists must have been completely shocked by an incident that occurred only a year later in San Carlos. Two slaves, Simon and Joaquín, set fire to the home of the captain of the militias, Manuel Correa, killing the captain; his wife, Francisca; their sixteen-year-old son, José; and four others. The assailants belonged to a Portuguese man, Domingo García, from Río Grande do Sul, and were in transit, staying at the captain's home. Although the two were captured only days later, the racial equilibrium (no matter how fragile) that had existed in the town had been broken; for the colonists, the uprising and attack on the captain's home was their first experience with the danger inherent in living in a slave society. However, this violent act was not an isolated incident.[45] At approximately the same time, an uprising occurred in Montevideo in which twenty slave and free African men fled the city and created a maroon community in the Río Yi. The authorities responded violently to this act of resistance, attacking the settlement, making examples of the survivors, returning the slaves to their masters, and executing some of the free blacks.[46] With this episode, the colonists learned that living in a slave society came with some substantial dangers.

From Colonists to *Vecinos*

Work and slavery were not the only means through which the colonists integrated into American society. Because of their complicated status as colonists, they relied on the establishment of the basic institutions of Spanish and Spanish American religious and political life to formalize their place in the Río de la Plata and to reconfigure their relationship with royal authorities.

When the colonists arrived, religious structures in the Buenos Aires countryside were flimsy at best. In 1780 the entire region outside of the city was served by only fifteen parishes. With the exception of those who lived near the town of Luján, which already had a parish, most of the inhabitants relied on the forts to provide for their spiritual needs until after the wars of independence. In fact, the Guardia de los Ranchos and other forts only became parishes after Buenos Aires's control of the region was consolidated and it became clear that the colonists' situation was permanent.[47]

Although there were plenty of secular clergy in the region, most held lay benefices and were not available for parish work. As a result, a combination of military chaplains and itinerant regular clergy administered the sacraments to the colonists and their families. Many of them were poorly trained in pastoral care and basic parish administration, as indicated by the visitations by Bishop Sebastián Malvar y Pinto in 1778 (who had come to the Río de la Plata on the *Princesa* along with the first colonists) and by Bishop Lué y Riega in 1803–1805. At the Guardia de los Ranchos, Bishop Lué y Riega had to remind the parish priest to give catechism classes and teach doctrine either before or after mass, to prohibit wandering or unlicensed clergy from administering the sacraments, and to correctly record information in the parish registers. He also noted the "extreme" poverty of the facilities. The fort chapel had no black vestments for funerals, and he described the baptismal font as "highly indecent." In the countryside outside of Buenos Aires, religious devotion had a markedly frontier character. Félix de Azara reported that rural parishioners sometimes heard mass from horseback.[48]

In the Banda Oriental, the situation was not much different. The Jesuits had been the dominant religious force in much of the region prior to their expulsion in 1767, but their work was focused on the indigenous population, not on establishing parishes for or administering the sacraments to the settlers. Observers found both urban and rural ecclesiastical structures in a state of disrepair. According to Diego de Alvear, even the main church in Montevideo, the *iglesia matriz*, which dated from the 1740s, was poor and dirty. Not surprisingly, the rural parishes were in no better shape. When Bishop Malvar y Pinto made his first official visit to the church at Maldonado just before colonists were settled there, he noted that there was no baptismal font.[49]

To remedy these deficits, after the colonists' homes were completed, Indians and local artisans began construction on new churches. By all accounts, the result at Minas was impressive. After giving a sermon in the new church, José Manuel Pérez Castellanos noted, "I never tired of looking at it" and that although Buenos Aires had its share of fine churches, "none were more splendid." As we have already seen, construction of a new church at San Carlos began in November 1792 using slave labor. Some of the colonists volunteered to haul building materials, but many parishioners were not happy about the weekly collections to fund the construction.[50] Work was slow and the church was not completed until 1801.

Facilities were not the only problem. Both clergy and parishioners engaged in activities that were less than orthodox. At both Maldonado and at Nuestra Señora de Guadalupe (Canelones), Bishop Malvar y Pinto chastised the clergy for administering "lesser" burials for the poor (without vigils or bells or other pomp), reminding them that the poor should be buried with the same solemnity as others. He also prohibited the "scandalous" wakes that occurred with the death of an infant, in which it was "customary to offend with fires and dances."[51] Faced with such "abuses," it was clear that the residents of the rural Río de la Plata required some religious education. Certainly, the colonists would benefit from regular sermons and catechism classes, as they had come from one of the most poorly served and poorly educated parts of the peninsula. Fortunately, they were settling down just as the region was experiencing a spiritual revival. In 1788 the city council of Buenos Aires suggested reviving the custom of sending missions to the rural areas, filling a gap left after the expulsion of the Jesuits. For the most part, this task was taken up by Franciscans, who had recently founded the Colegio de Misioneros de San Carlos in Santa Fe. For the next three years, missions took place regularly across the region, including the new communities of the colonists.[52] By all accounts, the religious event that attracted the most enthusiasm was the visit of Madre María Antonia Figueroa y Paz (known as Mama Antula), a Jesuit *beata*. She spent three years in and around Montevideo, bringing her version of the Spiritual Exercises to the masses, attracting throngs of people from both the city and the countryside.[53]

For the female colonists, regardless of their individual piety, the solidification of parish life allowed them to move beyond their official designation as colonists toward a more familiar and comfortable community identity—that of parishioner. Across the Spanish Empire, the church, with its regular rhythms of masses, holy days, and sacraments, structured everyone's, but particularly women's, public lives. No matter where they hailed from on the peninsula, the baptism of a child or marriage of a young couple initiated festivities organized by women that bound women to one another. Each time a woman had an infant baptized, she created or reinforced connections both with the parish as an institution and with other women and men in the community through godparentage. In addition to spiritual guidance, godparentage provided physical protection for children, so most mothers looked to women from their same age cohort to act as godmothers. Escolástica Cordero sought out her sister-in-law Casimira, her friend Lorenza Aparicio, whom she had known in Floridablanca, and Juana Fresco, a new friend in Minas,

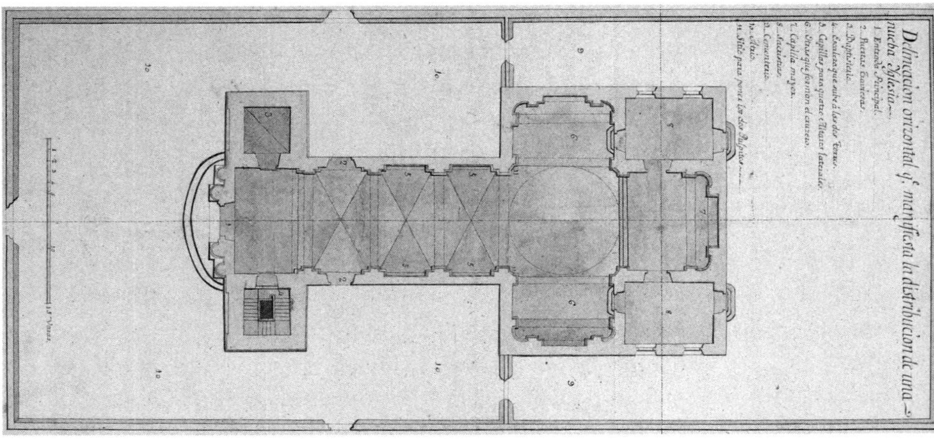

Figure 8.3. Plan for the new parish church in Maldonado (1796). España. Ministerio de Educación, Cultura y Deporte. Archivo General de Indias. AGI, MP-Buenos Aires, 195.

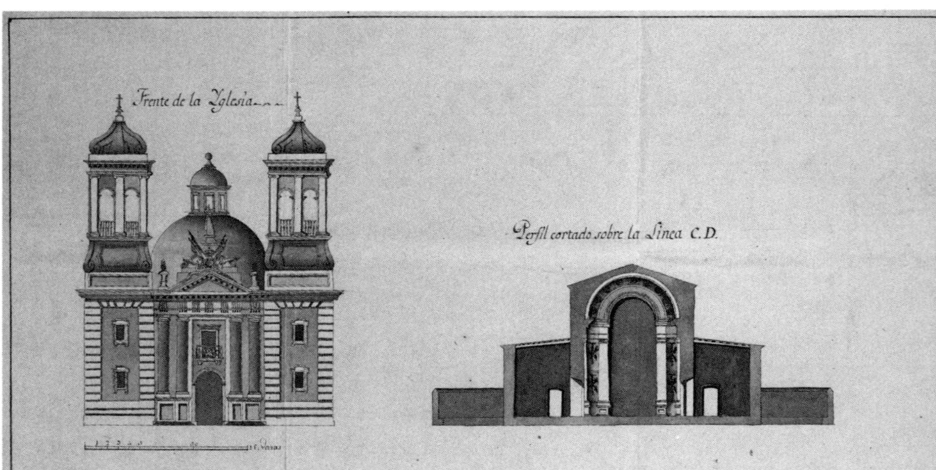

Figure 8.4. Design for the main facade of the new parish church at Maldonado (1796). España. Ministerio de Educación, Cultura y Deporte. Archivo General de Indias. AGI, MP-Buenos Aires, 196.

as godmothers for her many children, knowing that each of these women would be willing to care for their godchildren if tragedy struck.

Beyond baptism, parish life provided other opportunities for women to interact. At San Carlos, the death of a member brought out the confraternity of the Virgin of the Rosary, which included female members, to accompany the body to burial.[54] Local festivals in honor of patron saints created additional opportunities for female organizing and socializing. In 1787 the city council of Maldonado dedicated the parish to San Fernando with such a festival on May 30.[55] These events were as much social as religious affairs. Pérez Castellano recounted his visit to the parish festival at Canelones, at which he heard a funny ballad, composed by a Gallego (likely one of the colonists), and noted that lots of people came to the town not to participate in the festival, but to fool around on the way there.[56] Attendance at mass, no matter how regular, was an opportunity for women to gather, gossip, and pray. As was true across the Spanish Empire, women's contributions to parish life were present in other ways, including the production of the textiles that decorated the altars.

The regularization of their religious lives provided some continuity and stability for the colonists, but they continued to chafe at the Crown's unwillingness to resolve their status. Despite the fact that many were no longer receiving their government supplement, they were still beholden to the Crown through their contracts. Traditionally, Spaniards expected a certain reciprocity between themselves and the Crown. In return for their love and loyalty, Spanish subjects believed that the Crown would be responsive to their needs. As a consequence, far from being cowed by authority figures, peasants were accustomed to pursuing grievances against and denouncing injustices to both local officials and the monarchy.[57] The colonists believed that they had dutifully fulfilled the terms of their contracts by volunteering for the project, crossing the Atlantic, and being settled and then resettled around the Río de la Plata. Their inability to move out from under royal supervision and control their own destinies was both frustrating and emasculating.

In 1784 the colonists resolved to take political action, designating representatives to act on their behalf in a series of petitions to royal authorities. Bernabé de Cal, a farmer and carpenter from Galicia, represented the colonists from the Banda Oriental, and Adriano de la Infiesta, a farmer from the mountains of Asturias, represented the colonists settled at the forts outside of Buenos Aires and Colonia del Sacramento. Later, Ignacio de Otero, a

Gallego and one of the first colonists to arrive in the Río de la Plata, took over for Bernabé de Cal.

The petitions from the peasant colonists focused on the Crown's failure to meet its obligations to them.[58] They argued that despite having "conceded decisions about our subsistence" to the "State and the Republic," they had not received their due. They made their expectations and their sense of disappointment clear. According to one petition, having willingly abandoned their native lands for this project, the colonists had expected that "we would find in those lands the relief that the always merciful and generous hand of Your Majesty offered us; but on the contrary, we have come to this day with so much misfortune, that far from having found the remedy for our anxieties and surprises, we see ourselves without the few comforts to which we were reduced in our native lands." The Crown was not only obligated to provide for them financially, as detailed in their contracts, but they also expected "royal power" to "always be inclined to make your loyal vassals happy." Furthermore, they asserted the superiority of their understanding of justice over that espoused by the Crown, arguing that the reasons the Crown gave for not paying them were neither "right" nor "just."[59] They got the attention of at least lower-level authorities who complained that the colonists were bombarding them with complaints.

Beyond the Crown's failure to fulfill its obligations to the colonists, the petitions expressed two central grievances against royal authorities. The first, and without a doubt the most urgent, was their failure to be paid the daily real; the second was their lack of fixed residence—that they remained sin destino fixo. The failure of the Crown to pay the *real diario* created both practical and symbolic problems. As we have seen, some of the less successful families continued to rely on the supplement, a situation that had to be remedied for the health and well-being of their families; however, their reputations were also at stake. The petitions asserted that they were forced to rely on the credit provided by local retailers and could not support themselves by virtue of their own hard work. Good credit was an integral part of a Spanish man's sense of honor and identity, and the idea of credit did not differentiate between the two key meanings of the word: financial solvency and trustworthiness. The situation was made worse by the fact that some colonists had been paid, while many others had not.[60] The Crown was forcing these dutiful subjects into a socially unacceptable and inequitable situation that denied them their economic independence and impugned their reputations as respectable men.

The other grievance articulated by the colonists was that until they were designated as having a fixed residence, they could not permanently acquire property and or enjoy the rights of *vecindad* (citizenship), which many of them had on the peninsula and that was afforded to their neighbors.[61] Those rights might include access to communal lands, participation in local politics, and some economic privileges like lower tariffs in return for payment of taxes and participation in the militia. Lack of vecindad implied political and social limbo and a degree of personal liberty that peninsular Spaniards found dangerous in others and demeaning to themselves.[62] Indeed, their unclear status was plainly articulated in the documentation, both secular and ecclesiastical, in which the colonists were almost always referred to as *pobladores*, a denomination that clearly defined them by their contracts, rather than as vecinos (citizens). So, as the Crown was unwilling to grant them the desired citizenship, the colonists began to constitute themselves as citizens by making themselves vecinos through the formation of cabildos, or city councils.[63]

Peninsular Spaniards had a long history of municipal self-governance; however, as late as the 1780s such formalized government structures were rare in the Banda Oriental.[64] The formation of town councils not only gave the rural population the ability to regulate itself, but also allowed the peasants to eschew their status as colonists in favor of the more standardized rights and privileges of vecinos. In Maldonado, residents formed the first cabildo in 1784, although no colonists served, probably due to their interim status. The cabildo oversaw a variety of mundane tasks, from arranging celebrations for the births and deaths of royal family members to penalizing local artisans who insisted on working on holidays. At one point, they tried to regulate "diversions" both inside the home and in public, and they arranged for the extermination of the always-problematic wild-dog population.[65] However, the actual activities of the cabildos were much less important than the symbolic act of organizing one's own affairs, no matter how trivial.

Among the new communities, the residents of Santa Lucía were among the first to establish local governance; in the mid-1780s they formed a *medio cabildo*, a modified town council made up of an *alcalde* (magistrate), a *procurador* (solicitor), and an *aguacil mayor* (law enforcement officer).[66] For José Lavandera and José Costales, Asturian farmers who were among the first town councilmen in Santa Lucía, their participation in the town council reflected their change in status from poor men reliant on the Crown for subsistence to independent self-governing citizens.[67] For reasons that are not entirely clear, in San José the move toward self-governance was slower; residents did not form a medio cabildo until 1795. Nevertheless, when Manuel Fernández Félix, the first elected alcalde, and his Asturian neighbors Francisco Fernández Porley, who served as the first procurador, and Francisco Verde, elected as the first aguacil mayor, began their tenures in office, they also initiated a new relationship with both the administrators of the Patagonia project and the Crown.[68]

Upper-class men expected to use politics to advance their own gender and class interests, but lower-class men were also political actors and understood the importance of creating and participating in politics.[69] As they formed cabildos in their new communities, they created new corporate identities that moved them beyond their status as colonists and foreigners, while at the same time they wrestled away some of the authority of the royal and military officials who had overseen the project since its inception.[70] Moreover, the cabildos demonstrated their individual and corporate independence and asserted their ability to regulate and govern themselves, their families, and their communities. In all respects, the creation of cabildos reasserted the colonists' masculinity and their place in the Spanish Empire.

Despite the persistent complaints from the colonists, the Crown found it difficult to extricate itself from the Patagonia project. By the late 1780s, only a few peasants had managed to buy themselves out of their contracts, usually by repaying one year's worth of the daily real and the housing supplement. A few colonists had died and others had deserted, but the costs related to the project continued to spiral out of control. The Tribunal de Cuentas in Buenos Aires complained that it was spending more than forty thousand pesos annually on the colonists, an expenditure which they described as useless and "intolerable," despite the fact that it was approximately the same amount as the viceroy's salary. To help reduce costs, royal authorities even briefly considered allowing the colonists to return to Spain.[71] Only one took advantage of the offer. Juan Gallo, a single man from Asturias, had had his fill of America. He had been sent to San Julián, then to Santa Lucía after the Patagonian outposts were abandoned, and then to San José. In 1789 he departed for his native land. It is not surprising that others chose to remain. They had already been gone for a decade and, having sold off their lands and possessions, most had nothing to return to.

Just as some of the administrators were trying to resolve the colonists' situation, the new viceroy, Nicolás de Arredondo (r. 1789–1795), contemplated reviving the plan to colonize Puerto Deseado as a means to secure the territory and supply the growing number of vessels traversing the Straits of Magellan. After Alejandro Malaspina's expedition to the Patagonian coast reignited his enthusiasm for the project, Arredondo gave permission to the Real Compañía Marítima, the Royal Maritime Company, to establish outposts there, and he briefly considered moving some of the colonists back to Patagonia. However, Pérez del Puerto strenuously argued against moving the colonists yet again.[72] Nevertheless, in April 1794 the viceroy ordered that some colonists still living in Montevideo should be given only fifteen days to prepare to leave for a colony created by the Real Compañía Marítima in Puerto Deseado. In the end, nothing came of this effort, but in later petitions, the peasant colonists described "the terror" that they experienced after hearing that they might have to live in the "miserable state" that they believed awaited them in Patagonia.[73]

Finally, in February 1799 Viceroy Gabriel de Avilés (r. 1799–1801) initiated the process of liquidating the remaining colonists' contracts, more than twenty years after the project's inception. It was an accounting nightmare. Royal authorities made detailed notes of how many days of payments each colonist was owed, who had died, who had been born, and which women had married out of the colonist cohort and were therefore ineligible for any compensation after the date of their marriages.[74] They carefully tallied up the number of days and calculated the number of pesos, which ranged into the tens of thousands per family. It seems unlikely that all of the colonists received every peso that they were owed, but the Crown made a good faith effort to acknowledge its outstanding debts to the peasants.

For a few colonists, the colonizing adventure was still not over. Félix de Azara, fresh from his expedition to delineate the border with Brazil, suggested to Viceroy Avilés that he use the colonists to establish some new communities, in particular San Gabriel de Batoví, along the border for security purposes. Avilés concurred, noting that as recently as 1801 many of the colonists were still living without a permanent residence, "useless to the State" and a drain on the royal treasury. Azara tried to recruit volunteers from those who were living in Montevideo, but only eight or ten families expressed a willingness to be moved again. He tried to lure the colonists at Pando and Colonia del Sacramento to go, but they also refused. Instead, they requested that they be released from their contracts and given "complete freedom." Unimpressed with his handful of volunteers, whom he judged too old and not smart enough, Azara agreed to let some of them settle instead in the new town at Rocha, leaving only four families to go to Batoví. Yet, as moving day approached, even those four came up with all kinds of excuses not to move again.[75] The official in charge of the event waited all day only to have half the volunteers not show up.[76] In the end, only one Asturian family—Rosa Manzano, her husband, Diego Arias, and their children—moved to the new border town. Then, in May 1801 Joaquín del Pino, who had been governor of Montevideo and had supervised the settlement of the colonists in the early 1780s, became the new viceroy. Under his watch, twenty-three more families were settled at Batoví by Pérez del Puerto.[77] With this last move, the Patagonia project finally ended once and for all.

The final stages of the Patagonia project tested the peasant colonists' abilities to integrate into colonial society. In their new communities, most proved to be economically savvy and politically astute as they made the transition from poor laborers to slave owners and from colonists to vecinos. It also tested both the flexibility and the resiliency of their gender expectations. Permanently settled in the Río de la Plata, the most successful colonists adopted colonial labor norms that emphasized race over gender. At the same time, as they sought to redefine their status in relationship to the Crown, they looked to traditional peninsular mechanisms to define male and female subjects and to reestablish the women as parishioners and the men as citizens of the Spanish Empire.

Epilogue

THE PATAGONIA PROJECT FINALLY CAME TO A CONCLUSION MORE than a quarter century after it began. By the time the accountants finished tabulating the thousands of reales owed to the colonists, all of the royal officials originally associated with the project, save one, were dead. The main administrator on the peninsula, Jorge Astraudi, had died in 1795. While it is difficult to know whether he cared that only a few of his charges ever saw the coast of Patagonia, his successful administration of his end of the project certainly aided his advancement through the royal bureaucracy. After his interim appointment in La Coruña, he went on to serve first as intendant of Toro, then later of Jaén and Valladolid. The former viceroy in Buenos Aires, Juan José Vértiz, died in 1799, having retired to Madrid. For him, the Patagonia project was just an expensive and time-consuming problem during an otherwise transformative tenure as viceroy. Among other achievements, he brought the first printing press to the Río de la Plata, established the *Protomedicato* to oversee the provision of medical care, made the city safer by installing lights along Buenos Aires's main streets, and built a hospital for the city's abandoned children. In his review of his administration, he boasted about the beautiful, productive towns that he had founded for the colonists.[1] The only major official to survive beyond the project's liquidation was Francisco de Viedma, who died while serving as intendant in Bolivia in 1809. Viedma had remained a strong advocate of the Patagonian outposts, arguing that they should be revived as late as 1784, but with his promotion and move to Bolivia, his career took a different turn and his time in Patagonia became a distant memory. The Patagonia project was only a small, somewhat unfortunate blemish on their otherwise successful careers.

At the end of their lives, if any of these men had attempted to assess the Patagonia project in terms of its original goals, it would have been clear that its few successes were overshadowed by its failures. In retrospect, one of its few bright spots was that Enlightenment thinkers had formulated the Patagonia project as a means to secure peripheral territories by settling loyal peninsular subjects at the edges of the empire, and for the most part, despite the many detours, the peasant colonists fulfilled that expectation. As we have seen, with few exceptions they dutifully moved wherever the authorities demanded, settled and resettled into new homes, tilled the unfamiliar soil, brought Spanish ways to the rural areas, and bore plenty of Spanish children. They also remained unshakably loyal to the Crown at a critical juncture in Spanish imperial history.

International conflict tested the peasant colonists' ties to the monarchy soon after the end of the colonization project, when the English invaded the Río de la Plata. The invasion was the scheme of Sir Home Riggs Popham, an English naval captain who had convinced Prime Minister William Pitt the Younger that with little effort he could emancipate the Spanish colonies and set up friendly creole governments. When the project was delayed by other international concerns, Popham decided to undertake an unauthorized attack on Montevideo using troops from the Cape of Good Hope and St. Helena. Upon arrival in the Río de la Plata, he again changed his mind, and on 10 June 1806 a landing force of 1,635 men commanded by General Sir William Beresford stormed Buenos Aires.[2] Caught completely by surprise, Viceroy Rafael de Sobremonte ignominiously fled the city and found refuge in Córdoba. It took some time for the Spanish military to regroup. While English troops occupied Buenos Aires, in Montevideo Santiago Liniers, a French officer in the service of the Spanish Crown, organized a combination of soldiers and militiamen and set off to free the viceregal capital. The colonists had their first interactions with Liniers and his men while they were waylaid in Canelones during three days of torrential rains.[3] When the storms finally subsided, the troops left for Colonia del Sacramento. They then crossed the Río de la Plata to Buenos Aires on 28 July, where Liniers and his men quickly expelled the English forces. Popham and Beresford, however, were undeterred and attempted a second invasion in October 1806. This time, Popham returned to his original plan, using his 1,700 troops to attack Montevideo. When that effort was stymied, the English troops withdrew to San Carlos and Maldonado on 29 October, bringing the invasion to the colonists' doorsteps. Padre Amenedo, San Carlos's dutiful parish priest, kept an account of the invasion that vividly describes the impact of the fighting on his parishioners. As some of the male colonists and their neighbors fended off the invaders, the women also had their first taste of the violence, as they were forced to flee their homes, care for the wounded, and mourn the dead.

The colonists and their neighbors immediately took up arms to protect their homes and communities, but tragedy came quickly. Juan de la Fuente, a Castilian farmer who had uprooted his wife and four children to settle in the Río de la Plata, was shot by the English troops as they entered Maldonado. According to Padre Amenedo, as the situation became more dangerous, the women fled "the fury of the enemy," via the road to San Carlos, "where they spent the night amid of tears and moans."[4] Women endured the brunt of the English sacking that followed:

> That horrifying night, they [the English] not only stole clothing, money, jewelry and tools, they smashed the furniture and everything that was not useful to pieces, destroying many effigies and holy images in the houses . . . in some of [the houses] they searched the women without the least shame to see if they had some money hidden and they removed some of the clothes they had on, forcibly abusing others without regard for their tears, supplications, advanced age or virginity.[5]

In the midst of this terror, a soldier rode through town warning the inhabitants that more English were coming. The announcement frightened them so much that even more people fled to the safety of the countryside, leaving behind only Padre Amenedo, the mayor, fifteen or so of the town's elderly, and a few of the colonists' wives, including Agustina Quevedo. Now in her fifties, Agustina had enlisted for the Patagonia project along with her parents and siblings at the age of eighteen. They had traveled from their native village of Cevico de la Torre in the bishopric of Palencia to the port at La Coruña, crossed the ocean, and had been settled in San Carlos.[6] Soon after, she married Francisco Payán, an emigrant from Valencia, and bore three sons over five years during the last decade of the eighteenth century. Although she could have moved to the countryside where it was safer, Agustina proved remarkably resilient and determined to protect her home, for which she had traveled so far and worked so hard, against the English invaders.

Agustina and the other wives risked their lives by staying in the city. When the Battle of San Carlos began in earnest on 7 November, the leader of the popular militia, Agustín Abreu, was wounded by both an enemy bullet and a saber blow to the head. As crowds had gathered at the house where the dead and injured were being tended, Francisco Payán brought the commander to his home where he would be more comfortable. There, Agustina Quevedo cared for the gravely injured man until he died two days later.[7] In doing so, she drew the ire of the English. In his entry for 8 November 1806, Padre Amenedo again lamented "the fury of the English," as eight hundred to one thousand English troops encircled the town and officers ran down the street armed with pistols and swords. They rounded up Agustina and the other wives and threw the terrified women and children into the water. The Englishmen then took the captives back to their homes "consoling them and telling them that they had only come looking for the general and his troops." There had been some miscommunication. Evidently, a wandering Portuguese cleric had incorrectly told them that the missing viceroy, the Marqués de Sobremonte, had taken refuge there.[8]

The terror did not abate. The English ravaged the countryside, plundering livestock from local ranches. On 26 December, the fighting literally hit home when at 9:30 p.m., Agustina's house and kitchen caught fire, a result of either the barrage of canon fire or arson. In response to the ringing of the church bells, a crowd gathered to help put out the fire, but strong winds made it difficult to extinguish the flames and the house was seriously damaged.[9]

In early January 1807, Padre Amenedo threw himself on the mercy of the British commander, pleading that he end the siege and the pillaging of the town by his soldiers. Amenedo described how the troops had ransacked colonist José Borrego's farmhouse, taking the family's linens and clothing and forcing Borrego and his children to flee dressed only in rags. The priest then pressed the English commander to enforce the promises that the English had made to protect the inhabitants' property and allow them to worship freely. They were running out of food as the English prevented supplies from entering the town, leaving them "without a milk cow with which to feed themselves." The "most horrible" fact, according to Amenedo, was that on six different occasions buildings had been set on fire, frightening the remaining inhabitants and forcing most of them to flee. On behalf of himself and the remaining "old men," Amenedo begged for pity and protection and promised that they would not take up arms against the British. Among the signatories to this pitiful document were colonists Domingo de la Infiesta and Paulino Baeza, as well as Agustina Quevedo's husband and son.[10]

Although much of the violence occurred around San Carlos and Maldonado, the fighting affected the colonists living in other parts of the Banda Oriental as well. In January 1807 English soldiers attacked Montevideo. Ramona Villamil y Saavedra, one of the few unattached single women to enlist in the Patagonia project, had married Francisco Vila, a Gallego merchant, in Montevideo within a month of her arrival in 1783. She was left widowed by an English bullet on 19 January just before the city capitulated. On 1 May, three hundred English troops entered the undefended town of San José on their way to Colonia del Sacramento. The mostly Asturian inhabitants and their children were forced to swear allegiance to the British king.[11] Fortunately, their humiliating submission to the enemy would not last long. On 7 July 1807 Spanish troops, with the aid of the Tercios de Gallegos, a regiment made up of Galician residents of Buenos Aires, defeated the English and the war came to an abrupt halt.

The peasant colonists had bravely demonstrated their loyalty to the Spanish king under the most difficult of circumstances. It is ironic that, having withstood Indian attacks and slave uprisings, no sooner was their status in the Spanish Empire settled than they were forced to defend their homes against *European* invaders. It is hard to imagine that during the siege some did not regret the decision to move across the ocean. While their aunts, sisters, and cousins lived peacefully in rural northern Spain, the women of San Carlos and Maldonado fled their homes, watched their husbands die at the hands of an invading army, and felt the shame of strip searches by their English adversaries.

Although the English invasion ended almost as suddenly as it had begun, the Banda Oriental again was quickly consumed by violence, this time from within. The crisis began with the Napoleonic invasion of the Iberian peninsula. In response to the overthrow of King Ferdinand VII, political elites in Buenos Aires formed a ruling junta opposed to French rule. In 1810 they deposed the viceroy and declared independence from Spain; however, under the leadership of Governor Francisco Javier de Elío, Montevideo remained loyal to the Spanish monarchy, and Elío declared himself viceroy of Montevideo and the Banda Oriental.

Elío's defiance of Buenos Aires raised the ire of José Gervasio Artigas, an officer in the blandengues, who had been in charge of the resettlement of many of the colonists and was also an old friend of Padre Amenedo. The charismatic Artigas mobilized the rural inhabitants of the Banda Oriental in an uprising that supported the junta in Buenos Aires against Elío's royalist regime. Artigas and his army moved swiftly across the Banda Oriental, taking one town after another, including the colonists' communities. At the end of April 1811, first Minas fell, then San José, followed by San Carlos and Maldonado. At San José, with the defeat of the royalists (or the triumph of the revolution, depending on one's politics), dozens of men who had opposed Artigas were taken prisoner, among them the sons of many colonists. They were then expelled from the Banda Oriental for their opposition to the junta in Buenos Aires. After a brief intervention by the Portuguese, who supported Elío, just as Artigas was ready to march on Montevideo, the ruling junta betrayed the rebels by signing the Banda Oriental back to Spain.[12] Caught between the Spanish and Portuguese, Artigas and his troops withdrew to the western shore of the Río Uruguay. They were followed by thousands of supporters from the Banda Oriental who joined him in what became known as the Exodus of Artigas, or La Redota.

This enormous movement of people transformed the rural Banda Oriental. According to Artigas supporter (and the soldier who had been in charge of constructing the colonists' homes in Maldonado) José Rondeau, the countryside became "a desert." Yet, when Artigas and his "exiles" arrived at Salto, he took a census, and as far as I can tell, most of the colonists did not accompany him. On some level, Artigas's message probably did not appeal to them, focused as it was on the rights of Indians and federalism, but even if it did, who could blame them for remaining at home?[13] They had risked everything to come to the Americas, and some of them had moved four or more times over the last three decades. Barely settled into their new communities, it would have been difficult to convince them to abandon the lives that they had worked so hard to create. In fact, by remaining in their homes, they suffered miserably. Artigas and the exiles stole all their cattle and burned everything in their wake.[14] The Redota would become a critical moment in the history of the Banda Oriental and ultimately the nation of Uruguay, but most of the peasant colonists remained loyal subjects of the king and became the innocent victims of a revolution not of their own making.

As Artigas's uprising spiraled into an independence movement, many of the colonists experienced the humiliation of having their possessions embargoed by revolutionary troops. In the eyes of their neighbors, after more than thirty years in the Río de la Plata, they were still peninsular Spaniards and were designated as "enemies of the state." Luisa Magdalena Gándara and her husband, José Antonio Núñez, had both emigrated as children with the Patagonia project, and after their families settled in San Carlos, they wed in 1792. Although it is unlikely that either of them even had memories of Galicia (she had left at age three and he at age seven), on a terrifying June day in 1813 military officials entered their San Carlos home to inventory and embargo their possessions. They seem to have done well, owning slaves and cattle, but they had little furniture—only two tables and five chairs. Their neighbor María Clara Corbo faced the same intrusion by revolutionary forces. Ironically, María Clara was a true creole, one of the first children born to the newly arrived colonists in San Carlos. The officer conducting their inventory was less than impressed by her possessions. He declared María Clara's kitchen, one of her tables, and her chairs "useless." Interestingly enough, in both of these cases, the revolutionary forces entrusted the embargoed lands and possessions (including slaves) of the colonists to Luisa and María Clara, and allowed the women to continue working the lands. This act of mercy must have been a relief to the women, who otherwise would have had no means of support.

Some women fled rather than face the rebels. Andrea Castellote, who had made the journey from La Coruña as a child and later established herself as a single woman, abandoned her home in Maldonado for Montevideo. She may have left to avoid the banditry and lawlessness that plagued the region during the revolutionary crisis, or she may have moved to the city in support of the royalists.[15]

In general it is difficult to know how the remaining colonists and their children and grandchildren responded to the calls for independence. Having traveled far and toiled hard and still nursing the frustrations of more than twenty years of unfulfilled promises, some may have been energized by the prospect of a new regime in which they, and not royal authorities, controlled their destinies. Others, as dutiful Spaniards who had traveled halfway around the world in the service of the Crown, may have wholeheartedly rejected the notion of independence.[16] In her study of Arequipa, Peru, Sarah Chambers notes that most of the population maintained what she calls a "careful neutrality" during the independence wars. Although royalism was strong among the populace, many Arequipeños changed sides frequently, and when the republicans won, even loyalists swore allegiance to the new republic as enthusiastically as those who had supported it all along.[17] The same political pragmatism (or ambivalence) seems to describe many of the colonists. Most remained in their homes despite the violence, and although some fled to Montevideo, it is unclear whether they were determined to ally with the royalist cause or whether they merely hoped to escape retribution based on their status as peninsular Spaniards. Whatever the case, there is no indication that any of the families fled permanently, as happened in loyalist communities in other parts of Latin America.

Not only did the colonists' families stay in the Banda Oriental, having weathered the storm of independence, many of their children and grandchildren assumed leadership positions in the new republics, a strong indication of how easily most adapted to the new political circumstances. Among them, Agustina Quevedo's son, Cipriano Payán, served in the first Uruguayan legislative assembly in 1828.[18] Francisco Solano Antuña, who signed Uruguay's first constitution, was the grandson of María Antonia del Monte, a remarkably resilient woman. María had been widowed at the port of La Coruña but continued on to South America, where she forged a new life for her family, first in the rural areas outside of Buenos Aires and later in Montevideo.[19] Without a doubt, their parents' and grandparents' struggle to become vecinos laid the groundwork for their descendants' political ambitions. The sons and grandsons of peasants became the statesmen of a new generation.

In terms of its others goals, the Patagonia project was a failure. Strategically, although the establishment of the colonies may have temporarily dissuaded English interest in Patagonia, as we have seen it did not stop them from invading the Río de la Plata twice at the beginning of the next century. Moreover, the influence of the English in the region only grew after independence. The English provided loans to the new government, and English merchants participated extensively in the new national economy. Even the possibilities of colonization in the Río de la Plata were not lost on the English. With the support of the government, in 1825 a pair of English merchants tried their hand at the family colonization business, bringing more than two hundred Scots to establish an agricultural outpost called Monte Grande just outside of Buenos Aires, one of a number of such foreign colonies attempted during the nineteenth century.[20] Even Patagonia did not escape British influence. In 1832 Charles Darwin's ship, the *Beagle*, explored the coast, and in 1865 the first Welsh settlers traveled to the Chubut valley, where they established colonies that still exist today. From the beginning, keeping the British out of Patagonia was a primary goal of the colonization project and, as such, it was an abject failure.

Economically, the impact of the project was minimal. Although there was some expansion of the whaling industry and salt mining in Patagonia, the region remained (and remains) peripheral. In terms of extending Spanish control over the rural Río de la Plata, it was reasonably effective in both the outskirts of Buenos Aires and the Banda Oriental, in part because of the forts that were constructed in those areas and in part because of the colonists' settlements. After independence, Argentine campaigns against Indian groups in the Pampas and Patagonia intensified as a result of nineteenth-century nation building. These efforts culminated with the so-called "Conquest of the Desert" in the 1870s in which Argentine troops killed and displaced tens of thousands of Patagonian peoples.

On the peninsula, at least initially, the Patagonia project had no particular impact at all. A few northern villages experienced some decline as their inhabitants were lured by the call for volunteers, but there was no large-scale depopulation or redistribution of the population. However, the long-term impact of the project on the demography of northern Spain was substantial, as it played a critical role in altering migration patterns from that part of the peninsula. Although by the 1770s Buenos Aires already had a significant population of Gallegos, between 1779 and 1810 the number of Gallegos in the city (not counting the colonists) rose 200 percent, the number of Asturians by 100 percent, and northern Castilians 97 percent. Gallegos went from accounting for about one-quarter of the immigrants in Buenos Aires to about one-third.[21] In the next half century, those numbers would skyrocket with thousands of Gallegos streaming to Buenos Aires and Montevideo each year, so much so that *gallego* would become a generic and usually derogatory term for all Spanish immigrants. The gendered impact was also substantial. By the middle of the nineteenth century, there was a significant increase in the number of female immigrants, especially to Buenos Aires, demonstrating the degree to which the Patagonia project laid the foundation for the expansion of family migration from northern Spain.[22]

But the story of the Patagonia project is only partially about the Spanish Empire and the project's success or failure as one of the Bourbon reforms. From the outset, I wanted to use the colonization scheme to tell the stories of women who moved around the Spanish Empire and to analyze how their experiences inform our understanding of sex and gender at the end of the colonial period. One thing is clear. Far from being a homogenous, well-defined set of norms based on honor or chastity or anything else, gender expectations in the Spanish Atlantic world were fluid, contested, and ever negotiable.

Not surprisingly, the best articulated ideas about sex and gender came from officials like Astraudi who based their plans for the Patagonia project on eighteenth-century ideas about peninsular women's conduct and their ability to influence the behavior of others. Supposedly chaste and submissive, they could do what neither military, religious, nor administrative authorities could—make otherwise uncontrollable men into well-behaved fathers and husbands. To ensure that only women able to fulfill this expectation participated in the project, royal officials attempted to vet the conduct of the female volunteers. But their interest in women's deportment did not stop there. Astraudi and the other officials arranged marriages for the single women and intervened to keep couples together in order to ensure that as many of the female colonists as possible traveled and settled under male supervision. Even the layout of the forts in Patagonia allowed for the ongoing surveillance over the families to protect the women from sexual predation.

Most of the women adapted easily to the expectations of the officials; however, they resisted when the demands of the authorities conflicted with their own gender norms, at times forcing authorities to revise their expectations to ensure that the project went forward. When Galician peasant women failed to volunteer for the project because families rarely migrated out of the region, they unknowingly pressured Astraudi to alter both the marketing and the geography of his recruitment efforts. Once enlisted, the female volunteers influenced the administration of the project through their unrelenting demands for diapers, better housing, and medical care. They forced the royal treasury to spend excessively to meet their needs and constantly challenged Astraudi's ability to keep the project on track.

As they moved from their native villages to La Coruña and then to South America, the peasant women negotiated the changing gender scenarios in different ways. Take, for example, Escolástica Cordero, one of the peasant women who adapted easily to the changes in gender expectations that she encountered as a part of the Patagonia project. She was born in 1755 in tiny Rabanal Viejo, near Astorga in León, where men and women worked together to harvest rye.[23] When Astraudi extended the call for volunteers to her native lands, two families in the village found the king's offer enticing, one of which included Escolástica, her brother, José, and her widowed mother, Pascuala Rojo. She took the edict's stated preference for married women to heart and at twenty-four quickly married Pedro Prieto, a farmer and cousin from nearby Argañoso.[24] Then, accompanied by family and neighbors, Escolástica undertook the 270 kilometer trek to La Coruña. Astraudi must have been thrilled. She and Pedro were exactly the type of young, married, healthy colonists that Astraudi wanted for the new outposts. Yet, while she waited to depart, Escolástica saw the pressure that Astraudi put on the single women she knew. Within six months, Astraudi paid for her brother to marry seventeen-year-old Casimira Fernández, who had traveled with them from Rabanal Viejo, and for another Astorgan man to marry Casimira's nineteen-year-old sister. From Astraudi's perspective, single women's sexuality was so threatening to the goals of the project that only through marriage could they secure a place on the passenger list.

One month after the weddings, in May 1780, the entire extended family departed for Montevideo on the *Real Carlos*. Crowded tightly into the hold of the ship for nearly eleven weeks, all the adults made it safely across the ocean, but the voyage took a toll on the very young, and Escolástica witnessed the sea burials of twelve children. The ship arrived in Montevideo in August. While other families adjusted to the very masculine and racially diverse frontier town, within a couple of months Escolástica and her family all boarded a ship for the new outpost at San Julián, which was closer to Antarctica than to Montevideo.

From the outset, the new colony at Floridablanca was fraught with gender tensions. At first, those anxieties played out exclusively among men, as the large contingent of sailors, soldiers, and convicts sent to construct the outpost regularly defied the orders of their superiors, deserted, and fought among themselves. Each time the Tehuelches and their caciques took captives or provided food for the encampment, they reminded the Spaniards that Patagonia belonged to them, not the Spanish king, which led to even more violence. Rather than pacify the men, the women's arrival only complicated an already difficult situation, forcing the authorities to separate the colonists as soon as possible to protect them from sexual predation. Female fertility was central to the colony's survival, but only within the bounds of matrimony.

Life in Floridablanca tested Escolástica's physical and emotional endurance. She conceived her first child only a couple of months after arriving; however not only was her pregnancy marred by the deaths of dozens of soldiers and colonists during the first horrific winter, she suffered her own loss. Although her first son, Santiago, was born healthy, sometime the next year an infant girl died. She faced other challenges as well. Although the family had been poor in Spain, there was generally enough food. In Patagonia, the family's survival depended on Pedro's ability to harvest a little grain from the sandy soil and her ability to turn the unpredictable rations and tough guanaco meat into meals for the family.

The few women at Floridablanca had to rely on one another for all kinds of support, and Escolástica must have found some solace in having her mother close at hand. However, it quickly became clear that there was no place for aging women at the colony, and the authorities considered Pascuala a burden. Although she married a widower in an attempt to remain at the outpost, she was beyond her childbearing years, and he was too old for the hard work of establishing the settlement. Both were deemed "useless" and sent back to Montevideo.

Escolástica's separation from her mother did not last long. With the abandonment of Floridablanca, the family was reunited and resettled in the new town of Concepción de Minas. Fortunately, life in the Banda Oriental was much more stable and secure, and Escolástica gave birth to at least eight more children over the next fifteen years. With so many baptisms, she established her place in the new parish. She created a network of close relationships with other women through godparentage. Escolástica connected her children's future fortunes to those of her sister-in-law Casimira and other new friends and neighbors, and she in turn accepted spiritual responsibility for other children in the community. She suffered through the early deaths of at least three of her children, and their burials provided more moments for the women of the parish to gather and help her in her time of need.

Just as her eldest son, Pedro, was ready to marry, their lives were turned upside down first with the English invasion and then with the Artigas uprising. Through it all, the family remained loyal to the Spanish Crown. In 1811 Pedro Prieto (either her husband or her son) signed a petition to a Portuguese general asking for his protection against the insurgents who threatened the "sacred rights of our Catholic monarch."[25]

Despite the turmoil, Escolástica and Pedro prospered, and with their economic stability they purchased at least one slave, a woman named María. It is unclear whether María worked in their fields or in the house, but either way her labor freed Escolástica for other tasks and gave her some status in the community. Despite frequent admonishments from authorities to control the sexual activity of slaves, María bore at least three illegitimate children, all of whom were baptized. Escolástica's sister-in-law, Casimira, even administered an emergency baptism to one of the infants. It is certainly possible that Pedro or one of her sons fathered some of the slave's children, but the records are silent on that issue. Escolástica died in 1834, having received the sacraments at the ripe old age of seventy-six in the new Republic of Uruguay.

Independence movements in the Río de la Plata toppled more than just the Spanish monarchy. Scholars, including Jeffrey Shumway and Christine Hunefeldt, have noted that although colonial patriarchy was not dismantled with independence, it faced serious challenges in the new regimes.[26]

Shumway has attributed this challenge to "disgruntled women and children, idealistic reformers, and a growing state government eager to create a modern nation."[27] The "disgruntled women and children" to whom he refers no doubt included many of the daughters and grandchildren of the colonists who came to the Río de la Plata as a part of the Patagonia project. In their villages on the peninsula, the women had become accustomed to significant female independence. As they joined the project and settled in the Americas, they acclimated to elite gender expectations by marrying early and restricting most sexual activity to the marital bed; however, the fact that they made such accommodations during the migration process did not mean that they wholeheartedly submitted to such restrictive ideas of female behavior. Moreover, the colonists who came with the Patagonia project were far from alone. Although creole elites in the Río de la Plata may have been strongly invested in the maintenance of patriarchal authority, the rest of the population brought diverse ideas about gender based on the peninsular cultures in which they were raised, as well as on their migration and frontier experiences. During the transition from colony to nation, they worked to resolve the contradictions between their traditional ways, the expectations of those around them, and the opportunities of their new nations.

The Patagonia project demonstrates that no singular set of sex and gender norms existed in the Spanish Empire. Whether one lived near a fort on the Pampa or in a village in northern Spain, a complex interplay of prescribed ideals, regional cultures and economies, class, demography, and race framed both the expectations of women and their actions. The women of the Patagonia project were not bound to an inflexible set of expectations based on their chastity; rather, they were willing and able to both assert their own expectations and alter their behaviors when necessary in order to negotiate the complicated gender dynamic created by peninsular and colonial administrations, the pressures of migration, and the daily realities of life in Spain and its colonies. In that sense, they were not unlike the thousands of other women who moved around the Spanish Empire at the end of the colonial period. Through their adaptations, contestations, and negotiations, they defined and redefined gender in the Atlantic world.

Notes

Chapter One

1. The classic works on honor in Spanish society are Julian Pitt-Rivers, *The Fate of Shechem or the Politics of Sex: Essays in the Anthropology of the Mediterranean* (Cambridge: Cambridge University Press, 1977); and J. G. Peristany, *Honour and Shame: The Values of Mediterranean Society* (Chicago, IL: University of Chicago Press, 1966).
2. Allyson M. Poska, "Elusive Virtue: Rethinking the Role of Female Chastity in Early Modern Spain," *Journal of Early Modern History* 8, no. 1–2 (June 2004): 135–46; Poska, *Women and Authority in Early Modern Spain*; Renato Barahona, *Sex Crimes, Honour, and the Law in Early Modern Spain: Vizcaya, 1528–1735* (Toronto: University of Toronto Press, 2003), chap. 5; and Taylor, *Honor and Violence in Golden Age Spain*, chap. 5. On noblewomen and extramarital sex, see Grace E. Coolidge, "'A Vile and Abject Woman': Noble Mistresses, Legal Power, and the Family in Early Modern Spain," *Journal of Family History* 32, no. 3 (2007): 195–214. On nonmarital sexuality in Spanish America, see Moreno, "Sexo, matrimonio y familia," 68; Thomas Calvo, "Concubinato y mestizaje en el medio urbano: el caso de Guadalajara en el siglo XVII," *Revista de Indias* 44, no. 173 (1984): 211; Guiomar Dueñas-Vargas, *Los hijos del pecado: ilegitimidad y vida familiar en la Santa Fe de Bogotá colonial* (Bogotá: Universidad Nacional de Colombia, 1997), chap. 7; and Ann Twinam, *Public Lives, Private Secrets: Gender, Honor, Sexuality, and Illegitimacy in Colonial Spanish America* (Stanford, CA: Stanford University Press, 1999).
3. On the royal policy on women and migration, see Konetzke, "La emigración de mujeres españolas," 123–50. Such legislation initiated what historian Antonia Castañeda has referred to as Spain's "policy of domestic unity": see Castañeda, "Engendering the History of Alta California, 1769–1848," 239; and Altman, "Spanish Women in the Caribbean, 1493–1540," 60. On women and early migration to the Americas, see Konetzke, "La emigración de mujeres españolas"; and Altman, "Spanish Women and the Indies." On family migration, see Auke P. Jacobs, *Los movimientos migratorios entre Castilla e Hispanoámerica durante el*

reinado de Felipe III, 1598–1621 (Amsterdam: Rodopi, 1995), 72–89. For sex ratios, see Martínez Shaw, *La emigración española a América (1492–1824)*, 80; Jacobs, *Los movimientos migratorios*, 216; and Macías Domínguez, *La llamada del Nuevo Mundo*, 66.

4. Philippe Denis, "The Cape Huguenots and Their Legacy in Apartheid South Africa," in *Memory and Identity: The Huguenots in France and the Atlantic Diaspora*, ed. Randy J. Sparks and Bertrand Van Ruymbeke (Columbia: University of South Carolina Press, 2003), 285–311; and Coates, *Convicts and Orphans*, 175–76. Among other similar efforts, the French moved two hundred Acadian families to Cayenne in 1763 and to a settlement in the Malvinas in 1764: see Hodson, "'A Bondage So Harsh,'" 95–131. In a most remarkable feat, the Portuguese transported the entire town of Mazagão from West Africa to the Amazon in 1770: see Laurent Vidal, *Mazagão, la ville qui traversa l'Atlantique: du Maroc á l'Amazonie (1769–1783)* (Paris: Editions Aubier, 2005).
5. Enlightenment intellectual and military man José del Campillo y Cossío (1693–1743) urged Spain to imitate France and England, both of which encouraged colonial migration by paying for the migrants' transportation and providing them with land, tools, and any necessary artisanal instruction: see his *Nuevo sistema para el gobierno económico para la América*, 81. This text is reiterated word for word in Ward's *Proyecto económico: en que se proponen varias providencias dirigidas á promover los intereses de España* (1779), 236–37. There is considerable debate over Campillo y Cossío's authorship of the *Nuevo sistema*, as well as Ward's authorship and/or plagiarism of the text: see Weber, *Bárbaros*, 181, 337n28. According to David Brading, Campillo y Cossío's manuscript circulated between 1743 and 1762, when it was then incorporated into Ward's text: see Brading, *Miners and Merchants in Bourbon Mexico: 1763–1810* (Cambridge: Cambridge University Press, 1971), 25. Weber, *The Spanish Frontier in North America*, 192–94; Voss, *The Archaeology of Ethnogenesis*; Longo Formoso, *Expedición militar a las Californias, Sonoras y Cinaloa (1768–1771), expediciones de familias al Río de la Plata (1778–1784) y a la Costa de Mosquitos (1787)*; Bouvier, *Women and the Conquest of California, 1542–1840*; and Armando C. Alonzo, *Tejano Legacy: Rancheros and Settlers in South Texas, 1734–1900* (Albuquerque: University of New Mexico Press, 1998).
6. On the Bourbon reforms in Spain, see Antonio Domínguez Ortiz, *Sociedad y estado en el siglo XVIII español*, 3rd ed. (Barcelona: Editorial Ariel, 1988), chap. 18; and Paquette, *Enlightenment, Governance, and Reform*. The Bourbon reforms also attempted to resolve a variety of other problems, including the economic power of the Catholic Church, outmoded systems of landholding and taxation, and inefficiencies in agriculture.
7. Luis Navarro García, *La política americana de José de Gálvez según su "Discurso y reflexiones de un vasallo"* (Málaga: Editorial Algazara, 1998), 126. On Gálvez's *Discurso*, see Stanley J. Stein and Barbara H. Stein, *Apogee of Empire: Spain and*

New Spain in the Age of Charles III, 1759–1789 (Baltimore, MD: Johns Hopkins University Press, 2003), 227. On European conflicts with various Indian groups in Patagonia, see Leonardo León Solís, "Indios, piratas y corsarios en las costas de la Araucanía y Patagonia, 1557–1790," *Boletín de historia y geografía* 15 (2001): 117–51. For more on the conditions at Nombre de Jesús and Rey Don Felipe, see Jorge A. Suby, Ricardo A. Guichón, and M. Ximena Senatore, "Los restos óseos humanos de Nombre de Jesús: evidencias de la salud en el primer asentamiento europeo en Patagonia austral," *Magallania* (Chile) 37, no. 2 (2009): 23–40; and AGI, Buenos Aires 326, fol. 11v.

8. Mancke, "Early Modern Expansion and the Politicization of Oceanic Space," 233; S. Samuel Trifilo, "British Travel Accounts on Argentina before 1810," *Journal of Inter-American Studies* 2, no. 3 (July 1960), 243; and Weber, *Bárbaros*, 142, 323n22.
9. Jones, "Nineteenth-Century British Travel Accounts of Argentina," 197; Falkner, *A Description of Patagonia and the adjoining parts of South America . . . with a grammar and a short vocabulary, and some particulars relating to Falkland's Islands*, 85; and AGI, Buenos Aires 326, fol. 3.
10. Alden, "The Undeclared War of 1773–1777," 59, 68–69, 73.
11. José Cornide, "Observaciones sobre el establecimiento de colonias en las provincias del Río de la Plata, Paraguay y Tucuman," AGI, Buenos Aires 326, fol. 175.
12. Gálvez had a long-standing distrust of creoles: see Elliott, *Empires of the Atlantic World*, 320. On the creation of towns on the northern fringe, see Cruz, *Let There Be Towns*; in the Río de la Plata, see David J. Robinson and Teresa Thomas, "New Towns in Eighteenth-Century Northwest Argentina," *Journal of Latin American Studies* 6, no. 1 (May 1974): 1–33.
13. Castañeda, "Engendering the History of Alta California"; Chávez-García, *Negotiating Conquest*, 11ff; Bouvier, *Women and the Conquest of California*; and Reyes, *Private Women, Public Lives*, esp. 102–3. As Bianca Premo has argued, "The ideal-typical model of household authority, fashioned on the patriarchal family, was replicated in political ideology at the level of the Spanish empire, with the king taking the role of father and colonial subjects conceived of as children"(*Children of the Father King*, 10). On the creation of an idealized patriarchal order, see Martínez, *Genealogical Fictions*, 237. On Bourbon paternalism, see Premo, "'Misunderstood Love,'" 231–61. For a negative view of Charles III's paternalism, see Francisco Sánchez-Blanco, *El absolutismo y las luces en el reinado de Carlos III* (Madrid: Marcial Pons, 2002), 49.
14. "Informe del Padre Lizasoin sobre las provincias de Sonora y Nueva Vizcaya," in *Materiales para la historia de Sonora*, ed. Rafael Pérez Taylor and Miguel Ángel Paz Frayre (México, D.F.: Instituto de Investigaciones Antropológicas, Universidad Nacional Autónoma de México, 2007), 409.
15. On the centrality of women and children to Enlightenment debates and reforms in Spanish America, see Milton, *The Many Meanings of Poverty*; Arrom, *Containing the Poor*; González and Premo, eds., *Raising an Empire*;

Premo, *Children of the Father King*; and Martínez, *Genealogical Fictions*, 243–44.

16. Chávez-García, *Negotiating Conquest*, 8; Bouvier, *Women and the Conquest of California*, 46ff; Reyes, *Private Women, Public Lives*, 101; Voss, "Colonial Sex: Archaeology, Structured Space, and Sexuality," 39–41; Albert L. Hurtado, *Intimate Frontiers: Sex, Gender, and Culture in Old California* (Albuquerque: University of New Mexico Press, 1999), 13ff; Barr, *Peace Came in the Form of a Woman*; and Castañeda, "Sexual Violence in the Politics and Policies of Conquest," 15–33.
17. Cited in Bouvier, *Women and the Conquest of California*, 58; Gilbert C. Din, *The Canary Islanders of Louisiana* (Baton Rouge: Louisiana State University Press, 1988); and Antonio Acosta Rodríguez, *La población de la Luisiana española (1763–1803)* (Madrid: Ministerio de Asuntos Exteriores, 1979).
18. AGI, Buenos Aires 326, fol. 86.
19. Reyes, *Private Women, Public Lives*, 106; and Chávez-García, *Negotiating Conquest*, 20.
20. Cooper and Stoler, "Tensions of Empire: Colonial Control and Visions of Rule," 613. Miroslava Chávez-García has similarly noted, "Spanish-speaking women at the missions, like those at the pueblos and presidios, aided in reproducing not only the social and physical environment of Spanish society, but also the ideological and institutional bases of Hispanic life" (*Negotiating Conquest*, 21).
21. Castañeda, "Presidarias y Pobladoras," 120; and Chávez-García, *Negotiating Conquest*, 15.
22. Campomanes, *Reflexiones sobre el comercio español a Indias (1762)*, 227. On Campomanes, see Rodríguez Díaz, *Reforma e ilustración en la España del siglo XVIII*; and Castro, *Campomanes*. As Ondina González has argued, in the colonial context, "Childhood and child-rearing practice were highly politically charged. It *mattered* how one raised children. For, as adults, these children would have to accept a world in which they were subjects of distant political powers that knew little of the realities of the colonies" (*Raising an Empire*, 7). Many reformers believed that children were "agents of human perfectibility" and made their care a priority: see Joan Sherwood, *Poverty in Eighteenth-Century Spain: The Women and Children of the Inclusa* (Toronto: University of Toronto Press, 1988), 152. For colonial examples, see Arrom, *Containing the Poor*, esp. chap. 3; and Premo, *Children of the Father King*, chaps. 5 and 6.
23. Paquette, *Enlightenment, Governance, and Reform*, 98, 114ff; Voss, *The Archaeology of Ethnogenesis*, 45, 93; and Marysa Navarro, "Women in Pre-Columbian and Colonial Latin America and the Caribbean," in *Women in Latin America and the Caribbean: Restoring Women to History*, ed. Marysa Navarro and Virginia Sánchez Korrol (Bloomington: Indiana University Press, 1999), 42.
24. On population concerns, see Manuel Martín Rodríguez, *Pensamiento económico español sobre la población de Soto a Matanegui* (Madrid: Ediciones Pirámide,

1984); and Manuel Herrera Gómez, *Demografía e ilustración en España* (Granada: Universidad de Granada, 1999). A similar debate about population was occurring in France: see Carol Blum, *Strength in Numbers: Population, Reproduction, and Power in Eighteenth-Century France* (Baltimore, MD: Johns Hopkins University Press, 2002); and Leslie Tuttle, *Conceiving the Old Regime: Pronatalism and the Politics of Reproduction in Early Modern France* (Oxford: Oxford University Press, 2010). Officials in colonial Peru also viewed themselves as being in the midst of a population crisis: see Adam Warren, *Medicine and Politics in Colonial Peru: Population Growth and the Bourbon Reforms* (Pittsburgh, PA: University of Pittsburgh Press, 2010). For Galicia in 1752, see Eiras Roel, *La población de Galicia, 1700–1860*, 149. For regional population densities in 1787, see Gabriel Tortella, *The Development of Modern Spain: An Economic History of the Nineteenth and Twentieth Centuries*, trans. Valerie J. Herr (Cambridge, MA: Harvard University Press, 2000), 259.

25. Castro, "Informe de Campomanes sobre la emigración e industrialización de Galicia," 247; and Cornide, "Observaciones," AGI, Buenos Aires 326, fol. 179v.
26. John Adams, *The Works of John Adams, Second President of the United States*, vol. 3 (Boston, MA: Little, Brown, and Co., 1865), 244; Ana Hontanilla, "Images of Barbaric Spain in Eighteenth-Century British Travel Writing," *Studies in Eighteenth Century Culture* 37 (2008): 119–43; and Feijoo, "Honra y provecho de agricultura," in *Teatro crítico universal* (1726).
27. Dubert, "La mortalité en Galice, 1600–1850," 221–48, esp. 235; Antonio Meijide Pardo, "El hambre de 1768–1769 en Galicia y la obra asistencial del estamento eclesiástico compostelano," *Compostellanum* 10, no. 2 (1965): 213–56; Pérez Moreda, *La crisis de mortalidad en la España interior*, 366; and Alfredo Martín García, "Mortalidad ordinaria y mortalidad extraordinaria en el Ferrol de finales del antiguo régimen," *Studia historica, historia moderna* 23 (2001): 249–73, esp. 260.
28. Feijoo, "Honra y provecho de agricultura." For the data on northern emigration, see Ramón Lanza García, "De norte a sur: las migraciones de la fachada cantábrica en la España moderna," in *Movilidad interna y migraciones intraeuropeas en la península Ibérica*, vol. 1, ed. Antonio Eiras Roel (Santiago de Compostela: Universidad de Santiago de Compostela, 2002), 17–53; and Jacobo García Blanco-Cicerón, *Viajeros angloparlantes por la Galicia de la segunda mitad del siglo XVIII* (A Coruña: Fundación Pedro Barrie de La Maza, 2006), 206. Cited in Meijide Pardo, "La emigración Gallega intrapeninsular," 481. On the multiple uses of the word "slave" in the eighteenth century, see Michel Trouilliot, *Silencing the Past: Power and the Production of History* (Boston, MA: Beacon Press, 1995), 85–86.
29. Stelio Cro, ed., *Descripción de la Sinapia, península en la tierra austral*. For Sarmiento as the author, see José Santos Puerto, "*La Sinapia*: luces para buscar la utopía de la ilustración," *Bulletin Hispanique* 13, no. 2 (2001): 481–510. The

manuscript was found among Campomanes's papers. For Campomanes as author, see Miguel Avilés Fernández, ed., *Sinapia: una utopía española del Siglo de las Luces* (Madrid: Editora Nacional, 1976).

30. *Descripción de la Sinapia*, 67, 20.
31. Armando Alberola Romá and Enrique Giménez López, "El proyecto de poblar la isla de Cabrera a fines del siglo XVIII," *Investigaciones geográficas* 12 (1994): 86–87; and Francisco Javier Blanco Segarra, Mariano Galant Torregrosa, and Francisco Sala Aniorte, "Formación y crecimiento de Torrevieja," in *El mar y Torrevieja: estudios geo-históricos* (Murcia: Servicio de Publicaciones de la Universidad, 1997).
32. On Campomanes and the scheme to colonize the Sierra Morena, see Castro, *Campomanes*, 294–98; Alonso Soane, *Las "Nuevas poblaciones"*; and Avilés Fernández, *Carlos III y las "Nuevas poblaciones."*
33. The fuero for the new population is available at http://biblioteca2.uclm.es/biblioteca/CECLM/ARTREVISTAS/LaMancha/LM03_CottaFuero.pdf; AGI, Buenos Aires 326, fol. 87.
34. On changing ideas about work, see Mackay, *"Lazy, Improvident People"*; Campillo y Cossío discusses idleness in *Lo que hay de más y de menos en España, para que sea lo que debe ser y no lo que es* (1741); see also Cro, ed., *Descripción de la Sinapia*, 53.
35. William J. Callahan, *Honor, Commerce and Industry in Eighteenth-Century Spain* (Boston, MA: Harvard Graduate School of Business, 1972), 64; Mackay, *"Lazy, Improvident People,"* 170; and Ward, *Proyecto económico*, xvi. On women and textile production, see Rebecca Haidt, "The Wife, the Maid, and the Woman in the Street," in *Eve's Enlightenment: Women's Experience in Spain and Spanish America, 1726–1839*, ed. Catherine M. Jaffe and Elizabeth Franklin Lewis (Baton Rouge: Louisiana State University Press, 2009), 125ff.
36. Campomanes, *Discurso sobre el fomento de la industria popular* (1774), sección 8—he even pushed guilds to allow entrance to women (*Discurso sobre el fomento*, sección 15); Smith, *The Emerging Female Citizen*, 75–80; Sarasúa, "The Role of the State in Shaping Women's and Men's Entrance into the Labour Market," 347–71; and Mackay, *"Lazy, Improvident People,"* 170–72.
37. Campomanes, *Reflexiones sobre el comercio español a Indias* (1762), 227. Authors also urged the monarchy to resettle gypsies: see Antonio Gómez Alfaro, "La polémica sobre la deportación de los gitanos a las colonias de América," *Cuadernos hispanoamericanos* 386 (1982): 308–36; Laura Rodríguez, "The Spanish Riots of 1766," *Past & Present* 59 (May 1973): 117, 125; and José Miguel López García, *El Motín contra Esquilache: crisis y protesta popular en el Madrid del siglo XVIII* (Madrid: Alianza Editorial, 2006).
38. The alleviation of poverty was central to the Bourbon reforms: see Pérez Estévez, *El problema de los vagos en la España del siglo XVIII*; Elena Maza Zorrilla, *Pobreza y asistencia social en España, siglos XVI al XX: aproximación histórica* (Valladolid: Universidad de Valladolid, 1987); and William J. Callahan, "The

Problem of Confinement: An Aspect of Poor Relief in Eighteenth-Century Spain," *Hispanic American Historical Review* 51 (1971): 1–24. For Spanish America, see Milton, *The Many Meanings of Poverty*; Arrom, *Containing the Poor*; Ward, *Proyecto económico*, 59, 205; Campomanes, *Discurso sobre el fomento*, sección 8; and Ward, *Obra pia y eficaz modo para remediar la miseria de la gente pobre de España (1767)*, 104.

39. Ward, *Obra pia*, 131.
40. Campomanes, *Discurso sobre la educación popular de los artesanos y su fomento* (1775), sección 17.
41. Cornide, "Observaciones," AGI, Buenos Aires 326, fols. 179v, 190. For more on resettling peasants from northern Spain, see De Cristóforis, "Ideas y políticas migratorias españolas a fines del antiguo régimen," 117–50.

Chapter Two

1. On the intendancy system in Spain, including a brief biography of Astraudi, see Didier Fabrice Abbad, *Les intendants espagnols du XVIIIe siècle* (Madrid: Casa de Velázquez, 1992); and Enrique Orduña Rebollo, *Intendentes e intendencias* (Buenos Aires: Ediciones Ciudad Argentina, 1997).
2. AGI, Buenos Aires 326, fol. 88.
3. Archivo Municipal de La Coruña (AMC), Colección de la familia de Cayo Acha de Patiño, caja 6-1.
4. Apolant, *Génesis de la familia uruguaya*, 660.
5. Scholars of migration have argued that there was no direct correlation between any single factor (poverty, overpopulation, accessibility of land) and migration: see Moya, *Cousins and Strangers*, 92–93; and Antonio Eiras Roel, "Migraciones internas y medium-distance en España en la edad moderna," in *Migraciones internas y médium-distance en la península Ibérica, 1500–1900*, ed. Eiras Roel and Rey Castelao, 1:73.
6. Moya, *Cousins and Strangers*, 94–95; and Poska, *Women and Authority*, chap. 1.
7. Moya, *Cousins and Strangers*, 95; and Macías Domínguez, *La llamada del Nuevo Mundo*, chap. 4.
8. For a complete explanation of the foro system, see Saavedra, *La vida cotidiana*, 28–34.
9. Cornide, "Observaciones," AGI, Buenos Aires 326, fols. 178v–179.
10. Saavedra, *La vida cotidiana*, 23, 102; Isidro Dubert García, *Historia de la familia en Galicia durante la época moderna, 1550–1830 (Estructura, modelos hereditarios y conflictividad)* (A Coruña: Ediciós do Castro, 1992), 19–20; and Poska, *Women and Authority*, 35 and chap. 4.
11. Eiras Roel, *La población de Galicia*, 202–3, and app. 1, tables 29–41; and Poska, *Women and Authority*, chaps. 1–2.

12. In 1750 the Crown had decided to make the port city the home of the royal arsenal and the main base for the royal navy. As a result, between 1752 and 1767 the population increased some 190 percent: Martín García, *Demografía y comportamientos demográficos*, 43; AGI, Buenos Aires 326, fol. 124.
13. Lelo Bellotto, *Correio marítimo hispano-americano*, 247–55.
14. AGI, Buenos Aires 326, fol. 136v.
15. AGI, Buenos Aires 326, fol. 151; AGI, Buenos Aires 329, nf; and Apolant, *Operativo Patagonia*, 51–52. These prices were considerably less than the typical fares of two hundred pesos fuertes; see Lelo Bellotto, *Correio marítimo hispano-americano*, 247.
16. On migration and the European peasantry more broadly, see Moch, "The European Perspective," 115–40. On mobility among the Spanish peasantry, see Vassberg, *The Village and the Outside World in Golden Age Castile*, esp. chap. 4. For an overview of female migration in Spain, see Rey Castelao, "Las migraciones femeninas de antiguo régimen," 39–67.
17. Dudley Baines, "European Emigration, 1815–1930: Looking at the Emigration Decision Again," *Economic History Review*, New Series, 47, no. 3 (August 1994): 525–44; Eiras Roel, "Migraciones internas y médium-distance," 37–83; and Germán Rueda Hernanz et al., "Estudios en preparación sobre la emigración de Santander a las Américas," in *La emigración española a Ultramar*, ed. Antonio Eiras Roel (Madrid: Tabapress, 1991), 69. On the debate over women's motivations for migration, see Mirjana Morokvasic, "Women in Migration: Beyond the Reductionist Outlook," in *One Way Ticket: Migration and Female Labour*, ed. Annie Phizacklea (London: Routledge, 1983), esp. 28–29.
18. For an excellent discussion of the complex factors involved in migration, see David Tidswell, "Gender, Family, Work, and Migration in Early Nineteenth-Century Scotland," in *Women, Gender, and Labour Migration: Historical and Global Perspectives*, ed. Pamela Sharpe (London: Routledge, 2001), 127–44.
19. The easiest way to document female migration is to note that they bore children in places other than their native villages. The genealogical work completed by Juan Alejandro Apolant for *Operativo Patagonia* allowed me to trace the movements of most of the families. Leslie Moch makes a strong argument for the importance of local itineraries to understanding larger migration processes in "The Importance of Mundane Movements," 98.
20. Apolant, *Operativo Patagonia*, 227, 230.
21. Isidro Dubert, "Attraction urbaine et dynamiques migratoires du service domestique en Galice, 1752–1924," *Annales de démographie historique* 1 (2001): 155–76; and Dubert, "Modernity without Modernisation," 199–210.
22. There were only 82.5 men for every 100 women: see Vigo Trasancos, *A Coruña y el siglo de las luces*, 141; and Eiras Roel, "Demografía rural en la España moderna," 28.
23. Martín García, *Demografía y comportamientos demográficos*, 86.

24. Paul-André Rosental has argued that at a distance as short as twenty kilometers, a migrant entered an environment that was less familiar than that of her or his native village, in "La migration des femmes (et des hommes) en France au XIX siècle," 109–10.
25. Sebastián de Miñano, *Diccionario geográfico-estadístico de España y Portugal dedicado al Rey Nuestro Señor*, tomo 4 (Madrid: Imprenta Pierart-Peralta, 1827), 138.
26. See Baudilio Barreiro, *La Coruña 1752 según las respuestas generales del Catastro de Ensenada* (Madrid: Tabapress, 1990).
27. Apolant, *Operativo Patagonia*, 232, 239.
28. AGI, Buenos Aires 326, fols. 256, 284v–285.
29. Ibid., fol. 332.
30. Jacobs, "Legal and Illegal Immigration," 60–63.
31. AGI, Buenos Aires 326, fols. 350–53.
32. Ibid., fol. 139. For reasons that are unclear, the nephew did not make the voyage.
33. The licenses to go to the Indies included the same information: see Jacobs, "Legal and Illegal Immigration," 62. On this emphasis on physiognomy, see Joanne Rappaport, "'Asi lo paresçe por su aspeto': Physiognomy and the Construction of Difference in Colonial Bogotá," *Hispanic American Historical Review* 91, no. 4 (2011): 601–31.
34. On related issues, see Valentin Groebner, *Who Are You? Identification, Deception, and Surveillance in Early Modern Europe*, trans. Mark Kyburz and John Peck (New York: Zone Books, 2007).
35. AGI, Buenos Aires 326, fol. 300v; and Apolant, *Operativo Patagonia*, 248.
36. Poska, *Women and Authority*, chap. 3.
37. AGI, Buenos Aires 326, fol. 136.
38. AGI, Buenos Aires 410, nf.
39. Grace Coolidge has asserted that Spanish women's ability to waive these rights made them "legally male": see *Guardianship, Gender, and the Nobility in Early Modern Spain* (Burlington, VT: Ashgate Press, 2011), 31–32.
40. AGI, Buenos Aires 326, fols. 256, 283, 258ff.
41. Spaniards expected a certain reciprocity between themselves and the Crown. Since at least the reign of Isabel and Ferdinand, the monarchy had relied on the love and loyalty of its subjects, and in return Spanish subjects expected that the Crown would be responsive to their needs: see Corteguera, *For the Common Good*, 196. Similarly, Carla Rahn Phillips argues that "royal authority was strongest when it fulfilled the requirement to act for the well-being of the citizenry and when it rewarded steadfast loyalty with tangible benefits": see "The Organization of Oceanic Empires: The Iberian World in the Habsburg Period (and a Bit Beyond)," paper presented at Seascapes, Littoral Cultures, and Trans-Oceanic Exchanges symposium, Library of Congress, Washington, DC, 12–15 February

2003, www.historycooperative.org/proceedings/seascapes/phillips.html (accessed 21 November 2010).

42. Apolant, *Operativo Patagonia*, 244; and Apolant, *Génesis de la familia Uruguaya*, 658–59, 647.
43. For instance, Gozón and Siero: see Florentino López Iglesias, *El grupo doméstico en la Asturias del siglo XVIII* (Oviedo: Real Instituto de Estudios Asturianos, 1999), 57, 63. On the economy, see Gonzalo Anes, *Economía y sociedad en la Asturias del antiguo régimen* (Barcelona: Editorial Ariel, 1988).
44. AGI, Buenos Aires 326, fol. 228v.
45. María del Carmen Ansón Calvo, "Niños ilegítimos y niños expósitos en las Asturias del siglo XVIII: la propuesta de un ministerio de sanidad," in *Expostos e ilegítimos na realidade Ibérica do século XVI ao presente*, ed. Vicente Pérez Moreda (Porto, Portugal: Edições Afrontamento, 1993), 205–229, esp. 210–11. For a more general discussion of the agricultural problems of the period, see Domínguez Ortiz, *Sociedad y estado*, 402–28.
46. Detailed studies of these areas include Yun Casalilla, *Sobre la transición al capitalismo en Castilla*; Pérez García, *Un modelo social leonés en crecimiento*; and Marcos Martín, *Economía, sociedad, pobreza en Castilla*.
47. On poor harvests in the areas, see Yun Casalilla, *Sobre la transición al capitalismo en Castilla*, 591ff. For more on the climate and related crises, see Armando Alberola Romá, "Clima, crisis y reformismo agrario en tiempos del conde de Floridablanca," *Mélanges de la Casa de Velázquez* 93, no. 2 (2009): 105–25.
48. For some insight into the material conditions of these peasants, see Juan Manuel Bartolomé Bartolomé, "Condiciones de vida y privacidad cotidiana del campesinado leonés de Tierra de Campos: la comarca de Sahagún en el siglo XVIII," *Estudios humanísticos. Historia* 4 (2005): 37–52.
49. Eiras Roel, "Demografía rural," 36 (table); Vicente Pérez Moreda and David Reher, "Hacía una definición de la demografía urbana: España en 1787," *Revista de demografía histórica* 21, no. 2 segunda época (2003), cuadro 2; and López Iglesias, *El grupo doméstico*, 72ff. For the data on Siero and Langreo in 1787, see María del Carmen Ansón Calvo, *Asturias en la España del Carlos III: demografía y sociedad* (Oviedo, Spain: Universidad de Oviedo, 1999), 193–99. According to Baudilio Barriero Mallón, in the eighteenth century migration was largely confined to the coastal areas west of Gijón: "Ritmo, causas y consecuencias de la emigración asturiana a América, 1700–1850," in Eiras Roel, *La emigración española a Ultramar*, 43.
50. Apolant, *Operativo Patagonia*, 328, 247, 298.
51. AGI, Buenos Aires 410, nf.
52. Apolant, *Operativo Patagonia*, 332–33.
53. AGI, Buenos Aires 414, no. 50; and Apolant, *Operativo Patagonia*, 364.
54. AGI, Buenos Aires 415, no. 138.
55. Apolant, *Operativo Patagonia*, 340, 309, 349.

Chapter Three

1. José Mathías Escribano, *Itinerario español o guia de caminos para ir desde Madrid a todas las ciudades y villas más principales de España: y para ir de unas ciudades a otras, y a algunas Cortes de la Europa* (Madrid, 1767), www.archive.org/stream/itinerarioespaooescr#page/n3/mode/2up.
2. No doubt the roads were in worse repair after the Napoleonic wars, but the general problems of travel date from an earlier period: see Julián Francisco Suarez Freyre, *Viage de Galicia desde la villa de Benavente, ó breve descripción de sus dos carreteras: de la construída desde Astorga a La Coruña, y de la que debe construirse desde la villa de Benavente a la ciudad de Orense, Santiago y Vigo . . .* (Santiago de Compostela: Ayuntamiento Constitucional, 1813), 4, available at cervantesvirtual.com; and D. Gaspar Melchor de Jovellanos, "Carta tercera a Antonio Ponz," in *Obras publicadas é inéditas de D. Gaspar Melchor de Jovellanos*, tomo 2, *Colección hecho e ilustrada por don Cándido Nocedal* (Madrid, 1859), 281.
3. On the state of Spanish roads, see Shaw, "*El siglo de hazer caminos*," 413–34. On transportation more generally, see David R. Ringrose, *Transportation and Economic Stagnation in Spain, 1750–1850* (Durham, NC: Duke University Press, 1970).
4. On the state of roads and roadside inns, see Madrazo, *El sistema de transportes en España*, 1750–1850, 1:238–47, 247–54, 260–73; and 2:chap. 3. On how the poor roads impeded development in Galicia, see Hortensio Sobrado Correa, "Obstáculos estructurales al desarrollo de los intercambios comerciales en la Galicia de la edad moderna," *Obradoiro de historia moderna* 17 (2008): 303–24.
5. AGI, Buenos Aires 411, no. 396; and AGI, Buenos Aires 326, fol. 495.
6. AGI, Buenos Aires 326, fols. 475–477v, 489.
7. AGI, Buenos Aires 327, nf; and Apolant, *Operativo Patagonia*, 79–80n83.
8. AGI, Buenos Aires 327, nf.
9. AGI, Buenos Aires 326, fols. 313, 493–495v.
10. AMC, Colección de la familia de Cayo Acha de Patiño, caja 6 (2).
11. AGI, Buenos Aires 326, fols. 508, 909v; and Vigo Trasancos, *A Coruña y el siglo de las luces*, 36–37.
12. AGI, Buenos Aires 411, no. 207; AGI, Buenos Aires 326, fol. 508; and AGI, Buenos Aires 414, no. 39.
13. AMC, Colección de la familia de Cayo Acha de Patiño, caja 5 (1)1; and AGI, Buenos Aires 412, fol. 392.
14. AMC, Colección de la familia de Cayo Acha de Patiño, caja 5 (1)1, Libro de cuentas, 25 mayo hasta 31 julio 1779, and diciembre 1779. On female landlords in Galicia, see Serrana M. Rial García, *Las mujeres en la economía urbana del antiguo régimen: Santiago durante el siglo XVIII* (A Coruña: Ediciós do Castro, 1995).
15. AMC, Colección de la familia de Cayo Acha de Patiño, caja 5 (1)1, Libro de cuentas, noviembre 1779, and caja 5 (1)2; Vigo Trasancos, *A Coruña y el siglo de las*

luces, 36n39; Miguel Parrilla Hermida, "Los cuarteles de La Coruña," *Boletín de la Real Academia Galega* 25 (1953): 297–300, 437; and AMC, Colección de la familia de Cayo Acha de Patiño, caja 5 (1)2.

16. AGI, Buenos Aires 413, nf.
17. AGI, Buenos Aires 326, fol. 395.
18. AGI, Buenos Aires 411, nos. 125, 127, 133.
19. AGI, Buenos Aires 326, fols. 507, 576; and AMC, Colección de la familia de Cayo Acha de Patiño, caja 5 (1)2, enero 1780.
20. AGI, Buenos Aires 326, fol. 908; AGI, Buenos Aires 414, no. 1335; and AGI, Buenos Aires 412, fol. 415.
21. Apolant, *Operativo Patagonia*, includes the list of each company, 77–78.
22. AMC, Colección de la familia de Cayo Acha de Patiño, caja 6 (2); and AGI, Buenos Aires 326, fol. 321.
23. Anonymous, "Breve descripcion de las circumstancias en que se halla la provincia de Buenos Ayres y Yslas Malvinas y el modo facil de reparar la imprefeccion de su actualidad (1774)," AGI, Buenos Aires 326, fol. 63. The 1744 census indicates a significant excess of men (1.12), but the 1778 census indicates that the balance had changed and that there was a slight excess (.95) of women: see Johnson and Socolow, "Población y espacio en el Buenos Aires," 332.
24. AGI, Buenos Aires 326, fol. 568.
25. Apolant, *Operativo Patagonia*, 353, 303, 362.
26. AGI, Buenos Aires 411, no. 332.
27. This emphasis on marriage reflected the Bourbon monarchy's intensified intervention in the family. With the issuance of the Royal Pragmatic on Marriages (1776), state authority replaced ecclesiastical courts in arbitrating conflicts between parents and children over spousal choice: see Ann Twinam, *Public Lives, Private Secrets: Gender, Honor, Sexuality and Illegitimacy in Colonial Spanish America* (Stanford, CA: Stanford University Press, 1999), esp. 301–13; Saether, "Bourbon Absolutism and Marriage Reform in Late Colonial Spanish America," 475–509; and Seed, *To Love, Honor, and Obey in Colonial Mexico*, chap. 13.
28. During the annual migration from Galicia to the grain harvests of Castile, authorities were concerned about the large numbers of single women, whom they accused of falsifying familial relationships to men and even dressing like men in order to evade restrictions on their movement. Meijide Pardo, "Emigración gallega intrapeninsular," 533–34.
29. AGI, Buenos Aires 326, fol. 544.
30. For Galicia, see Eiras Roel, "Mecanismos autoreguladores, evolución demográfica y diversificación intrarregional," 71; and Eiras Roel, *La población de Galicia*, 197–98. For Asturias and Castilla la Vieja, see Dopico, "Nupcialidad y familia en España (siglos XVI–XX)." The average age of marriage was even higher in some parts of León: see María José Pérez Álvarez, "Estrategias matrimoniales en la provincia de León (siglo XVIII)," in *Actas del Congreso Internacional de la*

Población: V Congreso de la ADEH, vol. 4, *Matrimonio y nupcialidad: perspectivas interdisciplinares* (Logroño, Spain: Ediciones Instituto de Estudios Riojanos, 1999), 161–62. On younger husbands, see Eiras Roel, *La población de Galicia*, 200–201. There is significant evidence of economic equality as well. Not only was partible inheritance the legal and social norm, but in many areas (particularly on the Atlantic and northern coasts), women received supplements to their partible inheritance, and uxorilocal residence was common: see Poska, *Women and Authority*.

31. Of the couples, twelve were both Asturians, eleven were both Castilians, seven were Galician women and Castilian men, and six were other combinations, including a Basque couple.
32. Apolant, *Operativo Patagonia*, 289.
33. Ibid., 312, 344, 369–70.
34. Ibid., 306, 307, 351.
35. Ibid., 274, 314.
36. Ibid., 303.
37. Ibid., 377–78; AGI, Buenos Aires 413, no. 906; and Apolant, *Operativo Patagonia*, 320. There is no mention of her having a husband, and it is not clear what had become of her own child.
38. AGI, Buenos Aires 412, fol. 504.
39. AGI, Buenos Aires 414, no. 1310; and Apolant, *Operativo Patagonia*, 237.
40. AGI, Buenos Aires 414, no. 1311; and Apolant, *Operativo Patagonia*, 240–41.
41. Apolant, *Operativo Patagonia*, 376.
42. Ibid., 281, 262, 255, 252.
43. AGI, Buenos Aires 326, fols. 519, 494.
44. Mary Lindemann, *Health and Healing in Eighteenth-Century Germany* (Baltimore, MD: Johns Hopkins University Press, 1996), 321–22.
45. On Buen Suceso hospital, see Baudilio Barreiro Mallón and Ofelia Rey Castelao, *Pobres, peregrinos y enfermos: la red asistencial gallega en el antiguo régimen* (Santiago de Compostela: Ediciones Consorcio de Santiago, 1999), 89–90; and Vigo Trasancos, *A Coruña y el siglo de las luces*, 278, 281, 379. Like most hospitals of the period, Buen Suceso catered mainly to travelers, many of whom were pilgrims on the way to Santiago de Compostela: see Piedad Barreiro Barreiro, "Relación de peregrinos a Santiago que recibieron asistencia en el 'Hospital del Buen Suceso' de La Coruña desde 1696 a 1800," *Compostellanum* 11 (1966): 725–52.
46. AGI, Buenos Aires 326, fol. 581; AGI, Buenos Aires 411, no. 87; and AGI, Buenos Aires 412, fol. 401.
47. Posse Roybanes (also spelled Pose Roibanes) was later central to the introduction of smallpox vaccination to Galicia and the Balmis expedition to the Americas. For more on Roybanes, see Carlos M. Fernández Fernández, "El médico Pose Roibanes: un brigantino en los inicios de la lucha contra la viruela," *Anuario*

brigantino 30 (2007): 249–62; AGI, Buenos Aires 413, no. 921; and AGI, Buenos Aires 414, no. 1283.

48. AGI, Buenos Aires 413, no. 921.
49. AGI, Buenos Aires 411, no. 439.
50. AGI, Buenos Aires 411, no. 212; and AGI, Buenos Aires 412, fol. 163. This documentation includes many requests written by notaries on behalf of patients or their spouses that describe either their ailments or their treatments as they requested additional alms from Astraudi. They provide important descriptions of illness by nonelites. Studies of letters from literate Spanish patients to doctors include José Pardo-Tomás and Alvar Martínez Vidal, "Stories of Disease Written by Patients and Lay Mediators in the Spanish Republic of Letters (1680–1720)," *Journal of Medieval and Early Modern Studies* 38, no. 3 (Fall 2008): 467–91; and Alfons Zarzoso, "Medicine through Private Letters: The Eighteenth-Century Catalan Medical World," in *Cultural Approaches to the History of Medicine*, ed. Willem de Beécourt and Cornelie Usborne (Basingstoke, UK: Palgrave Macmillan, 2004): 108–26. AGI, Buenos Aires 412, fol. 314.
51. AGI, Buenos Aires 414, no. 1200.
52. AGI, Buenos Aires 411, no. 246.
53. Poska, "Babies on Board," 269–83.
54. AGI, Buenos Aires 327, nf.
55. Since 1750 midwives were regulated by the Royal Protomedicato, but none ever sought payment from Astraudi for their services nor did any colonist explicitly request additional alms to pay the costs of a midwife. On the Royal Protomedicato and midwives, see María Soledad Campos Díez, *El Real Tribunal del Protomedicato Castellano (siglos XVI–XIX)* (Cuenca: Ediciones de la Universidad de Castilla–La Mancha, 1999), 150. On midwives, see Teresa Ortiz Gómez, "From Hegemony to Subordination," 99; and "Protomedicato y matronas: una relación al servicio de la cirugía," *Dynamis* 16 (1996): 109–21. On childbirth more generally, see Jacques Gélis, *History of Childbirth: Fertility, Pregnancy, and Birth in Early Modern Europe*, trans. Rosemary Morris (Boston, MD: Northeastern University Press, 1991).
56. This evidence supports the argument that male practitioners intervened only in dangerous births and that outside of England, particularly southern Europe, male doctors did not usurp the role of women at births: see Lianne McTavish, *Childbirth and the Display of Authority in Early Modern France* (Aldershot, UK: Ashgate Press, 2005), 11; and the essays by Teresa Ortiz Gómez and Nadia Maria Filippini in *The Art of Midwifery*.
57. AGI, Buenos Aires 411, no. 396; AGI, Buenos Aires 414, no. 1283; and AGI, Buenos Aires 412, fol. 317v.
58. AGI, Buenos Aires 414, no. 1309.

59. Apolant, *Operativo Patagonia*, 365. It is difficult to know for certain that this was a caesarean birth, as the description of the operation comes from the husband, not the doctor. I consulted various experts in the field, but found no consensus. Jaime Alcalá Martínez reported a successful cesarean on a living woman in his *Disertación médico-chirúrgica, sobre una operación cesárea executada en muger y feto vivos, en la ciudad de Valencia* (Valencia, 1753), cited in José G. Rigau-Pérez, "Surgery at the Service of Theology: Postmortem Cesarean Sections in Puerto Rico and the Royal Cedula of 1804," *Hispanic American Historical Review* 75, no. 3 (1995): 383.
60. Apolant, *Operativo Patagonia*, 240.
61. On fathers and wet nurses, see Christiane Klapisch-Zuber, *Women, Family, and Ritual in Renaissance Italy*, trans. Lydia Cochrane (Chicago, IL: University of Chicago Press, 1985), 143–44.
62. AGI, Buenos Aires 413, nos. 906, 989. On wet-nursing, see Carmen Sarasúa, *Criados, nodrizas y amos: el servicio doméstico en la formación del mercado de trabajo madrileño, 1758–1868* (Madrid: Siglo XXI, 1994); Emilie L. Bergmann, "Milking the Poor: Wet-nursing and the Sexual Economy of Early Modern Spain," in *Marriage and Sex in Medieval and Early Modern Iberia*, ed. Eukene Lacarra Lanz (New York: Routledge, 2002), 90–114; Claude Larquié, "Les milieux nourriciers des enfants madrilènes au XVIIe siècle," *Mélanges de la Casa de Velásquez* 19 (1983): 95–118; Sherwood, *Poverty in Eighteenth-Century Spain*, chap. 4; Premo, *Children of the Father King*, 168; and Premo, "'Misunderstood Love.'"
63. AGI, Buenos Aires 326, fol. 581; AGI, Buenos Aires 411, nos. 285, 339; for child mortality rates in the region, see Saavedra, *La vida cotidiana*, 180–83.
64. Children who died were removed from the accounting lists, but not all newborns would have lived long enough to be placed on the lists in the first place. The total of forty-three children for whom I have evidence of their deaths at port is surely an undercount: AGI, Buenos Aires 411, nos. 284, 378; and AGI, Buenos Aires 412, fol. 105.
65. AMC, Colección de la familia de Cayo Acha de Patiño, caja 3 (2–7).
66. AGI, Buenos Aires 413, no. 891.
67. AGI, Buenos Aires 327, nf.
68. AGI, Buenos Aires 412, fol. 500.
69. AGI, Buenos Aires 413, nos. 995, 996; and AGI, Buenos Aires 327, nf.
70. AGI, Buenos Aires 327, nf.
71. Ibid.
72. Apolant, *Operativo Patagonia*, 77: those reminders go back as early as 1780; AGI, Buenos Aires 326, fol. 940; and Apolant, *Operativo Patagonia*, 86.
73. Apolant, *Operativo Patagonia*, 380, 88.
74. Due to discrepancies between the passenger lists created in La Coruña and those in Montevideo, it is impossible to be absolutely certain how many passengers made the transatlantic voyage.

Chapter Four

1. Lelo Bellotto, *Correio marítimo hispano-americano*, 248–51; Hernán Asdrúbal Silva, *El comercio entre España y el Río de la Plata (1778–1810)* (Madrid: Banco de España—Servicio de Estudios, Estudios de Historia Económica, nº 26—1993), 78–79. In addition to other cargo, the *Princesa* carried one hundred plows designed especially for the project. There is extensive and very interesting documentation about the design of these plows in AGI, Buenos Aires 326.
2. AGI, Buenos Aires 410, nf; quoted in Apolant, *Operativo Patagonia*, 75; and AGI, Buenos Aires 327, nf.
3. Apolant, *Operativo Patagonia*, 74; and AGI, Buenos Aires 327, nf.
4. AMC, Colección de la familia de Cayo Acha de Patiño, caja 3(2–6).
5. AGI, Buenos Aires 327, nf.
6. Cesáreo Fernández Duro, *Disquisiciones náuticas: la mar descrita por los mareados* (Madrid: Imprenta Estereotipia y Galvanoplastia de Aribau y Cª, 1877), 2:146–47, at archive.org.
7. AGI, Buenos Aires 410, nf.
8. Apolant, *Operativo Patagonia*, 239.
9. This is the description of the festivities before the second voyage, but the events were replicated prior to each embarkation: see AGI, Buenos Aires 326, fols. 313–15; and AGI, Buenos Aires 410. Celebrations surrounding the departure of the *Nuestra Señora del Socorro* are at AGI, Buenos Aires 326, fol. 313. Although the monarchy increasingly regulated and even prohibited many similar public festivities, these differed in that they were carefully orchestrated by Astraudi on behalf of the Crown. On Bourbon regulation of public events, see Linda A. Curcio-Nagy, *The Great Festivals of Colonial Mexico City: Performing Power and Identity* (Albuquerque: University of New Mexico Press, 2004), chap. 5; and Juan Pedro Viqueira Albán, *Propriety and Permissiveness in Bourbon Mexico*, trans. Sonya Lipsett-Rivera and Sergio Rivera Ayala (Wilmington, DE: Scholarly Resources, 1999).
10. AGI, Buenos Aires 412, fols. 255–58.
11. AGI, Buenos Aires 412, fols. 255–58; and AGI, Buenos Aires 413, no. 896.
12. See Bolufer, *Mujeres e ilustración*, 244; Bolufer, "Actitudes y discursos sobre la maternidad en la España del siglo XVIII"; Sally-Ann Kitts, *The Debate on the Nature, Role, and Influence of Woman in Eighteenth-Century Spain* (Lewiston, PA: Edwin Mellon Press, 1995), 85–87; and Elizabeth Franklin Lewis, *Women Writers in the Spanish Enlightenment: The Pursuit of Happiness* (Aldershot, UK: Ashgate Press, 2004), 44–46. Breastfeeding also cut costs and the weight of supplies on ship, but as Astraudi spent generously at all other points, expense does not seem to have been an issue. Breastfeeding also suppressed fertility. Scholars assume from demographic data that Galician women typically breastfed for one to two years: see Saavedra, *La vida cotidiana*, 182.

13. AGI, Buenos Aires 327, nf. Although it is possible that the lactating mothers wanted more rations for themselves, an inability to breastfeed on ship seems to have been common on ocean voyages: see Haines and Shlomowitz, "Explaining the Modern Mortality Decline," 31–32.
14. AGI, Buenos Aires 327, nf.
15. AGI, Buenos Aires 329, nf.
16. Diario de navegación del paquebot "La Princesa," AGI, Correos, 192B, R.4; Malvar y Pinto, quoted in Apolant, *Operativo Patagonia*, 48n34; and Diario de navegación del paquebot "El Real Carlos," AGI, Correos, S, 194B, R.5.
17. On the elaborate "baptism of the tropics" performed on a French ship, see Marc-Antoine Caillot, *A Company Man: The Remarkable French-Atlantic Voyage of a Clerk for the Company of the Indies*, ed. Erin M. Greenwald and trans. Teri F. Chalmers (New Orleans, LA: The Historic New Orleans Collection, 2013), 29–34; and Robert W. Harms, *The Diligent: A Voyage through the Worlds of the Slave Trade* (New York: Basic Books, 2002), 105–6; Jaime Rodrigues, "A New World in the Atlantic: Sailors and Rites of Passage crossing the Equator, from the 15th to the 20th centuries," *Revista brasileira de história* 33, no. 65 (2013): 235–76, http://dx.doi.org/10.1590/S0102-01882013000100010.
18. Pérez-Mallaína, *Spain's Men of the Sea*, 137.
19. Porro Gutiérrez, *La emigración asturiana y castellano-leonesa*, 62.
20. Diario de navegación del paquebot "El Cortés," AGI, Correos, 194B, R.7-4 recto.
21. AGI, Buenos Aires 327, nf.
22. Apolant, *Operativo Patagonia*, 87.
23. AGI, Buenos Aires 326, fol. 972.
24. Diario de navegación del paquebot "El Real Carlos," AGI, Correos, 194B, R.5-7 verso and 69 recto.
25. AGI, Buenos Aires 327, nf. Hernán Silva implies that the captain's decision to throw the paperwork overboard was a tactic to hide the fact that he was transporting illicit goods: see *El comercio entre España y el Río de la Plata*, 79.
26. AGI, Buenos Aires 328, nf.
27. Porro Gutiérrez, *La emigración asturiana y castellano-leonesa*, 64.
28. On ship life during an earlier period, see Antonio de Guevara, *Arte del marear y de los inventores de ella: con muchos avisos para los que navegan en ellas* (Valladolid, 1539), www.filosofia.org/cla/gue/gueam.htm; and Pérez-Mallaína, *Spain's Men of the Sea*.
29. AGI, Buenos Aires, 327, nf; and Apolant, *Operativo Patagonia*, 87.
30. David Northrup, *Indentured Labor in the Age of Imperialism, 1834–1922* (Cambridge: Cambridge University Press, 1995), 84; and Klaus J. Bade, *Migration in European History*, trans. Allison Brown (Malden, MA: Blackwell Pubs, 2003), 86.
31. Thanks to Carla Rahn Phillips for examining the descriptions of the ships and helping me understand how the ships were reconfigured to lodge the peasant

passengers. For a comparison with the space on slave ships, see Garland and Klein, "The Allotment of Space for Slaves aboard Eighteenth-Century British Slave Ships," 238–48. On the living space on galleons, see Fernández Duro, *Disquisiciones náuticas*, vol. 2, 144ff.

32. Vicente Lardizábal, *Consideraciones político-médicas sobre la salud de los navegantes, en que se exponen las causas de sus mas frecuentes enfermedades, modo de precaverlas, y curarlas*, 16; Pedro González, *Tratado de enfermedades de la gente de mar en que se exponen sus causas, y los medios de precaverlas* (1805), 378; Phillips, *Six Galleons for the King of Spain*, 156–57; and Alfredo Martín García, "Entre el mar y la muerte: procedencias, condiciones de vida y mortalidad de los navegantes en el Real Servicio (1776–1804)," *Espacio, tiempo y forma, serie IV, historia moderna*, t. 12 (1999), 431–32. On lice, see Fernández Duro, *Disquisiciones náuticas*, 408, and on fleas, 436.
33. Certainly, the advent of the steamship and the overcrowding of the mass migrations of the nineteenth century had a negative effect on the voyage; however, it is hard to imagine that by that point transatlantic travel was less comfortable than it had been a century earlier: see Juaco López Álvarez, "Cartas desde América: la emigración de asturianos a través de la correspondencia, 1899–1925," *Revista de dialectología y tradiciones populares*, tomo 55, cuaderno 1 (2000), 89. For an eighteenth-century German servant's account of the transatlantic voyage, see Susan E. Klepp, Farley Grubb, and Anne Pfaelzer de Ortiz, eds., *Souls for Sale: Two German Redemptioners Come to Revolutionary America; The Life Stories of John Frederick Whitehead and Johann Carl Büttner* (University Park: Pennsylvania State University Press, 2006). For a Frenchman's account, see Caillot, *A Company Man*. For the most recent work on the subject, see Stephen R. Berry, *A Path in the Mighty Waters: Shipboard Life and Atlantic Crossings to the New World* (New Haven, CT: Yale University Press, 2015).
34. Pérez-Mallaína, *Spain's Men of the Sea*, 136.
35. AGI, Buenos Aires 326, fol. 146.
36. Lardizábal, *Consideraciones político-médicas*; and slightly later, González, *Tratado de enfermedades*. For a discussion of foodstuffs on ship, see Fernández Duro, *Disquisiciones náuticas*, 2:133ff; and Phillips, *Six Galleons for the King of Spain*, 96ff, 163ff. Juan Cartaya Baños, "La alimentación de la Armada española en la Edad Moderna: una visión distinta de la batalla de Trafalgar," *Historia, instituciones, documentos* 35 (2008): 127–48.
37. On chocolate as a medicine, see Marcy Norton, *Sacred Gifts, Profane Pleasures: A History of Tobacco and Chocolate in the Atlantic World* (Ithaca, NY: Cornell University Press, 2008).
38. Apolant, *Operativo Patagonia*, 54–55.
39. AGI, Buenos Aires 326, fol. 805; AGI, Buenos Aires 327, nf; and Caillot, *A Company Man*, 23.
40. Feijoo, *Teatro crítico universal*, "Honra y provecho de la agricultura."

41. Joseph Townsend, *A Journey through Spain in the Years 1786 and 1787 with Particular Attention to the Agriculture, Manufactures, Commerce, Population, Taxes, and Revenue of That Country* (London: C. Dilly, 1791), 2:14.
42. On peasant diets, see Saavedra, *La vida cotidiana*, chap. 5.
43. Adolfo I. Arbelo García, ed., *Al recibo de esta . . . relaciones epistolares canario-americanas del siglo XVIII* (Santa Cruz de Tenerife: Ediciones Idea, 2010), 133.
44. AGNA, Sala IX, Montevideo 2.3.6, fols. 701–3.
45. Manuel Gracia Rivas, "La sanidad naval española: de Lepanto a Trafalgar," *Cuadernos de historia moderna*, Anejos 5 (2006): 167–85. For a discussion of British maritime surgeons, see Haines, *Doctors at Sea*, 56ff.
46. Mikel Astrain Gallart, *Barberos, cirujanos y gente de mar: la sanidad naval y la profesión quirúrgica en la España ilustrada* (Madrid: Ministerio de Defensa, 1996), 133ff, and chap. 3; for another discussion of ship doctors, see Robin Haines, "Medical Superintendence and Child Health on Government-Assisted Voyages to South Australia in the Nineteenth Century," *Health and History* 3, no. 2 (2001): 1–29.
47. Astrain Gallart, *Barberos, cirujanos y gente de mar*, 142–43, 108.
48. AGI, Buenos Aires 326, fols. 812–13v. The list of pharmaceuticals on the *Nuestra Señora de los Dolores* appears in Apolant, *Operativo Patagonia*, 55; see the lists of medications in the appendix of J. L. Valverde López, F. Sánchez, L. Vinuesa, and R. Gómez Villalba Ballesteros, *La dotación de medicamentos en los buques de la armada durante los siglos XVII y XVIII* (Granada: Universidad de Granada, 1979).
49. Diario de navegación del paquebot, "La Princesa," AGI, Correos, 192B, R.4-5 recto; Lardizábal, *Consideraciones político-médicas*, 54–56; and González, *Tratado de enfermedades*, 113.
50. Fernández Duro, *Disquisiciones náuticas*, 2:159.
51. Arbelo García, *Al recibo de esta . . .*, 124.
52. González, *Tratado de enfermedades*, 104ff, 113. On seasickness in an earlier period, see Phillips, *Six Galleons for the King of Spain*, 155–57; and Pérez-Mallaína, *Spain's Men of the Sea*, 135–37.
53. González, *Tratado de enfermedades*, 104ff; and Klepp, Grubb, and Pfaelzer de Ortiz, *Souls for Sale*, 133.
54. Phillips, *Six Galleons for the King of Spain*, 174; and Julián de Zulueta and Lola Higueras, "Health and Navigation in the South Seas: The Spanish Experience," in *Starving Sailors: The Influence of Nutrition upon Naval and Maritime History*, ed. J. Watt, E. J. Freeman, and W. F. Bynum (Bristol, UK: National Maritime Museum, 1981), 85–99.
55. Apolant, *Operativo Patagonia*, 96–98.
56. The captain does not note the cause of death for the other passenger.
57. On children's illnesses during ocean voyages, see Haines and Shlomowitz, "Causes of Death," 51, 53.
58. This mortality rate is comparable to the rate of 9 percent for German immigrant children on the Atlantic voyage: see Grubb, "Morbidity and Mortality," 570. But

the rates are lower than the 13.1 percent of children who died on nineteenth-century voyages to Australia: see Haines and Shlomowitz, "Deaths of Babies Born," 117. For more on babies and ocean voyages, see Shlomowitz and McDonald, "Babies at Risk on Immigrant Voyages," 86–101. Note the numerical difference between these figures and those in my article "Babies on Board," 269–83. The discrepancy is due to different definition of "child." Both the ship captains and Juan Alejandro Apolant use the word "child" as a status rather than an age category, thus they included at least two "children" over the age of eighteen in their accounting of shipboard deaths. In this work, I have refined the definition to focus on children under age six.

59. Apolant, *Operativo Patagonia*, 298, 356, 309.
60. AGI, Buenos Aires 326, fol. 317v; and AGI, Buenos Aires 326, fols. 464v–65; see also Porro Gutiérrez, *La emigración asturiana y castellano-leonesa*, 67. For a more extensive discussion, see Poska, "Babies on Board."
61. AGI, Buenos Aires 328, nf.
62. Vidart, *El discípulo instruido*.
63. On the impact of seasickness on pregnant women, see Haines and Shlomowitz, "Causes of Death," 204.
64. For a discussion of privacy on ship, see Pérez-Mallaína, *Spain's Men of the Sea*, 139–40. In the nineteenth century, women who gave birth on Australia-bound ships reported that because of the quality of care, confinement was easier on ship than on land: see Haines and Shlomowitz, "Causes of Death," 201.
65. Apolant, *Operativo Patagonia*, 240.
66. I do not know the date of one birth.
67. Apolant, *Operativo Patagonia*, 326, 327, 343, 291, 328. Estimates of maternal mortality on land range from 1–2 percent to 8–15 percent. For the two extremes, see Roger Schofield, "Did the Mothers Really Die? Three Centuries of Maternal Mortality in 'the world we have lost,'" in *The World We Have Gained*, ed. Lloyd Bonfield, Richard M. Smith, and Keith Wrightson (Oxford: Basil Blackwell, 1986), 231–60; and Edward Shorter, *Women's Bodies: A Social History of Women's Encounter with Health, Ill-Health, and Medicine* (New Brunswick, NJ: Transaction Publishers, 1997), 97. The only data that exists on immigrant women's maternal mortality during ocean crossings is from the nineteenth century in Haines and Shlomowitz, "Causes of Death," 200. For a brief discussion of slave women and shipboard childbirth, see Emma Christopher, *Slave Ship Sailors and their Captive Cargoes, 1730–1807* (Cambridge: Cambridge University Press, 2006), 187.
68. Here too there is a slight discrepancy in the number of total deaths from my previously published work. This time, I counted those passengers who were eighteen years old and older as adults and included those who died while still on ship but before disembarking at Montevideo.

69. In the only truly comparable study—that of white, voluntary, civilian German immigrants to Philadelphia—Farley Grubb found a passage mortality rate of 3.8 percent: see "Morbidity and Mortality," 570; see also Berry, *Path in the Mighty Waters*, 40.
70. Apolant, *Operativo Patagonia*, 333, 291, 326, 359.
71. AGI, Buenos Aires 327, nf.
72. AGI, Buenos Aires 326, fols. 849, 927.
73. By the eighteenth century, children regularly made the transatlantic crossing, and not only as a part of the family resettlement projects discussed in chapter 1 and the military deployments discussed in chapter 2. See for instance, the recent work of Daniel Livesay about Jamaicans who regularly sent their children to England during this period and Jane Mangan's forthcoming work on mixed-race Spanish children making the voyage during the sixteenth century.
74. Berry, *Path in the Mighty Waters*, 60.
75. See for instance, Arbelo García, *Al recibo de esta . . .* ; Rosario Márquez Macías, *Historias de América: la emigración española en tinta y papel* (Huelva: Ertoil, 1994); Isabelo Macías and Francisco Morales Padrón, *Cartas desde América, 1700–1800* (Sevilla: Andalucía 92, 1991); and Caillot, *A Company Man*, 21.
76. Apolant, *Operativo Patagonia*, 368, 365, 262, 255, 262. For a discussion of bonding during the transatlantic voyage by slaves, see Walter Hawthorne, "'Being now, as it were, one family': Shipmate Bonding on the Slave Vessel *Emilia*, in Rio de Janeiro and throughout the Atlantic World," *Luso-Brazilian Review* 45, no. 1 (2008): 53–77.
77. Diario de navegación del paquebot "El Real Carlos," AGI, Correos, 194B, R.5; and Diario de navegación del paquebot "La Princesa," AGI, Correos, 192B, R.4, 42 recto, and 5 recto.
78. Diario de navegación del paquebot "La Princesa," AGI, Correos, 192B, R.4, 42 recto, and 5 verso ff; and AGI, Buenos Aires 327, nf.
79. Apolant, *Operativo Patagonia*, 347, 381, 343.
80. Ibid., 267, 354.
81. Diario de navegación del paquebot "La Princesa," AGI, Correos, 192B, R.4, 44 recto.

Chapter Five

1. Miguel Molina Martínez, "El giennense Antonio Viedma, colonizador y cronista de la costa patagónica," *Boletín del Instituto de Estudios Giennenses* 132 (1987): 39–62; and Senatore, *Arqueología e historia*, 46n97.
2. Diario de navegación del paquebot "La Diana," AGI, Correos, 195B, R9; and Diario de navegación del paquebot "La Diligencia," AGI, Correos, 193A, R7.

3. Biographical information on Vértiz is scattered, but one source is José Torre Revello, *Juan José de Vértiz y Salcedo gobernador y virrey de Buenos Aires ensayo basado en documentos inéditos del Archivo General de Indias* (Buenos Aires: Imprenta de la Universidad, 1932).
4. Gorla, *Los establecimientos españoles en la Patagonia*, 37–38. Although at times Piedra and the Viedma brothers would try to exploit this division of authority, in his account of his tenure as viceroy Vértiz spoke favorably about his interactions with the intendant and the two appear to have worked well together. Juan José de Vértiz y Salcedo, "Memoria a su sucesor Marqués de Loreto, Buenos Aires, 12 de marzo 1784," in *Memorias de los virreyes del Río de la Plata*, ed. Sigfrido Augusto Radaelli (Buenos Aires: Editorial Bajel, 1945), 28.
5. Vértiz, "Memoria a su sucesor," 60. Many years later and in order to distance himself from the project, Vértiz claimed that when Piedra presented his commission, it was the first that he had heard of the Patagonia project. However, it seems clear that he was being disingenuous, as the Crown had promulgated the royal decree at the end of March and it had arrived in the Río de la Plata in early June. In fact, Vértiz had sent a letter to Gálvez dated 16 July saying that he had received the decree and would put it in action as soon as spring arrived: see AGI, Buenos Aires 326, fols. 22–23. The letter is reprinted in Vicente G. Quesada, *La Patagonia y tierras australes del continente americano* (Buenos Aires: Imprenta y Librerías de Mayo, 1875), 582.
6. AGI, Buenos Aires 326, fol. 26ff.
7. James S. Cunningham, Jr., "Spanish Colonization in Patagonia, 1778–1783," unpublished PhD diss. (University of California, Berkeley, 1946), 26.
8. Cunningham, "Spanish Colonization," 26, 27; AGI, Buenos Aires 331, fol. 62; and AGI, Buenos Aires 326, fols. 227–28.
9. "Carta del Virrey Vértiz al Ministro Gálvez, del 30 noviembre de 1778," *Revista de la Biblioteca Nacional (Buenos Aires)* (*RBN*) tomo 2, no. 5 (enero–marzo 1938), 363.
10. AGI, Buenos Aires 326, fols. 199–207.
11. AGI, Buenos Aires 331, fol. 41ff.
12. On masculinity in early modern Europe, see Hendrix and Karant-Nunn, eds., *Masculinity in the Reformation Era*; and Susan Broomhall and Jacqueline Van Gent, eds., *Governing Masculinities in the Early Modern Period: Regulating Selves and Others* (Farnham, UK: Ashgate, 2011). On this masculine hierarchy, see Stern, *The Secret History of Gender*, 161ff; Poska "A Married Man Is a Woman," 8; and Taylor, *Honor and Violence in Golden Age Spain*, chap. 4.
13. According to Scott Taylor, "Male honor was less a static set of values or beliefs than an idea that could be invoked in order to defend oneself when challenged" (*Honor and Violence in Golden Age Spain*, 153).
14. Borreguero Beltrán, "Del tercio al regimiento," 75; Raúl O. Fradkin, "Tradiciones militares coloniales: el Río de la Plata antes de la revolución," in *Experiências*

nacionais, temas transversais: subsídios para uma história comparada da América Latina, comp. Flavio Heinz (São Leopoldo: Editora Oikos, 2009), 81n19; José Maréa Imízcoz Beunza, "Militares ilustrados: parentesco, amistad y afinidades políticas en la formación de 'elites estatales' en el siglo XVIII," in *Soldados de la ilustración: el ejército español en el siglo XVIII*, ed. Manuel Reyes-García Hurtado (A Coruña: Universidade da Coruña, 2012): 165–214.

15. Apolant, *Génesis de la familia uruguaya*, 1026.
16. Cristina Borreguero Beltrán, "La vida de los soldados en el siglo de las luces," in *Soldados de la Ilustración*, 15.
17. Pérez Estévez, *El problema de los vagos en la España*, 236ff. Some of them may have been vagrants taken up in the conscriptions of 1779: see Pedro-Alejo Llorente de Pedro, "La deserción militar y las fugas de los presidiarios en el antiguo régimen: especial estudio de su incidencia en los presidios norteafricanos," *Anuario de la facultad de derecho (Universidad de Alcalá)* (2006), 110.
18. Pérez, *En busca de mejor fortuna*, 190.
19. Chambers, "Masculine Virtues and Feminine Passions," 24, 26; and Matthew Brown, "Soldier Heroes and the Colombian Wars of Independence," *Hispanic Research Journal* 7, no. 1 (February 2006): 41–56.
20. Senatore, *Arqueología e historia*, 150–51.
21. Martínez de Gorla, "La presencia de Negros en la Nordpatagonia," 178; for more on royal slaves, see María Elena Díaz, *The Virgin, the King and the Royal Slaves of El Cobre* (Stanford, CA: Stanford University Press, 2000).
22. Núria Sala i Vila, "'Son más embusteros y trapalistas que los Gitanos de Cataluña': la imagen de los grupos pre-andinos del Cusco por los franciscanos del Colegio de Propaganda Fide de Monquegua," in *De la etnohistoria a la historia en los andes*, ed. John Fisher and David Cahill (Quito: Ediciones Abya-Yala, 2008), 44.
23. Antonio Comajuncosa, "Manifiesto histórico de lo que han trabajado los misioneros de Tarija así entre los fieles como entre los infieles desde el año de 1775 hasta el de 1810," in *El colegio franciscano de Tarija y sus misiones*, ed. A. M. Corrado (1884), 80.
24. Johnson, *Workshop of Revolution*, 68–75.
25. Falkner, *A Description of Patagonia*, 86–87.
26. AGI, Buenos Aires 331, fols. 145–46.
27. Pérez, *En busca de mejor fortuna*, 203, 201.
28. AGI, Buenos Aires 331, fols. 147–49.
29. Llorente de Pedro, "La deserción militar," includes Carlos III's regulations on deserters in appendix 3; and Pérez, *En busca de mejor fortuna*, 203ff.
30. Francisco de Viedma, *Memoria dirigida al señor Márquez de Loreto, virrey y capitán general de las provincias del Río de la Plata, sobre los obstáculos que han encontrado, y las ventajas que prometen los establecimientos proyectados en la Costa Patagónica* (1784).

31. Comajuncosa, "Manifiesto histórico de lo que han trabajado los misioneros de Tarija," 81.
32. AGI, Buenos Aires 331, fol. 51.
33. AGI, Buenos Aires 326, fols. 199–207.
34. Cited in Fradkin, "Tradiciones militares coloniales," 17; and AGI, Buenos Aires 331, fol. 140.
35. Álvaro Jara and John Jay TePaske, eds., *The Royal Treasuries of the Spanish Empire in America*, vol. 4, *Eighteenth-Century Ecuador* (Durham, NC: Duke University Press, 1990), xviff. For a discussion of *contadores* in Buenos Aires, see Socolow, *The Bureaucrats of Buenos Aires, 1769–1810*.
36. AGI, Buenos Aires 331, fol. 83; and Taylor, *Honor and Violence*, 111–12, 131.
37. AGI, Buenos Aires 331, fols. 93v, 163.
38. Vértiz, "Memoria a su sucesor," 61.
39. "Carta de Francisco de Viedma al Virrey Vértiz del 4 de junio de 1779," *RBN*, 409.
40. Gorla, *Los establecimientos españoles*, 56–57nn91–92.
41. "Carta del Virrey Vértiz al Ministro Gálvez del 3 de febrero de 1781," *RBN*, 473.
42. AGI, Buenos Aires 326, fol. 670.
43. See www.jameslindlibrary.org/illustrating/articles/james-lind-and-scurvy-1747-to-1795.
44. Phillips, *Six Galleons for the King of Spain*, 174.
45. AGI, Buenos Aires 326, fols. 626ff, 682–85.
46. Comajuncosa, "Manifiesto histórico de lo que han trabajado los misioneros de Tarija," 81.
47. AGI, Buenos Aires 326, fol. 700. Thanks to Alison Weber for help on the translation.
48. AGI, Buenos Aires 331, fol. 405; Juan Marchena Fernández, "Sin temor de rey ni de Dios: violencia, corrupción y crisis de autoridad en la Cartagena colonial," in *Soldados del Rey: el ejército borbónico en América colonial en vísperas de la independencia*, ed. Juan Marchena Fernández and Allan J. Kuethe (Castellón: Editorial Universitat Jaume I, 2005), 49–50.
49. AGNA, Sala IX, Montevideo 2.3.5, fol. 392; Apolant, *Operativo Patagonia*, 241.
50. AGI, Buenos Aires 326, fol. 636; and Apolant, *Operativo Patagonia*, 101n115.
51. AGI, Buenos Aires 326, fol. 634ff.
52. AGI, Buenos Aires 326, fol. 690; and Entraigas, *El fuerte del Río Negro*, 89.
53. AGNA, Sala IX, Montevideo 2.3.5, fol. 720.
54. Apolant, *Operativo Patagonia*, 242, 105.
55. AGI, Buenos Aires 326, fol. 769.
56. Antonio de Viedma, *Descripción de la costa meridional del sur, llamada vulgarmente Patagónica, relación de sus terrenos, producciones, brutos, aves y peces; indios que la habitan, su religión, costumbres, vestidos y trato; desde el puerto de*

Santa Elena en 44 grados, hasta el de la Virgen en 52, y boca del Estrecho de Magallanes (1783).

57. Mandrini and Ortelli, "Los 'Araucanos' en las Pampas (c. 1700–1850)," 237–57. For more on the Spanish designations for different Pampas and Patagonian peoples, see Nacuzzi, "Social Strategies in a Situation of Interethnic Contact," 89–102.
58. Antonio de Viedma, *Diario de un viaje a la costa de la Patagonia, para reconocer los puntos en donde establecer poblaciones con una descripción de la naturaleza de los terrenos, de sus producciones y habitantes; desde el puerto de Santa Elena hasta la boca del Estrecho de Magallanes* (1780).
59. AGI, Buenos Aires 327, nf.
60. A. Viedma, *Diario de un viaje*, 21–25 noviembre.
61. Apolant, *Operativo Patagonia*, 108.
62. Gorla, *Los establecimientos españoles*, 232–33.
63. Ibid., 92n172.
64. Buscaglia, "Los marinos malditos (Patagonia, siglo XVIII)," 46; Michael Lacombe makes a strong argument for the relationship between provisioning and authority in *Political Gastronomy*, 66.
65. AGI, Buenos Aires 327, nf; for other examples of the role of alcohol, see Johnson, "Dangerous Words, Provocative Gestures, and Violent Acts," 132.
66. Taylor, *Honor and Violence*, 111. On violence and card games, see Johnson, *Workshop of Revolution*, 72.
67. Gorla, *Los establecimientos españoles*, 108, 93.
68. Entraigas, *El fuerte del Río Negro*, 138.
69. AGI, Buenos Aires 327, nf.
70. Ibid.
71. On peasant male violence, see Stern, *The Secret History of Gender*, chap. 7.
72. AGI, Buenos Aires 327, nf. It is likely that Francisca Xaviera was an Indian.
73. AGNA, Sala IX, Costa Patagónica 16.3.8, nf.
74. AGI, Buenos Aires 326, fols. 204–5; on Spanish/Indian relations during this period, see Weber, *Bárbaros*.
75. Lidia R. Nacuzzi, "Francisco de Viedma, un 'cacique blanco' en tierra de indios," in *Funcionarios, diplomáticos, guerreros: miradas hacia el otro en las fronteras de pampa y Patagonia (siglos XVIII y XIX)*(Buenos Aires: Sociedad Argentina de Antropología, 2002), 30.
76. On the use of food to define masculine dominance in European/Indian relations, see Brown "The Anglo-Algonquian Gender Frontier," 37–38.
77. LaCombe, *Political Gastronomy*, 9–10, and chap. 4; on the connection between Tehuelche hunting and masculinity, see Graciela B. Hernández, "Orden cósmico, roles de género y relaciones interétnicas en la mitología tehuelche," *Cuadernos del sur, historia* 32 (2003): 195–219.

78. Lacombe, *Political Gastronomy*, 70.
79. A. Viedma, *Descripción de la costa meridional del sur*; for a discussion of this type of colonial discourse in the French colonial context, see Sara E. Melzer, *Colonizer or Colonized: The Hidden Stories of Early Modern French Culture* (Philadelphia: University of Pennsylvania Press, 2012). Quote in Buscaglia, "La representación de las relaciones interétnicas," 29. Michael Lacombe has noted that Indians were not a "passive audience for English claims of authority" (*Political Gastronomy*, 19). The same was true of Spanish authority.
80. Buscaglia, "La representación de las relaciones interétnicas," 25; and AGI, Buenos Aires 328, nf.
81. AGI, Buenos Aires 327, nf. For more on the redemption of captives, see Lauren Benton, *Law and Colonial Cultures: Legal Regimes in World History, 1400–1900* (Cambridge: Cambridge University Press, 2002), 75–77; and Operé, *Indian Captivity in Spanish America.*
82. The text erroneously says Cañadas: see AGI, Buenos Aires 327, nf.

Chapter Six

1. "Informe sin fecha ni firma," *RBN*, 613. By 1784 some of the inhabitants were forced to live in nearby caves in order to protect themselves from the elements: see Martínez de Gorla, "El primer asentamiento de colonos en el Río Negro," 42–56.
2. Apolant, *Operativo Patagonia*, 113–14.
3. Entraigas, *El fuerte del Río Negro*, 101.
4. Gorla, *Los establecimientos españoles*, 107.
5. AGNA, Criminales 32.3.6, leg. 17, no. 1.
6. Johnson, *Workshop of Revolution*, 69; and Stern, *The Secret History of Gender*, 175–76.
7. On the ships as sites of discipline and punishment, see Buscaglia, "Los marinos malditos," 48.
8. Other than ellipses to remove some short, untranslatable passages, I have not added punctuation so as to maintain the quality of the text. The text is reprinted in Haurie, *Mujeres en tierra de hombres*, 27–29. Thanks to María Laura Bocaz-Leiva for her help in translating this text. Palacios was Ana María's mother's surname.
9. It is impossible to know exactly who wrote the letter. Although they seem to have been Ana María's words, it was very unusual for a peasant woman to know how to write. She could have received some basic schooling in her hometown of Portugalete in Vizcaya or maybe her father taught her to write. It seems more likely that a soldier in the jail might have written it for her.
10. "Documento relativo a la expedición," *RBN*, 375; Entraigas, *El fuerte del Río Negro*, 101; and Gorla, *Los establecimientos españoles*, 92.

11. Gorla, *Los establecimientos españoles*, 92–93.
12. AGNA, Sala IX, Montevideo 2.3.7, fol. 307.
13. Buscaglia, "Los marinos malditos," 42–44, 52.
14. AGNA, Sala IX, Costa Patagónica 16.3.8, nf; and Senatore et al., "Una arqueología de las prácticas cotidianas en la colonia española de Floridablanca," 91–92. On the nuclear family as an organizational structure at the colony, see Senatore, *Arqueología e historia*.
15. Buscaglia et al., "To Project an Order," 4–5.
16. AGNA, Sala IX, Costa Patagónica 16.3.8, nf.
17. Senatore, *Arqueología e historia*, 202.
18. A. Viedma, *Diario de un viaje*, febrero, abril, and julio 1781; and Apolant, *Operativo Patagonia*, 311.
19. Antonio de Viedma actually reports that María Ferrera died, and the next day the wife of Bartolomé Tamame died. María Herrero was Tamame's wife, but lists of the dead in San Julián refer only to María Ferrera.
20. AGNA, Sala IX, Costa Patagónica 16.3.8, nf; and A. Viedma, *Diario de un viaje*, mayo 21 hasta el 31.
21. AGNA, Sala IX, Costa Patagónica 16.3.8, nf; and Apolant, *Operativo Patagonia*, 307, 289.
22. Apolant, *Operativo Patagonia*, 305.
23. AGI, Buenos Aires 328, nf, reprinted in Apolant, *Operativo Patagonia*, 124–26.
24. AGNA, Sala IX, Costa Patagónica 16.3.8, nf.
25. AGI, Buenos Aires 328, nf, reprinted in Apolant, *Operativo Patagonia*, 124–26.
26. A. Viedma, *Diario de un viaje*, septiembre 1781.
27. AGNA, Sala IX, Costa Patagónica 16.3.8, nf; AGI, Buenos Aires 328, nf.
28. Entraigas, *El fuerte del Río Negro*, 268–69.
29. Francisco de Viedma, "Continuación del diario de los acaecimientos," AGI, Buenos Aires 327, nf.
30. Senatore, *Arqueología e historia*, 204.
31. Apolant, *Operativo Patagonia*, 298, 302.
32. Ibid., 305.
33. Senatore, *Arqueología e historia*, 146.
34. Apolant, *Operativo Patagonia*, 267; and Nuestra Señora del Carmen, Carmen de Patagones, *Libro de matrimonios, 1780–1884*.
35. Apolant, *Operativo Patagonia*, 313; and Nuestra Señora del Carmen, Carmen de Patagones, *Libro de matrimonios, 1780–1884*.
36. AGNA, Sala IX, Montevideo 2.4.2, fol. 41.
37. Apolant, *Operativo Patagonia*, 247.
38. Senatore et al., "Una arqueología de las prácticas cotidianas," 101–2; and Marschoff, *Gato por liebre*, 107.
39. AGI, Buenos Aires 328, nf.
40. Marschoff, *Gato por liebre*, 210; AGNA, Sala IX, Costa Patagónica 16.3.8, nf; and Bianchi Villelli, *Organizar la diferencia*, 79.

41. AGI, Buenos Aires 328, nf, reprinted in Apolant, *Operativo Patagonia*, 124–26
42. Marschoff, *Gato por liebre*, 113.
43. Images of the plows are available in AGI, Buenos Aires 326, fol. 105. For a more detailed discussion of the agricultural problems, see Gorla, *La agricultura en la Patagonia*.
44. AGI, Buenos Aires 328, nf.
45. AGNA, Sala IX, Costa Patagónica 16.3.9, nf.
46. Gorla, *Los establecimientos españoles*, 105; and AGNA, Sala IX, Costa Patagónica 16.3.9, nf.
47. AGI, Buenos Aires 328, nf.
48. Gorla, *Los establecimientos españoles*, 99.
49. AGI, Buenos Aires 328, nf.
50. Johnson, *Workshop of Revolution*, 68.
51. AGI, Buenos Aires 328, nf.
52. Ibid.
53. Ibid., reprinted in Apolant, *Operativo Patagonia*, 124–26, 127.
54. Juan José Vértiz, "Informe del Virrey Vértiz, para que se abandonen los establecimientos de la Costa Patagónica."
55. Senatore, *Arqueología e historia*, 286.
56. Vértiz, "Informe del Virrey Vértiz."
57. AGI, Buenos Aires 329, nf.
58. Apolant, *Operativo Patagonia*, 276; on these additional structures, see Senatore et al., "Una arqueología de las prácticas cotidianas," 103ff.
59. Among the late defenses of the Patagonia colonies are Custodio Sá y Farías, "Segundo informe sobre el Puerto de San José," in *Viajes por las costas de la Patagonia y los campos de Buenos Aires: informes, diarios y cartas de viajeros (s. xviii)*, ed. Pedro de Angelis (Buenos Aires: Ediciones Continente, 2007), 127–35.
60. Francisco de Viedma, *Memoria dirigida al señor Márquez de Loreto, virrey y capitán general de las provincias del Río de la Plata*.
61. See, for instance, "Real Orden del 5 de junio de 1784," *RBN*, 618; and "Real Orden del 2 de octubre de 1784," *RBN*, 623.
62. Gorla, *Los establecimientos españoles*, 116.
63. "Real Orden del 8 de febrero de 1784," *RBN*, 614; and "Real Orden del 2 de octubre de 1784," *RBN*, 623–24.
64. AGI, Buenos Aires 328, nf.
65. Apolant, *Operativo Patagonia*, 128. The outpost became penal colony and now is known as Carmen de Patagones.
66. Sorsby, "Spanish Colonization of the Mosquito Coast, 1787–1800," 145–53; Santana Pérez and Sánchez Suárez, "Repoblación de Costa de Mosquitos en el último cuarto del siglo XVIII," 695–712.

Chapter Seven

1. Apolant, *Operativo Patagonia*, 343, 327, 318.
2. Ibid., 315, 331, 358.
3. Diego de Alvear, *Diario de la segunda división de límites al mando de D. Diego de Alvear con la descripción de su viaje desde Buenos-Aires . . . , n.d.*
4. Thomas Kinder, *War, Revolution and Society in the Rio de la Plata 1808–1810*, 130–33; *Anonymous notes on the viceroyalty of La Plata, in South America; with a sketch of the manners and character of the inhabitants, collected during a residence in the city of Monte Video* (1808), 76, 77.
5. AGNA, Sala IX, Montevideo 2.4.1 (31 julio 1781).
6. AGNU, caja 87, documento 6; AGNA Sala IX, Montevideo 2.3.7, fol. 679ff; and John J. TePaske et al., *The Royal Treasuries of the Spanish Empire in America*, vol. 3, *Chile and the Río de la Plata* (Durham, NC: Duke University Press, 1982), 289ff.
7. AGNU, caja 87, documento 6.
8. Ibid., documentos 24, 36.
9. AGI, Buenos Aires 328, nf.
10. AGI, Buenos Aires 327, no. 319; AGNA, Sala IX, Montevideo 2.3.7, fol. 307; and AGI Buenos Aires 327, no. 348.
11. AGNA, Sala IX, Montevideo 2.3.6, fols. 687, 675.
12. AGNA, Sala IX, Montevideo 2.3.7, fol. 731.
13. AGNA, Sala IX, Montevideo 2.4.1, fol. 821.
14. Apolant, *Operativo Patagonia*, 119–20; and AGNA, Sala IX, Montevideo 2.4.2, fol. 903.
15. Weber, *Bárbaros*, 62–68; and AGI, Buenos Aires 327, nf.
16. Weber, *Bárbaros*, 68; Richard W. Slatta, "Spanish Colonial Military Strategy and Ideology," in *Contested Ground*, ed. Guy and Sheridan; and Eugenia Alicia Néspolo, "La 'Frontera' bonaerense en el siglo XVIII un espacio políticamente concertado: fuertes, vecinos, milicias y autoridades civiles-militares," *Mundo agrario: revista de estudios rurales* 7, no. 13 (2006): 2, 5, 7, www.redalyc.org/articulo.oa?id=84501308. On Spanish-Indian relations in an earlier period, see Maria Andrea Campetella, "At the Periphery of Empire: Indians and Settlers in the Pampas of Buenos Aires, 1580–1776," unpublished PhD diss. (Rutgers University, 2008), http://mss3.libraries.rutgers.edu/dlr/showfed.php?pid=rutgers-lib:24124; and *Documentos para la historia del Virreinato del Río de la Plata*, 1:218.
17. Operé, *Indian Captivity in Spanish America*, 70–71; and Weber, *Bárbaros*, 172.
18. AGNA, Sala IX, Comandancia de fronteras 1.4.3, nf; on these caciques, see Nacuzzi, "Social Strategies in a Situation of Interethnic Contact"; Bibiana Andreucci, "Familia, redes y poder en la Guardia de Luján," *Mundo agrario: revista de estudios rurales* 11, no. 21 (2010): 3–4, www.redalyc.org/articulo.oa?id=84518824016; and Mayo and Latrubesse, *Terratenientes, soldados y cautivos*, 25.

19. Nuestra Señora de Luján, *Libro de defunciones*, 1731–1799, fols. 102–3. A transcription of the letter can be found in Jorje María Salvaire, *Historia de Nuestra Señora de Luján: su origen, su sanctuario, su villa, sus milagros y su culto* (Buenos Aires: Imprenta de Pablo E. Coni, 1885), 425–27.
20. Nuestra Señora de Luján, *Libro de defunciones*, 1731–1799, fol. 158. As a result of this incident, Our Lady of Luján became famous as a redeemer of captives: see Salvaire, *Historia de Nuestra Señora de Luján*, esp. chap. 23.
21. Quoted in León Solís, *Maloqueros y conchavadores en Araucanía y las Pampas, 1700–1800*, 52; and *Documentos para la historia del Virreinato del Río de la Plata*, 1:305.
22. For these accounts, see Mayo, *Fuentes para el estudio de la frontera*, 38–40, 40–42, 47–50.
23. Socolow, "Spanish Captives in Indian Societies," 79; and Mayo, *Fuentes para el estudio de la frontera*, 43, 41, 65. For more on Pedrosa, see Weber, *Bárbaros*, 221ff.
24. Apolant, *Operativo Patagonia*, 232, 234; and AGNA, Sala IX, Interior 30.3.4, fols. 78v–79.
25. Thomas D. Hall, "The Río de la Plata and the Greater Southwest: A View from World-System Theory," in *Contested Ground*, ed. Guy and Sheridan, 159; Socolow, "Spanish Captives in Indian Societies," 83–89; Weber, *Bárbaros*, 226; Jones, "Conflict and Adaptation in the Argentine Pampas," 63–64; and Operé, *Indian Captivity*, 78–79.
26. Weber, *Bárbaros*, 226; and Operé, *Indian Captivity*, 74. Some scholars have speculated that female captives may have been ashamed by the loss of honor that resulted from their captivity. It is also likely that there was no market for such works, as the region's urban elites demonstrated little interest in the stories of poor, rural women: see Rotker, *Captive Women*, 50–51.
27. The strategic nature of the questions is evident from the many texts in Mayo, *Fuentes para el estudio de la frontera*.
28. Mayo, *Fuentes para el estudio de la frontera*, 44–45. For more on this incident, see Silvia Ratto, "Para qué quieren tener cautivas si no estamos en guerra? las variadas formas del cautiverio interétnico en la campaña bonaerense (primera mitad del siglo XIX)," *Boletín del Instituto de Historia Argentina y Americana Dr. Emilio Ravignani* no. 32 (ene./jun. 2010), www.scielo.org.ar/scielo.php?pid=S0524-97672010000100002&script=sci_arttext.
29. Carlos A. Mayo, "La frontera: cotidianidad, vida privada e identidad," in *Historia de la vida privada en Argentina*, vol. 1, *País antiguo: de la colonia a 1870*, ed. Fernando Devoto and Marta Madero (Buenos Aires: Editorial Taurus, 1999), 97; Kristine L. Jones, "Comparative Raiding Economies," in *Contested Ground*, ed. Guy and Sheridan, 105; Weber, *Bárbaros*, 221–22; and Socolow, "Spanish Captives in Indian Societies," 88.
30. AGNA, Sala IX, Interior 30.3.4, fols. 78v–79.
31. AGNA, Sala IX, Comandancia de fronteras 1.4.6, no. 89.

32. Cited in Mariana Canedo, "Fortines y pueblos en Buenos Aires del siglo XVIII ¿Una política de urbanización para la frontera?," *Mundo agrario: revista de estudios rurales* 7, no. 13 (2006): 12, www.redalyc.org/articulo.oa?id=84501309; and Vértiz, "Memoria a su sucesor," 62–63.
33. On gauchos, see Slatta, *Gauchos and the Vanishing Frontier.* Across the region, the population was 55.5 percent male and 44.5 percent female, and white women made up 46.6 percent of the total: see José Luis Moreno, "Población y sociedad en el Buenos Aires rural a mediados del siglo XVIII," *Desarrollo económico* 29, no. 114 (1989): 268; Susan M. Socolow, "Women of the Buenos Aires Frontier, 1740–1810 (or the Gaucho Turned Upside Down)," in *Contested Ground*, ed. Guy and Sheridan; and Mayo, *Estancia y sociedad en la Pampa*, 179, 167.
34. Félix de Azara, *Viajes por el América del Sur de Don Félix de Azara* (1850), 278.
35. Azara, *Descripción e historia del Paraguay y del Río de la Plata* (1847), 1:302–6; Laura Leonor Cabrejas, "Vida material en la frontera bonaerense (1736–1870)," in *Vivir en la frontera, ed.* Mayo, 61; and AGNA, Sala IX, Interior 30.3.4, fol. 74.
36. Apolant, *Operativo Patagonia*, 331–32.
37. AGNA, Sala IX, Interior 30.3.4, fol. 73ff; on property ownership in the area, see Banzato, *La expansión de la frontera bonaerense*; see the many discussions of drought in AGNA, Sala IX, Comandancia de fronteras (Chascomús) 1.4.3; and *Documentos para la historia del Virreinato del Río de la Plata*, 1:287, 291.
38. The landowners included Martín Jose Altolaguirre, Cecilio Sánchez de Velasco, Manuel Basavilbaso, and Pedro Medrano: Apolant, *Operativo Patagonia*, 140. On Altolaguirre and Medrano, see Socolow, *The Bureaucrats of Buenos Aires.* For later texts about the colonists by Altolaguirre and his widow, see AHPBA, 13.1.4.1, fol. 17; see also De Cristóforis, *Proa al Plata*, 89–90. Some forty families eventually returned to Montevideo: nineteen families in 1783, sixteen in 1784 (eight of whom were sent to Colonia del Sacramento), and five in 1786, who were to be sent to a new settlement named Solís Grande that was never established.
39. AGNA, Sala IX, Comandancia de fronteras (Luján) 1.6.3, nf.
40. AGNA, Sala IX, Montevideo 2.4.2, fol. 616 (30 septiembre 1782); and AGNA, Sala IX, Interior 30.3.4, fol. 79.
41. Apolant, *Los primeros pobladores españoles de la Colonia del Sacramento*, 34–35.
42. On the founding of Maldonado, see Fajardo Terán, "Los orígenes históricos de la ciudad de San Fernando de Maldonado," 98–114.
43. *Transcripción de las ordenanzas de descubrimiento, nueva población y pacificación de las Indias* (Madrid: Ministerio de la Vivienda, 1973). For an English translation of the *Ordenanzas*, see http://cbp.arc.miami.edu/Resources/Laws%20°f%20the%20Indies.html.
44. AGNA, Sala IX, Maldonado 3.7.4, fol. 513.
45. AGNA, Sala IX, Maldonado 3.7.4, fol. 547; for more on the foundation of Minas, see Fajardo Terán, "Historia de Minas," 130–31; AGNA, Sala IX, Interior 30.3.4, fol. 53ff; and AGNA, Sala IX, Maldonado 3.7.4, fols. 544, 547; on the suffering of

the Indians, see AGNA, Sala IX, Maldonado 3.7.4, fol. 625; Fajardo Terán, "Historia de la cuidad de Minas," 103–4; Barrios Pintos, *Minas: dos siglos de su historia*, 1: 147; and Fajardo Terán, "Historia de Minas," 132.

46. Apolant, *Operativo Patagonia*, 287; and Nuestra Señora de Guadalupe, Canelones, *Libro de bautismos*, 1776–1794.
47. Apolant, *Operativo Patagonia*, 253, 308; and San Carlos Borromeo, San Carlos Maldonado, *Libro de bautismos*, 1.
48. Santa María Magdalena, *Libro de bautismos*, 1776–1826.
49. Eiras Roel, "Demografía rural," 36.
50. Catedral de la Inmaculada Concepción de Minas, *Libro de bautismos*, 1: 1783–1799, and 2: 1799–1804; Apolant, *Operativo Patagonia*, 349, 344; and Apolant, *Los primeros pobladores españoles*. On the high fertility in the region, see Mónica Ghirardi, "Las edades de la vida: niños y ancianos de Córdoba a comienzos del siglo XIX," in *Población y sociedad en tiempos de lucha por emancipación: Córdoba, Argentina, en 1813, ed.* Sonia E. Colantonio (Córdoba: CIECS, 2010), 354ff.
51. Moreno, "La infancia en el Río de la Plata," 559. On children and childhood in Latin America, see González and Premo, *Raising an Empire*; Premo, *Children of the Father King*; and Tobias Hecht, ed., *Minor Omissions: Children in Latin American History and Society* (Madison: University of Wisconsin Press, 2002). On children in the Río de la Plata, see Moreno, *Historia de la familia en el Río de la Plata*, chap. 2.
52. AGNU, Escribanía de gobierno y hacienda, caja 49 (1802).
53. San Fernando de Maldonado, *Libro de defunciones, 1765–1823*; and Apolant, *Operativo Patagonia*, 308.
54. Apolant, *Operativo Patagonia*, 362, 310, 325; Catedral de la Inmaculada Concepción de Minas, *Libro de defunciones*, 1783–1805; Apolant, *Operativo Patagonia*, 392, 258; and San Carlos Borromeo, San Carlos Maldonado, *Libro de defunciones, 1771–1821*, 1.
55. Mariquita Sánchez de Thompson, *Intimidad y política: diario, cartas y recuerdos*, ed. María Gabriela Mizraje (Buenos Aires: Adriana Hidalgo Editora, 2010), 145. Mariquita Sánchez is famous for marrying against her parents will in 1801: see Shumway, *The Case of the Ugly Suitor*, chap. 4. On the issue of love, see Carlos A. Mayo, *Porque la quiero tanto: historia del amor en la sociedad rioplatense (1750–1860)* (Buenos Aires: Editorial Biblos, 2004). See, for instance, Seed, *To Love, Honor, and Obey*; and Poska, *Women and Authority*, 119.
56. Moreno, *Historia de la familia*, 109; and Socolow, "Acceptable Partners," 212. Age at first marriage declined further during the nineteenth century to around seventeen: see Mark D. Szuchman, *Order, Family, and Community in Buenos Aires, 1810–1860* (Stanford, CA: Stanford University Press, 1988), 199.
57. Apolant, *Operativo Patagonia*, 370, 282, 331, 333, 308.
58. Francisco García González, "La historia de la familia en el interior castellano: estado de la cuestión y esbozo bibliográfico (ss. XVI–XIX)," in *La historia de la*

familia en la península ibérica: balance regional y perspectivas (Homenaje a Peter Laslett), coord. Francisco García González (Cuenca: Ediciones de la Universidad de Castilla–La Mancha, 2008), 306.

59. Apolant, *Operativo Patagonia*, 288, 289, 294, 378.
60. Apolant, *Operativo Patagonia*, 279, 283; and Nuestra Señora de Guadalupe, Canelones, *Libro de matrimonios*, 1.
61. Bentancur, "Patrimonios locales y metropolitanos de inmigrantes gallegos en el Montevideo colonial," *Anuario del Centro de Estudios Gallegos* (2001), 148.
62. I know the ages of both spouses in 326 (out of 402) of the couples who enlisted as colonists. On Buenos Aires elites, see Socolow, *The Merchants of Buenos Aires, 1778–1810*, 39–40; and *The Bureaucrats of Buenos Aires*, 207. However, large age differences were not the norm everywhere in Latin America, and they were generally less common among the nonelite population. For instance, in late colonial Mexico City, husbands and wives tended to be very close in age: see Arrom, *The Women of Mexico City*, 117; and Pérez, *En busca de mejor fortuna*, 153.
63. Arturo Bentancur has also found large age differences among couples in the Gallego population in Montevideo: see "Solitarios y grupos familiares en la sociedad colonial tardía," 171.
64. For more on this, see Poska, *Women and Authority; and* Moreno, "Sexo, matrimonio y familia," 83.
65. The availability of single women is evident in Montevideo's 1778 padrón at www.siniestro.com.uy/pueblosynumeros/index.php; Anonymous, "Breve descripcion de las circumstancias en que se halla la provincia de Buenos Ayres (1774)," AGI, Buenos Aires 326, fol. 63; Nadia De Cristóforis also found that at the beginning of the nineteenth century, half of the Asturian and Gallego immigrant men were single: see *Proa al Plata*, 181; on single Gallegos in Montevideo, see Bentancur, "Vida de solteros en el Montevideo tardocolonial," 9–26; Bentancur, "Solitarios y grupos familiares"; and Poska, *Women and Authority*, 30–31.
66. Apolant, *Operativo Patagonia*, 325; and Catedral de la Inmaculada Concepción de Minas, *Libro de matrimonios*, 1784–1805, fol. 14.
67. Gary M. Miller, "Bourbon Social Engineering: Women and Conditions of Marriage in Eighteenth-Century Venezuela," *The Americas* 46, no. 3 (1990): 264; and Pérez, *En busca de mejor fortuna*, 194.
68. Apolant, *Operativo Patagonia*, 231; Apolant, *Génesis de la familia uruguaya*, 1223; and AGNA, Sala IX, Protocolos, Escribano Pedro Núñez (1792–1793), fol. 195.
69. *El amor de la estanciera*, www.cervantesvirtual.com.
70. Astigarraga, "Un cura de 1800: Manuel de Amenedo Montenegro," pt. 1, 20.
71. San Fernando de Maldonado, *Libro de matrimonios*, 1–2.
72. Mayo, *Estancia y sociedad*, 182; Socolow, "Women of the Buenos Aires Frontier," 75; Mayo, "Amistades ilícitas," 3–9; and Moreno, "Sexo, matrimonio y familia"; Félix de Azara, *Viajes por la América meridional* (1969), 286. However, white illegitimacy rates in the Pago de Costa between 1731 and 1744 were 9.1 percent:

see Olivero, *Sociedad y economía en San Isidro colonial*, 171–72; see also Sandra Olivero, "Legitimidad e ilegitimidad en los nacimientos de blancos rioplatenses: indicador de aceptación a las normas socio-culturales de la Iglesia y el Estado," *Revista de demografía histórica* 26, no. 1 (2008): 56–85. White illegitimacy was very rare in the Pago de Magdalena (1738–1765): see César A. García Belsunce, *El Pago de La Magdalena, su población (1600–1765)* (Buenos Aires: Academia Nacional de Historia, 2003), 87–89. For a brief discussion of nonmarital sexuality in the rural Río de la Plata, see Mayo, *Estancia y sociedad*, chap. 11.

73. Ferreyra, "La ilegitimidad en la ciudad y en el campo a finales del siglo XVIII en Córdoba," 423, table 5; and Bernd Schröter, *Der heiratsmarkt im kolonialen Uruguay: geschlechterbeziehungen in einer grenzregion Spanisch-Amerikas, 1727–1810* (Stuttgart: Heinz, 2001), 312, graphic 27. He does not, however, have data for the years immediately preceding the arrival of the colonists. In late seventeenth-century Guadalajara, upwards of one-third of Spanish children were illegitimate: see Thomas Calvo, "Concubinato y mestizaje en el medio urbano: el caso de Guadalajara en el siglo XVII," *Revista de Indias* 44, no. 173 (1984): 211. Twenty-nine percent of Spanish children in eighteenth-century Valladolid (Mexico) were born out of wedlock: see Claude Morin, "Age at Marriage and Female Employment in Colonial Mexico," www.hist.umontreal.ca/U/morin/pub/CIDHInd97.htm.
74. Apolant, *Operativo Patagonia*, 244.
75. Brenda Pagola, "*. . . Y ellos le dieron vida" San Carlos: fundadores y vecinos* (Montevideo: Arca, 1998), 34–40; excerpts from the case can be found in Astigarraga, "Un cura de 1800," pt. 4, apéndice 2, 1–6; and San Carlos Borromeo, San Carlos Maldonado, *Libro de bautismos*, 1.
76. Apolant, *Operativo Patagonia*, 280–81.
77. Ibid., 380, 315.
78. Ibid., 261, 239; Apolant, *Los primeros pobladores*, 34; San Carlos Borromeo, San Carlos Maldonado, *Libro de bautismos*, 1; and Pagola, "*. . . Y ellos le dieron vida*," 301–2, 131.
79. Apolant, *Operativo Patagonia*, 227.
80. AGNA, Sala IX, Montevideo 2.3.5, fol. 1029.
81. Apolant, *Operativo Patagonia*, 179n221. Female mobility was often the source of conflict among couples: see Chambers, *From Subjects to Citizens*, 103. On the issue of official surveillance, see Black, *The Limits of Gender Domination*, 120.
82. AGNA, Sala IX, Tribunales 35.7.4, 1790, nf.
83. AGNA, Sala IX, Tribunales 37.7.4, legajo 153, expediente 10.
84. Apolant, *Operativo Patagonia*, 228.
85. For sex ratios in Galicia, see Eiras Roel, *La población de Galicia*, 124; and "Mecanismos autoreguladores," 70.
86. Moreno, *Historia de la familia*, chap. 4; and Socolow, "Women of the Buenos Aires Frontier," 78–81.

87. Poska, *Women and Authority*, 79–87.
88. Apolant, *Operativo Patagonia*, 260.
89. AGNA, Sala IX, San Carlos 7.10.4, nf., and Montevideo 2.4.3.
90. AGNU, Acuerdos del Cabildo de Maldonado, 1784–1801, libro 269, doc. 51; Apolant, *Operativo Patagonia*, 270; and Apolant, *Los primeros pobladores*, 32.

Chapter Eight

1. José Manuel Pérez Castellanos, "Montevideo y la campaña de la Banda Oriental en 1787," 16, 18; and AGNU, Caja 217, del fondo de ex archivo histórico, Cabildo y juzgado de Santa Lucía, carpeta 7. This dispute was part of a broader conflict between large landowners and settlers in the region: see Djenderedjian, "Roots of Revolution," 652ff.
2. Apolant, *Operativo Patagonia*, 268, 295; for the original text, see AGNA, Sala IX, Hacienda 34.6.1; on small farms in the area, see Garavaglia, *Pastores y labradores de Buenos Aires*, 159ff; much of the document is reprinted in Fajardo Terán, *Historia de la Ciudad de San Carlos*, 318–26; on these two colonists, see pages 324–25.
3. Fajardo Terán, *Historia de San Carlos*, 319, 323, 320.
4. Ibid., 319, 320, 324.
5. AGNA, Sala IX, Div. Colonia Hacienda 34.6.1, fol. 28ff.
6. Apolant, *Operativo Patagonia*, 253; and AGNA, Sala IX, Div. Colonia Hacienda 34.6.1, fols. 29, 33, cited in Djenderedjian, "Roots of Revolution," 645.
7. For an overview of the scholarship on slavery on the peninsula, see William D. Phillips, *Historia de la esclavitud en España* (Madrid: Editorial Playor, 1990); and more recently, Rocío Periáñez Gómez, "La investigación sobre la esclavitud en España en la edad moderna," *Norba: revista de historia* 21 (2008): 275–82. Although much work has been done on slavery in sixteenth-century Spain, very few studies deal with the eighteenth century. Some recent studies include Pedro Parrilla Ortíz, *La esclavitud en Cádiz durante el siglo XVIII* (Cádiz: Diputación de Cádiz, 2001); A. M. González Díaz, *La esclavitud en Ayamonte durante el Antiguo Régimen (siglos xvi, xvii y xviii)* (Huelva: Diputación Provincial de Huelva, 1997); and Eloy Martín Corrales, "La esclavitud en la Cataluña de fines del siglo XVIII y primera mitad del XIX: los 'amados' sirvientes de indianos y negreros," *Historia moderna, historia en construcción*, coord. Pierre Vilar and Carlos Martínez Shaw (Lleida: Editorial Milenio, 1999): 1: 133–50. On Gallegos in Cádiz, see María José de la Pascua Sánchez, "Los Gallegos en el Cádiz de la Carrera de Indias: balance secular de un proceso migratorio (1682–1778)," in *Migraciones internas y medium-distance*, ed. Eiras Roel and Castelao, 2: 851; on emigration to Portugal and Andalucía, see Meijide Pardo, "La emigración gallega," chap. 5.

8. *Documentos para la historia Argentina*, tomo 12, *Territorio y población*, 389; and Francisco Millau, *Descripción de la provincia del Río de la Plata* (1772), 109. As late as 1808, Englishman Thomas Kinder mused, "There are no white domestics in either Montevideo or Buenos Aires, but the quantity of negroes is by no means so striking as in Rio de Janeiro" (*War, Revolution and Society in the Río de la Plata*, 133).
9. On the complicated nature of race relations in colonial society see R. Douglas Cope, *The Limits of Racial Domination: Plebian Society in Colonial Mexico City, 1660–1720* (Madison: University of Wisconsin Press, 1994); on race relations among workers in Buenos Aires, see Johnson, *Workshop of Revolution*; and Bentancur, "Familia, esclavos y libertos," 83.
10. Mayo, *Estancia y sociedad*, 41; Goldberg and Mallo, "La población Africana en Buenos Aires y su campaña," 45–46; Banzato, *La expansión de la frontera bonaerense*, 91; Fogelman, "Población de color en una villa en la frontera bonaerense," 14; Nuestra Señora de Luján, *Libro de matrimonios*, 1769–1796, fols. 93–94; and Nuestra Señora de Pilar, General Paz (Ranchos), *Libro de defunciones*, 1788–1860, fol. 14.
11. AGNA, Sala IX, Maldonado 3.7.4, fol. 261ff.
12. On the role of pulperías in urban socialization, see Johnson, *Workshop of Revolution*, 75ff; and Pilar González Bernaldo, "Las pulperías de Buenos Aires: historia de una expresión de sociabilidad popular," *Siglo XIX revista de historia* 13 (1993): 27–54.
13. Socolow, *The Merchants of Buenos Aires*, 77; and AGNA, Sala IX, Maldonado 3.7.4, fols. 443–61.
14. Johnson, *Workshop of Revolution*, 36; and Alex Borucki "The Slave Trade to the Río de la Plata, 1777–1812: Trans-Imperial Networks and Atlantic Warfare," *Colonial Latin American Review* 20, no. 1 (2011): 83–88. Portuguese trading networks were critical to this expansion: see Prado, "In the Shadows of Empires," unpublished PhD diss. (Emory University 2009); and Borucki et al., *Esclavitud y trabajo*," 19.
15. Apolant, *Operativo Patagonia*, 311; Díaz de Guerra, *Documentación relativa a esclavos*, 20; and San Fernando de Maldonado, *Libro de defunciones*, 1765–1823. Their household, including slaves, can be found in Excel files of the 1803 padrón, which were available (but no longer) online at http://pueblosynumeros.fcs.edu.uy. In Buenos Aires, female household slaves were common even in homes of poorer Spanish immigrants, indicating that they were a sign of status: Johnson, *Workshop of Revolution*, 203; Pagola, "*. . . Y ellos le dieron vida*," 426; and Apolant, *Operativo Patagonia*, 243.
16. AGNU, libro 278, *Padrones de San José*, 1791.
17. AGNU, libro 279, *Padrones de Canelones y su jurisdicción*, Partido de Pando, 1791.
18. For Prieto, see Pagola, "*. . . Y ellos le dieron vida*," 534; for Huertas and Pérez Brañas, see Apolant, *Operativo Patagonia*, 245, 253; for their slaves' deaths, see

San Carlos Borromeo, San Carlos Maldonado, *Libro de defunciones*, 1771–1821; Pagola, "*. . . Y ellos le dieron vida*," 53; and Díaz de Guerra, *Documentación relativa a esclavos*, 21, 25.

19. Celton, *La población de Córdoba a fines del siglo XVIII*, 272; Johnson, *Workshop of Revolution*, 39; and San Fernando de Maldonado, *Libro de defunciones*, 1765–1823.
20. San Fernando de Maldonado, *Libro de defunciones*, 1765–1823; and Apolant, *Operativo Patagonia*, 271.
21. Apolant, *Operativo Patagonia*, 353; and Luis Fernando Loriente Brian and Luis Alberto Pintos Anza, eds., *Libro primero de matrimonios de la iglesia de San Juan Bautista, 1782–1845*, 32.
22. On gauchos, see Slatta, *Gauchos and the Vanishing Frontier*; on the difference in the labor force, see Garavaglia, *Pastores y labradores de Buenos Aires*, 89; and Garavaglia, "Un siglo de estancias en la campaña de Buenos Aires," 704; on the rural workforce, see Salvatore and Brown, "Trade and Proletarianization in Late Colonial Banda Oriental," 431–59.
23. Rial García, "Trabajo femenino y economía de subsistencia," 86; on Asturias, see Jesús García Fernández, *Sociedad y organización tradicional del espacio en Asturias* (Oviedo, Spain: Instituto de Estudios Asturianos, 1976), 167; and Patricia Suárez Álvarez and Alberto Morán Corte, "Más allá del telar: el mundo del trabajo femenino en la Asturias del siglo XVIII," *El futuro del pasado: revista electrónica de historia* 2 (2011): 483–98; quote from Rial García, "Trabajo femenino," 86.
24. Apolant, *Operativo Patagonia*, 273; and Rial García, "Trabajo femenino," 85, 88; for women harvesting for wages, see Meijide Pardo, "La emigración gallega," 532ff; Félix de Azara, *Memorias sobre el estado rural del Rio de la Plata en 1801*, 5, http://bibliotecavirtual.aragon.es/bva/i18n/consulta/registro.cmd?id=1610; and Azara, *Descripción e historia del Paraguay y del Río de la Plata* (1847), 1: 306–7; for a brief discussion of women's work, see Mayo, *Estancia y sociedad*, chap.10; on rural households, see Cabrejas, "Vida material en la frontera bonaerense"; Slatta, *Gauchos and the Vanishing Frontier*, chap. 4; Donna J. Guy, "Women, Peonage, and Industrialization: Argentina, 1810–1914," *Latin American Research Review* 16, no. 3 (1981): 66; and Socolow, "Women of the Buenos Aires Frontier," 76–77.
25. Mayo, *Estancia y sociedad*, chap. 10; and Rial García, "Trabajo femenino," 86.
26. Scholars have engaged in considerable debate over treatment of slaves in the Río de la Plata. For decades, many scholars asserted that, unlike plantation slavery, the more extensive mobility of slaves and the fact that masters and slaves often lived together in similar conditions led to a more benign form of slavery; however, based on archival evidence about maltreatment of slaves, others have argued that violence was inherent in all slave regimes. On this debate, see Bentancur and Aparicio, *Amos y esclavos en el Río de la Plata*; and Mario Rufer, *Historias*

negadas: esclavitud, violencia y relaciones de poder en Córdoba a fines del siglo XVIII (Córdoba, Argentina: Ferreyra Editor, 2005), 50ff, and chap. 4.

27. For more on the slave law, see Manuel Lucena Salmoral, "La instrucción sobre educación, trato, y ocupaciones de los esclavos de 1789: una prueba del poder de los amos de esclavos frente a la debilidad de la Corona española," *Estudios de historia social y económica de América* 13 (1996): 155–78, http://hdl.handle.net/10017/5928; and María Eugenia Chaves Maldonado, "Paternalismo, iluminismo y libertad: la vigencia de la instrucción esclavista de 1789 y su impacto en la sociedad colonial," *Historia y sociedad* 21 (julio–diciembre 2011): 61–93.
28. On the opposition from slave owners in Cuba, see Matt D. Childs, *The 1812 Aponte Rebellion in Cuba and the Struggle against Atlantic Slavery* (Chapel Hill: University of North Carolina Press, 2006), 36–37; for Louisiana, see Jennifer M. Spear, *Race, Sex and Social Order in Early New Orleans* (Baltimore, MD: Johns Hopkins University Press, 2009), 103ff; and Bentancur and Aparicio, *Amos y esclavos*, 18.
29. On merchants and slaves, see Socolow, *The Merchants of Buenos Aires*, 77.
30. Astigarraga, "Un cura de 1800," pt. 3, apéndice 1, 180–90; and Díaz de Guerra, *Documentación relativa a esclavos*, 24. For more on the clergy's use of slave labor, see Mayo, *Los Betlemitas en Buenos Aires*.
31. San Carlos Borromeo, San Carlos Maldonado, *Libro de bautismos*, 1801, 1804.
32. The provisions on slave marriage appear in part 4, title 5, in *Las Siete Partidas*, vol. 4, *Family, Commerce, and the Sea: Worlds of Women and Merchants*, ed. Robert I. Burns, SJ, and trans. Samuel Parsons Scott (Philadelphia: University of Pennsylvania Press, 2001), 901; on the multiple meanings of slave marriage in Mexico during an earlier period, see Bennett, *Africans in Colonial Mexico*, chap. 4, and 128–29.
33. Catedral de la Inmaculada Concepción de Minas, *Libro de matrimonios, 1784–1805*, fol. 15; San Fernando de Maldonado, *Libro de bautismos*, 1798, 1800; and Apolant, *Operativo Patagonia*, 300, 351, 347; the marriage record for these slaves appears in Loriente Brian and Pintos Anza, eds., *Libro primero de matrimonios de la Iglesia de San Juan Bautista*, 25.
34. San Carlos Borromeo, San Carlos Maldonado, *Libro de bautismos*, 1797, 1805; and Apolant, *Operativo Patagonia*, 287.
35. Schwartz, "Opening the Family Circle," 142; and San Carlos Borromeo, San Carlos Maldonado, *Libro de bautismos*, 1802.
36. Catedral de la Inmaculada Concepción de Minas, *Libro de defunciones*, 1783–1805, fol. 18; San Carlos Borromeo, San Carlos Maldonado, *Libro de defunciones*, 1771–1821; and Apolant, *Operativo Patagonia*, 287.
37. Schwartz, "Opening the Family Circle," 140; on black confraternities, see Miguel A. Rosal, "La religiosidad católica de los afrodescendientes de Buenos Aires (Siglos XVIII–XIX)," *Hispania Sacra* 60, no. 122 (julio–diciembre 2008): 597–633; Norberto Pablo Cirio, "Antecedentes históricos del culto a San Baltazar

en la Argentina: 'La Cofradía de San Baltazar y Animas' (1772–1856)," *Latin American Music Review / Revista de música latinoamericana* 21, no. 2 (Autumn–Winter 2000): 190–214; and San Fernando de Maldonado, *Libro de defunciones*, 1788.

38. In Luján at least half of the marriages of nonwhites were to spouses from other racial categories: see Fogelman, "Población de color," 31; and Celton, "Selección matrimonial y mestizaje en Córdoba," 327–44. White endogamy remained strong even as the white percentage of the population declined toward the end of the eighteenth century and the beginning of the nineteenth century: see Mónica Ghirardi et al., "Hogares, familias y trabajo en dos zonas rurales de Córdoba, Argentina, a comienzos del siglo XIX," *Revista de demografía histórica* 25, no. 2 (2007): 76; Ferreyra, "Matrimonio de 'Españoles' en la ciudad de Córdoba en el siglo XVIII," 290; and Socolow, "Acceptable Partners," 235. A copy of Vértiz's issuance of the Pragmatic can be found in *Documentos para la historia del Virreinato del Río de la Plata*, 1:242. For more on the Royal Pragmatic on Marriages, see Twinam, *Public Lives, Private Secrets*; Saether, "Bourbon Absolutism and Marriage Reform"; Seed, *To Love, Honor, and Obey;* and Olivero, *Sociedad y economía en San Isidro colonial*, 112.
39. Apolant, *Operativo Patagonia*, 295; and AGNA, Sala IX, Hacienda 34.6.1, fol. 35.
40. AGNA, Sala IX, Comandancia de Buenos Aires 1.7.5, fol. 507.
41. Catedral de la Inmaculada Concepción de Minas, *Libro de bautismos*, 1799–1804, fol. 145v; Sarah Chambers also notes the absence of racial identifiers in Peru in *From Subjects to Citizens*, 84.
42. In 1779 Viceroy Vértiz petitioned the Crown for the establishment of a foundling home in Buenos Aires that received 685 children in its first decade: see José Luis Moreno, "El delgado hilo de la vida: los niños expósitos de Buenos Aires, 1779–1823," *Revista de Indias* 60, no. 220 (2000): 667. Of course, not all abandoned children were the products of illicit relationships; at least in urban areas, some parents abandoned their children for economic reasons: see Celton, "Abandono de niños e ilegitimidad," 231–50. On Montevideo, see Diana Bianchi, "Componentes ilustrados en la práctica de la exposición en el Montevideo tardo-colonial," *Investigaciones históricas: época moderna y contemporánea* 20 (2000): 67–88.
43. In some ways, this scenario might be parallel to that described by Barbara Voss regarding the surveillance over the sexual activity of colonizers at the presidio of San Francisco in *The Archaeology of Ethnogenesis*, 93–94.
44. AGNU, Escribanía de gobierno y hacienda, caja 49, fol. 9ff.
45. San Carlos Borromeo, San Carlos Maldonado, *Libro de defunciones*, 1803; and Díaz de Guerra, *Documentación relativa a esclavos*, 30–32.
46. Roberto Pacheco, "Invisible But Not Forgotten: The Afro-Argentine and Afro-Uruguayan Experience from the Sixteenth to the Twentieth Centuries," unpublished MA thesis (Florida International University, 2001), 69.

47. Di Stefano, *El púlpito y la plaza*, chap. 1; and Barral, *De sotanas por la Pampa*, 24–29.
48. Di Stefano, *El púlpito y la plaza*, 40; Nuestra Señora de Pilar, General Paz (Ranchos), *Libro de bautismos*, 1788–1852, fol. 102ff; and Azara, *Descripción e historia del Paraguay*, 303.
49. Alvear, *Diario de la segunda división*, chap. 2; and Astigarraga, "Un cura de 1800," pt. 1, 15.
50. AGNA, Sala IX, Montevideo 2.4.2, fol. 1012; Pérez Castellanos, "Montevideo y la campaña de la Banda Oriental," 17; and Astigarraga, "Un cura de 1800," pt. 3, 182.
51. Astigarraga, "Un cura de 1800," pt. 1, 16, 21, 27.
52. Barral and di Stefano, "Las 'misiones interiores' en la campaña de Buenos Aires," 641–44. The missions took place in 1786 (to the west and north of Buenos Aires, Santa Fe, and the Banda Oriental), 1787 (Entre Ríos and the Banda Oriental), 1788 (north of Buenos Aires and Santa Fe), 1789 (around Buenos Aires and Río Tercero), 1790 (the northern and southern frontiers outside of Buenos Aires), 1791 (Corrientes), and 1793 (the Banda Oriental and Buenos Aires). On these missions, see, "Ceremonial de las misiones del Colegio Apostólico de San Carlos del Carcarañal, año 1792," *Nuevo Mundo* 3–4, Instituto Teológico Francisco Fr. Luis Bolaños (2002–2003): 99–124.
53. Fraschina, "A Jesuit Beata at the Time of the Suppression in the Viceroyalty of Rio de la Plata," 758–71; Marcos Ezcurra, *Vida de Sor María Antonia de la Paz* (Buenos Aires: S. de Amorrortu, 1947), 87.
54. On popular religious practice in the region, see Barral, *De sotanas por la Pampa*, chap. 7.
55. AGNU, Acuerdos del cabildo de Maldonado, 1784–1801, libro 269, doc. 87; on the role of festivals, see Barral, *De sotanas por la Pampa*, chap. 6.
56. Pérez Castellano, "Montevideo y la campaña de la Banda Oriental," 30.
57. Corteguera, *For the Common Good*, 196, 47; for examples of rural peasants defending their rights against abuses by royal officials, see Tomás Antonio Mantecón Movellán, *Conflictividad y disciplinamiento social en la Cantabria rural del Antiguo Régimen* (Santander: Universidad de Cantabria, 1997), 290ff.
58. As Alejandro Cañeque has pointed out, the Spanish monarchy was "built on the base of a profound respect for corporate structures and for the traditional rights, privileges, and customs of the different territories that made up the monarchy": *The King's Living Image: The Culture and Politics of Viceregal Power in Colonial Mexico* (New York: Routledge, 2004), 10; on the expectation of reciprocity, 68.
59. AGNA, Sala IX, Interior 30.3.4, fol. 73–74v; and AGI, Buenos Aires 329, nf (20 octubre 1790).
60. AGI, Buenos Aires 329 nf; AGNA, Sala IX, Tribunales Civiles 34.1.6, fol. 44; Taylor, *Honor and Violence*, 120; and AGI, Buenos Aires 329.
61. Herzog, *Defining Nations*, 6.
62. Herzog, "Early Modern Spanish Citizenship," 209.

63. "Through making use of their rights and fulfilling their obligations, vecinos thus indicated that they were socially and politically members of the local community" (Herzog, *Defining Nations*, 7).
64. Laureano M. Rubio Pérez, "Poder o poderes: señorios, concejos y relaciones de poder en el mundo rural durante la Edad Moderna," in *El mundo rural en la España moderna*, coord. Francisco José Aranda Pérez, 2: 1081–1155; Mantecón Movellán, *Conflictividad y disciplinamiento social*, esp. 123–130; and Pegerto Saavedra, *Economía, política y sociedad en Galicia: la provincia de Mondoñedo, 1480–1830* (Madrid: Xunta de Galicia, 1985), 487–97.
65. AGNU, Acuerdos del cabildo de Maldonado, 1784–1801, libro 269, docs. 2, 144, 152v.
66. A similar process occurred on the northern frontier of Mexico: see Omar S. Valerio-Jiménez, "Neglected Citizens and Willing Traders: The Villas del Norte (Tamaulipas) in Mexico's Northern Borderlands, 1749–1846," *Mexican Studies* 18, no. 2 (Summer 2002): 257; see also Cruz, *Let There Be Towns*, 75.
67. AGNU, Fondo de ex archivo histórico, cabildo y juzgado de Santa Lucía, caja 217, carpeta 3.
68. Carlos Larriera Bonavita, *San José: su origen y fundación 1 de junio de 1783* (Montevideo: n.p., 1961), 72.
69. Arlene Diaz, *Female Citizens, Patriarchs, and the Law in Venezuela, 1786–1904* (Lincoln: University of Nebraska Press, 2004), 12–13.
70. In his case study of Mexico, Peter Guardino calls the town council of Antequera "the maximum local expression of corporatist society and political culture," in *The Time of Liberty: Popular Political Culture in Oaxaca, 1750–1850* (Durham, NC: Duke University Press, 2005), 29; see also Djenderedjian, "Roots of Revolution," 647.
71. Apolant, *Operativo Patagonia*, 193, 188, 191.
72. Ibid., 192; and Andrew David et al., eds., *The Malaspina Expedition 1789–1794: The Journal of the Voyage by Alejandro Malaspina*, vol. 1, *Cádiz to Panama* (London: Hakluyt Society, 2001).
73. Apolant, *Operativo Patagonia*, 196n248; on this final colonization attempt in Patagonia, see Carlos Martínez Shaw, "Economía e imperio: los establecimientos de la Real Compañía Marítima en América," *Anuario de estudios atlánticos* 54, no. 1 (2008): 593–630.
74. Apolant, *Operativo Patagonia*, 201; and AGI, Buenos Aires 330.
75. Azara, *Memorias sobre el estado rural*, 18; Don Gabriel de Avilés y Del Fierro, Marqués de Avilés, "Memoria de Avilés," in *Memorias de los virreyes*, ed. Radaelli, 496–47; and Apolant, *Operativo Patagonia*, 208ff.
76. AGNU, caja 246, doc. 149.
77. Apolant, *Operativo Patagonia*, 215.

Epilogue

1. Vértiz, "Memoria a su sucesor," 64.
2. Street, *Artigas and the Emancipation of Uruguay*, 80; see also John Charles Chasteen, *Americanos: Latin America's Struggle for Independence* (Oxford: Oxford University Press, 2008), 38–42.
3. Oscar Abadie-Aicardi, "En los 200 años de la invasión inglesa al Plata," *Humanidades* 4, no. 1 (diciembre 2006): 76.
4. This account is reprinted as an appendix in Roberto L. Elissalde, "El Pbro. Manuel Tomás de Amenedo Montenegro y su 'Conquista de la ciudad de Maldonado por los ingleses y demás ocurrencias acaecidas en esta villa de San Carlos,'" 33–175: the text appears on 111–35 and the quote on 113. Apolant, *Operativo Patagonia*, 293.
5. This document is reprinted in Francisco Bauzá, "Exposición de los vecinos de Maldonado al Cabildo de Montevideo sobre la conducta de los ingleses," *Humanidades* 7, no. 1 (2007): 101–211, the quote is on page 104.
6. Elissalde, "Amenedo y su 'Conquista de la ciudad de Maldonado,'" 113; Apolant, *Operativo Patagonia*, 147.
7. Elissalde, "Amenedo y su 'Conquista de la ciudad de Maldonado,'" 117.
8. Ibid., 118.
9. Ibid., 132.
10. Ibid., 104–5.
11. Apolant, *Operativo Patagonia*, 377; and Anibal Barrios Pintos, *San José: de la historia a nuestros días* (Montevideo: Ministerio de Educación y Cultura, 1986), 2: 284.
12. Barrios Pintos, *San José*, 2:290; and Nicolas Shumway, *The Invention of Argentina* (Berkeley: University of California Press, 1991), 53.
13. *Archivo Artigas*, tomos 6, 11, www.bibliotecadelbicentenario.gub.uy/innovaportal/v/53049/51/mecweb/archivo_artigas; see also Chasteen, *Americanos*, 87; *Exodo del Pueblo Oriental*; and Jeremy Adelman, *Sovereignty and Revolution in the Iberian Atlantic* (Princeton: Princeton University Press, 2006), 281.
14. Street, *Artigas and the Emancipation of Uruguay*, 151.
15. Pagola, ". . . *Y ellos le dieron vida*," 426–27, 461; see also *Archivo Artigas*, tomo 13:395ff for these inventories; Ana Frega, "Caudillos y montoneras en la revolución radical artiguista," *Andes* 13 (2002): unpaged, www.redalyc.org/pdf/127/12701304.pdf.
16. For insight into some of these issues, see Djenderedjian, "Roots of Revolution," 665ff.
17. Chambers, *From Subjects to Citizens*, 37.
18. Pagola, ". . . *Y ellos le dieron vida*," 472.
19. Apolant, *Operativo Patagonia*, 147, 340.

20. Vera Blinn Reber, *British Mercantile Houses in Buenos Aires, 1810–1880* (Cambridge: Harvard University Press, 1979), 131.
21. Pérez, *En busca de mejor fortuna*, 38.
22. Nadia Andrea De Cristóforis, "Políticas y prácticas migratorias: los flujos de gallegos y asturianos a Buenos Aires (1840–1860)," *Revista de Indias* 68, no. 244 (2008): 86; and Moya, *Cousins and Strangers*, 257, 502n94; see also the work of Pilar Cagiao Vila.
23. The response to the Catasto de Ensenada for Rabanal Viejo, AGS_CE_RG_L361_119.jpg, at pares.mcu.es.
24. Eiras Roel, "Demografía rural," 36.
25. "Representación suscrita por vecinos de Minas solicitando a Diego de Souza un destacamiento para mantener el orden el aquella villa," *Archivo Artigas*, tomo 6:296.
26. Shumway, *The Case of the Ugly Suitor*, 150n20; and Christine Hunefeldt, *Liberalism in the Bedroom: Quarreling Spouses in Nineteenth-Century Lima* (University Park: Penn State University Press, 2000), 111.
27. Shumway, *The Case of the Ugly Suitor*, 7.

Bibliography

Selected Primary Sources

Archivo General de Indias (AGI), Sevilla, Spain
Archivo General de la Nación (AGNA), Buenos Aires, Argentina
Archivo General de la Nación (AGNU), Montevideo, Uruguay
Archivo Histórico de la Provincia de Buenos Aires (AHPBA), La Plata, Argentina
Archivo Municipal (AMC), La Coruña, Spain
Parish registers available at familysearch.org
    Nuestra Señora de la Merced, Chascomús, Argentina
    Nuestra Señora del Carmen, Carmen de Patagones, Argentina
    Nuestra Señora de Luján, Luján, Argentina
    Nuestra Señora de Pilar, General Paz (Ranchos), Argentina
    Santa María Magdalena, Magdalena, Argentina
Microfilms of parish registers provided by the Church of the Latter Day Saints of Jesus Christ
    Catedral de la Inmaculada Concepción de Minas, Uruguay
    Nuestra Señora de Guadalupe, Canelones, Uruguay
    San Carlos Borromeo, San Carlos Maldonado, Uruguay
    San Fernando de Maldonado, Maldonado, Uruguay

Alvear, Diego de. *Diario de la segunda división de límites al mando de D. Diego de Alvear con la descripción de su viaje desde Buenos-Aires . . .* n.d. www.cervantes-virtual.com.

Azara, Félix de. *Viajes por la América meridional.* Madrid: Espasa-Calpe, 1969.

———. *Viajes por el América del Sur de don Félix de Azara.* Montevideo, Uruguay: Comercio del Plata, 1850.

———. *Descripción e historia del Paraguay y del Río de la Plata.* Tomo 1. Madrid: Imprenta de Sánchez, 1847.

———. *Memorias sobre el estado rural del Río de la Plata en 1801, demarcación de límites entre el Brasil y el Paraguay á últimos del siglo XVIII, e informes sobre varios particulares de la América meridional española.* Madrid: Imprenta de Sánchez, 1847.

Campillo y Cossío, José del. *Nuevo sistema para el gobierno económico para la América.* Madrid: Benito Cano, 1789.

———. *Lo que hay de más y de menos en España, para que sea lo que debe ser y no lo que es.* 1741. www.cervantesvirtual.com.

Campomanes, Pedro Rodríguez. *Discurso sobre la educación popular sección de los artesanos y su fomento.* 1775. www.cervantesvirtual.com.

———. *Discurso sobre el fomento de la industria popular.* 1774. www.cervantesvirtual.com.

———. *Reflexiones sobre el comercio español a Indias. 1762.* Edited by Vicente Llombart Rosa. Madrid: Ministerio de Hacienda, 1988.

Castro, Manuel de, OFM. "Informe de Campomanes sobre la emigración e industrialización de Galicia." *Cuadernos de estudios gallegos,* tomo 13, fasículo 40 (1958): 242–54.

Comajuncosa, Antonio. "Manifiesto histórico de lo que han trabajado los misioneros de Tarija así entre los fieles como entre los infieles desde el año de 1775 hasta él de 1810." In *El colegio franciscano de Tarija y sus misiones: noticias históricas recogidas por dos misioneros del mismo colegio,* edited by A. M. Corrado. Florence: Quaracchi, 1884.

Cro, Stelio, ed. *Descripción de la Sinapia, península en la tierra austral.* Hamilton, Ont: McMaster University, 1975.

Documentos para la historia Argentina. Tomo 12, *Territorio y población.* Buenos Aires: Compañía Sud-Americana de Billetes de Banco, 1919.

Documentos para la historia del Virreinato del Río de la Plata. 3 vols. Buenos Aires: Compañía Sud-Americana de Billetes de Banco, 1912.

Elissalde, Roberto L. "El Pbro. Manuel Tomás de Amenedo Montenegro y su 'Conquista de la ciudad de Maldonado por los ingleses y demás ocurrencias acaecidas en esta villa de San Carlos.'" *Boletín histórico del ejército* 331–34 (2007): 33–175.

Encyclicas o cartas circulares del P. Fray Antonio Comajuncosa (1794–1801). www.franciscanosdetarija.com.

Exodo del Pueblo Oriental. Montevideo, Uruguay: Museo Histórico Nacional, 1968.

Falkner, Thomas. *A description of Patagonia and the adjoining parts of South America . . . with a grammar and a short vocabulary, and some particulars relating to Falkland's Islands.* Hereford: C. Pugh, 1774.

Feijoo y Montenegro, Benito Jerónimo. *Teatro crítico universal.* 1726. www.cervantesvirtual.com.

Fernández Duro, Cesáreo. *Disquisiciones náuticas: la mar descrita por los mareados.* Vol. 2. Madrid: Imprenta Estereotipia y Galvanoplastia de Aribau y C^{a}, 1877. archive.org.

González, Pedro. *Tratado de enfermedades de la gente de mar en que se exponen sus causas, y los medios de precaverlas.* Madrid, 1805.

Kinder, Thomas. *War, Revolution and Society in the Rio de la Plata, 1808–1810: Thomas Kinder's Narrative of a Journey to Madeira, Montevideo and Buenos Aires.* Edited by Malyn Newitt. Oxford: Signal Books, 2010.

Lardizábal, Vicente. *Consideraciones político-médicas sobre la salud de los navegantes, en que se exponen las causas de sus mas frecuentes enfermedades, modo de precaverlas, y curarlas.* Madrid: Antonio Sanz, 1769.

Loriente Brian, Luis Fernando, and Luis Alberto Pintos Anza, eds. *Libro primero de matrimonios de la iglesia de San Juan Bautista, 1782–1845.* Montevideo, Uruguay: Instituto de Estudios Genealógicos del Uruguay, 2003.

Millau, Francisco. *Descripción de la provincia del Rio de la Plata (1772).* Buenos Aires: Espasa-Calpe, 1947.

Pérez Castellanos, José Manuel. "Montevideo y la campaña de la Banda Oriental en 1787." In *Selección de escritos, crónicas históricas, 1787–1814.* Biblioteca Artigas Colección de clásicos uruguayos, vol. 130. Montevideo, Uruguay: Departamento de Investigaciones Históricas del Museo Histórica Nacional, 1968.

Pueblos y números Río de la Plata, 1760–1860. http://pueblosynumeros.fcs.edu.uy/.

Radaelli, Sigfrido Augusto, ed. *Memorias de los virreyes del Río de la Plata.* Buenos Aires: Editorial Bajel, 1945.

Real Cédula de su Magestad sobre la educación, trato y ocupaciones de los esclavos. 1789. www.afehc-historia-centroamericana.org/index.php?action=fi_aff&id=1109.

Revista de la Biblioteca Nacional (Buenos Aires). Tomo 2, no. 5 (enero–marzo 1938).

Somoza de Monsoriu, Francisco. *Estorbos i remedios de la riqueza de Galicia: discurso político legal.* Santiago, Spain: Ignacio Aguayo, 1775.

Vértiz, Juan José. "Informe del Virrey Vértiz, para que se abandonen los establecimientos de la Costa Patagónica." n.d. www.cervantesvirtual.com.

Vidart, Pedro. *El discípulo instruido en el arte de partear . . . / dispuesta en dialogo.* Madrid: Imprenta Real, 1785.

Viedma, Antonio de. *Descripción de la Costa Meridional del Sur, llamada vulgarmente Patagónica; relación de sus terrenos, producciones, brutos, aves y peces; indios que la habitan, su religión, costumbres, vestidos y trato; desde el puerto de Santa Elena en 44 grados, hasta el de la Virgen en 52, y boca del Estrecho de Magallanes.* 1783, www.cervantesvirtual.com.

———.*Diario de un viaje a la costa de la Patagonia, para reconocer los puntos en donde establecer poblaciones con una descripción de la naturaleza de los terrenos, de sus producciones y habitantes; desde el puerto de Santa Elena hasta la boca del Estrecho de Magallanes.* 1780, www.cervantesvirtual.com.

Viedma, Francisco de. *Memoria dirigida al señor Márquez de Loreto, virrey y capitán general de las provincias del Río de la Plata, sobre los obstáculos que han encontrado, y las ventajas que prometen los establecimientos proyectados en la Costa Patagónica.* 1784, www.cervantesviritual.com.

Ward, Bernardo. *Proyecto económico: en que se proponen varias providencias dirigidas á promover los intereses de España . . .* Madrid: Joaquin Ibarra, 1779.

——. *Obra pia y eficaz modo para remediar la miseria de la gente pobre de España . . .* Madrid: Imprenta Antonio Marin, 1767.

Selected Secondary Sources

Alden, Dauril. "The Undeclared War of 1773–1777: Climax of Luso-Spanish Platine Rivalry." *Hispanic American Historical Review* 41, no. 1 (February 1961): 55–74.

Alonso Soane, María José et al. *Las "Nuevas poblaciones" de Carlos III en Sierra Morena y Andalucía.* Córdoba, Argentina: Universidad de Córdoba, 1985.

Altman, Ida. "Spanish Women in the Caribbean, 1493–1540." In *Women of the Iberian Atlantic*, edited by Sarah E. Owens and Jane E. Mangan, 57–81. Baton Rouge: Louisiana State University Press, 2012.

——. "Spanish Women and the Indies: Transatlantic Migration in the Early Modern Period." In *New Perspectives on Women and Migration in Colonial Latin America*, PLAS Cuadernos no. 4, edited by M. Anore Horton, 21–45. Princeton, NJ: Program in Latin American Studies, 2001.

——. *Transatlantic Ties in the Spanish Empire: Brihuega, Spain, and Puebla, Mexico, 1560–1620.* Stanford, CA: Stanford University Press, 2000.

Apolant, Juan Alejandro. *Operativo Patagonia: historia de la mayor aportación demográfica masiva a la Banda Oriental.* 2nd ed. Montevideo, Uruguay: Ediciones El Galeón 1999.

——. *Los primeros pobladores españoles de la Colonia del Sacramento.* Montevideo, Uruguay: Ministerio de Educación y Cultura, 1971.

——. *Génesis de la familia uruguaya: los habitantes de Montevideo en sus primeros 40 años, filiaciones, ascendencias, entronques, descendencias.* Montevideo, Uruguay: Imprenta Vinaak, 1966.

Arrom, Sylvia Marina. *Containing the Poor: The Mexico City Poor House, 1774–1871.* Durham, NC: Duke University Press, 2000.

——. *The Women of Mexico City, 1790–1857.* Stanford, CA: Stanford University Press, 1985.

Astigarraga, Luis. "Un cura de 1800: Manuel de Amenedo Montenegro." *Boletín histórico del estado mayor del ejército.* In four parts: 251–54 (1978), pt. 1, 1–66; 255–58 (1978); pt. 2, 3–84; 259–62 (1978); pt. 3, 179–192; 263–66 (1978); pt. 4, 1–86.

Avilés Fernández, Miguel et al. *Carlos III y las "Nuevas poblaciones."* Córdoba, Argentina: Universidad de Córdoba, 1988.

Banzato, Guillermo. *La expansión de la frontera bonaerense: posesión y propiedad de la tierra en Chascomús, Ranchos y Monte, 1780–1880.* Buenos Aires: Universidad Nacional de Quilmes Editorial, 2005.

Barr, Juliana. *Peace Came in the Form of a Woman: Indians and Spaniards in the Texas Borderlands.* Chapel Hill: University of North Carolina Press, 2007.

Barral, María Elena. *De sotanas por la Pampa: religión y sociedad en el Buenos Aires rural tardocolonial.* Buenos Aires: Prometeo Libros, 2007.

Barral, María Elena, and Roberto di Stefano. "Las 'misiones interiores' en la campaña de Buenos Aires entre dos siglos: de los Borbones a Rosas." *Hispania Sacra* 60, no. 122 (julio–diciembre 2008): 635–58.

Barrios Pintos, Anibal. *San José: de la historia a nuestros días.* 2 vols. Montevideo, Uruguay: Ministerio de Educación y Cultura, 1986.

———. *Minas: dos siglos de su historia.* Tomo 1. Montevideo, Uruguay: Ministerio de Educación y Cultura, 1983.

Bennett, Herman L. *Africans in Colonial Mexico: Absolutism, Christianity, and Afro-Creole Consciousness, 1574–1640.* Bloomington: Indiana University Press, 2003.

Bentancur, Arturo Ariel. "Vida de solteros en el Montevideo tardocolonial: vínculos, intereses y sentimientos al interior de la colectividad gallega." *Anuario del Centro de Estudios Gallegos* (2007): 9–26.

———. "Familia, esclavos y libertos: algunas pautas sobre el relacionamiento de la colonia gallega con los afromontevideanos." *Anuario del Centro de Estudios Gallegos* (2003): 81–94.

———. "Solitarios y grupos familiares en la sociedad colonial tardía: una mirada al interior de los hogares gallegos montevideanos." *Anuario del Centro de Estudios Gallegos* (2002): 155–73.

———. "Patrimonios locales y metropolitanos de inmigrantes gallegos en el Montevideo colonial: riqueza, pobreza y solidaridad con la tierra de origen." *Anuario del Centro de Estudios Gallegos* (2001): 145–62.

———. *El puerto colonial de Montevideo.* Tomo 1, *Guerras y apertura comercial: tres lustros de crecimiento económico (1791–1806).* Montevideo, Uruguay: Universidad de la República, 1997.

Bentancur, Arturo A., and Fernando Aparicio. *Amos y esclavos en el Río de la Plata.* Montevideo, Uruguay: Planeta, 2006.

Bianchi Villelli, Marcia. *Organizar la diferencia: prácticas de consumo en Floridablanca (costa patagónica, siglo XVIII).* Buenos Aires: Editorial Teseo, 2007.

Black, Chad Thomas. *The Limits of Gender Domination: Women, the Law, and Political Crisis in Quito, 1765–1830.* Albuquerque: University of New Mexico Press, 2010.

Bolufer, Mónica. *Mujeres e ilustración: la construcción de la feminidad en la España del siglo XVIII.* Valencia: Disputació de Valencia, 1998.

———. "Actitudes y discursos sobre la maternidad en la España del siglo XVIII: la cuestión de la lactancia." *Historia Social* 14 (1992): 3–24.

Borreguero Beltrán, Cristina. "Del tercio al regimiento." *Estudis* 27 (2001): 53–89.

Borucki, Alex. "The Slave Trade to the Río de la Plata, 1777–1812: Trans-Imperial Networks and Atlantic Warfare." *Colonial Latin American Review* 20, no. 1 (2011): 81–107.

Borucki, Alex, Karla Chagas, and Natalia Stalla. *Esclavitud y trabajo: un estudio sobre los afrodescendientes en la frontera uruguaya (1835–1855)*. Montevideo, Uruguay: Pulmón Ediciones, 2004.

Bouvier, Virginia M. *Women and the Conquest of California, 1542–1840: Codes of Silence*. Tucson: University of Arizona Press, 2001.

Brown, Kathleen M. "The Anglo-Algonquian Gender Frontier." In *Negotiators of Change: Historical Perspectives on Native American Women*, edited by Nancy Shoemaker, 26–48. New York: Routledge, 1995.

Burns, Kathryn. *Into the Archive: Writing and Power in Colonial Peru*. Durham, NC: Duke University Press, 2010.

Buscaglia, Silvana. "La representación de las relaciones interétnicas en el discurso de Antonio Viedma (Patagonia meridional, siglo XVIII)." *Magallania* (Chile) 39, no. 2 (2011): 15–35.

———. "Los marinos malditos: identidad, poder y materialidad (Patagonia, siglo XVIII)." *Vestigios: revista latinoamericana de arqueología histórica* 2, no. 1 (2008): 35–62.

Buscaglia, Silvana, et al. "To Project an Order: Interdisciplinary Perspectives on Spatial Construction in the Spanish Colony of Floridablanca (Patagonia, Eighteenth Century)." *Historical Archaeology* 42, no. 4 (2008): 1–20.

Castañeda, Antonia. "Engendering the History of Alta California, 1769–1848: Gender, Sexuality, and the Family." *California History* 76, no. 2/3, *Contested Eden: California before the Gold Rush* (Summer–Fall, 1997): 230–59.

———. "Sexual Violence in the Politics and Policies of Conquest: Amerindian Women and the Spanish Conquest of Alta California." In *Building with Our Hands: New Directions in Chicana Studies*, edited by Adela de la Torre and Beatriz M. Pesquera, 15–33. Berkeley: University of California Press, 1993.

———. "Presidarias y Pobladoras: Spanish-Mexican Women in Frontier Monterey, Alta California, 1770–1821." PhD diss., Stanford University, 1990.

Castro, Concepción de. *Campomanes: estado y reformismo ilustrado*. Madrid: Alianza Editorial, 1996.

Celton, Dora. "Abandono de niños e ilegitimidad: Córdoba, Argentina, siglos XVIII–XIX." In *Familias iberoamericanas ayer y hoy: una mirada interdisciplinaria*, edited by Mónica Ghirardi, 231–50. Rio de Janeiro: Asociación Latinoamericana de Población, 2008.

———. "Selección matrimonial y mestizaje en Córdoba." In *III Jornadas de historia de Córdoba*, 327–44. Cordoba: Junta Provincial, 1997.

———. *La población de Córdoba a fines del siglo XVIII*. Buenos Aires: Academia Nacional de la Historia, 1993.

Chambers, Sarah C. "Masculine Virtues and Feminine Passions: Gender and Race in the Republicanism of Simón Bolívar." *Hispanic Research Journal* 7, no. 1 (February 2006): 21–40.

———. *From Subjects to Citizens: Honor, Gender, and Politics in Arequipa, Peru, 1780–1854*. University Park, PA: Penn State University Press, 1999.

Chávez-García, Miroslava. *Negotiating Conquest: Gender and Power in California, 1770s–1880s*. Tucson: University of Arizona Press, 2004.

Coates, Timothy J. *Convicts and Orphans: Forced and State-Sponsored Colonizers in the Portuguese Empire, 1550–1755*. Stanford, CA: Stanford University Press, 2001.

Cooper, Frederick, and Ann L. Stoler. "Tensions of Empire: Colonial Control and Visions of Rule." *American Ethnologist* 16 (1989): 609–21.

Corteguera, Luis R. *For the Common Good: Popular Politics in Barcelona, 1580–1640*. Ithaca, NY: Cornell University Press, 2002.

Cruz, Gilbert R. *Let There Be Towns: Spanish Municipal Origins in the American Southwest, 1610–1810*. College Station: Texas A&M University Press, 1985.

De Cristóforis, Nadia Andrea. *Proa al Plata: las migraciones de gallegos y asturianos a Buenos Aires (fines del siglo XVIII y comienzos del XIX)*. Madrid: CSIC, 2009.

———. "Ideas y políticas migratorias españolas a fines del Antiguo Régimen: el caso astur-galaico." *Anuario de estudios americanos* 63 (2006): 117–50.

Díaz de Guerra, María A. *Documentación relativa a esclavos en el departamento de Maldonado, siglos XVIII y XIX*. Montevideo, Uruguay: Imprenta Cooperativa Gaboto, 1983.

Di Stefano, Roberto. *El púlpito y la plaza: clero, sociedad y política de la monarquía católica a la república Rosista*. Buenos Aires: Siglo Veintiuno Editores, 2004.

Djenderedjian, Julio. "Roots of Revolution: Frontier Settlement Policy and the Emergence of New Spaces of Power in the Río de la Plata Borderlands, 1777–1810." *Hispanic American Historical Review* 88, no. 4 (November 2008): 639–68.

Domínguez Ortiz, Antonio. *Sociedad y estado en el siglo XVIII español*. 3rd ed. Barcelona: Editorial Ariel, 1988.

Dopico, Fausto. "Nupcialidad y familia en España (siglos XVI–XX)." *Revista migratio* 1 (junio 2005). http://migratio.cesga.es/IMG/pdf/fausto2-2.pdf.

———. *A ilustración e a sociedade galega: a visión de Galicia dos economistas ilustrados*. Vigo, Spain: Galaxia, 1978.

Dubert García, Isidro. "Modernity Without Modernisation: The Evolution of Domestic Service in North-West Spain, 1752–1900." *Gender and History* 18, no. 2 (2006): 199–210.

———. "La mortalité en Galice, 1600–1850." *Annales de démografie historique* 1 (1996): 221–48.

Eiras Roel, Antonio. "Demografía rural en la España moderna: evolución, variantes y problemas." In *El mundo rural en la España moderna*, VII[a] Reunión Científica de la Fundación Española de Historia Moderna, edited by Francisco José Aranda Pérez, vol. 2, 19–78. Cuenca, Spain: Ediciones de la Universidad de Castilla–La Mancha, 2004.

———. *La población de Galicia, 1700–1860: crecimiento, distribución espacial y estructura de la población de Galicia en los siglos XVIII y XIX.* Santiago de Compostela: Fundación CaixaGalicia, 1996.

———. *La emigración española a Ultramar.* Madrid: Tabapress, 1991.

———. "Mecanismos autoreguladores, evolución demográfica y diversificación intrarregional: el ejemplo de la población de Galicia a finales del siglo XVIII." *Boletín de la Asociación de Demografía Histórica* 8/2 (1990): 51–72.

Eiras Roel, Antonio, and Ofelia Rey Castelao, eds. *Migraciones internas y médium-distance en la península Ibérica, 1500–1900.* 2 vols. Santiago de Compostela: Xunta de Galicia, 1994.

Elliott, J. H. *Empires of the Atlantic World: Britain and Spain in America, 1492–1830.* New Haven, CT: Yale University Press, 2006.

Entraigas, Raúl A. *El fuerte del Río Negro.* Buenos Aires: Libería Don Bosco, 1960.

Fajardo Terán, Florencia. "Historia de la cuidad de Minas, capítulos IV a VI." *Boletín histórico del estado mayor del ejército* 92–95 (1962): 103–26.

———. "Historia de Minas." *Boletín histórico del estado mayor del ejército* 75–76 (1958): 113–33.

———. "Los orígenes históricos de la ciudad de San Fernando de Maldonado." *Boletín histórico del estado mayor del ejército* 73–74 (julio–diciembre 1957): 98–114.

———. *Historia de la Ciudad de San Carlos (orígenes y primeros tiempos).* Montevideo, Uruguay: n.p., 1953.

Ferreyra, María del Carmen. "Matrimonio de 'Españoles' en la ciudad de Córdoba en el siglo XVIII: el uso de fuentes diversas para su estudio." In *Poblaciones históricas: fuentes, métodos y líneas de investigación*, edited by Dora Celton, Mónica Ghirardi, and Adrián Carbonetti. *Serie Investigaciones N° 9*, 271–310. Rio de Janeiro: ALAP Editor, 2009. www.alapop.org/2009/index.php?option=com_content&view=article&id=532.

———. "La ilegitimidad en la ciudad y en el campo a finales del siglo XVIII en Córdoba." In *Cambios demográficos en América Latina: la experiencia de cinco siglos.* Córdoba, Argentina: International Union for the Scientific Study of Population and Universidad Nacional de Córdoba, 1998.

Fogelman, Patricia A. "Población de color en una villa en la frontera bonaerense: Luján, 1771–1815." *Signos históricos* 1. no. 2 (diciembre 1999): 9–34.

Fraschina, Alicia. "A Jesuit Beata at the Time of the Suppression in the Viceroyalty of Río de la Plata." In *The Jesuits II: Cultures, Sciences, and the Arts 1540–1773.* Edited by John O'Malley, 758–71. Toronto: University of Toronto Press, 2006.

Garavaglia, Juan Carlos. *Pastores y labradores de Buenos Aires: una historia agraria de la campaña bonaerense, 1700–1830.* Buenos Aires: Ediciones de la Flor, 1999.

———. "Un siglo de estancias en la campaña de Buenos Aires: 1751 a 1853." *Hispanic American Historical Review* 79, no. 4 (November 1999): 703–34.

Garland, Charles, and Herbert S. Klein. "The Allotment of Space for Slaves aboard Eighteenth-Century British Slave Ships." *William and Mary Quarterly*, 3rd ser., 42, no. 2 (1985): 238–48.

Goldberg, Marta B., and Silvia C. Mallo. "La población Africana en Buenos Aires y su campaña: Formas de vida y de subsistencia (1750–1850)." *Temas de África y Asia* 2 (1993): 15–69.

González, Ondina E., and Bianca Premo, eds. *Raising an Empire: Children in Early Modern Iberia and Colonial Latin America*. Albuquerque: University of New Mexico Press, 2007.

Gorla, Carlos María. *Los establecimientos españoles en la Patagonia: estudio institucional*. Seville: Centro de Estudios Hispano-Americanos, 1985.

———. *La agricultura en la Patagonia (1779–1810)*. Viedma, Argentina: n.p., 1984.

Grubb, Farley. "Morbidity and Mortality on the North Atlantic Passage: Eighteenth-Century German Immigration." *Journal of Interdisciplinary History* 17, no. 3 (Winter 1987): 565–85.

Guy, Donna J., and Thomas E. Sheridan, eds. *Contested Ground: Comparative Frontiers on the Northern and Southern Edge of the Spanish Empire*. Tucson: University of Arizona Press, 1998.

Haines, Robin. *Doctors at Sea: Emigrant Voyages to Colonial Australia*. Basingstoke, UK: Palgrave-Macmillan, 2005.

Haines, Robin, and Ralph Shlomowitz. "Deaths of Babies Born on Government-Assisted Emigrant Voyages to South Australia in the Nineteenth Century." *Health and History* 6, no. 1 (2004): 113–24.

———. "Causes of Death among British Emigrants on Voyages to South Australia, 1848–1885." *Social History of Medicine* 16 (2003): 194–208.

———. "Explaining the Modern Mortality Decline: What Can We Learn from Sea Voyages?" *Social History of Medicine* 11 (1998): 15–48.

Haurie, Virginia. *Mujeres en tierra de hombres: historias reales de la Patagonia invisible*. Buenos Aires: Editorial Sudamericana, 1996.

Hendrix, Scott H., and Susan C. Karant-Nunn, eds. *Masculinity in the Reformation Era*. Kirksville, MO: Truman State University Press, 2008.

Herzog, Tamar. "Early Modern Spanish Citizenship: Inclusion and Exclusion in the Old and the New World." In *New World Orders: Violence, Sanction, and Authority in the Colonial Americas*, edited by John Smolenski and Thomas J. Humphrey, 205–25. Philadelphia: University of Pennsylvania Press, 2005.

———. *Defining Nations: Immigrants and Citizens in Early Modern Spain and Spanish America*. New Haven, CT: Yale University Press, 2003.

Hodson, Christopher. "'A Bondage So Harsh': Acadian Labor in the French Caribbean, 1763–1766." *Early American Studies: An Interdisciplinary Journal* 5 (2007): 95–131.

Jacobs, Auke Pieter. "Legal and Illegal Immigration from Seville, 1550–1650." In *"To Make America": European Emigration in the Early Modern Period*, edited by Ida Altman and James Horn, 59–84. Berkeley: University of California Press, 1991.

Johnson, Lyman L. *Workshop of Revolution: Plebian Buenos Aires and the Atlantic World, 1776–1810*. Durham, NC: Duke University Press, 2011.

———. "Dangerous Words, Provocative Gestures, and Violent Acts." In *The Faces of Honor: Sex, Shame, and Violence in Colonial Latin America*, edited by Lyman L. Johnson and Sonya Lipsett-Rivera, 127–151. Albuquerque: University of New Mexico Press, 1998.

Johnson, Lyman L., and Susan M. Socolow. "Población y espacio en el Buenos Aires del siglo XVIII." *Desarollo económico* 20, no. 79 (1980): 329–49.

Jones, Kristine L. "Nineteenth-Century British Travel Accounts of Argentina." *Ethnohistory* 33, no. 2 (Spring 1986): 195–211.

———. "Conflict and Adaptation in the Argentine Pampas." PhD diss., University of Chicago, 1984.

Konetzke, Richard. "La emigración de mujeres españolas a América durante la época colonial." *Revista internacional de sociología* (1945): 123–50.

Lacombe, Michael A. *Political Gastronomy: Food and Authority in the English Atlantic World*. Philadelphia: University of Pennsylvania Press, 2012.

Lelo Bellotto, Manoel. *Correio marítimo hispano-americano: a carreira de Buenos Aires (1767–1779)*. Assis, Brazil: Faculdade de Filosofia, Ciências e Letras de Assis, 1971.

León Solís, Leonardo. *Maloqueros y conchavadores en Araucanía y las Pampas, 1700–1800*. Temuco, Chile: Ediciones Universidad de la Frontera, 1990.

Longo Formoso, Miguel. *Expedición militar a las Californias, Sonoras y Cinaloa (1768–1771), expediciones de familias al Río de la Plata (1778–1784) y a la Costa de Mosquitos (1787)*. A Coruña, Spain: M. Longo, 2002.

Luque Azcona, Emilio José. *Ciudad y poder: la construcción material y simbólica del Montevideo colonial (1723–1810)*. Seville: CSIC, 2007.

Macías Domínguez, Isabelo. *La llamada del Nuevo Mundo: la emigración española a América (1701–1750)*. Seville: Universidad de Sevilla, 1999.

Mackay, Ruth. *"Lazy, Improvident People": Myth and Reality in the Writing of Spanish History*. Ithaca, NY: Cornell University Press, 2006.

Madrazo, Santos. *El sistema de transportes en España, 1750–1850*. 2 vols. Madrid: Ediciones Turner, 1984.

Mancke, Elizabeth. "Early Modern Expansion and the Politicization of Oceanic Space." *Geographical Review* 89, no. 2, *Oceans Connect* (April 1999): 225–36.

Mandrini, Raúl, and Sara Ortelli. "Los 'Araucanos' en las Pampas (c. 1700–1850)." In *Colonización, resistencia y mestizaje en las Américas (siglos XVI–XX)*, edited by Guillaume Boccara, 237–57. Quito: Ediciones Abya-Yala, 2002.

Marcos Martín, Alberto. *Economía, sociedad, pobreza en Castilla: Palencia, 1500–1814*. Palencia, Spain: Diputación Provincial de Palencia, 1985.

Márquez Macías, Rosario. *La emigración española a América (1765–1824)*. Oviedo, Spain: Universidad de Oviedo, 1995.

Marschoff, María. *Gato por liebre: prácticas alimenticias en Floridablanca*. Buenos Aires: Editorial Teseo, 2007.

Martínez, María Elena. *Genealogical Fictions: Limpieza de Sangre, Religion and Gender in Colonial Mexico*. Stanford, CA: Stanford University Press, 2008.

Martínez de Gorla, Dora Noemí. "La presencia de Negros en la Nordpatagonia, 1779–1837." *Memoria y sociedad* 7, no. 15 (2003): 176–92.

———. "El primer asentamiento de colonos en el Río Negro en Patagonia." *Temas americanistas* 6 (1986): 42–56.

Martínez Shaw, Carlos. *La emigración española a América (1492–1824)*. Colombres, Spain: Archivo de Indianos, 1994.

Martín García, Alfredo. *Demografía y comportamientos demográficos en la Galicia moderna: la villa de Ferrol y su tierra, siglos XVI–XIX*. León: Universidad de León, 2005.

Mayo, Carlos A. *Estancia y sociedad en la pampa (1740–1820)*. Buenos Aires: Editorial Biblos, 2004.

———. *Fuentes para el estudio de la frontera: voces y testimonios de cautivos, fugitivos y renegados. Fuentes para el estudio de la frontera bonaerense, 1752–1790*. Mar del Plata, Argentina: Universidad de Mar del Plata, 2002.

———, ed. *Vivir en la frontera: la casa, la dieta, la pulpería, la escuela (1770–1870)*. Buenos Aires: Editorial Biblos, 2000.

———. *Los Betlemitas en Buenos Aires: convento, economía y sociedad (1748–1822)*. Seville: Publicaciones de la Excma, Diputación Provincial de Sevilla, 1991.

———. "Amistades ilícitas: las relaciones extramatrimoniales en la campana bonaerense, 1750–1810." *Cuadernos de historia regional* 2 (1985): 3–9.

Mayo, Carlos A., and Amalia Latrubesse. *Terratenientes, soldados y cautivos: la frontera (1730–1815)*. Mar del Plata, Argentina: Universidad Nacional de Mar del Plata, 1993.

Meijide Pardo, Antonio. "La emigración gallega intrapeninsular en el siglo XVIII." In *Estudios de historia social de España*. Tomo 4, vol. 2, 463–606. Madrid: CSIC, 1960.

Milton, Cynthia E. *The Many Meanings of Poverty: Colonialism, Social Compacts, and Assistance in Eighteenth-Century Ecuador*. Stanford, CA: Stanford University Press, 2007.

Moch, Leslie Page. "The European Perspective: Changing Conditions and Multiple Migrations, 1750–1914." In *European Migrants: Global and Local Perspectives*, edited by Dirk Hoerder and Leslie Page Moch, 115–40. Boston, MA: Northeastern University Press, 1996.

———. "The Importance of Mundane Movements: Small Towns, Nearby Places, and Individual Itineraries in the History of Migration." In *Migrants in Modern*

France: Population Mobility in the Later 19th and 20th Centuries, edited by Philip E. Ogden and Paul E. White, 97–117. Boston, MA: Unwin Hyman, 1989.

Moreno, José Luis. *Historia de la familia en el Río de la Plata*. Buenos Aires: Editorial Sudamericana, 2004.

———. "La infancia en el Río de la Plata: ciudad y campaña de Buenos Aires, 1780–1860." In *Cambios demográficos en América Latina: la experiencia de cinco siglos*, 559–79. Córdoba, Argentina: Universidad de Córdoba, 1998.

———. "Sexo, matrimonio y familia: la ilegitimidad en la frontera pampeana del Río de la Plata, 1780–1850." *Boletín del Instituto de Historia Argentina y Americana "Doctor Emilio Ravignani"* 16–17 (1998): 61–84.

———. "Población y sociedad en el Buenos Aires rural a mediados del siglo XVIII." *Desarrollo económico* 29, no. 114 (1989): 265–82.

Moya, José C. *Cousins and Strangers: Spanish Immigrants in Buenos Aires, 1850–1930*. Berkeley: University of California Press, 1998.

Nacuzzi, Lidia R. "Los desertores de la expedición española a la costa patagónica de fines del siglo XVIII y la circulación de personas en los espacios de frontera." *Nuevo Mundo Mundos Nuevos*. Debates 2011. http://nuevomundo.revues.org/61394.

———. "Social Strategies in a Situation of Interethnic Contact: The Fort del Carmen, Río Negro, Case Study." In *Archaeological and Anthropological Perspectives on the Native Peoples of Pampa, Patagonia, and Tierra del Fuego to the Nineteenth Century*, edited by Claudia Briones and José Luis Lanata, 89–102. Westport, CT: Bergin and Garvey, 2002.

Olivero, Sandra. *Sociedad y economía en San Isidro colonial: Buenos Aires, siglo XVIII*. Seville: Universidad de Sevilla, 2006.

Operé, Fernando. *Indian Captivity in Spanish America: Frontier Narratives*. Translated by Gustavo Pellón. Charlottesville: University of Virginia Press, 2008.

Ortiz Gómez, Teresa. "From Hegemony to Subordination: Midwives in Early Modern Spain." In *The Art of Midwifery: Early Modern Midwives in Europe*, edited by Hilary Marland, 95–114. London: Routledge, 1993.

Paquette, Gabriel B. *Enlightenment, Governance, and Reform in Spain and Its Empire, 1759–1808*. Basingstoke, UK: Palgrave-MacMillan, 2008.

Pérez, Mariana Alicia. *En busca de mejor fortuna: los inmigrantes españoles en Buenos Aires desde el Virreinato a la Revolución de Mayo*. Buenos Aires: Prometeo Libros, 2010.

Pérez Estévez, Rosa María. *El problema de los vagos en la España del siglo XVIII*. Madrid: Confederación Española de Cajas de Ahorros, 1976.

Pérez García, José Manuel. *Un modelo social leonés en crecimiento: la Vega Baja del Esla entre 1700 y 1850*. León, Spain: Universidad de León, 1998.

Pérez-Mallaína, Pablo E. *Spain's Men of the Sea: Daily Life on the Indies Fleets in the Sixteenth Century*. Translated by Carla Rahn Phillips. Baltimore, MD: Johns Hopkins University Press, 1998.

Pérez Moreda, Vicente, ed. *La crisis de mortalidad en la España interior (siglos XVI–XIX)*. Madrid: Siglo Veintiuno, 1980.

Phillips, Carla Rahn. *Six Galleons for the King of Spain: Imperial Defense in the Early Seventeenth Century*. Baltimore, MD: Johns Hopkins University Press, 1986.

Porro Gutiérrez, Jesús María. *La emigración asturiana y castellano-leonesa para el poblamiento de la Patagonia en época de Carlos III*. Valladolid, Spain: Sever Cuesta, 1995.

Poska, Allyson M. "Campesinas transatlánticas: las mujeres y la migración en el imperio español al fin del siglo XVIII." *Nuevo Mundo Mundos Nuevos*. Debates 2012. http://nuevomundo.revues.org/63354.

———. "Public Health, Peasant Bodies, and the Spanish Colonization of Patagonia." *Social History of Medicine* 25, no. 2 (2012): 290–306.

———. "Babies on Board: Women, Children, and Imperial Policy in the Spanish Empire." *Gender and History* 22, no. 2 (August 2010): 269–83.

———. "A Married Man Is a Woman: Negotiating Masculinity in Early Modern Northwestern Spain." In *Masculinity in the Reformation Era*, edited by Scott H. Hendrix and Susan C. Karant-Nunn. Kirksville, MO: Truman State University Press, 2008.

———. *Women and Authority in Early Modern Spain: The Peasants of Galicia*. Oxford: Oxford University Press, 2005.

———. "From Peasants to Slave Owners: Race, Class, and Gender in the Spanish Empire." In *The Early Modern Hispanic World: Transnational and Interdisciplinary Approaches*, edited by Kimberly Lynn and Erin Rowe. New York: Cambridge University Press, forthcoming.

Prado, Fabrício. "In the Shadows of Empires: Trans-Imperial Networks and Colonial Identity in Bourbon Rio de la Plata (c. 1750–1813)." PhD diss., Emory University, 2009.

Premo, Bianca. *Children of the Father King: Youth, Authority, and Legal Minority in Colonial Lima*. Chapel Hill: University of North Carolina Press, 2005.

———. "'Misunderstood Love': Children and Wet Nurses, Creoles and Kings in Lima's Enlightenment." *Colonial Latin American Review* 14 (2005): 231–61.

Rey Castelao, Ofelia. "Las migraciones femeninas de Antiguo Régimen en su contexto Europeo." In *Mujer y emigración: una perspectiva plural*, edited by Julio Hernández Borge and Domingo L. González Lopo, 39–67. Santiago de Compostela: Universidade de Santiago de Compostela, 2008.

Reyes, Bárbara O. *Private Women, Public Lives: Gender and the Missions of California*. Austin: University of Texas Press, 2009.

Rial García, Serrana Mercedes. "Trabajo femenino y economía de subsistencia: el ejemplo de la Galicia moderna." *Manuscrits* 27 (2009): 77–99.

Rodríguez Díaz, Laura. *Reforma e ilustración en la España del siglo XVIII: Pedro Rodríguez de Campomanes*. Madrid: Fundación Universitaria Española, 1975.

Rosental, Paul-André. "La migration des femmes (et des hommes) en France au XIX siècle." *Annales des démografie historique* 107 (2004): 107–36.

Rotker, Susana. *Captive Women: Oblivion and Memory in Argentina*. Translated by Jennifer French. Minneapolis: University of Minnesota Press, 2002.

Saavedra, Pegerto. *La vida cotidiana en la Galicia del Antiguo Régimen*. Barcelona: Crítica, 1994.

Saether, Steinar A. "Bourbon Absolutism and Marriage Reform in Late Colonial Spanish America." *The Americas* 59 (2003): 475–509.

Salvatore, Ricardo, and Jonathan C. Brown. "Trade and Proletarianization in Late Colonial Banda Oriental: Evidence from the Estancia de las Vacas, 1791–1805." *Hispanic American Historical Review* 67, no. 3 (August 1987): 431–59.

Sanguinetti de Bórmida, Amalia C., María Ximena Senatore, and Silvana Buscaglia. "Patagonia en los confines de la sociedad moderna: fronteras materiales en Floridablanca." In *La frontera: realidades y representaciones*, edited by Ariel Guiance, 69–84. Buenos Aires: CONICET, 2005.

Santana Pérez, Juan Manuel, and José Antonio Sánchez Suárez. "Repoblación de Costa de Mosquitos en el último cuarto del siglo XVIII." *Revista de Indias* 67, no. 241 (2007): 695–712.

Sarasúa, Carmen. "The Role of the State in Shaping Women's and Men's Entrance into the Labour Market: Spain in the Eighteenth and Nineteenth Centuries." *Continuity and Change* 12, no. 3 (1997): 347–71.

Schwartz, Stuart B. "Opening the Family Circle: Godparentage in Brazilian Slavery." In *Slaves, Peasants, and Rebels: Reconsidering Brazilian Slavery*. Urbana: University of Illinois Press, 1992.

Seed, Patricia. *To Love, Honor, and Obey in Colonial Mexico: Conflicts over Marriage Choice, 1574–1821*. Stanford, CA: Stanford University Press, 1988.

Senatore, María Ximena. *Arqueología e historia en la colonia española de Floridablanca (Patagonia, siglo XVIII)*. Buenos Aires: Editorial Teseo, 2007.

Senatore, María Ximena et al. "Una arqueología de las prácticas cotidianas en la colonia Española de Floridablanca (Patagonia, siglo XVIII)." In *Arqueología del extremo sur del continente americano: resultados de nuevos proyectos*, edited by Luis Alberto Borrero and Nora Viviana Franco, 81–117. Buenos Aires: CONICET, 2008.

Shaw, Michael Crozier. "*El siglo de hazer caminos:* Spanish Road Reforms during the Eighteenth Century. A Survey and Assessment." *Dieciocho* 32, no. 2 (Fall 2009): 413–34.

Shlomowitz, Ralph, and John McDonald. "Babies at Risk on Immigrant Voyages to Australia in the Nineteenth Century." *Economic History Review*, New Series, 44, no. 1 (February 1991): 86–101.

Shumway, Jeffrey M. *The Case of the Ugly Suitor and Other Histories of Love, Gender, and Nation in Buenos Aires, 1776–1870*. Lincoln: University of Nebraska Press, 2005.

Slatta, Richard W. *Gauchos and the Vanishing Frontier*. Lincoln: University of Nebraska Press, 1992.

Smith, Theresa Ann. *The Emerging Female Citizen: Gender and Enlightenment in Spain*. Berkeley: University of California Press, 2006.

Socolow, Susan Migden. "Spanish Captives in Indian Societies: Cultural Contact along the Argentine Frontier, 1600–1835." *Hispanic American Historical Review* 72, no. 1 (1992): 73–99.

———. "Acceptable Partners: Marriage Choice in Colonial Argentina, 1778–1810." In *Sexuality and Marriage in Colonial Latin America*, edited by Asunción Lavrin, 209–51. Lincoln: University of Nebraska Press, 1989.

———. *The Bureaucrats of Buenos Aires, 1769–1810: Amor al Real Servicio*. Durham, NC: Duke University Press, 1987.

———. "Women and Crime: Buenos Aires, 1757–1797." *Journal of Latin American Studies* 12, no. 1 (May 1980): 39–54.

———. *The Merchants of Buenos Aires, 1778–1810: Family and Commerce*. Cambridge: Cambridge University Press, 1978.

Sorsby, William S. "Spanish Colonization of the Mosquito Coast, 1787–1800." *Revista de historia de América* 73–74 (1972): 145–53.

Stern, Steven J. *The Secret History of Gender: Women, Men, and Power in Late Colonial Mexico*. Chapel Hill: University of North Carolina Press, 1995.

Street, John. *Artigas and the Emancipation of Uruguay*. Cambridge: Cambridge University Press, 1959.

Taylor, Scott K. *Honor and Violence in Golden Age Spain*. New Haven, CT: Yale University Press, 2008.

Vassberg, David E. *The Village and the Outside World in Golden Age Castile: Mobility and Migration in Everyday Rural Life*. Cambridge: Cambridge University Press, 1996.

Vigo Trasancos, Alfredo. *A Coruña y el siglo de las luces: la construcción de una ciudad de comercio (1700–1808)*. A Coruña: Universidade de A Coruña, 2007.

Voss, Barbara L. *The Archaeology of Ethnogenesis: Race and Sexuality in Colonial San Francisco*. Berkeley: University of California Press, 2008.

———. "Colonial Sex: Archaeology, Structured Space, and Sexuality in Alta California's Spanish-Colonial Missions." In *Archaeologies of Sexuality*, edited by Robert A. Schmidt and Barbara L. Voss, 35–62. New York: Routledge, 2000.

Weber, David J. *Bárbaros: Spaniards and Their Savages in the Age of Enlightenment*. New Haven, CT: Yale University Press, 2005.

———. *The Spanish Frontier in North America*. New Haven, CT: Yale University Press, 1992.

Yun Casalilla, Bartolomé. *Sobre la transición al capitalismo en Castilla: economía y sociedad en Tierra de Campos (1500–1830)*. Valladolid, Spain: Junta de Castilla y León, 1987.

Zusman, Perla. "Entre el lugar y la línea: la constitución de las fronteras coloniales patagónicas, 1780–1792." *Fronteras de historia* 6 (2001): 41–67.

Index